INTERVENTION WITH AT-RISK AND HANDICAPPED INFANTS

INTERVENTION WITH AT-RISK AND HANDICAPPED INFANTS
From Research to Application

Edited by
Diane D. Bricker, Ph.D.
Professor, Special Education
Director, Early Intervention Program
Center on Human Development
University of Oregon

University Park Press
Baltimore

UNIVERSITY PARK PRESS
International Publishers in Science, Medicine, and Education
300 North Charles Street
Baltimore, Maryland 21201

Typeset by Britton Composition
Manufactured in the United States of America by
The Maple Press Company

Library of Congress Cataloging in Publication Data
Main entry under title:
Intervention with at-risk and handicapped infants.
Includes index.
1. Handicapped children—Rehabilitation—Congresses.
I. Bricker, Diane D.   [DNLM: 1. Handicapped—Congresses.
2. Child development disorders—Prevention and control—Congresses.
3. Disability evaluation—In infancy and childhood—Congresses.
WS 350 I63 1980]
HV888.I57   362.4'048   82-7018
ISBN O-8391-1738-8   AACR2

CONTENTS

CONTRIBUTORS

Lynne Baker-Ward
Frank Porter Graham Child
  Development Center
Highway 54 Bypass West 071A
Chapel Hill, North Carolina 27514

Bennett I. Bertenthal
Department of Psychology
University of Virginia
Charlottesville, Virginia 22901

Diane D. Bricker, Ph.D.
Center on Human Development
University of Oregon
Eugene, Oregon 97403

Joseph J. Campos, Ph.D.
Department of Psychology
University of Denver
Denver, Colorado 80208

Rosemary G. Campos
Department of Psychology
University of Denver
Denver, Colorado 80208

Laurel Carlson, Ph.D.
Center on Human Development
University of Oregon
Eugene, Oregon 97403

Jill G. de Villiers, Ph.D.
Department of Psychology
  and Philosophy
Smith College
Northampton, Massachusetts
  01063

Gerald Gratch, Ph.D.
Department of Psychology
University of Houston
Houston, Texas 77004

Marci J. Hanson, Ph.D.
Department of Special Education
San Francisco State University
1600 Holloway Avenue
San Francisco, California 94132

Anne Henderson, Ph.D.
Occupational Therapy
Boston University-Sargent College
  Allied Health Professions
Boston, Massachusetts 02215

Ken G. Jens, Ph.D.
Biological Sciences
Research Center
University of North Carolina
Chapel Hill, North Carolina 27514

Nancy M. Johnson, Ph.D.
Biological Sciences
Research Center
University of North Carolina
Chapel Hill, North Carolina 27514

Claire B. Kopp, Ph.D.
Department of Education
Project REACH
University of California
  at Los Angeles
Los Angeles, California 90024

Michael Lewis, Ph.D.
Department of Pediatrics
Rutgers Medical School-UMDNJ
Piscataway, New Jersey

Karen E. O'Donnell
Department of Psychology
University of North Carolina
Chapel Hill, North Carolina 27514

Ross D. Parke, Ph.D.
Department of Psychology
University of Illinois
Urbana-Champaign, Illinois 61820

Craig T. Ramey, Ph.D.
Frank Porter Graham Child
  Development Center
Highway 54 Bypass West 071A
Chapel Hill, North Carolina 27514

Cordelia C. Robinson, Ph.D.
Meyer Children's Rehabilitation
  Institute
University of Nebraska
  Medical Center
Omaha, Nebraska 68105

Arnold J. Sameroff, Ph.D.
Institute for the Study of
  Developmental Disabilities and
  Department of Psychology
University of Illinois at Chicago
Chicago, Illinois 60608

Robert Sheehan, Ph.D.
Department of Child Development
  and Family Studies
Purdue University
West Lafayette, Indiana 47907

Marilyn J. Svejda
School of Nursing
University of Michigan
Ann Arbor, Michigan

Barbara R. Tinsley, Ph.D.
Department of Educational
  Psychology
University of Illinois
Urbana-Champaign, Illinois 61820

Jeanette A. Walker, Ph.D.
Department of Special Education
University of Illinois
Urbana-Champaign, Illinois 61820

Aileen Wehren
Early Childhood Personnel
  Training Project
Indiana University
South Bend, Indiana 46615

Philip R. Zelazo, Ph.D.
Tufts New England Medical
  Center Hospital
  Center for Behavioral Pedi-
  atrics and Infant Development
Tufts University
School of Medicine
171 Harrison Avenue
Boston, Massachusetts 02111

PREFACE

The recognition of the need for communication between researchers and practitioners is not new (see, for example, Tjossem, 1976; Minifie and Lloyd, 1978; Schiefelbusch and Bricker, 1981); however, establishing a reciprocal dialogue may have been an unemphasized dimension. The transactional model so popular in describing caregiver-infant interactions seems a perspective that is also applicable to the research and intervention efforts underway for handicapped and at-risk infants. A need exists to develop a dialogue between researcher and practitioner that is reciprocal and affects change in both partners. In an effort to meet this need a conference entitled "Handicapped and At-Risk Infants: Research and Application" was held in the Asilomar Conference Center, Pacific Grove, California, in May, 1980. The goal of this conference was to examine strategies to enhance the dialogue between researchers and interventionists working with populations of nonhandicapped, handicapped, and at-risk infants. This conference brought together a talented group of laboratory scientists and field researchers to address the issues surrounding translation of research outcomes to intervention efforts and the articulation of problems facing practitioners that need attention from the research community.

The Asilomar environment provided conference participants a rustic, peaceful setting that produced an atmosphere of cooperation, enthusiasm, and willingness to tackle the issues attendant to the conference goal. Each participant presented a prepared paper, which was followed by discussion. These presentations, the discussions throughout the conference, and the participants' subsequent reflections form the substance of this volume.

Claire Kopp, Ken Jens, and Marci Hanson assisted in the development of the conference themes and the selection of the participants. Their time and efforts were important to the balance and success of the conference.

The Office of Special Education, USOE provided the support for the conference. In particular Nick Certo, then Project Officer for the Division of Innovation and Development, William Swan, then Acting Branch Chief for the Handicapped Children's Early Education Program and Edward Sontag, then Acting Division Director, Division of Innovation and

Development, were exceptionally responsive and helpful in the planning and execution of the conference.

A number of individuals from the Center on Human Development, University of Oregon were instrumental in the development of the conference and this volume. In particular, Carol Sims was responsible for the arrangements of a smoothly executed meeting. Gregg Halley and Laurel Carlson assisted in a number of ways that contributed to the excellence of the meeting. Robert Schwarz, Director of the Center on Human Development, provided support and thoughtful advice that helped maintain a balanced perspective throughout the project. Finally, acknowledgment and thanks are due Susan Edginton for assistance in editing the manuscripts and Connie Nosbisch for her patience and care in preparation of the manuscripts.

The quality of the conference and this volume is due in large part to the effort expended by each of the participants. Their support for the concept of the conference and this volume has been heartening. These individuals share in providing leadership and direction for the field, and their concern for establishing a dialogue between researchers and practitioners surely lends credibility to the effort.

The goal of the Asilomar Conference was to expand the communicative network between researchers and practitioners focused on handicapped and at-risk infants. The goal of this volume is to share this dialogue with a larger audience.

INTERVENTION WITH AT-RISK AND HANDICAPPED INFANTS

Introduction

FROM RESEARCH
TO APPLICATION

Diane D. Bricker

The child development and early intervention literature contain frequent, though passing, reference to issues surrounding the translation
of research findings to clinical practice or the identification of important
clinical problems for the research community. Such discussions, however, rarely go beyond the recognition of problems in the practice-
research exchange. In addition, Clarke (1977) noted in his presidential
address to the Fourth Congress of the International Association for the
Scientific Study of Mental Deficiency, ". . . an ominous and, I fear,
growing gap between our knowledge and our practice" (p. A-16). This
is a particularly unfortunate state of affairs in these days of diminishing
resources when there is greater need for effective collaboration and
the development of cost-effective research and intervention strategies.
Efforts directed toward isolating the conditions responsible for this
"growing gap" between researchers and practitioners (e.g., clinicians,
teachers, interventionists) seem a paramount goal.

Conditions preventing effective collaboration efforts or the exchange of information seem to be: 1) a generally mistaken assumption
that the flow of data must be from laboratory to field and not the
reverse; 2) an unwillingness or inability to establish effective communication among individual practitioners or researchers or local,
state, and federal agencies; and 3) an absence of effective translators
or mechanisms to enhance exchange between researchers and
practitioners.

Many researchers and practitioners seem to assume that information flows unilaterally from the laboratory to field application for
the eradication of social ills, the enhancement of general knowledge,
or for the implementation of specific rehabilitative procedures for the
benefit of specific populations. Some writers have questioned whether
the unilateral flow from researcher to practitioner produces the greatest
positive clinical impact, the most enlightened social policies, or the

1

most effective governmental policies toward social issues. Baumeister (1981) wrote:

> In short, the view commonly held by researchers is that public policy needs science. That proposition is not only false, but its converse is true. Research is the product of public policy (p. 450).

Focusing specifically on developmental research, Achenbach (1978) claimed that the more applied form of research (i.e., mission-oriented):

> . . . is likely to remain the primary medium through which developmental research and theory influence social policy. Furthermore, mission-oriented research has and will continue to enrich the methodological repertoire of developmental researchers as well as exposing the gaps and ambiguities in existing theory (p. 195).

Butterfield (1978) argued:

> The clinician can and should draw on the understandings produced by scientific research, but he need not be at the mercy of the scientist (p. 585).

Butterfield emphasized that the practitioner need not play the role of an empty vessel waiting to be filled with selected information provided by the research community. Rather, the practitioner should actively seek and apply a variety of therapies and procedures as they seem useful and relevant to the problems at hand—even if such procedures lack a strong empirical or scientific base.

The thrust of this discussion is not that information and social policy emanate exclusively from the field but rather to suggest that both practitioner and researcher contribute to the understanding of human development in the social environment. The generation of ideas, information, and strategies that may enhance the quality of life for individuals and groups comes from both the practitioner and researcher.

Recognition of the bilateral flow of information between researchers and practitioners and social and governmental agencies may lead to increased mutually beneficial collaboration. A more balanced and perhaps more useful approach would be to strive for a reciprocity of communication in which information, ideas, and even inspiration travel between researchers and practitioners.

Communication is a second source of difficulty leading to the "growing gap between our knowledge and our practice." Researchers and practitioners, with rare exceptions, form camps whose inhabitants talk and write predominately for each other. As Baumeister (1981) commented, communication among colleagues tends to be horizontal rather than vertical. Conversations occur among individuals with similar thoughts and modes of operations rather than with persons from the other camp. Moving vertically into other domains, paradigms, or information bases occurs infrequently. Observation of "convention-going" behavior among professionals supports Baumeister's conclusion.

Fortunately, researchers and practitioners seem to be recognizing the need for rapproachment, and a number of solutions have been offered to eliminate current practice-research dichotomies. For example, in 1979 Parke remarked that ". . . the current lab/field controversy, often arises not out of legitimate disagreement but due to misunderstandings and confusion concerning the meaning of certain scientific distinctions." Parke suggested that mere useful distinctions should focus on the research setting, the research design, and the data collection procedures as independent dimensions. Equating laboratory settings with experimental efforts and field settings with nonexperimental efforts leads to unproductive conceptual and practical dilemmas. Achenbach (1978) offered a different view of the research practice distinction. He suggested that:

> . . . theoretically oriented research aims for precise statements about the operation of isolated variables under conditions chosen by the researcher, whereas mission-oriented research must yield answers about behavior under conditions of naturally occurring complexity within deadlines for making policy decisions (p. 194).

Such reformulations of the research-practice dichotomy should lead to more useful collaborative and integrative efforts.

Although it is probably safe to surmise that barriers to the flow of information and communication have hindered the research-practice exchange, the literature does contain examples of productive reciprocity between researcher and practitioner. Tyler and Kogan (1977) conducted an investigation using 18 preschool cerebral palsied children in which the focus was on providing the child's mother with a special training program to enhance mother-child interactions. The content of the training program was derived from previous clinical observations of increasing negative behavior by the child and decreasing positive interactions between mother and child as therapy progressed over time. By implementing an intervention program under controlled conditions, these investigators were able to produce a positive impact on behaviors that have clinical importance to young cerebral palsied children and their mothers. Conversely, procedures developed under controlled conditions have found relevant and useful clinical application. For example, Eilers, Wilson, and Moore (1977) developed a procedure to examine speech discrimination in infants. This operant procedure, termed the *visually reinforced infant speech discrimination (VRISD),* has subsequently been adopted for hearing evaluation of young children in clinical settings (Northern & Downs, 1978).

Such examples suggest the potency of a reciprocal relationship between practitioner and researcher; however, caution is in order. Thoughtful application, and in many cases restraint, should be employed by clinicians and teachers in applying procedures that have been shown to produce desired effects under controlled conditions. In a paper discussing the significant events of infants' cognitive-perceptual development, Watson (1971) raised the issue of indiscriminate application of laboratory findings to clinical settings. In particular, he pointed to the possible problems of employing contingent stimulation that is artificial and mechanical. He suggested that infants may develop an unfortunate sense of control during the laboratory procedure, which they would not obtain in their usual environment. Practitioners must guard against the application of training procedures that may produce undesirable effects in young children.

The third major barrier to preventing effective collaboration and information exchange between researcher and practitioner is the lack of articulate and credible individuals to function as translators of research and clinical findings. In addition, few well-defined mechanisms or procedures are available that facilitate the systematic movement of useful research outcomes into the practitioner's realm. A functional communication system should include strategies for selecting the research findings that have the greatest probability of enhancing intervention efforts. Once that selection is made, a commitment to operationalize or field test these research outcomes is necessary. New approaches that are found to be uninterpretable for practitioners or overly expensive in terms of resource allocation should be eliminated from the practitioner's repertoire or be modified to fit criteria of usefulness in applied settings. The final step in the translation process is the application of the new content or technique by practitioners with an attendant evaluation system to produce information for researchers on its effectiveness in applied settings. At this final level, comparisons of new procedures with existing strategies would be ideal. Often such comparisons are impossible because of the methodological and resource problems described by Baer (1981).

Equally important to the development of a systematic link between research and application is alerting the laboratory scientist and field researcher to the problems confronting interventionists and practitioners. The articulation and documentation of problems that interfere with the progress of intervention efforts is the responsibility of the practitioner, and problems—once isolated—must be communicated to the researcher. Some research efforts should concentrate on major difficulties confronting interventionists.

A further problem arises for individuals as translators. The literature on child development, intervention, and relevant environmental factors is vast and scattered (Hayden, 1978). Considerable time and effort are required if one is to maintain some currency with the array of material that may be potentially useful to practitioners. In addition, sufficient attention must be given to the details of investigations to ensure that critical aspects are not overlooked or that potential dangers are adequately perceived (Watson, 1971).

Because of the complexity of the research-practice exchange, the practitioner must weigh the application of new information and procedures to habilitation efforts against the potential risk inherent in using undocumented strategies. Such complexity and risk provide further reason for increasing current levels of communication between researcher and practitioner.

Although there are examples of effective communication between the researchers and practitioners, undue optimism seems unwarranted. Phillips (1980) cautioned:

> There is a gap between the world of fundamental research in the sciences and the everyday world in which human activity takes place. The researchers use sophisticated techniques and their world is a theoretical one in which findings do not automatically apply to the everyday world because everyday terms do not appear in their theories; links of some sort have to be established (p. 19).

Phillips shifted the emphasis from the dichotomy between researcher and practitioner to establishing "links" between laboratory and field settings and procedures. From a similar perspective, Butterfield (1978) offered a number of suggestions for forging such links. Suggestions for the practitioner include: 1) identifying reasons that current intervention strategies are ineffective; 2) isolating elements that are effective in intervention regimes; and 3) suggesting alternatives that may produce greater impact on the target population. Suggestions for the researcher include: 1) describing procedures clearly so that practitioners can judge their applicability and usefulness; 2) documenting the reliability of procedures; 3) making empirical and theoretical arguments for areas of selected research; and 4) suggesting methods for clinical application of relevant findings.

The Asilomar conference, from which this book has evolved, was undertaken because the participants acknowledged the need to establish more functional and productive exchanges between research conducted in controlled settings to its application in the field. The need for building a bridge from research to practice was articulated throughout the conference and again in this book. Although the construction of the bridge is just beginning, certain requisites have been established. The bridge must be broad in order to handle a frequent and varied flow of information, the bridge must have multiple access and exit points that allow reciprocity between a variety of individuals and agencies, and the flow of traffic (information) across the bridge must be regulated by adopting some common language and/or guidelines in order to avoid chaotic and unproductive exchanges. A primary goal of this volume is to establish a foundation for increasing useful exchanges between practitioners and researchers.

The contributors to this volume have confronted the research-to-practice exchange through a variety of topics. In the first section, Theory to Practice, Kopp discusses the neglect of theory in the area of handicapped and at-risk populations and the subsequent yield of a fragmented research literature that is exceedingly difficult for practitioners to interpret and apply. She argues convincingly for the need to be guided by theory to acquire objective data about the population and for the integration of findings to formulate effective intervention efforts. Arguing for an equally important perspective, Jens and O'Donnell articulate the need for interventionists to adopt an "as if" attitude when confronted with problems of daily programming with populations of at-risk and handicapped infants. They suggest that waiting for formal documentation of the effectiveness of new procedures and approaches may result in unnecessarily slow progress toward improving intervention efforts. They advocate caution and flexibility, however, in the implementation of unproved methods.

Section two, Assessment Issues, contains four diverse perspectives on the assessment of populations of at-risk and handicapped infants. Sheehan reviews current assessment strategies for infants. He delineates the significant problems confronted when applying current assessment methods to handicapped infants. Given these problems, he speculates on the future directions that will assist in the development of more adequate strategies for handicapped populations. Johnson discusses in more detail problems confronting interventionists using norm-referenced, criterion-referenced and Piagetian-based scales with handicapped populations. She emphasizes the importance of the link between evaluation and the intended goals of a program whether they are prediction, identification, or monitoring of child progress. Lewis and Wehren concisely and clearly describe the hazards of using measures of central tendency to evaluate the impact of interventions on populations of at-risk and handicapped infants. They point to population variability as a dimension that often renders the mean and similar measures of central tendency suspect in terms of actual outcomes for individuals or sub-groups of individuals. This reality has significant relevance for the practitioner as well as the researcher working with heterogeneous populations. Gerald Gratch addresses an equally important but different assessment problem. He urges caution in thinking that the use of Piagetian-based scales with handicapped infants overcomes the problems inherent in more traditional assessment measures. Following a discussion of action and perception in relationship to sensorimotor intelligence, Gratch warns against the wholesale adoption of any one assessment strategy. He suggests the need for continued individualization when dealing with handicapped infants.

The discussion of serious problems of accurately assessing at-risk and handicapped infants is followed by section three, Assessment Strategies, in which innovative assessment procedures are analyzed. Zelazo and his colleagues have developed a reliable method for differentiating between children with central and peripheral neuromotor deficits. This technique, which holds promise for assisting interventionists in acquiring more appropriate diagnostic information about motorically impaired infants, offers an explicit example of the research-to-practice exchange. Acknowledgment of the importance of reflexive behavior is the basis of the Henderson chapter. She describes the need for the conduct of careful investigation of reflex activity and further operationalizes this need by reporting an investigation in which she and a colleague examined procedural variables associated with eliciting the Asymmetrical Tonic Neck Reflex.

Section four, Environmental Context, emphasizes the importance of expanding the traditional context in which assessment and intervention usually occur. Sameroff suggests that adopting the transactional model entails a commitment to evaluating the daily interactions between the infant and caregiver in the broader societal context. He stresses the importance of understanding community and cultural variables that may influence the infant-caregiver relationship. Parke and Tinsley expand on this perspective by reviewing the impact of a variety of sources on the premature infant and his or her family. These authors provide convincing support for the need of interventionists to broaden their approaches to include parents, siblings, and extended family and to understand cultural expectations and their potential impact when an atypical infant is introduced into the family constellation.

The chapters in section five, Social and Developmental Issues, illuminate the service-research exchange. deVilliers focuses on the methodological problems associated with the field of pragmatics. In particular, she discusses the beginning of intentional communication, the categories for analysis, the order of emergence of these categories, and the relationship between the form and function of early communication. All these topics are of concern and interest to researchers and practitioners. Walker's chapter provides dramatic evidence of the reciprocal and beneficial relationship that can be developed between researchers and practitioners. Her study of dyadic interaction between handicapped infants and their caregivers provides rich data. These data in turn offer concrete suggestions for effective intervention techniques. Analyzing data from their own laboratory as well as from other sources, Campos, Svejda, Campos, and Bertenthal construct a convincing case for the impact of self-produced locomotion on specific emergent cognitive, emotional, and social behaviors of infants. These authors voice concern for young handicapped children with limited mobility and suggest that further work with motor impaired infants may produce valuable information about the effects of motor behavior on subsequent psychological development. The Robinson chapter attacks the problem of response substitution when handicapping conditions preclude typical response modes. She argues for the need to define behavioral targets more broadly so that infants are encouraged to explore their environment and develop communicative behavior as best they can. Robinson emphasizes the practitioner's need for expanded research focusing on the longitudinal impact of response substitution on handicapped infants.

The final section, Intervention, includes a chapter by Hanson, which presents a comprehensive review of the current research literature on at-risk, handicapped, and nonhandicapped infants. Through this review, Hanson suggests direction and content for the who, how, and what of intervention. Ramey and Baker-Ward present a comprehensive discussion of the early intervention paradigm, which they conclude is incomplete. They suggest that the field adopt an emphasis on the transactional model with the clear acknowledgment that early experience and intervention is only a small portion of the individual's life span. The final chapter by Carlson and Bricker sketches a picture of early communicative development, which is synthesized from the available research. Understanding the acquisition of early communicative responses provides a basis for formulating an intervention strategy to be employed with infant-caregiver dyads that present problems of effective dialogic exchanges.

A few readers may be disappointed to find that the contributors to this (or any other) book can offer few immediate solutions to the many dilemmas posed by the research-practice exchange. An arsenal of workable solutions still eludes us and therefore the goal of this volume is necessarily more modest. Each contributor focuses on the central theme from an individual perspective evolved through years of research and practical experience. The content offered in this volume may establish the basis for a dialogue between researchers and practitioners that will produce more powerful and effective collaborative efforts in the future.

REFERENCES

Achenbach, T. *Research in developmental psychology*. New York: The Free Press, 1978.
Baer, D. The nature of intervention research. In R. Schiefelbusch & D. Bricker (Eds.), *Early language: Acquisition and intervention*. Baltimore: University Park Press, 1981.
Baumeister, A. Mental retardation policy and research: The unfulfilled promise. *American Journal of Mental Deficiency*, 1981, 85, 449–456.
Butterfield, E. Behavioral assessment of infants: From research to practice. In F. Minifie & L. Lloyd (Eds.), *Communicative and cognitive abilities: Early behavioral assessment*. Baltimore: University Park Press, 1978.
Clarke, A. From research to practice. In P. Mittler (Ed.), *Care and intervention*. Baltimore: University Park Press, 1977.
Eilers, R., Wilson, W., & Moore, J. Developmental changes in speech discrimination in infants. *Journal of Speech and Hearing Research*, 1977, 20, 766–780.
Hayden, A. The implications of infant intervention research. *Allied Health and Behavioral Sciences*, 1978, 1, 583–599.
Northern, J., & Downs, M. *Hearing in children*. Baltimore: Williams and Wilkins, 1978.
Parke, R. Interactional designs. In R. Cairns (Ed.), *The analysis of social interactions: Methods, issues, and illustrations*. Hillsdale, N.J.: Lawrence Erlbaum Associates, 1979.
Phillips, D. What do the researcher and the practitioner have to offer each other? *Educational Researcher*, 1980, 9, 17–20.
Tyler, N., & Kogan, K. Reduction of stress between mothers and their handicapped children. *The American Journal of Occupational Therapy*, 1977, 31, 151–155.
Watson, J. Cognitive-perceptual development in infancy: Setting for the seventies. *Merrill-Palmer Quarterly*, 1971, 17, 139–152.

Section I
THEORY
TO PRACTICE

Chapter 1

THE ROLE OF THEORETICAL FRAMEWORKS IN THE STUDY OF AT-RISK AND HANDICAPPED YOUNG CHILDREN

Claire B. Kopp

The study of biologically based risk factors has expanded significantly during the past 2 decades. Developmentalists have played a key role in this growth by contributing to a variety of studies. Among the most visible endeavors are follow-up or outcome studies focused upon the intellectual, social, and behavioral sequelae of children exposed to diverse kinds of risk events. Graham and her colleagues' classic follow-up research of anoxic infants (Corah, Anthony, Painter, Stern, & Thurston, 1965; Graham, Ernhart, Thurston, & Craft, 1962) has been succeeded by many other outcome studies of infants born preterm, or with chromosome and genetic abnormalities, structural lesions, and so forth.

Other investigations have been directed toward examination of developmental processes—perception, cognition, social interactions—that may be affected by risk conditions. Dozens of studies are now available, but at one time the seminal work of Fantz, Fagan, and Miranda on visual preferences and recognition memory of preterm and Down's syndrome infants stood virtually alone (see summary in Fantz et al., 1975).

Still other research efforts have converged upon amelioration of risk and handicapping conditions. These attempts are exemplified by the numerous intervention studies that have been provided to preterm infants (see summary in Cornell & Gottfried, 1976). An expanded focus has occurred in public policy research, some of which emanates from the newly established Bush Foundation Training Programs in Child

Preparation of this paper was supported in part by BEH Contract #300-77-0306 to the Graduate School of Education, University of California, Los Angeles. An abbreviated version of this chapter was presented at the biennial meeting of the Society for Research in Child Development, Boston, April 1981.

Development and Social Policy. One of their emphases is on families of handicapped.

In a period of rapid growth, it is often difficult to step back and appraise the direction and nature of research efforts. This situation prevails in research focused on at-risk and young, handicapped children. With the exception of Sameroff and Chandler's (1975) discussion of the interrelationship of biological risk and environmental conditions, and Gibson's (1978) volume on Down's syndrome, the gaps in our self-appraisal process continue.

This author has examined an extensive number of studies in the risk and handicapped literature, pursuant to writing a chapter on risk factors in development (Kopp, in press). A concern arose about the approaches employed in the formulation of developmentally oriented research. That is, many studies designed to elucidate the characteristics of young handicapped and at-risk children have not been guided by an explicit, well-articulated, theoretical formulation. This, in part, has contributed to an exceedingly fragmented research literature.

The neglect of theory is all the more remarkable because in recent decades the study of normally developing children has been enriched by the use of theoretical underpinnings (e.g., Piaget, Bowlby, Bandura). Collectively, theories have been the framework around which an impressive body of developmental findings have been generated. Theories serve us well because they have moved the field from sole reliance upon descriptive, cataloging studies of behavioral units (e.g., activity, locomotion) to more diverse probing analyses of cognitive, social, perceptual, and affective phenomenon.

It would be foolhardy to suggest that theories always provide a well-defined research guide. This clearly has not been the case with studies of normally developing children, nor will it be true of studies of handicapped and at-risk children. Challenges arise because some theories are broad, others singularly narrow, and a few frustratingly difficult to translate into operational terms (Zigler, 1963). Stated another way, theories rarely contain the whole truth about phenomena. Some theories contain a smaller content than the phenomena themselves, others imply conclusions that are not really so, and still others fail to report phenomena that are true (Simon & Newell, 1963). Those of us who are concerned with development issues often find that theories provide incomplete accounts of developmental change, instead they give theoretically derived frames of reference or points-of-view (Achenbach, 1978).

Despite these shortcomings, theoretical viewpoints play an important role in generating the questions and tentative answers around which developmental research is organized (Achenbach, 1978). Research that is not guided by theory leads to scientific information that is difficult to categorize and synthesize into existing perspectives (Lerner, 1976).

Unfortunately, one does not have to search far in the risk and handicapped literature to find confirmation of Lerner's statement. Instructive examples can be obtained from many domains of inquiry. Because this state of affairs severely constrains the growth of knowledge, and because knowledge needs to be applied to very real problems, the remainder of this chapter is focused upon a discussion of theoretical frameworks and research on handicapped and at-risk young children.

Two points are made. First, theory must be used at this time because relatively little "hard" information is available about the developmental parameters of handicapped and at-risk young children. As Brainerd (1981) noted, when a science is young and facts are few, theories suggest potentially interesting areas of investigation.

Second, theoretically derived studies, however diverse, invariably can be integrated in a meaningful way to describe, at least partially, the nature of early development. In the absence of theory, one has to find a tool or strategy that can help organize the data. This quest may lead to a problematic outcome because organizational tools are rarely elastic enough to encompass all manner of research.

This chapter begins with a discussion about research specifically concerned with Down's syndrome infants and young children. In the first part, theoretically derived studies are examined in terms of the insights gained about development. Then, non-theoretically based studies are briefly examined. Because this research lacks an underlying unity, the theme of "deceleration in development" is used as an organizational tool. Several studies are then examined from this perspective.

The second half of this chapter moves away from empirical findings; instead, a hypothetical, theory-derived study focused upon questions related to delays in development is proposed. Delays are commonly found among many handicapping conditions, thus the question has widespread applicability.

RESEARCH: DOWN'S SYNDROME INFANTS AND YOUNG CHILDREN

Of all the diagnostic groups, young Down's syndrome children have been the subjects of most of the developmentally oriented research. The reasons for this seem to be twofold. First, Down's syndrome is identified early and the outcome for intellectual retardation is fairly straightforward. Thus, the group is often selected to provide a developmental marker of sorts. Second, many intervention programs have been initiated for Down's syndrome infants and their parents. Parents in these programs frequently encourage research with the hope that findings will facilitate developmental potentials.

Theory-Guided Studies

Very specific questions have been posed about social development (Bowlby, 1969) and sensorimotor development (Piaget, 1952, 1954) of Down's syndrome infants and young children. Often, the questions that have been asked stem directly from principles or precepts found in the theory.

For example, attachment theory (described by Bowlby, 1969, and extended by Ainsworth & Wittig, 1969; Ainsworth, Bell, & Stayton, 1974; Serafica, 1978; Sroufe & Waters, 1978) includes the following postulates: 1) proximity and contact are important in the formation of the mother-infant bond; 2) the infant has a set of goal corrected patterns of behavior that elicit similar patterns of maternal behavior; 3) differential behaviors are directed to the primary caregiver by the end of the first year; 4) the need to feel secure prompts the infant's use of signalling and approach behaviors; and 5) the feeling of security allows the infant to use the mother as a base from which to explore the environment.

Taking their cue from these statements, investigators have explicitly or implicitly asked: What kinds of signals are displayed by Down's syndrome infants? What effect do these signals have upon the mother-infant relationship? Do Down's syndrome children show differential response to their caregivers following exposure to strangers? What is the interrelationship between attachment and other behavioral systems?

Overall, examining the findings from four rather diverse studies reveals considerable similarity in the attachment behavior manifested by Down's syndrome and normally developing infants (Cicchetti & Serafica, 1981; Cytryn, 1975; Markowitz, 1980; Serafica & Cicchetti, 1976). For example, the range and patterning of signals is equivalent; moreover, both groups use their mothers as a base from which to explore, and a stranger evokes affiliative behaviors. Irrespective of diagnosis, in the presence of mothers, infants approach strangers, and when mothers leave, the behavior to strangers changes. On the basis of these data, it can be inferred that the primary features and the organization of attachment are maintained despite the presence of Down's syndrome. The implications of this inference are profound.

Despite the fact that important similarities in social development have been noted, differences in other manifestations of attachment have been observed. For example, variability has been noted in the age of emergence of signal behaviors (Cytryn, 1975) and in degree of intensity of displayed behaviors (Cicchetti & Serafica, 1981). Being left with a stranger or in an unfamiliar setting did not provoke as much distress in 2–3-year-old Down's syndrome children as it generally does with normally developing children. Whereas the latter tend to cry and show other signs of upset, Down's syndrome children merely averted their eyes.

To the extent that maternal behaviors were explored in these attachment studies, maternal responses seem to be congruent with the principles of the theory. For example, Markowitz (1980) found infant *enface* vocalizations highly salient for mothers of Down's syndrome and normally developing 5–7-month-olds who were observed in a structured play situation over a 3-month period. All mothers were silent during infant *enface* vocalization, and all mothers utilized tactile play when infants became quiet. This maternal response to signals was evident despite variations in amount of infant behavior. In general, mothers exhibited active patterns of interaction when their infants were nonactive.

Mothers were, however, highly tuned to the level of developmental skills displayed by their infants. Maternal response to infant visual orientation to mother's body (which was evidenced by the infants of *younger developmental ages* irrespective of diagnosis) elicited maternal hand play. This pattern of hand play was rarely used with older infants who demonstrated considerable amounts of *enface* activity.

In actuality, Markowitz found a greater number of differences in maternal behavior as a function of infant developmental age, than as a function of diagnosis. This finding is congruent with Buckhalt, Rutherford, and Goldberg's (1978) observation that mothers adjust the complexity of their language to the maturity level of their infants. These authors noted that this adjustment was made with both Down's syndrome and normally developing infants.

Overall, the data from the studies described above can be integrated into a meaningful characterization of the early social-affective development of Down's syndrome children. At least for the ages that were studied, inferences can be made about the organization and sequence of the behavioral repertoire of attachment behaviors. Furthermore, despite the presence of a major handicapping condition, these young children have the means (e.g., signals) to draw their caregivers to them. In turn, caregivers respond to these signals even though they know their children are handicapped. In a sense, the pull of child to parent, and parent to child, overrides the saliency of the handicap. This phenomenon is not unique to Down's syndrome infants and their parents; Roskies (1972) wrote of the startling force eye-to-eye contact had for parents of thalidomide infants. The force was so powerful that in one case it overcame the mother's initial reluctance to accept her limbless infant.

The studies described above also point to differences (e.g., the rate of acquisition of behaviors, or the intensity with which behaviors are expressed) that might have ramifications for later socialization training or development. Additional research is needed to elucidate the nature and meaning of these differences.

The study of Down's syndrome infants using Piagetian theory has also yielded important insights. Object permanence, imitation, means-ends problem-solving develop much the same way for Down's syndrome infants as for others (see Kopp, in press). These very fundamental abilities permit the child to learn about the world of objects and of people, and to assume a modest independence from others. In these sensorimotor studies, differences are reported in the rate of acquisition of behaviors, the frequency in which behaviors are deployed, and their intensity. I do not want to belittle these differences (or those noted above) because their implications are not yet understood. Again, additional research is warranted.

In summary, because theory was used as a guide, it was possible to take four rather different studies, integrate their findings, and make some intelligible inferences about young Down's syndrome children and their parents. The data also point to additional questions that need answers.

Atheoretical Research

Turning from theory-guided research to studies that have not been explicitly tied to theory, or are avowedly atheoretical, one finds some instances of elegant, rigorous research. The problem is how to fit this research, which includes emotional expressiveness, self-recognition, pre-linguistic communications, auditory and visual processing, attention, recognition memory, and mother-child interaction (see Kopp, in press), into a comprehensible developmentally based synthesis. This problem is all the more challenging because these studies also vary in the methodological approaches that were employed, ages of infants that were studied, response indices, and the degree of differences reported between Down's syndrome and normally developing samples. The magnitude of this diversity looms large in the absence of theory because there are no obvious directions that show how the pieces of information should go together.

Because some of the data from the atheoretical studies have value, some of the findings are integrated into an explanation of a puzzling aspect of development in Down's syndrome children. In effect, the "puzzle" became an ideational framework (an organization tool) around which to explore the deceleration in rates of development that is frequently shown by Down's syndrome infants.

Some background information may be helpful here. During the first few months of life many Down's syndrome children average 3 months of change for every 4 months shown by normally developing infants. By the end of the first year, however, the ratio is often down to a 2-month growth in 4 months actual time. This deceleration continues for about 3 to 4 years and then levels off (Carr, 1975; Dameron, 1963; Dicks-Mireaux, 1972; Share, Koch, Webb, & Graliker, 1964).

The essential question is what occurs in the first and second years that is related to this deceleration pattern? Earlier Kopp and Parmelee (1979) noted that the deceleration in development appeared at about the same that normally developing infants were hypothesized to show a qualitative surge in cognition (Collins & Hagen, 1979; Kagan, 1972; McCall, Eichorn, & Hogarty, 1977; Piaget, 1952, 1954; Werner, 1957; Zelazo, 1980). Terms such as intentionality, consciousness, adaptive type behavior, and "hypothesis testing" have been used to describe the nature of the child's "new" abilities.

Do Down's syndrome infants show the full complement of these emergent skills? If not, why not? Could a limited repertoire be related to deceleration? Do problems with processing information have any bearing on deceleration?

This last question stemmed from findings that suggested that Down's syndrome infants had difficulty handling subtleties in their object and social world (see Fantz et al., 1975; Cicchetti & Sroufe, 1976). Yet studies with normally developing infants showed that visual discrimination, for example, markedly improves in the latter quarter of the first year (e.g., Ruff, 1978).

In the Fantz et al. studies on visual preferences and recognition memory, data revealed that 2- to 4-month-old Down's syndrome and normally developing infants showed similar preferences for novel over familiar stimuli, and equivalent decreases in fixation time over age. Significant differences emerged toward the latter part of the first year, however, when normally developing infants were capable of making differential responses to novel stimuli involving complex arrangement of elements, shadings, or patterns, whereas the Down's syndrome infants had particular difficulty with the element stimuli, which were quite complex. Although the authors reported these differences in terms of an age lag, they also depicted graphically the pattern of responses seen at 8–16, 17–29, and 30–40 weeks chronological age. The finding most germane to speculations about processing deficits was that recognition memory responses of the Down's syndrome sample to the element stimuli never rose above chance level at any age. That is, even the oldest Down's syndrome infants never responded to the stimuli in the way that normally developing children did.

In the last few years, three other studies have appeared that lend credence to the thesis that Down's syndrome infants may either be unaware of subtleties or complexities in their milieu or may not process them accurately. In one study, Jones (1977, 1980) examined the prelinguistic communications of six Down's syndrome and six normally developing infants matched for sex, socioeconomic status, ordinality, and developmental age. Chronological age ranged from 8 to 24 months, developmental age from 8 to 19 months. Jones coded eye contact, vocalizations, and communicative events in home observations over a 3-month period.

In many ways, both groups of children evidenced similar behavioral repertoires. One of the striking group differences that did emerge, however, was the attenuated use of referential eye contact by the Down's syndrome sample. Jones described this type of visual contact as the infant's way of inviting the mother to engage in mutual activity. He commented that the Down's syndrome child "apparently has not developed a full understanding of the potential communicative role" of referential eye contact, and could not "cope cognitively with the complexities" of the referential system. Congruent with this finding, the mothers of the Down's syndrome children in this sample reported they had difficulty in attracting their infants' attention.

In a second set of studies, Cicchetti and Sroufe (1976, 1978) extended their initial investigations of the affective behavior of Down's syndrome infants by examining responses to visual loom and visual cliff situations. Few differences emerged in the loom condition, and those that did seemed to be related to the slower development of the Down's syndrome sample. By 16 months, responses to the loom were virtually indistinguishable from those of normally developing 12-month olds. In contrast, the visual cliff condition led to findings that were not solely a function of developmental age. Although the Down's syndrome infants rarely crossed the cliff end of the stimulus, few cried and few showed the heart rate acceleration and fearfulness commonly found with younger normally developing infants. Thus it may be that the Down's syndrome infants appreciated the more obvious characteristics of the visual cliff, but had difficulty in processing its more subtle ramifications.

Patterns of attention demonstrated by normally developing and Down's syndrome infants in the second year of life were studied (Krakow and Kopp ,in press). Attention was defined as the child's ability to remain engaged with a set of toys in an unstructured play situation.

The sample included normally developing and Down's syndrome infants with mean developmental ages of 16 to 17 months.

The results indicate that both groups of children responded with interest to toys and showed similar types of play activities. The Down's syndrome infants, however, were distinguished by 1) low levels of monitoring of the environs, 2) attenuated social engagement of mothers in play, and 3) high amounts of stereotypic play. It was surmised that stereotypic play acts as a deterrent to efficient engagement with the milieu because it creates an imbalanced awareness of one's own activities in contrast to events occurring in the external environment. Whether this hypothesis is valid remains to be seen; however, the Down's syndrome children in this sample did not seem to be taking in as much information as their peers.

In summary, a deceleration phenomenon emerges toward the end of the first year of life of Down's syndrome infants. This slow-down appears at about the same time that normally developing infants show a major qualitative transformation in abilities. Questions are asked about the repertoire of abilities of Down's syndrome infants, and the quality of their performing skills. Some data are available about visual processing, and these findings are summarized above. There is, as yet, no direct link between these findings and deceleration.

Nevertheless, because an organization theme could be discerned (i.e., deceleration), it was possible to unite several diverse studies. Some commonalities in findings emerged that can be explored more fully in subsequent studies.

Challenges for the Future

It is evident from the discussions above that considerably more research is necessary in order for us to obtain a comprehensive developmental picture of the young Down's syndrome child. In addition to pursuing the issue of deceleration, at least two other major challenges await us. One is the documentation of the growth of developmental functions (see McCall, 1979). This line of inquiry is best pursued with theory-guided research questions. With theories that are currently available it ought to be possible to examine and document the developmental course of affective, social, cognitive, and motor competencies. Figure 1, adapted from McCall (1979) and Wohlwill, (1973) shows an hypothesized approximation of the growth of attachment behaviors of Down's syndrome and normally developing infants. With additional research (and schematics of this type), it should be possible to make meaningful interpretations about the growth of developmental functions of Down's syndrome samples.

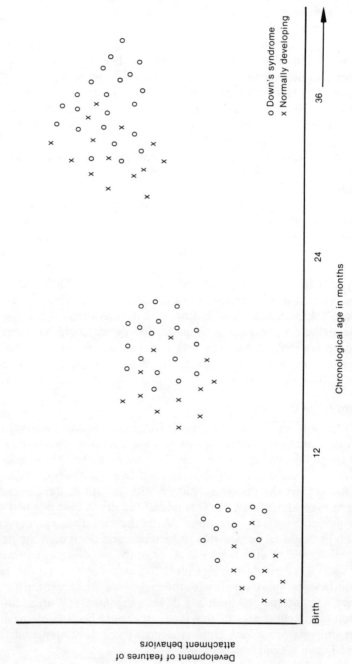

Figure 1. Hypothesized growth of developmental function related to attachment.

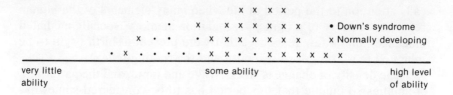

Figure 2.   Hypothetical example of individual and group differences in the ability to handle complex stimuli at 2 years of age: developmental age equivalents.

The second challenge confronting us is to obtain a sense of the variability within and between samples of Down's syndrome and normally developing infants and young children, and, to determine the implications of this variability. The "grand" developmental theories of Piaget or Bowlby may be less useful here as research guides; however, other mini-theories and approaches are available and can be used for the study of individual differences.

At present, very little is known about when and under what conditions the range of performance or patterns of behavior for Down's syndrome infants overlaps, or is distinct from, the range of behaviors demonstrated by normally developing infants (see Figure 2). It is necessary to pull apart differences that are identified, determine which are meaningfully related to ongoing and future development, and which are amenable to training. At that point, it will be possible to understand some of the underlying reasons for the intellectual impairments of Down's syndrome children.

Finally, although the preceding discussion focuses solely on young Down's syndrome children, much of what was said is pertinent to the study of other diagnostic groups. The use of theory is not only warranted, its value has already been demonstrated. (Witness the classic studies by Decarie (1969) on the development of object permanence and attachment of thalidomide children.)

THEORY-DERIVED RESEARCH
WITH YOUNG HANDICAPPED CHILDREN

In this section, concern is directed toward an issue that cuts across many handicapping conditions. Specifically, the issue is how the understanding of developmental delays can be increased. Developmental theories can have an important role in this endeavor.

Before turning to the role of theory, key terminology needs to be defined. First, in the phrase, *young handicapped* child, the word *young* calls attention to the period in life when many elements of the human repertoire emerge (e.g., grasp, recognition memory, socially mediated language), and a few responses that were present at birth begin to be inhibited (e.g., the Moro response and the rooting reflex).

The density of change is so extensive and rapid, and the patterning of abilities so unique that this period has to be considered somewhat apart from the school-age period when growth is more incremental (i.e., quantitative) and less rapid. This fundamental development difference between young organisms and their more mature counterparts influences the developmental perspectives that are employed and some of the research questions that are asked. This, in turn, has implications for studies of young handicapped children, a point that is discussed below.

The term *handicapped* is generic and encompasses many conditions including physical and sensory impairments, and cognitive, emotional/social, language, and motor delays in development. The diversity of functional limitations found within and between groups of handicapped children is extensive. For example, among children with structural lesions of the spine (spina bifida), some have lesions that are relatively minor and associated with virtually no physical impairment and others have lesions that are extensive and lead to paralysis of the lower limbs and bladder and bowel incontinence. Similarly, a wide range of cognitive abilities is found in spina bifida. Some children are severely retarded, others show mild retardation, and still others have normal intellectual skills. There is, moreover, some association between site of the lesions and cognitive problems, in that lesions closest to the head (children with encephaloceles) on the average have more problems than children with more distal lesions.

Although children who have sensory and motor impairments are the most visible of the young handicapped groups, there are other children whose development has gone awry in a less obvious way. These are the children with emotional disorders and/or developmental delays. When formally tested using developmental examinations, some of these children show delay in all areas of functioning (e.g., language, social, motor), whereas others have deficits in only one domain such as language. A sizable number of children who are developmentally delayed and who have no physical, sensory, or neurological signs, do not have an identifiable etiology.

Given that the term *handicap* connotes such diversity, it is not surprising that researchers studying even a well-defined handicapped group (e.g., homogeneous on developmental age, diagnosis) find variability in the ways that the young handicapped children are similar to, and differ from, normally developing children. As noted above, sorting out *similarities* and *differences* and examining if and how each *differ-*

ence is tied to ongoing performance will help us understand the long-term development of handicapped children.

One of the most obvious ways that many young handicapped children differ from their normally developing peers is the former's slower rate of developmental growth. Some delays are consistently evident and obvious (e.g., 2 to 3 months' change for every 12 months of actual time). This group is not the focus here; rather, the concern is with children who have less severe delays. Many of these higher functioning children have an uncertain outcome. Some will eventually be mentally retarded, others will catch up and show developmental capabilities that are expected for their chronological ages. Given our present level of expertise, it is often difficult to predict the outcome for any given child.

The interesting point about developmental delays (as diagnosed by performance on a standardized test) is that the diagnosis per se provides few clues about the child. Will, for example, further development be compromised because of the delay (or associated factors), or is the delay relatively benign, being a slow motion version of "normal development?"

One of the ways to get a better handle on the implications of delay is to examine the performance of delayed children using principles derived from developmental theory. In effect, the strategy is to embed an individual difference issue into a developmental framework.

Developmental Theory

Among contemporary developmental theorists, Piaget (1952, 1954), Bowlby (1969), Werner (1957), Kagan (1972), Emde (Emde, Gaensbauer, & Harmon, 1976), Erickson (1950), and Spitz (1959) all have postulated that development in the first months and years of life shows qualitative change. New competencies emerge, and the behaviors in the child's repertoire are patterned into new organizational systems, while the less mature modes of functioning are "phased out." These views emphasize the *transformative* nature of early development.

Research with normally developing children has provided some evidence for the transformation of neurophysiological and affective organization at about 3 months of age (Emde et al., 1976). Other studies show the emergence of new patterns of cognitive-affective-social systems at about 9–12 months (McCall, Eichorn, & Hogarty, 1977). Still others indicate that a new cognitive-language-affective organization emerges at about 18 months of age.

These transformations have important developmental significance. Each shift is associated with a child who is becoming a more effective processor of information about the world of objects, people, and the self.

Question 1 The first question that ought to be posed about children who are delayed is: What happens to developmental transformations and the organization of behavior when a young child's development is delayed across all domains of functioning (e.g., cognitive, motor, language, etc.)? Does development that is in "slow motion"— an individual difference issue—have any bearing on the patterning or organization of a behaviorial transformation—a developmental issue?

Stated another way, when a child is, for example, 12 months chronological age and functioning at 12 months developmental age, we know that an organizational relationship exists among cognitive domains (e.g., the ability to plan a behavioral sequence), social domains (e.g., awareness of some dictums of caregivers), motor domains (e.g., some control of upright locomotion), and affiliative domains (e.g., proximity seeking in the face of the unknown). The beauty of this interrelationship is that it gives the child a richer repertoire of resources to draw upon than would otherwise be available. With these resources, the child can experiment with different options to meet new challenges.

Is this interrelationship mirrored in the behavior of a child who is functioning at 12 months developmental age but is actually 18 months chronological age? No research currently exists that can help provide answers. In the absence of data, however, a clinical observation may be useful. In our laboratory, when developmentally delayed subjects are equated on developmental age with normally developing peers, the organization of behavior seems fragmented, and indeed the repertoire of spontaneously generated responses seems to be impoverished. For example, there seems to be an imbalance between object and social interactions. Does delayed development foster repetitiveness of certain kinds of behaviors, which in turn lead to a concomitant reduction of the repertoire?

Interestingly, two opposing points of view have addressed the issue of delay. Schnierla (1957), for example, suggested that delay and experiences inevitably have an effect on the development of subsequent behavior. Alternatively, Zigler (1968) argued that the organization of behavior is essentially unmodified in the face of mild delays. Zigler's position is supported, in part, by Cicchetti and Sroufe (1976) who showed that a parallel trend existed in the increasing ability of Down's syndrome infants to respond affectively to complex stimuli that required increasing sophistication in cognitive skills. Because only two domains of functioning were explored, it is difficult to generalize from this study.

Question 2 A second question has to do with the effect of uneven delays in development (e.g., delay in one or two areas) upon developmental transformations and overall organization of behavior. Consider the normally developing child of 18 months of age who displays an integrated pattern of problem solving object-oriented behaviors (cognitive domain), expressive communication (language domain), and affiliative bids to a caregiver (social-affective domain). This child shows a finely tuned balance between exploration, goal setting, communication, and use-of-another as a resource. Symbolic representation becomes an increasingly important mode of interaction.

The fact that this cognitive-linguistic-social-affective balance is periodically upset by fatigue or the press of a strong stimulus seems not to have deleterious effects if caregivers act to impose an external balance on the child. Suppose, however, there is a consistent imbalance as is found with many delayed children. For example, some 24-month-old children demonstrate locomotor abilities commensurate with their chronological age, but show cognitive and language abilities at an 18-month level. Will the transformative shift to a representational mode of functioning be compromised because the child shows a disparity between levels of mental and motor functioning?

Some examples will make this question clearer. There are suggestions in the clinical literature to the effect that nonhandicapped children who manifested major development imbalances such as marked motor precocities (Heider, 1966), or who showed accelerated motor development with a significant delay in language development (see discussions in Rexford, 1978) demonstrated problems in "control" of behavior. It was as if these children did not have the cognitive resources to think about their actions, or did not have the means to understand what was expected of them, or could not verbally tell themselves what to do (e.g., don't touch). Stated another way, it seems that representation of rules and do's and don't's lagged behind the refinement of motor abilities.

A similar type of problem functioning seems to arise with some young deaf children. In those instances where caregivers have not adopted alternative means of communication (e.g., a sign language system instead of spoken words), the child does not learn how words are assigned to categories, are used to convey rules, and so forth. Not surprisingly, problems in cognitive functioning and impulse control have been documented (Harris, 1978).

A Summary

This section focused upon the young handicapped child. It was pointed out that many of these children are developmentally delayed during early life. Some, however, subsequently show normal cognitive development, while others become mentally retarded. This suggested that additional study about the ramifications of developmental delays is warranted.

As a point of departure, several developmental theorists were mentioned who stressed the transformative nature of early development. Speculations concerning how two different kinds of developmental delays might influence qualitative transformations were provided.

A Cautionary Note

This article argues for the use of theory in the study of young handicapped children. Moreover, it suggests that developmental perspectives are the most appropriate guides for the study of the young. But it must be emphasized that slavish adherence to a theory that is vague and imprecise cannot further our quest for knowledge. Furthermore, slavish adherence to a theory that has not been supported by sound research will clearly move us backward rather than forward.

We need to select our theories judiciously, use them to help us find what we have to know, and turn to alternatives when the questions we want to ask have to be broadened.

REFERENCES

Achenbach, T. M. *Research in developmental psychology: Concepts, strategies, methods.* New York: The Free Press, 1978.

Ainsworth, M. D., & Wittig, B. A. Attachment and exploratory behavior of one-year-olds in a strange situation. In B. M. Foss (Ed.), *Determinants of infant behavior* (Vol. 4). London: Methuen, 1969.

Ainsworth, M. D., Bell, S. M., & Stayton, D. J. Infant-mother attachment and social development: "Socialization" as a product of reciprocal responsiveness to signals. In M. P. M. Richards (Ed.), *The integration of a child into social world.* London: Cambridge, 1974.

Bowlby, J. *Attachment and loss, Vol. 1. Attachment.* London: Hogarth, 1969.

Brainerd, C. J. Stages II: A review of beyond universals in cognitive development. *Developmental Review,* 1981, *1,* 63–81.

Buckhalt, J. A., Rutherford, R. B., & Goldberg, K. E. Verbal and nonverbal interaction of mothers with their Down's syndrome and non-retarded infants. *American Journal of Mental Deficiency,* 1978, *82,* 337–343.

Carr, J. *Young children with Down's Syndrome.* London: Butterworth, 1975.

Cicchetti, D., & Serafica, F. C. Interplay among behavioral systems: Illustrations from the study of attachment, affiliation, and wariness in young children with Down's syndrome. *Developmental Psychology,* 1981, *17,* 36–49.

Cicchetti, D., & Sroufe, L. A. The emotional development of the infant with Down's Syndrome. *Child Development,* 1976, *47,* 920–929.

Cicchetti, D., & Sroufe, L. A. An organizational view of affect: Illustration from the study of Down's syndrome infants. In M. Lewis & L. Rosenblum (Eds.), *The development of affect.* New York: Plenum Press, 1978.

Collins, J. T., & Hagen, J. W. A constructivist account of the development of perception, attention, and memory. In G. A. Hale & M. Lewis (Eds.), *Attention and cognitive development.* New York: Plenum Press, 1979.

Corah, N. L., Anthony, E. J., Painter, P., Stern, J. A., & Thurston, D. L. Effects of perinatal anoxia after seven years. *Psychological Monographs,* 1965, *79*(3) (Whole No. 596).

Cornell, E. H., & Gottfried, A. W. Intervention with premature human infants. *Child Development,* 1976, *47,* 32–39.

Cytryn, L. Studies of behavior in children with Down's Syndrome. In E. J. Anthony (Ed.), *Explorations in child psychiatry.* New York: Plenum Press, 1975.

Dameron, L. E. Development of intelligence of infants with mongolism. *Child Development,* 1963, *34,* 733–738.

Decarie, T. G. A study of the mental and emotional development of the thalidomide child. In B. M. Foss (Ed.), *Determinants of infant behavior* (Vol. 4). London: Methuen, 1969.

Dicks-Mireaux, M. J. Mental development of infants with Down's Syndrome. *American Journal of Mental Deficiency,* 1972, *77,* 26–32.

Emde, R. N., Gaensbauer, J., & Harmon, R. J. Emotional expression in infancy: A biobehavioral study. *Psychological Issues,* 1976, Vol. X, Monograph 37.

Erikson, E. H. *Childhood and society.* New York: W. W. Norton & Co., 1950.

Fantz, R. L., Fagan, J. F., & Miranda, S. B. Early visual selectivity. In L. B. Cohen & P. Salapatek (Eds.), *Infant perception: From sensation to cognition,* Vol. 1. *Basic visual processes.* New York: Academic Press, 1975.

Graham, F. K., Ernhart, C. B., Thurston, D., & Craft, M. Development three years after perinatal anoxia and other potentially damaging newborn experiences. *Psychological Monographs,* 1962, *76*(3) (Whole No. 522).

Gibson, D. *Down's Syndrome: The psychology of mongolism.* Cambridge: Cambridge University Press, 1978.

Harris, R. I. Impulse control in deaf children: Research and clinical issues. In L. S. Liben (Ed.), *Deaf children: Developmental perspectives.* New York: Academic Press, 1978.

Heider, G. M. Vulnerability in infants and young children: A pilot study. *Genetic Psychology Monographs,* 1966, *73,* 1–216.

Jones, O. Mother-child communication with prelinguistic Down's Syndrome and normal infants. In R. Schaffer (Ed.), *Studies in mother-infant interaction.* New York: Academic Press, 1977.

Jones, O. Prelinguistic communication skills in Down's syndrome and normal infants. In T. M. Field (Ed.), *High risk infants and children.* New York: Academic Press, 1980.

Kagan, J. Do infants think? *Scientific American,* 1972, *226,* 74–82.

Kopp, C. B. Risk factors in development. In M. Haith & J. Campos (Eds.), *Infancy and the biology of development,* Vol. II. From P. Mussen (Ed.), *Manual of child psychology.* New York: John Wiley & Sons, in press.

Kopp, C. B., & Parmelee, A. H. Prenatal and perinatal influences on infant behavior. In J. Osofsky (Ed.), *Handbook of infant development.* New York: John Wiley & Sons, 1979.

Krakow, J. B., & Kopp, C. B. Sustained attention in young Down Syndrome children. Topics in Early Childhood Special Education. In press.

Lerner, R. M. *Concepts and theories of human development.* Reading, Mass.: Addison-Wesley, 1976.

Markowitz, S. L. Mother-infant interaction with Down Syndrome and normal infants. Unpublished doctoral dissertation, University of California, Los Angeles, 1980.

McCall, R. B. The development of intellectual functioning in infancy and the prediction of later I.Q. In J. Osofsky (Ed.), *Handbook of infant development*. New York: John Wiley & Sons, 1979.

McCall, R. B., Eichorn, D. H., & Hogarty, P. S. Transitions in early mental development. *Monographs of the Society for Research in Child Development*, 1977, *42* (serial #171).

Piaget, J. *The origins of intelligence in children*. New York: International Universities Press, 1952.

Piaget, J. *The construction of reality in the child*. New York: Basic Books, 1954.

Rexford, E. N. *A developmental approach to problems of acting out* (Rev. Ed.). New York: International Universities Press, 1978.

Roskies, E. *Abnormality and normality. The mothering of thalidomide children*. Ithaca: Cornell University Press, 1972.

Ruff, H. A. Infant recognition of the invariant form of objects. *Child Development*, 1978, *49*, 293–306.

Sameroff, A. J., & Chandler, M. J. Reproductive risk and the continuum of caretaking casualty. In F. D. Horowitz, M. Hetherington, S. Scarr-Salapatek, & G. Siegel (Eds.), *Review of Child Development Research*, (Vol. 4.) Chicago: University of Chicago Press, 1975.

Schnierla, T. C. The concept of development in comparative psychology. In D. B. Harris (Ed.), *The concept of development*. Minneapolis: University of Minnesota, 1957.

Serafica, F. The development of attachment behaviors: An organismic-development perspective. *Human Development*, 1978, *21*, 119–140.

Serafica, F. C., & Cicchetti, D. Down's syndrome children in a strange situation: Attachment and exloration behaviors. *Merrill-Palmer Quarterly*, 1976, *22*, 137–150.

Share, J., Koch, R., Webb, A., & Graliker, B. The longitudinal development of infants and young children with Down's Syndrome (mongolism). *American Journal of Mental Deficiency*, 1964, *68*, 685–692.

Simon, H. A., & Newell, A. The uses and limitations of models. In M. H. Marx (Ed.), *Theories in contemporary psychology*. New York: MacMillan Publishing Co., 1963.

Spitz, R. A. *A genetic field theory of ego formation: Its implications for pathology*. New York: International Universities Press, 1959.

Sroufe, L. A., & Waters, E. Attachment as an organizational construct. *Child Development*, 1978, *48*, 1184–1199.

Werner, H. The concept of development from a comparative and organismic view. In D. Harris (Ed.), *The concept of development*. Minneapolis: University of Minnesota Press, 1957.

Wohlwill, J. F. *The study of behavioral development*. New York: Academic Press, 1973.

Zelazo, P. R. The year-old infant: A period of major cognitive change. In T. Bever & C. Trevarthen (Eds.), *Regressions in development: Basic phenomena and theoretical alternatives*. Hillsdale, N.J.: Lawrence Erlbaum Associates, 1980.

Zigler, E. Metatheoretical issues in developmental psychology. In M. H. Marx (Ed.), *Theories in contemporary psychology*. New York: MacMillan Publishing Co., 1963.

Zigler, E. Development versus difference theories of mental retardation and the problem of motivation. *American Journal of Mental Deficiency*, 1968, *73*, 536–556.

Chapter 2

BRIDGING THE GAP BETWEEN RESEARCH AND INTERVENTION WITH HANDICAPPED INFANTS

Ken G. Jens and Karen E. O'Donnell

Researchers and intervention personnel in the fields of child development and special education generally perceive themselves as different from one another and as being engaged in separate and somewhat disparate tasks. Whether one is engaged primarily in the provision of treatment/intervention services or in basic research, however, it has become increasingly clear that the two processes cannot logically be isolated from each other. If intervention personnel are to maximize their effectiveness and credibility, they must attempt to understand and use the research literature that undergirds intervention; in turn, researchers must be responsive to both the perceived needs of those attempting to provide intervention services and to the results of their efforts. This chapter directs itself to one important aspect of the relationship between the researcher and the practitioner—the translation and movement of research findings into practice. It acknowledges the existence of a gap between the development of knowledge and putting that knowledge into practice; it also acknowledges that the usefulness of research findings on which practitioners must base intervention efforts may not be either obvious or durable. This problem is referred to herein as the practitioner's dilemma. Suggestions for resolving this dilemma and affecting intervention efforts with newly generated knowledge as rapidly as possible are offered.

Role responsibilities that have traditionally been delineated for persons assuming intervention responsibilities have differed considerably from those for the person who has chosen primarily to do developmental research. The practitioner has the task of managing daily intervention efforts on behalf of young handicapped children and is generally concerned with the day-to-day problems of facilitating the development of specific skills and abilities. The researcher, on the other hand, is primarily concerned with clarifying and expanding our understanding of the various components of development and with the creation of knowledge that will, it is hoped, underpin intervention efforts.

In responding to the task of providing appropriate experiences for handicapped children, the practitioner has two basic sources of information to use for making programming decisions. First, ecological information regarding specific children is employed. Children live with and are affected by a family; they may or may not attend school; and they, with their families, probably live in communities of complex social interactions. Second, the practitioner is confronted with an ever expanding set of theoretical and experimental literature on child development in general, and on the development of handicapped children in particular.

THE PRACTITIONER'S DILEMMA

As practitioners are asked to create programs for children with various handicapping conditions or to assess existing programs, two questions must constantly be addressed: "What kind of intervention is appropriate for children with differing handicaps?" and "Is current programming for both individual and groups of children reasonable and adequate?" The more an individual child deviates from what is considered normal behavior, the more significant are these questions and the greater is the need to be able to utilize current research findings as a basis for intervention efforts. The practitioner must, therefore, be constantly involved in a decision-making process that will maximize the quality of services being offered. This process is, in turn, dependent upon the practitioner's ability to make maximum use of information presented by the child, his or her family, and the knowledge that is provided by current scientific literature.

Thus, the practitioner is presented with a complex problem wherein he or she must ask "What knowledge exists regarding developmental processes and how can I use this knowledge in making decisions regarding the current developmental status and/or the intervention needs of a particular child?" A simplistic answer would suggest that the practitioner has responsibility for knowing and being able to use the variety of developmental assessment tools that have been marketed (e.g., Bayley Scale, Vulpe, HELP, Denver) as well as accepted intervention strategies (e.g., knowledge of Piagetian developmental concepts, behavior modification principles). These, in fact, constitute subsets of information typically provided future teachers in early childhood/special education programs at our universities. A more complex, but also more logical answer to the question points to the importance and relevance of a vast body of current research in child development, which is not available in the format of packaged assessment tools and/ or widely accepted intervention strategies. The practitioner's task, then, is to apply this kind of information to programming for children who are not developing according to normative expectations.

It is suggested that current research findings, although tentative, can make a substantial contribution to the assessment and intervention processes utilized for educators and psychologists in the field. Developmental research presents various landmarks of normal growth for children that are, as yet, reported only as hypotheses, trends, or patterns. In the areas of affective development, for example, there are data to support that: children smile to a human face at 6 weeks; they show surprise when a covered object is found to be missing upon uncovering at 16 weeks; by 4–6 months children laugh in response to various auditory and tactile stimuli; between 7 and 9 months children laugh more in response to social and visual stimuli; the first instances of stranger and separation anxieties occur at about 8 months of age; and, fear of perceived depth (the visual cliff) has been found to occur between 7 and 12 months and to be closely related to the development of locomotion in normal children.

Although these landmarks have been found useful in treating handicapped and at-risk children, the practitioner's dilemma becomes immediately evident. That is, the practitioner must cope with ongoing inconsistencies and shifts in the theoretical and experimental work. To illustrate, Campos and Stenberg (1980) pointed out that any theory of affective development must address at least five different processes. They demonstrated how, historically, the focus of the study of affective development has shifted among these processes since the early focus on the conscious awareness of emotional states (James, 1890; Lange, cited in Grossman, 1967). They proposed that the role of memory in theories of emotion has been overemphasized and that appraisal (social referencing, in particular) has been heretofore neglected. They suggested that perceptual learning and vicarious learning need to be studied more carefully. Similarly, Parke (1979) reflected that, over the past decade, the study of social-emotional development has changed in a variety of significant ways. He cited an increasing emphasis on the active role of the child, the need for multiple theories, recognition of cultural, contextual and social influences, the need for multiple research strategies and, finally and perhaps most relevant, the need for a close link between the research process and turning it to useful application.

The multiplicity of landmarks and shifts in theoretical focus that occur present a dilemma. Educators and psychologists who are trying to be responsive to new developments in the field frequently find themselves in a bind; they want to integrate the latest research information into assessment and programming, but the utility and application of new constructs and/or strategies is neither obvious nor direct. The usability of new constructs is constantly being evaluated by the practitioner and applications are made on the basis of that evaluation.

THE "AS IF" SOLUTION

How then does the interventionist approach the literature provided by theoreticians and researchers when attempting to garner information for day-to-day problem solving? Proposed here is the adoption of an "as if" model to bring resolution to the practitioner's dilemma, wherein the practitioner deals with current views and literature "as if" they were true. This "as if" approach is based conceptually on the work of Kuhn (1970) and Watson (1979) who suggested that we structure our understanding of the world according to currently accepted principles rather than with universal laws because there is, in fact, doubt as to the validity of such laws. Kuhn suggested that within any area of professional development there are paradigms that compete for viability in determining the course that professional intervention, treatment, and research models follow. Because any given paradigm gathers advocates on the basis of its apparent validity, it may offer strong competition to paradigms in use and change the course of intervention and research for a period of time. Such shifts are not unusual and they are most frequently seen as signs of progress. The shifts are not absolute either; a new paradigm may have greater face validity and thus credibility for immediate practice than the one that it replaces, but elements of the latter may still be maintained long into the future.

Examples of such paradigmatic shifts are obvious within several areas of special education. One of the most obvious is that which saw the shift from self-contained classrooms to "mainstreaming" within regular education as the expected way of providing educational programs for mildly handicapped children within the public schools. Another area wherein even greater conceptual shifts have occurred and in which the competition between paradigms has been most obvious within special education is the area of learning disabilities. Earliest work in the area of learning disabilities was founded upon a neuropsychological or "brain process dysfunction" model. This early work, although of value and importance, was enhanced by shifts within the neuropsychological paradigm so that it came to include the use of sensory stimulation, megavitamin therapy, and orthomolecular medicine.

While shifts were occurring within the neuropsychological model for explaining and ameliorating learning difficulties, so were new paradigms beginning to compete for use. In the early 1960s the psycholinguistic model took on greater importance as a basis for intervening with children manifesting learning problems. Although the aforementioned models persisted as bases for intervening with the learning disabled, in the late 1960s and early 1970s a fourth model, applied behavior analysis, began to evolve as a pragmatic way of dealing with learning difficulties. This model arose, in part, because of the lack of success demonstrated through use of the other models.

Over the years, models in child development, as illustrated here in learning disabilities, have continued to compete for credibility. As such, groups of practitioners have utilized them "as if" each were representative of truth. This phenomenon allows intervention to occur on the basis of a given model, providing direction to the efforts of practitioners although not ignoring the possibility that other models might, at the same time or in the future, provide a more logical basis for intervention. A shift in perspective for either intervention or research emphasis is seen as acceptable for the moment on the basis of consensus if it is seen as useful in application, but it is always subject to rejection by a changing consensus. Our new views may be as distorted as our old ones. While they last, though, they provide us with a model against which we can reappraise and test fundamental assumptions and with which we can adopt a confident scientific stance even though it may have only temporary validity.

An "as if" approach is proposed because it seems to best meet the twofold need of the practitioner who is working with handicapped and at-risk infants. First, the practitioner needs the security, comfort, and structure of a currently acceptable framework for understanding development in children. A current working hypothesis gives the practitioner a useful model from which to formulate the assessment and intervention needs of a particular child. Second, the practitioner, especially one dealing with handicapped children, also needs freedom and flexibility within a model. The "as if" approach gives the practitioner permission not to throw out the model or the child when current theory and research fail to be useful clinically. The practitioner is also allowed to be creative when using a model in an "as if" way, rather than holding to more inflexible rules when a model is seen as representing a universal truth.

USING RESEARCH FINDINGS IN CLINICAL SETTINGS

The individual working with at-risk or handicapped children has at least four major tasks: 1) to accurately assess the developmental status of the youngster; 2) to create appropriate intervention strategies congruent with goals for change and progress; 3) to become involved in the interactive process going on between parent and child; and 4) to provide ongoing evaluation of developmental progress and program effectiveness. These tasks are never discrete; one cannot intervene with a child without assessment and one cannot assess a child without intervening in some way. For the sake of organization, however, the practitioner's task is divided in this way and the division is used to provide examples of the usefulness of the "as if" model in applying current research findings to clinical work.

Assessment

When any manner of assessment is initiated, it is likely that the psychologist and educator are trying to gather information about a child in three areas. First, the clinician is trying to form hypotheses about the child's current ability to process information to ensure that intervention strategies are geared to an appropriate developmental level. Second, the clinician tries out various materials and techniques in assessment in attempting to predict sets of stimuli that will be attractive to a particular child and that will subsequently maximize his or her responding to the teaching task. Third, any assessment includes prognoses, that is, hypotheses about the probable course of development for a particular child. Prognosticating, therefore, affects both the short- and long-term goals that structure specific intervention attempts.

Given these assumptions about the assessment process, an example of the use of recent research findings in the clinical assessment of one child is presented. Kathleen is a young girl with cerebral palsy of a quadraplegic nature. She entered the intervention program at 10 months of age with few responses in her repertoire besides eye movement and smiling. While traditional intellectual assessment was impossible because of her psychomotor impairment, her mother was able to provide the following information: at 3 months, Kathleen seemed to be exhibiting a social smile; at 8 months she was attempting to attract others' attention through smiling; and at 9 months she was showing obvious discrimination of her mother from other persons as well as expressing distress when being left with individuals other than her mother.

Using empirical findings (reported in the child development literature) that suggest that cognitive and social-emotional aspects of development are inseparable (Kagan et al., 1978; McCall, 1972; Shultz & Zigler, 1970; Sroufe & Wunsch, 1972; Zelazo & Komer, 1971; Sroufe & Waters, 1976; Cicchetti & Sroufe, 1976; Gallagher, 1979), Kathleen's teachers were able to postulate that she was showing elements of cognitive functioning within expected limits for her age despite her limited repertoire of responses. The amount of data used to form this hypothesis was, of course, quite minimal; but the "as if" model for using research findings makes it possible to use available information for hypothesis formulation and, ultimately, for decision-making. The intervenor can assume, for example, that the statement made by Cicchetti and Sroufe (1976) and confirmed by Gallagher (1979) that the age at which an infant's first laugh appears is highly predictive of performance on the Bayley Mental Scales at 16 months and the Uzgiris-Hunt Scales at 13 months is a useful index. Similarly, the intervenor acts "as if" the studies of Bell (1970) and Lester et al. (1974), which demonstrated that the development of person permanence is closely related to the development of object permanence and that both relate to the expression of separation distress, are accurate.

Although researchers are often somewhat tentative in their statements about the clinical usefulness of their findings, it is possible to make use of their findings in generating hypotheses and intervention decisions about handicapped children. In this case, the assumptions about Kathleen's cognitive functioning proved to be warranted. By the time Kathleen was 2 years old, other measures of her cognitive abilities, for example, receptive language, appeared well within normal limits for her age.

Intervention

Intervention should follow naturally from the assessment process. If, in fact, an assessment has explored strengths and weaknesses of a child it has also set forth hypotheses about the way that child processes information, about the nature of appropriate intervention, and about the likelihood that specific strategies will be effective. Because many handicapped children, like Kathleen, are unable to provide the verbal and motoric responses required by traditional assessment paradigms, their information processing skills may be significantly underestimated. This frequently leads to a situation with which most educators and clinicians are unhappily familiar—children being taught at a developmentally young level with the realization at a later date that they were capable of processing information at a much higher level.

Use of developmental markers provided by recent work in the development of infant smiling and laughing (Cicchetti & Sroufe, 1976; Sroufe & Waters, 1976), perceptual-cognitive information processing using sequential visual and auditory stimuli (Kagan, Kearsley, & Zelazo, 1978; Zelazo, 1977), and the development of visual preference (Fantz, 1958) has helped alleviate this situation somewhat; it has permitted the practitioner to use markers "as if" they were true and to form new hypotheses with the additional developmental information they provide. It was apparent with Kathleen that there was a considerable discrepancy between her level of affective responding and her ability to demonstrate cognitive abilities in traditional ways. Using the aforementioned information, her parents and teachers were able to structure intervention experiences geared to a higher cognitive level than they would have otherwise. Without the affective information and the use of current, albeit tenuous, assumptions about its relationship to cognitive abilities, teaching would have focused on an entirely inappropriate developmental level and been less effective.

Entering the Parent-Child Relationship

The importance of assessment and intervention in the relationship between the child and his or her caregivers has been highlighted repeatedly in the child development literature of the past decade (Sameroff & Chandler, 1975; Bell, 1970; Parke, 1979). Brazelton (1979), for example, suggested that the primary task of the practitioner is to enter into the process between the child and the parent, thereby increasing the plasticity in the child's subsequent development. Specifically, he calls attention to the processes whereby the mother captures the child's attention and engages him or her in communicative acts. He also insists on the importance of the child's ability to engage the mother, to elicit care and contact from the mother, and thus to reinforce interactions that will ultimately facilitate development in other areas as well. The emphasis placed on parent-child interaction should be exciting to the practitioner in that it provides validation of his or her potential for effecting changes in the development of a child by intervening in the caregiving environment.

A major vehicle for entering into the caregiver-child interaction is provided by the literature on affective development. One significant perspective in this literature is an emphasis on the need for clarity of emotional signaling on the part of both the child and the parent. Emde (1979) points out that the continuance of interactions is dependent upon "emotional reciprocity" which, in turn, is a function of the "emotional availability" or capacity for emotional involvement manifested by both the child and caregiver.

Clinical experiences have shown that severely/multiply handicapped children have much greater problems than normal children providing signals that are readily understandable by caregivers. For illustrative purposes, consider the following comments on Paul. Paul is 3 years old and severely handicapped with athetoid cerebral palsy. For some time, his teacher was concerned about Paul's seeming lack of affective signals and the effect this might have on his relationship with his mother and other members of his family. Through ongoing observations of his affective responses in a preschool classroom, his teacher was able to share with his mother and to explore with her the possibility that Paul does respond emotionally, but not in ways readily identifiable. With these clinical observations and with information provided by Paul's mother about his behavior in other situations, it was possible to arrive at a joint hypothesis that an unusual facial grimace was, indeed, a smile. Not only has this hypothesis facilitated his development in the preschool situation, but it has had a significant effect on Paul's affective relationship with his parents. At least one of his emotional signals is clarified, and it is likely that more will be identified. His mother now sees him as emotionally available and able to respond to her signals. This quite probably resulted in increased maternal accessibility, which is seen as critical to developing and maintaining essential social interactions.

Demonstrating Developmental Progress

Parents are generally overwhelmed following the birth of a youngster who has been identified as having disabilities that may result in a handicapping condition. At a time that is supposed to be filled with excitement about the future, they are forced to deal with a series of traumatic events, all of which repeatedly point out that their youngster is different. This frequently results in a great many questions such as: Is it okay to handle him like other normal babies? How should I interact with him? What should I expect from him as he's developing? Parents do not know what to expect with regard to the development of a child once they have been told that he or she is different, and they have intense needs to see early signs of developmental progress.

Billy, a youngster with Down's syndrome, was 3 months old when he entered an infant treatment group. At that time, his mother demonstrated extreme anxiety with regard to Billy's developmental progress. She observed his responses to various affect-eliciting stimuli (Cicchetti & Sroufe, 1976). Although 85 percent of Billy's responses were neutral and another 10 percent indicated distress, the situation still provided a setting wherein it could be pointed out that Billy was attending to some of the stimuli and that there did seem to be an emerging smile at times. Although this information was not part of a standardized test instrument, it was readily available in the research literature. A less adequate assessment would have occurred if it had not been used "as if" it were valuable because of its current format. In addition, it was comforting to Billy's mother to know that there were first signs of an emerging smile at 3 months and to know that Billy's development in this area seemed similar to that of other babies in the group with Down's syndrome who were now older and whom Billy's mother perceived as making reasonable developmental progress.

Re-administration of the affect-eliciting stimuli at 5½ months showed Billy's mother that he was smiling to a significantly larger number of items, but she was also able to notice and point out that Billy was showing much better visual attention and that his visual tracking skills had increased noticeably since the last assessment.

At this time, Billy's mother was told that he was smiling in response to specific stimuli at which normal children generally begin to smile when they are 3 to 4 months of age. He was responding to auditory and tactile types of stimulation but not to visual and social items, responses that generally appear at a later time developmentally. This provided her with a developmental reference point, and perhaps more importantly, with a hypothesis regarding intervention. Thus, she began to attend to the frequency and type of stimulation that she was providing for Billy, and much more reciprocal play involving the two of them ensued.

LIMITATIONS AND PROBLEMS IN THE "AS IF" USE OF CURRENT DEVELOPMENTAL RESEARCH

Through the clinical examples described herein, it can be argued that experimental data regarding development can be useful in psycho-educational interactions with handicapped and at-risk children. Application of the "as if" approach is limited, however, because of the problems and limitations inherent in the introduction of tentative research data into teaching and treatment settings. Specifically, few findings are initially clear and discrete. One developmental landmark that could be clinically useful, for example, is the development of fear on the visual cliff, which generally occurs between 9 and 12 months of age (Campos et al., 1978). Its use is complicated by the fact that the onset of fear on the cliff is also apparently tied to the development of locomotion and social referencing (Campos & Stenberg, 1980).

In addition, some of the experimental methods used to estimate developmental level are cumbersome, to say the least. The visual cliff is not likely to be packaged for use by the itinerant psychologist working with preschool programs. Various affective-eliciting items, however, are more portable. Their use, unfortunately, raises parallel problems regarding the maintenance of interrater reliability in behavioral observations.

Furthermore, negative findings are difficult to interpret when using experimental strategies. If a youngster shows surprise when a covered object is found to be missing upon uncovering it, and laughs in response to auditory and tactile stimuli, a hypothesis that his or her developmental level falls in the 3-to 5-month range is reasonable, and one can plan interventions on that basis. If these responses are absent, however, more questions must be asked. Is the lack of responding a function of impaired perceptual development, lack of responsiveness to socially significant releasors of affect, lack of cognitive prerequisites for learning, or is it a function of the interaction among all three? Lack of responding on the part of a child makes hypothesizing and planning much more difficult.

The study of development in normal children does not always lead to useful application with handicapped children. For example, studies by Cicchetti and Sroufe (1976) and Gallagher (1979) demonstrated the importance of evaluating muscle tone in handicapped children before using affect-eliciting terms. Gallagher, Jens, and O'Donnell (1981) demonstrated that the effects of muscle tone impairment are independent of other factors and that as tone impairment increases, irrespective of the type of involvement, handicapped children's ability to laugh decreases. Obviously, much caution must be exercised when using affective responding in a prognostic way.

BRIDGING THE GAP BETWEEN RESEARCH AND PRACTICE

Use of the "as if" model helps to bridge the gap between persons engaged in intervention with handicapped children and those primarily interested in advancing knowledge regarding the development of handicapped children through research. Throughout this chapter, emphasis is put on the task of the practitioners in using experimental data in a clinical setting. Researchers, however, can also facilitate the bridging process in several ways. Scholarly journals are the major source of information for practitioners. It would be helpful for experimentally oriented individuals to show increased awareness of the fact that they are communicating, not only with their research colleagues, but also with practitioners who are frequently unschooled in much of the professional jargon. Similarly, it is beneficial when investigators are willing to offer their thoughts about the possible application of the research data. This would facilitate the establishment of the link between research and the improvement of educational and/or clinical practice. In addition, the presentation of findings in comprehensive articles facilitates their translation into practice; separating results into several publications can result in misinterpretation by and frustration on the part of the clinician trying to make use of the data.

What are some responsibilities clinicians and practitioners might better assume than they have in the past? First, they might accept half of the responsibility for communication with the research community;

communication is, after all, a two-way process. Just as the research community must go to the service community as the source for its data, the practitioner can also call upon the researcher for clarification of ideas or to explore new ideas.

Second, there is a wealth of information regarding normal and abnormal child development available in the professional literature, which many practitioners do not read on a regular basis; practitioners must invest in the quest for available information. It is possible that those who have to make daily decisions regarding service to youngsters may be overwhelmed by the abundance of literature available. If we are willing to adopt an "as if" model, we can use the literature in a cafeteria manner and make choices from it. We do not have to understand fully all that is presented; we can trust and try to make use of those portions of the literature that seem useful.

SUMMARY

This chapter addresses a major problem in the field of child development—the translation and movement of research findings from laboratory settings into everyday practice. It suggests that the gap between the development of new knowledge and its perceived usability presents a dilemma for practitioners. They need and want to respond to new developments in the field to improve assessment and intervention practices, but the potential application of new constructs and/or strategies is not always obvious or direct. The suggestion is made that the practitioner deal with this dilemma by using an "as if" model in utilizing current research findings and moving them into intervention settings. Examples of how the "as if" model is applicable to the areas of infant assessment and intervention are provided.

REFERENCES

Bell, S. The development of the concept of object as related to infant mother attachment. *Child Development,* 1970, *41,* 291–316.

Brazelton, T. Identifying assessment techniques for enhancing infant development. Paper presented at the meeting of The National Center for Clinical Infant Programs, Washington, D.C., 1979.

Campos, J. J., Hiatt, S., Ramsay, D., Henderson, C. & Svejda, J. The emergence of fear on the visual cliff. In M. Lewis and L. Rosenblum (Eds.). *The development of affect.* New York: Plenum Press, 1978.

Campos, J., & Stenberg, C. Perception, appraisal and emotion: The onset of social referencing. In M. Lamb, and L. Sherrod, (Eds.), *Infant Social Cognition.* Hillsdale, N.J.: Lawrence Erlbaum Associates, 1980.

Cicchetti, D., & Sroufe, L. The relationship between affective and cognitive development in Down's Syndrome infants. *Child Development,* 1976, *47,* 920–929.

Emde, R. The importance of affect in infant assessment. In Brazelton, T. (Chair), Identifying assessment techniques for enhancing infant development. Discussion presented at the meeting of the National Center for Clinical Infant Programs, Washington, D.C., 1979.

Fantz, R. Pattern vision in young infants. *The Psychological Record*, 1958, *8*, 43–47.

Gallagher, R. Positive affect in multiply handicapped infants: Its relationship to developmental age, temperament, physical status, and setting. Unpublished doctoral dissertation, University of North Carolina at Chapel Hill, 1979.

Gallagher, R., Jens, K., & O'Donnell, K. The effect of physical status on the affective expression of handicapped infants. Manuscript submitted for publication, 1981.

Grossman, S. *A textbook of physiological psychology*. New York: John Wiley & Sons, 1967.

James, W. *Principles of psychology*. New York: Henry Holt, 1890.

Kagan, J., Kearsley, R., & Zelazo, P. *Infancy: Its place in human development*. Cambridge: Harvard University Press, 1978.

Kuhn, T. *The structure of scientific revolutions* (2nd Ed.) Chicago: University of Chicago Press, 1970.

Lester, B., Kotelchuck, M., Spelke, E., Sellers, M., & Klein, R. Separation protest in Guatemalan infants: Cross cultural and cognitive findings. *Developmental Psychology*, 1974, *10*, 79–85.

McCall, R. Smiling and vocalization in infants as indices of perceptual-cognitive processes. *Merrill-Palmer Quarterly*, 1972, *18*, 341–348.

Parke, R. Emerging themes for social-emotional development. *American Psychologist*, 1979, *34*(10), 930–931.

Sameroff, A., & Chandler, M. Reproductive risk and the continuum of caretaking casualty. In F. D. Horowitz, M. Hetherington, S. Scarr-Salapatek & G. Siegel (Eds.), *Review of child development research* (Vol. 4). Chicago: University of Chicago Press, 1975.

Shultz, T., & Zigler, E. Emotional concomitants of visual mastery in infants: The effects of stimulus movement on smiling and vocalizing. *Journal of Experimental Child Psychology*, 1970, *10*, 390–402.

Sroufe, L., & Waters, E. The ontogenesis of smiling and laughter: A perspective on the organization of development in infancy. *Psychological Review*, 1976, *83*, 173–189.

Sroufe, L., & Wunsch, J. P. The development of laughter in the first year of life. *Child Development, 1972, 43*, 1326–1344.

Watson, L. *Lifetide*. New York: Simon and Schuster, 1979.

Zelazo, P. Reactivity to perceptual-cognitive events: Application for infant assessment. In R. Kearsley and I. Sigel (Eds.), *Infants at risk: The assessment of cognitive functioning*. Hillsdale, N.J.: Lawrence Erlbaum Associates, 1977.

Zelazo, P., & Komer, J. Infant smiling to nonsocial stimuli and the recognition hypothesis. *Child Development*, 1971, *42*, 1327–1329.

Section II
ASSESSMENT ISSUES

Chapter 3

INFANT ASSESSMENT:
A Review and Identification
of Emergent Trends

Robert Sheehan

The last decade has seen an upsurge of interest in handicapped and at-risk infants. This current focus is building upon an older tradition of research and assessment with nonhandicapped infants. Current intervention activities for handicapped infants are resulting in significant transformations of infant research efforts and a corresponding reformulation of infant assessment strategies.

This chapter is divided into three sections. The first presents a summary review of current assessment strategies for handicapped and nonhandicapped infants. Section two identifies controversial issues in current assessment activities that give rise to problems, inconsistencies, and ambiguities. The third section addresses five directions that professionals in the field may pursue in order to resolve the controversies surrounding infant assessment.

CURRENT INFANT ASSESSMENT STRATEGIES

An extensive review process is underway in the field of infant assessment. This review, which began approximately 5 years ago (Brooks & Weinraub, 1976), will likely provide the impetus necessary to make changes in infant assessment over the next decade. This review process can be divided into two related but somewhat independent types of activity. The first addresses the purposes of infant assessment. The second type of review process addresses the psychometric properties of existing infant assessment measures. That a differentiation can be made between purposes and psychometric properties is an indication of controversy that needs resolution because, in theory, the reliability and validity of a measure should be stated in terms of its purpose.

The writing of this chapter was supported by Contract No. 300-77-0306, from the U.S. Office of Education, Bureau of Education for the Handicapped to Project REACH, UCLA Graduate School of Education.

The review process occurring throughout the field of infant assessment is a sign that the field is in a period of transition. Support for this claim can be found in the area of early intervention for disadvantaged children. Hodges and Smith (1978) pointed out that early education for disadvantaged children has gone through several stages including a period of conception during which the problem became recognized; a period of reconstruction during which significant theory building occurred; a period of revolution during which there was a rush to provide services; and finally a period of reflection during which the efficacy of the services provided was analyzed.

The period of reflection in the education of young disadvantaged children is marked by comments and conclusions that are familiar to early childhood educators. Reviews by Bronfenbrenner (1974), Hunt (1975), Horowitz and Paden (1972), White et al. (1973), and Ryan (1974) contributed to the current value placed on ecological intervention, social competence, and family support. It is hoped that the current period of reflection on infant assessment will evoke changes of similar magnitude.

Purposes of Infant Assessment

Some insight into the purposes of infant assessment can be provided by the historical reviews of Honzik (1976) and Brooks and Weinraub (1976). These writers point out that the primary purpose of infant measures was the description of normal development. Only in recent years have infant measures been used to predict specific developmental patterns of atypical infants and to diagnose and suggest intervention for the handicapped and at-risk population. Unfortunately, the utility of infant measures to serve purposes other than general descriptions of normal developmental patterns still remains questionable.

The limited ability of infant assessment techniques to predict later intelligence in the nonhandicapped child has been documented (Honzik, 1976; Uzgiris, 1976). Lewis (1976) summarized this perspective by arguing that infant intelligence is not unitary, not predictive of later intelligence, and not generalizable from one specific instrument to other infant measures.

Scarr (Scarr-Salapetak, 1976) theorized that this limited predictability may be explained by an evolutionary interpretation that recognizes that sensorimotor functioning (a primary content of many infant instruments) may evolve earlier, and hence may be nondetermining of symbolic functioning (the content of later tests), resulting in limited predictive ability between assessment of both constructs. Goodman and Cameron's (1978) recent data qualify Scarr's interpretations by concluding that accuracy of prediction is inversely related to an infant's level of functioning. As the level of retardation increases, the usefulness of traditional assessment data for prediction also increases (MacRae, 1955). At best, however, these data indicate that an infant is functioning in a manner different from that of the general population.

A different purpose for infant assessment is reflected by the growing interest in assessment instruments that focus on the development of infant sensorimotor behavior. These measures are based on Piagetian theory and include scales by Uzgiris and Hunt (1975), Casati and Lezine (1968) and Corman and Escalona (1969). These assessment measures serve the purpose of theory development and validation in which current knowledge of the structure and sequence of sensorimotor development is refined. The usefulness of these measures for handicapped infants awaits future validation.

In addition to the purposes commonly acknowledged for infant assessment, there is an additional purpose that is receiving increasing attention in intervention programs. This purpose is built on assumptions of prediction, diagnosis, and theory testing and springs from political rather than academic impetus. This purpose is the documentation of infant progress, which is clearly related to but not synonymous with program evaluation. Documentation of progress is the gathering of data on one or more infants over a period of time (e.g., 1–3 years) in order to describe that progress to others. Although the gathering of child progress data for monitoring purposes and instructional planning is not new, there is an increasing emphasis on these data to determine whether an intervention program has produced suitable progress in the target population and should receive continuing support. The Office of Special Education now requires that demonstration projects gather such data.

Psychometric Properties of Infant Assessment Instruments

The second type of review process focuses on the psychometric properties of infant assessment instruments. An immediate conclusion that can be drawn from these reviews is that the large proportion of infant assessment instruments lacks adequate reliability, validity, and standardization data. Johnson and Kopp (undated) report that for 67 instruments specifically identified as infant measures, 46, or 69%, provide no reliability data. Even fewer provide validity data and norms are available on only a negligible fraction of those instruments.

Walls, Werner, Bacon, and Zane (1977) reported that 80% (131 out of 163) of the behavior checklists that they reviewed, many of which apply to infancy, lack reliability or validity information. Cross and Johnston (1977) also reported in their bibliography of 98 instruments that few instruments provide psychometric data. Their conclusion is that "reliability and validity studies are still incomplete" (p. 80). Of equal concern is their conclusion that "norms are based on other tests" (p. 75). This procedure entails the development of a test by selecting items from other existing instruments. The methodological hazard that can be encountered by this type of reasoning is obvious. One cannot claim that instruments developed in such a fashion are psychometrically sound because the norms for most tests are computed on an overall basis, rather than on an item basis. Utilizing only selected items in new tests invalidates those norms.

The absence of psychometric data for published infant assessment instruments portrays a bleak picture to academicians who have been trained to expect reliability, validity, and normative data. Many infant intervention programs have also developed their own assessment instruments (Pefly & Smith, 1976). The professionals in these programs argued that because the items are drawn from standardized instruments, the newly developed scales have adequate reliability and validity. The flaw in this argument has just been pointed out.

An additional concern is that in most cases in which psychometric data are reported for infant assessment measures, the data reflect non-handicapped infants. This factor becomes crucial when the instruments are used for purposes other than identification. It could be argued that data on nonhandicapped infants should form the basis of a comparison to determine if other infants are atypical. A problem occurs if, once identification is made, data on nonhandicapped children are used to compare progress with handicapped children. At present, this problem is not completely resolvable because appropriate instruments for atypical children do not exist and infant intervention projects are forced to use as a reference the normal standardization samples.

At first glance these conclusions regarding the psychometric properties of infant measures are of grave concern. Partial resolution is possible, however. First, a review of twenty-seven early intervention programs by Pefley and Smith (1976) suggests that most intervention programs are using more than one assessment measure. Most programs are using a battery of measures including at least one measure for which reliability and validity data on nonhandicapped infants exist. It would be encouraging to report that the infant intervention projects are actually correlating the standardized measures with the nonstandardized measures utilizing genuine data, but unfortunately this is often not the case. In most cases the multiple instruments are not being intercorrelated. Nevertheless, the projects are relying on multiple measures and referring to the more psychometrically sound measures when disagreement exists.

A second useful perspective is provided by the work of Cohen, Gross, and Haring (1976) who reviewed twenty-four assessment instruments. These instruments focus on developmental functioning from birth to approximately 6 years. Each item of each test was reviewed and identified the age at which that item was projected to emerge in the normal child. This comparison is encouraging because of the reported agreement between developmental age norms for the similar items across the tests during the birth-to-24-months developmental period. For these instruments, the range in age at which similar items were normally passed is approximately 1 month. A conclusion from this review is that with few exceptions, the twenty-four instruments are in general agreement at an item level.

A third positive perspective regarding the psychometric state of the art of infant assessment is that limited reliability and validity data for each of the many instruments in existence may be viewed as more of a problem for those assessment efforts that are normative in function (i.e., screening and diagnosis). Many projects are using infant assessment instruments to develop individual educational plans (IEPs) and to set objectives. In these instances, the sequence of items in assessment measures is far more important than the specific age emergence of each skill. As long as projects are using instruments that are based on standardized measures, and as long as the professionals using the measures are sensitive to the question of ordinal ranking of items, instruments currently in use are likely to be helpful for educational programming for atypical infants.

ISSUES RAISED BY CURRENT INFANT ASSESSMENT STRATEGIES

The approach taken in this chapter is to categorize the issues raised by current assessment strategies into four separate but related areas. This categorization is certainly arbitrary, but it is done in an attempt to provide a structure for discussing the multiple issues raised by current activities in the field of infant assessment.

Desirable and Actual Characteristics of Infant Measures

The first issue raised by current assessment activity is the conflict between the actual and desired characteristics of infant measures. This conflict occurs because although there has been a significant expansion in the purpose of infant assessment, current measures were originally designed to meet the limited purpose of describing normal developmental functioning. The problem is that the characteristics of infant measures strongly influence their usefulness for different purposes.

Ease of administration is important for an instrument to be useful for screening (or initial identification). Screening measures must also have low probability of missing atypical infants, resulting, therefore, in few false negatives. Screening measures need not be totally comprehensive, but they must be representative enough to ensure adequate coverage of developmental domains. The content of screening measures must be predictive of later performance. As a consequence, qualitatively different items are found in screening measures including items an intervenor might desire to teach and items useful simply because of the regularity of emergence.

A useful diagnostic instrument, on the other hand, should reflect accurately the etiology of an infant's condition. Such measures need not be as quickly administered as screening measures because relatively few infants must be diagnosed. A diagnostic measure must, however, have a low probability of mislabelling or falsely identifying infants. They should result in few false positives. Diagnostic measures must be comprehensive to provide a thorough assessment of an infant's strengths and limitations. Items must have construct validity, accurately reflecting the theoretical construct or trait being measured. These items need not necessarily be teachable but must go beyond simply predictability of later performance.

Instruments useful for educational planning, must be manageable for frequent assessment of the same child, must be relatively easy to administer yet must also cover an age span broad enough to be used for a given child across a significant time period. Despite the need for ease of administration, educational planning instruments must be comprehensive enough to provide concrete evidence for educational planning. The problem of error rates with educational planning measures is now significantly lessened as infants have already been identified as in need of intervention. Instruments useful for educational planning must have high content validity closely matching the goals and practices of intervention. These instruments should also have approximately equal intervals between items so that planning can be conducted at regular intervals. Thus such instruments must be specific, manageable, and prescriptive for the instructional staff.

The conflict between desirable and actual characteristics of infant measure becomes all the more apparent when one asks just how much information should be derived from assessment. The answer to this question is dependent upon the purpose of the assessment. For example, the most useful data for a screening or identification instrument should result in a unitary numerical score that has high predictive validity. Diagnostic, educational planning, and documentation instruments should, however, maximize the information they generate. They should, for example, convey far more information than the ceiling level of performance achieved by an infant. An intervention program's impact may not be on the attainment of a ceiling level, but some other aspect of functioning. An interventionist might want to know about the presence of developmental scatter, the performance on items that have high teachability, and so forth.

The conflict between standardization populations and assessed populations is a concern shared by many professionals. In addition, the conflict exists between the assumptions made by assessment measures that are "developmental" (i.e., they are scalar, progressing from simple to complex) and the actual performance of children. On these tests, the normal infant should exhibit a pattern of complete success up to a certain point (his or her developmental age) and then fail every item after this. The range from basal to ceiling, therefore, should always be 1.

As many clinicians are aware, performance on developmental tests is not completely scalar. Normal infants often miss several items before and after their ceiling. Quantitative estimates of existent ranges in the normal population and corresponding data regarding the handicapped and at-risk population are lacking. A project currently underway is estimating patterns of variability in child performance (Sheehan, Keogh, & Watson[1]). The preliminary analyses suggest large ranges between the lowest item that handicapped preschool children miss and their highest passed item on the Bayley Scales. These ranges vary from 11 items to 102 items across children on the same measure. In addition, there seems to be relative stability of these ranges within each child across administrations. Our initial conclusion is that variability in the sequence of development, as measured by infant instruments, does exist among populations of children. The meaning of this variability and its long term stability within children must be explored further.

Focus of Existing Measures

The third set of issues surrounding current infant assessment strategies is the focus of existing measures. That many assessment efforts are now directed at documentation rather than identification and diagnosis poses problems. These problems are reflected in the argument that many existing infant measures are not responsive to intervention activities (Kopp, 1979). As a result, these instruments should not be the outcome measures utilized in documentation efforts. Kopp (1979) fur-

---

[1] Sheehan, R., Keogh, B., & Watson, P. Research currently underway at UCLA's Project REACH, Study DP-79-S, funded by Contract No. 300-77-0306, from the U.S. Office of Education, Bureau of Education for the Handicapped.

ther proposes that such intervention with infants should be directed toward parents rather than the infant. Therefore, Kopp (1979) argued that more appropriate measures at the time of intervention would be those assessing impact on parents.

This argument regarding the focus of existing measures is supported by Wohlwill's (1973) plea for more dimensionalized instruments to assess progress over time. This argument is also supported by the sharp attacks on the limited scope of measures of many of the participants in the national Follow-Through evaluation (Haney, 1977; Hodges & Sheehan, 1978). These critics of the Follow-Through evaluation argue that the use of relatively few standardized measures in the national Follow-Through evaluation proved a narrow and fragmented estimate of program impact.

Traditional developmental data are necessary but insufficient for educational planning and documentation purposes for several reasons. A strong relationship does exist between the intervention activities of many educators in infant programs and the normal developmental model. Many infant programs are attempting to "teach" developmental skills to handicapped infants. The efficacy of this approach remains to be validated but standard developmental data are necessary for this validation effort.

A second reason for continuing to use existing assessment measures to document infant progress is pragmatic. Documentation of progress is used primarily for the political arena of program evaluation. Intervenors need to "cover all their bases" and therefore the collection of developmental data is necessary while more responsive data are sought. Unfortunately, instrument development is a lengthy process. The initial development of the Bayley Scales began in the 1920s and the codification of this scale did not occur until 1969. Reliable and valid measures of impact on parents will not be available for some time. During the interval, intervenors must use what they have.

Expected Magnitude of Treatment Effects

If treatment effects are defined as documentable changes in infants that are caused by intervention procedures, one conclusion that can be drawn from a review of current activities is that the expected magnitude of such effects, for a majority of intervention programs, is quite small. This generalization is in sharp contrast to the much heralded research of Skeels and Dye (1939) and equally impressive effects shown by Heber and Garber (1975). Both of these studies began intervention with infants at an early age. The treatment effects demonstrated in these two programs is on the magnitude of 30 points gain in IQ (or DQ). Current infant intervention data are yet to approach this magnitude of change.

The issue of small treatment effects is not brought up to criticize the efforts of current infant intervenors. The magnitude of the treatment provided by Heber and Garber (1975) was costly. This research relied heavily upon parent surrogate, minimizing the actual contact between infants and their mothers. The orphanage system existing when the Skeels and Dye research was conducted is not a social service system of most current mental health programs. Professionals using current infant assessment strategies should recognize that small treatment effects are the rule rather than the exception, and they must take action to ensure that the small documented effects are not further minimized by inconsistent data gathering techniques. For example, Durham and Black (1978) reported that infants assessed in the home score higher than when the same infants were assessed in the laboratory, provided that they are assessed in the home first. If these findings prove to be replicable, data gathering that occurs in both the home and the laboratory might further minimize the estimated treatment effects.

NEW DIRECTIONS IN ASSESSMENT STRATEGIES

The period of reflection in the assessment of handicapped and at-risk infants is a period that can have a beneficial impact on the activities of professionals in the field. There are at least five new directions toward which professionals are moving in the area of infant assessment. Over the course of the next decade, movement in these five directions might radically alter both the purposes and strategies of infant assessment.

Modification of Infant Measures

The first direction evident is the development of procedures to allow modifications in assessment of handicapped infants. Anyone working with severely handicapped infants and infants with specific handicapping conditions is aware that modifications are necessary when conducting a thorough assessment. In discussing this topic DuBose (1979) suggested that one purpose of assessment is to test childrens' limits, which may require adaptations in the assessment process. DuBose (1979) further points out that once adaptations are made, norm referenced comparisons become dubious.

The problem of the invalid norm-referenced comparisons because of adaptations is one that certainly confronts any assessment effort. Cautioning professionals who make adaptations not to refer to norms is inadequate. One recent development of interest is the funding by the Office of Special Education of a 3-year grant to develop an instrument and analytic system for the developmental period birth to 2 years (CAPE, 1978). This instrument called the Adaptive Performance Instrument (API) was developed to accommodate systematic modifications. This instrument is currently being field tested on handicapped infants and children. Suggested and novel adaptations are possible in the way in which tasks are presented and the possible responses that are considered acceptable. Modifications were developed for visually impaired, hearing impaired, visual/hearing impaired, and orthopedically involved children and infants.

Development of the API is an important step in the combination of adaptations and a norm-referenced perspective. This is also a first step in recognizing that instruments for documenting the progress of handicapped and at-risk infants require a large number of program-relevant items. The API, which extends from birth to 2 years, contains over 400 developmental items, all of which are considered teachable by the designers of the instrument. A 400-item instrument will be too time consuming for repeated documentation efforts. With systematic sampling of items, however, this instrument may be useful for both educational planning and documentation of child progress.

The API is only partially a "new instrument" because the API draws heavily from items contained within existing instruments. The API was designed to include those items that were educationally meaningful as opposed to being simply developmental markers. This instrument has been sequenced in a scalar fashion, and this sequence is one of the variables being examined in the field test effort. Repeated testing on at least 3,000 to 5,000 children is necessary before the instrument should be considered psychometrically sound. The development of this instrument has combined new concepts with many standard developmental items. The use of instruments such as the API may help resolve the problem of the "elusive bridge" from assessment to intervention to which Keogh and Kopp (1978) referred.

Considerable basic research is required in the area of adaptations with handicapped infants. For example, adaptations must be tested by administering adapted items to nonhandicapped infants. If the item is really being assessed in its generic sense, such an administration should not yield different results for the nonhandicapped infants. A more realistic approach would be to conduct such research with the goal of identifying the directions of the bias which is sure to occur through adaptations. If the bias does not penalize the normal infant, the implication would be that an adapted assessment of handicapped infants would at least be a conservative assessment.

Conducting Current Reliability and Validity Studies

A second new direction in the field of infant assessment is the conduct of current reliability and validity studies on existing measures with handicapped infants. Rentz (1977) recently completed a review of "Trends, Activities and Problems Related to Education of the Handicapped" for the Educational Testing Service. She concluded that "Rather than developing another screening instrument, a preferable strategy would be to conduct validity studies on some of the more promising popular instruments." This approach would seem to have great merit.

Developing New Assessment Strategies

The third direction is the development of new assessment strategies. Although a number of assessment instruments exist, there is a need for new instrumentation as our understanding of infant behavior increases. There is also a need to develop infant assessment strategies that pertain to the infants' home environments (Kopp, 1979). Bradley and Caldwell (1975) have extended the preschool version of the HOME Inventory downward to the 6 months age range. This instrument has been tested longitudinally with parents of normal infants (Elardo, Bradley, & Caldwell, 1976) but data pertaining to the environments of atypical infants have not been reported. Bromwich (1976) developed a six-stage progression of maternal-infant interaction, which is being used in several infant intervention programs around the country.

Reexamining Traditional Research Strategies

The fourth area of new development in infant assessment is in the reexamination of traditional assessment strategies to determine whether they might yield additional information. There seems to be genuine disagreement between clinicians who identify infants for intervention and evaluators who document the progress of those infants. This disagreement concerns the amount and quality of information yielded by traditional assessment efforts. A clinician administering an assessment will view the obtained developmental age score as only one of several useful indices. In addition, throughout the course of the assessment the clinician may attend to a variety of other variables such as the state and motivation of the infant. These data may be observed but not quantified by the clinician. An evaluator gathering documentation data will have access only to the quantified indices. These include raw scores, developmental ages, scale scores, and developmental quotients. As a result of this, the documentation of child progress will reflect only a small portion of the information available to the clinician. Reexamination of this situation calls for an attempt to define and quantify such concepts as developmental scatter, item profiling, and range of responses. Reexamination also requires a refinement of concepts of state and motivation.

Methodologies need to be developed that view an infant's performance as a topography rather than a single point. These methodologies must weave a delicate balance between the need for mathematical complexity (e.g., Joreskog, 1973) to capture the complexity of growth and the relatively low level of technical expertise of the professionals utilizing assessment information (e.g., project directors, teachers, funding agents).

Utilizing Rasch-type Latent Trait Psychometric Models

A fifth new direction that has potential for assessors involves the utilization of latent trait psychometric models. One of these models has been developed by Rasch (1966) and more recently discussed by Wright (1968). These psychometric models have been referenced as being appropriate for the school-age population in the area of achievement testing (Passmore, 1973). The assumptions made in the model, however, do not limit its useability and in fact suggest that the model may be very appropriate for infants and preschool populations.

A common concern regarding existing infant assessment measures is that they do not completely complement the goals of intervention programs. As a result, many intervenors have extracted items from existing measures and collated the items together into new, nonstandardized measures. The concern of these intervenors is that they need instruments that have content validity and the corresponding concern among researchers is that the new instrument must have reliability.

What is needed in the field of early intervention is for measures that are neither population bound (i.e., specific to any particular population) nor test bound (i.e., yielding statistics that cannot be compared to different measures). These requirements are both met by the Rasch psychometric model, which creates an interval scale measure yielding statistics independent of the specific test that generated them.

Space does not permit a full explication of the Rasch model but the two major assumptions are: that students (or infants) can be measured on a graduated scale, and that the success that students have in passing an item depends upon their achievement level and the difficulty of the item. The infant assessment process meets both of these assumptions.

SUMMARY

In summary, the field of infant assessment is in transition. This transition is indicated by the review process that has been occurring for the past 5 years and by dissatisfaction with the current state of infant assessment. The likely result of this transition will be the development and refinement of more useful techniques for documenting the progress of handicapped and at-risk infants across time. This transition is also resulting in the identification of more realistic expected treatment effects and the realization that infant intervention is having an impact on the total environment of the infant. The field of infant assessment is changing, and will likely continue to change, for the better, over the course of the next decade.

REFERENCES

Bradley, R., & Caldwell, B. Home observation for measurement of the environment: A revision of the preschool scale. *American Journal of Mental Deficiency*, 1975, 84, 235–244.

Bromwich, R. Focus on maternal behavior in infant intervention. *American Journal of Orthopsychiatry*, 1976, *46*, 439–446.

Bronfenbrenner, U. *A report on longitudinal evaluations of preschool programs.* Vol. II. Is early intervention effective? Washington, D. C.: Department of Health, Education and Welfare, Publication No. (OHD) 74-25, 1974.

Brooks, J., & Weinraub, M. A history of infant intelligence testing. In M. Lewis (Ed.), *Origins of intelligence.* New York: Plenum Press, 1976.

CAPE, Consortium on Adaptive Performance Evaluation. *Adaptive assessment for evaluating the progress of severely/profoundly handicapped children functioning between birth and 2 years.* The annual report of a field initiated research project funded by The Bureau of Education for the Handicapped, Grant No. G007702139, 1978–1979.

Casati, I., & Lezine, I. Les etapes de L'Intelligence Sensorinotrice, Les Edition's du Centre psychologie Appliquee, Paris, 1968.

Cohen, M., Gross, P., & Haring, N. Developmental pinpoints. In N. Haring & L. Brown (Eds.), Teaching the severely handicapped (Vol. 1). New York: Grune & Stratton, Inc., 1976.

Corman, H., & Escalona, S. Stages of sensorimotor development: A replication study. *Merrill-Palmer Quarterly*, 1969, *15*, 351.

Cross, L., & Johnston, S. A bibliography of instruments. In L. Cross & K. Goin (Eds.), Identifying handicapped children: A guide to casefinding, screening, diagnosis, assessment, and evaluation. New York: Walker Publishing Co., 1977.

DuBose, R. Adaptations in measurement procedures: Should you make alterations for handicapped children? In T. Black (Ed.), *Perspectives on measurement: A collection of readings for educators of young handicapped children,* Chapel Hill, NC: TADS, 1979.

Durham, M., & Black, K. The test performance of 16 to 21 month-olds in home and laboratory settings. *Infant Behavior and Development*, 1978, *1*, 216–223.

Elardo, R., Bradley, R., & Caldwell, B. The relation of infant's home environment to mental test performance from six to thirty-six months: A longitudinal analysis. *Child Development*, 1976, *46*, 71–76.

Goodman, J., & Cameron, J. The meaning of IQ constancy in young retarded children. *Journal of Genetic Psychology*, 1978, *132*, 109–119.

Haney, W. *A technical history of the national Follow Through evaluation,* Cambridge, Mass.: Huson Institute, 1977. (Also issued by the U.S. Office of Education as *The Follow Through Evaluation: A technical history, Vol. II* of the Follow Through Planned Vacation Experiment series).

Heber, R., & Garber, H. The Milwaukee project: A study of the use of family intervention to prevent cultural-familial retardation. In B. Friedlander, F. Sterritt & G. Kirk (Eds.), *Exceptional infant: Assessment and intervention* (Vol. 3). New York: Brunner/Mazel, 1975.

Hodges, W., & Sheehan, R. Follow through as 10 years of experimentation. *Young Children,* 1978, *34,* 4–14.

Hodges, W., & Smith, L. Retrospect and prospect in early childhood and special education. Presented at 1978 Annual Convention of the American Psychological Association, San Francisco. Sept. 1978.

Honzik, M. Values and limitations of infant tests: An overview in M. Lewis (Ed.), *Origins of intelligence.* New York: Plenum Press, 1976.

Horowitz, F., & Paden, L. The effectiveness of environmental intervention programs. In B. Caldwell & H. Ricciuti (Eds.), *Review of child development research* (Vol. 3). New York: Russel Sage Foundation, 1972.

Hunt, J. McV. Reflections on a decade of early education. *Journal of Abnormal Child Psychology,* 1975, *3,* 275–230.

Johnson, K., & Kopp, C. A bibliography of screening and assessment measures for infants. Project REACH, UCLA Graduate School of Education, Los Angeles.

Joreskog, K. A general method for estimating a linear structural equation system. In A. S. Goldberger & O. D. Duncan (Eds.), *Structural equation models in the social sciences.* New York: Seminar Press, 1973.

Keogh, B., & Kopp, C. From assessment to intervention: An elusive bridge. In F. Minifie & L. Lloyd (Eds.), *Communicative and cognitive abilities— Early behavioral assessment.* Baltimore: University Park Press, 1978.

Kopp, C. Mildly to moderately handicapped infants: What should influence your approach to measurement: In T. Black (Ed.), *Perspectives on measurement: A collection of readings for educators of young handicapped children,* Chapel Hill, NC: TADS, 1979.

Lewis, M. What do we mean when we say "infant intelligence scores?" A sociopolitical question. In M. Lewis (Ed.), *Origins of intelligence.* New York: Plenum Press, 1976.

MacRae, J. Retests of children given mental tests as infants. *Journal of Genetic Psychology,* 1955, *87,* 111.

Passmore, D. Objective measurement in occupational education. *Journal of Industrial Teacher Education,* 1973, *10*(4), 15–21.

Pefley, D., & Smith, H. *It's Monday morning.* Chapel Hill, NC: Technical Assistance Development System (TADS), 1976.

Rasch, G. An individualistic approach to item analysis. In P. Lazarsfeld & N. Henry (Eds.), *Readings in mathematical social science.* Chicago: Science Research Associates, 1966.

Rentz, C. Trends, activities and problems related to education of the handicapped. A paper prepared for Educational Testing Service, Atlanta: October, 1977.

Ryan, S. A report on longitudinal evaluations of preschool programs, Vol. I: Longitudinal evaluations. Washington, D.C.: DHEW Publication No. (OHD) 74024, 1974.

Scarr-Salapetak, S. An evolutionary perspective on infant intelligence: Species patterns and individual variations. In M. Lewis (Ed.), *Origins of intelligence.* New York: Plenum Press, 1976.

Skeels, H., & Dye, H. A study of the effects of differential stimulation of mentally retarded children. *Proceedings of the American Association on Mental Deficiency,* 1939, *44,* 114–136.

Uzgiris, I. Organization of sensorimotor intelligence. In M. Lewis (Ed.), *Origins of intelligence.* New York: Plenum Press, 1976.

Uzgiris, I., & Hunt, J. McV. *Assessment in infancy.* Urbana: University of Illinois Press, 1975.

Walls, R., Werner, T., Bacon, A., & Zane, T. Behavior checklists. In J. Cone & R. Hawkins (Eds.), *Behavioral assessment: New directions in clinical psychology.* New York: Brunner/Mazel, 1977.

White, S., Day, M., Freeman, P., Harman, S., & Messenger, K. *Federal programs for young children: Review and recommendations, Vol. III. Recommendations for federal program planning.* Washington, D.C.: Superintendent of Documents, 1973.

Wohlwill, J. The study of behavioral development. New York: Academic Press, 1973.

Wright, B. Sample-free test calibration and person measurement. In *Proceedings of the 1967 Invitational Conference on Testing Problems.* Princeton, N.J.: Educational Testing Service, 1968.

Chapter 4

ASSESSMENT PARADIGMS
AND ATYPICAL INFANTS:
An Interventionist's Perspective

Nancy M. Johnson

One of the major challenges facing the interventionist working with young handicapped children is finding accurate, reliable, and useful ways to describe the developmental status of these youngsters. Such a description is critical for all phases of service: identifying those in need of intervention, determining the goals for intervention, charting developmental progress, and evaluating the effectiveness of intervention.

Traditionally, three basic paradigms have been available for assessing developmental skills in children under 3 years of age. The first is through the use of norm-referenced, standardized psychological tests that yield one or two scores describing the child's status in terms of deviance from age expectancy or deviance from the mean performance of other children his or her age. Most of these tests were developed specifically to measure mental development although many of the items seem to involve more motor than cognitive skill. These tests were normed on samples of children deliberately chosen to exclude youngsters with known biological handicaps but nonetheless are widely used to describe the skills of just such populations. Interventionists have become frustrated with the single score categorization of youngsters provided by norm-referenced tests and the limitations of these tests for describing specific strengths and weaknesses in handicapped children. They continue to rely on these instruments, however, because of the scientific respectability associated with their standardization.

The second paradigm, criterion-referenced assessment, involves the use of instruments that contain lists of developmental skills and the criteria defining skill mastery. The lists are usually organized around several areas or domains such as cognition, language, gross motor, fine motor, and personal-social. A child's status is described in terms of the skills mastered in each of the domains. Criterion-referenced instruments were developed, in part, as a reaction against deviance scores, the rigidity of test administration, and the inappropriateness of many of the items in norm-referenced tests for the handicapped population. Yet, ironically, criterion-referenced tests include primarily (or exclusively) items taken directly from the standardized tests they were designed to replace. Furthermore, in an attempt to draw profiles of strengths and weaknesses in handicapped children, an age level is usually assigned to each skill included in the test. These age levels are also taken from the norm-referenced tests and are based on the mean age of children mastering the skill. Children are once again described in terms of age level or deviance from age expectancy, although with five or six scores instead of one or two. Furthermore, the scores may be less reliable than those obtained from any one standardized test because they are often derived from several tests, each based on a different standardization sample.

The third assessment paradigm frequently employed for use with handicapped children is ordinal scales based on Piaget's theory of cognitive development. (For example, Uzgiris and Hunt's Ordinal Scales of Development, 1975; and Escalona and Cormen's Albert Einstein Scales of Sensorimotor Development, 1966.) These scales have become popular within the last decade as interventionists have become disenchanted with the ability of items from other infant tests to provide a description of a child's cognitive capabilities. These instruments also seem to provide a better rationale for selecting intervention goals than simply teaching specific items that have long been included in infant intelligence tests. The greater flexibility in item administration allows for the description of children's cognitive development along process dimensions rather than only in terms of skill attainment. In practice, however, the ordinal scales are often used as another criterion-reference assessment with estimated age levels attached to each of the items and children again described in terms of age levels or deviance from expectancy.

As the interventionist evaluates these paradigms, he or she finds that none are adequate to describe the unique development of many of the handicapped children for whom he or she is responsible. These children do not fit simply on a continuum from profoundly retarded to mildly retarded as scores from norm-referenced tests might suggest. Neither can their cognitive processes be understood by assessment with criterion-referenced tests or ordinal scales where the sensory and/or motor demands of the items are inappropriate to the physical capabilities of the youngsters.

Because of these problems, interventionists are constantly in search of new assessment procedures, often accepting procedures as necessarily better without critically evaluating the usefulness of the information they provide. To avoid repeated disappointments with new procedures and premature discarding of traditional ones, it is necessary to recognize that assessment is a complex process, not a single event. To understand the process, assessment must be viewed as serving a variety of purposes or objectives with different objectives requiring different assessment strategies. Any assessment paradigm, new or old, should be evaluated for the validity of its underlying assumptions and its usefulness for particular objectives at specific times.

In any intervention setting the basic objectives for assessment may be designated as: 1) diagnosis or prediction of future status, 2) the identification of intervention goals, and 3) the evaluation of child progress or program effectiveness. At any time one, two, or all of these objectives may be the target of an assessment. Before assessment procedures are chosen, the particular objectives for that assessment should be specified and each procedure evaluated critically against these objectives. The question is not What test can I use? but What is it I want to know?

DIAGNOSIS OR PREDICTION OF FUTURE STATUS

Historically, interest in infant assessment in this country was based on a desire to predict future intellectual status. Only norm-referenced, standardized assessment paradigms are appropriate for this objective. Standardized infant tests were constructed to reflect the emergence of developmental skills in the infancy period. The items selected were those that discriminated between normal children of different ages and those that were believed to be relatively unaffected by environmental experiences. These items were arranged either in a sequence determined by the mean age at which normal children passed them (e.g., the Bayley Scales) or in groups of items reflecting the typical skills developed by children at different ages (e.g., the Cattell Infant Intelligence Scale). Because of the limited behavioral repertoire of infants, the tests are composed almost entirely of items based on sensorimotor behaviors at the earlier ages with language items gradually being added after the 10-month level and contributing significantly to the scores after the 24-month level.

Using these tests to predict later intellectual status seems to be based on the underlying assumptions that: 1) the rate of acquiring sensorimotor skills in infancy is the same as or similar to the rate of later cognitive development, 2) retarded and other atypical children will develop the same skills as normal youngsters but at a slower rate, and 3) the rate of development is relatively constant over time. That such "mental" tests account for less than 25% of the variance of later IQ measures suggests these assumptions be questioned (Thomas, 1970).

Among others, Kagan, Kearsley, and Zelazo (1978), Zelazo (1977), and Kopp and Shaperman (1973) have effectively pointed out the limitations of the assumption that particular sensorimotor skills are necessary for subsequent cognitive development or that sensorimotor skills necessarily accurately reflect underlying cognitive development. They cite evidence for the development of adequate and even superior intellectual abilities in individuals with limited sensory and/or motor skills.

Interventionists recognize that many significantly handicapped infants and toddlers are not simply "retarded" or "slow." These children do not develop the same skills as normal youngsters. Rather, they exhibit patterns of development that are rarely or never seen in normal children of any age. They may never master some skills considered elementary in normal children while mastering others considered more difficult; and they evidence much lower concordance between motor, language, cognitive, and social development than is apparent in the normal population.

In addition, McCall (1979) cited evidence from longitudinal studies to support the proposition that the predominant structure of mental performance changes from one developmental stage to another, making untenable the assumption of a relatively constant rate of cognitive development across stages. He and other stage theorists (e.g., Uzgiris & Hunt, 1975) suggest that an infant mental test can accurately describe an infant's current standing relative to his peers within a particular developmental stage but cannot be expected to describe the child's relative position on the different mental skills which will be assessed as he progresses to another developmental stage.

Before standardized mental tests are discarded as being of little use in predicting future status, however, it is important to recognize that while they are inadequate predictors of later IQ for the population as a whole, they do predict developmental outcomes remarkably well for clearly deviant populations (Erickson, 1968; Illingsworth & Birch, 1959; Knobloch et al., 1956). For example VanderVeer and Schweid (1974) reported that infants and toddlers identified as borderline, mildly, or moderately-profoundly retarded on the basis of Bayley scores between 18 and 30 months, all continued to fall in the retarded range 1 to 3 years later (on the basis of Stanford Binet or Bayley Scales). In a study involving prediction over a longer time period, Werner, Honzik, and Smith (1968) found that 89% of the 20-month infants who scored below 80 on the Cattell demonstrated a variety of significant school problems at age 10. What this may suggest is that infant tests identify which children are handicapped, but these tests are not sufficiently comprehensive to define the nature of the handicap. The handicap may be a learning disability, emotional disturbance, mental retardation, or some form of sensory or motor impairment. Thus, such tests are useful predictive instruments, but might better be described as tests of general development than as intelligence tests.

More refined and accurate predictive statements could be made if it were possible to specify the source of a child's poor performance on an infant test. It is in this area where the interventionist might consider using some of the alternative assessment procedures suggested by Zelazo (1977), Cicchetti and Sroufe (1976), and Johnson et al. (1980).

These alternative assessment procedures rely on child behaviors that are relatively motor-free and are less apt to produce negativism in youngsters than items demanding specific performances on standardized tests. Cicchetti and Sroufe's (1976) procedure involves recording whether a child laughs or smiles to a specific series of tactile, auditory, visual, and social stimuli. They found that young normal infants smile and laugh primarily to intrusive stimuli such as tickling, bouncing, or unusual sounds. Older infants smile and laugh to more cognitively complex stimuli such as game playing and recognition of discrepant events (e.g., mother sucking a baby bottle). Their sample of Down's syndrome youngsters demonstrated this same sequence of development, but demonstrated the responses at older ages. The same progression has been demonstrated and related to mental age in other handicapped young children by Gallagher (1979). This assessment paradigm may provide a window into the cognitive capabilities of children who cannot produce the motor responses necessary for more traditional assessment.

A second example of an alternative assessment procedure is the perceptual-cognitive battery developed by Kagan et al. (1978) and Zelazo (this volume). It makes use of heart rate and behavioral changes to indicate cognitive processing of sequential visual and auditory events. A youngster is presented with a standard series of events (for example, a car runs down a ramp to knock over a snowman); this is followed by a short series of discrepant events (the car runs down the ramp but the snowman does not fall down); and finally there is a return to the standard (the snowman falls again). There is a predictable developmental sequence both in heart rate changes associated with the trials in each series and in the behavior exhibited by the children, suggesting increasingly higher levels of problem-solving and assimilation of information. This paradigm also seems to provide a different look at levels of cognitive skill development in handicapped children than is available through standardized tests.

Given the availability of these alternative paradigms, it may be possible to identify youngsters who perform more than two standard deviations below the mean on a norm-referenced "mental" test but smile and laugh to stimuli appropriate to his or her age level and/or demonstrate age appropriate assimilation of sequential visual and auditory information. For these youngsters the label *retarded* and its particular implications for future development may not be applicable.

Two factors need attention, however, if one hopes to improve prediction by such alternative cognitive assessment procedures. First, the alternative procedures suggest only that the problem is not mental retardation; they do not define what the problem is. The child may have apraxia, specific sensory deficits, poor sensory integration, language problems, or emotional disturbance; all conditions that can be as handicapping as mental retardation and are in need of intervention. The discrepancy between performance on the two assessment procedures does not negate the value of the standardized test; it may only rule out one possible cause of poor performance and identify a need for still further assessment to improve the specificity of the diagnosis.

Second, it may be just as dangerous to assume that a child is cognitively intact because of an appropriate performance on an alternative assessment procedure as it is to assume he or she is retarded because of poor performance on a standardized test. Intelligence or cognition has many facets, and existing knowledge about the interdependence or independence of each facet is sketchy at best. It may be possible, for example, for an infant to be able to assimilate information from sequential visual and auditory events at an age appropriate level and yet to have immature or retarded spatial concepts. One would not expect to find this discrepancy in biologically normal children; however, if self-directed movement is a significant factor in the development of spatial concepts (Campos & Stenberg, 1980), it might be relatively common in children with cerebral palsy or other motor deficits. If assessment of cognition is focused only on concepts that develop readily in the absence of motor behaviors, it may be incorrectly concluded that cognition is intact when, in fact, some aspects of cognition are seriously impaired and in need of intervention.

IDENTIFICATION OF INTERVENTION GOALS

In most intervention programs standardized tests are not used as the primary assessment for planning intervention although many clinicians using a test for diagnostic purposes will write educational recommendations based on the particular items a child passed or failed, thereby using it as a starting point for planning intervention. More often "criterion-referenced" assessment tools like the Learning Accomplishment Profile (Sanford, 1976), the Hawaii Early Learning Profile (Furuno et al., 1979), or the Early Intervention Developmental Profile

(Rogers et al., 1977) are used for describing developmental status and setting intervention objectives. These instruments divide developmental tasks into domains: gross motor, fine motor, language, cognition (or sensorimotor), social, and self-help. The tasks that a child has mastered in each domain are checked off and the easiest items failed become the objectives for intervention. These instruments used as a basis for planning treatment are problematic in that they are primarily amalgamations of items taken from a variety of standardized developmental tests. They are an improvement over a standardized test only in that more items are included and the items are divided into developmental domains, making it easier to identify the strengths and weaknesses of the child. They suffer the same limitations as the standardized tests, however, in that sensorimotor skills pervade the items in the cognitive and language areas, making it difficult to develop reasonable intervention goals for youngsters with significant sensory and/or motor problems.

In addition, the way that some of these instruments have been developed and used can be criticized because of the assumptions underlying such development and use. Four examples are illustrative. First, in many criterion-referenced tests the sequence of the skills in a particular domain is determined by the mean ages at which these skills are observed in normal children. Many interventionists use the sequence to determine the order in which skills are to be taught. Assuming that skills should be taught to handicapped infants in an order determined by the mean ages at which normal children master the skills is questionable because most normal children do not develop all skills in the order they appear on the Gesell, Cattell, or Bayley tests. Furthermore, such an ordering does not necessarily provide a logical teaching sequence in which recently learned skills are practiced as a more difficult skill is learned. In the cognitive area, particularly, the items adjacent to one another often have little in common. For example, a sequence of skills may read: recovers rattle dropped on chest, makes gestural response to familiar gesture, looks for dropped object, finds partially hidden object. It is difficult to ascertain either a common cognitive basis for this sequence or common sensory or motor prerequisites.

Second, if standardized test items become criterion-referenced items there is a danger that teaching will become situation specific, altering the significance of accomplishing the item. For example, on almost every standardized infant test and on almost every criterion-referenced assessment there is the item, "places three blocks in a cup." If a child can put three blocks into a cup after 30 training trials, it may represent something different in terms of cognitive development than if a child does it spontaneously or after only one demonstration and few past experiences with combining cups and blocks. The latter child could be expected to be able to put a variety of objects into a variety of containers and to imitate a variety of simple motor tasks. The same could not be expected of the child who needed extensive training unless efforts had been made to build in generalization of the skill.

Third, when a standardized test item becomes a criterion-referenced test item, there is an assumption that the skill represented can be taught using reasonable educational and behavioral methods. Yet, an item that was selected for the standardized test because it discriminated between children of different ages may represent a skill that is primarily dependent on neurological maturation rather than on learning per se. Educational intervention targeted to develop such skills may be relatively fruitless. Examples of such skills might be the visual search for sounds that occurs in blind as well as sighted children and the pincer grasp that facilitates the child's ability to pick up small objects. Even in relatively motor-free areas it remains quite unclear which developmental tasks can readily be taught using a behavioral paradigm, which are primarily dependent on physiological maturation, and which are triggered by maturation but can be facilitated by appropriate teaching.

Finally, if the criterion-referenced test is entirely made up of items that occur on norm-referenced, standardized tests, there is an assumption that the items on these tests represent the most important or the only skills that should be taught. With such an assumption skills may be neglected that are important to later learning but have never been included in standardized tests because they are not age specific; for example, simple contingency learning (moving to activate a mobile) is rarely assessed on norm-referenced tests, but has been demonstrated to be important for learning later, more complex contingencies (Watson & Ramey, 1972). Furthermore, skills that are not "normal" but that allow handicapped individuals to make adaptations to the world around them may be ignored, for example, manual signing or manipulating a switch or pedal that could later be used to operate a communication board.

One alternative to using amalgamations of items from standardized tests for program planning in the cognitive domain has been to use scales based on Piaget's stage theory such as the Uzgiris and Hunt Ordinal Scales of Psychological Development (1975). These scales were designed to assess and describe a child's development in each of six decalages or domains of cognitive functioning. Because the ordering of items in each decalage provides a logical sequence for teaching and because there is flexibility in the materials used for assessment, interventionists have used the scales as a criterion-referenced instrument for intervention planning. Using the scales in this way, however, involves some of the same assumptions questioned above, that is, that a trained-in skill has the same generalizability across situations and materials as one developed through a variety of natural experiences and that the skills assessed can, in fact, be taught. Furthermore, the items on these scales are as dependent on visual and motor skills as items on all other infant tests, making them equally inappropriate for planning intervention for children impaired in these areas.

It is in considering assessment specifically directed toward the development of an intervention plan that alternative procedures like those of Cicchetti and Sroufe (1976) or Kagan et al. (1978) create excitement. Interventionists always operate on the assumption that if they had more information about a handicapped child they could intervene more effectively. Particularly, if they know a multiply handicapped child is not retarded, they can select more appropriate intervention goals. Yet, at this stage of our knowledge, it seems that the alternative strategies may be more beneficial to diagnosis than treatment. This is particularly true for the more severely handicapped children where it may be difficult to know what to do with the additional information. For example, if one can determine that a severely physically handicapped 2-year-old is processing visual and auditory sequential information like a normal 15- to 18-month-old when standardized tests suggest skills no higher than 5 months, what does it mean for that child? A normal child between 15 and 18 months is saying single words and parents are talking to him or her in short sentences, expanding on those words. Can one assume that this is the optimum language environment for the handicapped child? Similarly, can we assume that the object concepts of the handicapped child are like those of the normal 15-18 month old child? More importantly for the physically handicapped child's future, does the additional information suggest effective methods for teaching him or her, or indicate that he or she is ready to begin training in augmentative communication? These questions do not suggest that the information from the alternative assessment is useless. On the contrary, it is important to know that a child has some cognitive skills that are not as delayed as the child's motor development and that we may expect to teach him or her more than we previously believed. The specifics, however, must still be determined by trial and error.

It should also be recognized that for appropriate intervention it is critical that cognition not remain the only focus of alternative assessment strategies in defining intervention goals. Paradigms must be designed to assess receptive language, preverbal communication, motor status, and play skills. Steps in this direction have been made by Vulpe (1977) in her assessment battery; by Attermeier, Gallagher, and Anderson (1978) in their experimental Physical Status Form; by Simeonsson (1978) in the Carolina Record of Infant Behavior; and in the Adaptive Performance Instrument developed by the Consortium on Adaptive Performance Evaluation (CAPE, 1980). Nonetheless, we are some distance from using alternative assessment procedures for developing intervention plans that are comprehensive and sound both theoretically and practically.

EVALUATION OF CHILD PROGRESS

Ongoing assessment of handicapped children in programs is an essential part of accountability. Yet, there are major roadblocks to the development of good assessment procedures for this purpose. Although it is simple to check off items a child has mastered between two assessments and thereby indicate his or her developmental progression, it is by no means simple to demonstrate that the mastery of any of the items is a direct function of intervention. Progress attributable to intervention is usually defined as development that is greater than one would expect if no intervention had taken place. Because experimental and control groups are neither ethically or practically available to the clinician, the search is for assessment procedures that will identify changes in the rate of development in individual children after intervention is begun.

Standardized, norm-referenced tests have often been selected to demonstrate rate changes because the quotients they provide purportedly reflect developmental rate. With some regularity these tests suggest that intervention is more effective with mildly handicapped than severely handicapped children. In the National Collaborative Project, for example, progress as measured by Bayley or Denver scores was more related to degree of handicap than to any program characteristics that could be defined (Meisel, 1976). The most severely handicapped children made practically no measurable progress even after 24 months of intervention. Considering the shortcomings of such norm-referenced, standardized tests, these findings are not surprising. Most severely handicapped children have sensory and motor impairments that prevent appropriate responding to the test demands. Moreover, the predictive power of standardized tests for the moderately and severely handicapped population suggests that they are unlikely to be sensitive to intervention effects.

Some proponents of criterion-referenced assessments (e.g., Sanford, 1976) have attempted to monitor rate changes more effectively by treating each area of development (gross motor, fine motor, cognitive, etc.) separately. An age level is assigned to each item in the assessment, based on the age at which normal children are expected to pass the item. The assessment is treated as a norm-referenced test, and developmental ratios (developmental age/chronological age) are computed for each section of the test. The five or six ratios obtained each time the child is assessed purportedly increase the likelihood of monitoring rate changes in some skill areas.

Such a procedure is highly questionable both because the age levels for items in the test are estimates based on a variety of samples of normal children and because ratios based on developmental and chronological age are notably unreliable (hence, the preference of deviation IQs over ratio IQs). Furthermore, one must question the validity of statements about rate changes on the basis of McCall's (1979) discussion of the discontinuous nature of development across developmental stages. Other proponents of criterion-referenced instruments (e.g., White & Haring, 1979) suggested that developmental progress be evaluated by computing the percent of items passed in an assessment instrument at each assessment point. These percentage changes can be compared with changes expected on the basis of the development of normal children, some specific handicapped population, or a control group. Percentage changes in developmental domains where intervention has occurred may also be compared with those in domains where intervention has not occurred. Although these procedures eliminate the problem of unreliable age levels and unreliable developmental-chronological age ratios, they introduce yet another source of variability; that is, the percentages are based on items of unequal difficulty. Wherever there is a grouping of relatively easy items, progress will seem to be rapid just as it will seem to be slow when there is a grouping of relatively difficult items. Before percentage changes can be used as adequate indicators of progress it will be necessary to scale items to produce intervals of equal difficulty. This is no easy task because intervals made equal for task difficulty in normal children may not be equal for children who are blind, motor-impaired, or multiply handicapped. Some of the alternative assessment procedures noted above may eventually solve some of the problems in assessing child progress. At this point we know that when used longitudinally they are sensitive to change in children. We do not know, however, if particular environmental experiences will accelerate the rate of change nor what that acceleration would mean to the basic adaptation of a handicapped youngster.

SUMMARY

It is evident that we are a long way from solving the problems of assessing handicapped youngsters. Simeonsson et al. (1980) are undoubtedly correct in insisting that a variety of assessment procedures will be necessary for most handicapped youngsters because each provides only a partial picture and is useful for only limited objectives. Current procedures used in laboratory settings to explore developmental phenomena in normal children surely have applicability for the handicapped. This applicability, however, must be tempered by the degree to which these procedures can become transportable, available to interventionists in the field, and interpretable as indicators of developmental status, progress or the appropriateness of treatment methods.

In spite of the problems involved in adequate assessment, optimism is warranted. Research expertise has been growing among interventionists and an increasing number of those involved in normal developmental research have become interested in the questions raised by the atypical development of handicapped children. A merger of the knowledge and skills of these two groups of professionals should contrbute significantly to solving assessment problems. As the merger takes place it will be apparent that the "normal model" is not always applicable to many handicapped youngsters. Assessment procedures that focus only on the skills that seem important in normal growth and development may miss skills that are of particular importance to the adaptation of groups of handicapped youngsters. To be most helpful to the handicapped child's future, research will need to focus on questions raised by the assessment and treatment of handicapped youngsters, not only the questions raised by observations of normal children. This will involve not only collecting extensive longitudinal data on handicapped youngsters but asking different questions in the study of normal children. The assessment issue is less one of finding the best assessment paradigm than one of approaching each assessment with the questions: 1) What specific information needs to be gained from this assessment? and 2) What collection of procedures is most likely to produce that information? With these questions in mind the interventionist can be creative with assessment techniques, serve children more effectively, and, with careful documentation of his or her procedures, contribute data and ideas for further exploration of assessment issues by those involved in laboratory research.

REFERENCES

Attermeier, S., Gallagher, R., & Anderson, J. Physical Assessment Form (Unpublished instrument available from the Frank Porter Graham Child Development Center, Chapel Hill, NC 27514), 1978.
Campos, J., & Stenberg, C. Perception, appraisal and emotion: The onset of social referencing. In M. Lamb & L. Sherrod (Eds.), *Infant social cognition.* Hillsdale, N.J.: Lawrence Erlbaum Associates, 1980.

CAPE, Consortium on Adaptive Performance Evaluation. Adaptive Performance Instrument. Unpublished Assessment Instrument, Dept. of Special Education, University of Idaho, Boise, 1980.

Cicchetti, D., & Sroufe, A. The relationship between affective and cognitive development in Down's Syndrome infants. *Child Development*, 1976, *47*, 920–929.

Erickson, M. The predictive validity of the Cattell Infant Intelligence Scales for young mentally retarded children. *American Journal of Mental Deficiency*, 1968, *72*, 727–733.

Escalona, S., & Corman, H. Albert Einstein Scales of Sensori-Motor Development, unpublished test manual, Albert Einstein School of Medicine, New York, 1966.

Furuno, S., O'Reilly, K., Hosaka, C., Inatsuka, T., Allman, T., & Zeisloft, B. *Hawaii Early Learning Profile*, Palo Alto: VORT Corporation, 1979.

Gallagher, R. Positive affect in physically handicapped mentally retarded infants: Its relationship to developmental age, temperament, physical status and setting. Unpublished dissertation, University of North Carolina, 1979.

Illingsworth, R., & Birch, L. The diagnosis of mental retardation in infancy: A follow-up study. *Archives of Diseases in Childhood*, 1959, *34*, 269–273.

Johnson, N., Jens, K., Gallagher, R., & Anderson, J. Cognition and affect in infancy: Implications for the handicapped. In J. Gallagher (Ed.), *New directions for exceptional children: Young exceptional children*, San Francisco: Jossey-Bass, 1980.

Kagan, J., Kearsley, R., & Zelazo, P. *Infancy: Its place in human development*. Cambridge: Harvard University Press, 1978.

Knobloch, H., Riter, R., Harper, P., & Pasamanick, B. Neuropsychiatric sequelae of prematurity: A longitudinal study. *Journal of the American Medical Association*, 1956, *161*, 581–585.

Kopp, K., & Shaperman, J. Cognitive development in the absence of object manipulation during infancy. *Developmental Psychology*, 1973, *9*, 430.

McCall, R. The development of intellectual functioning in infancy and the predictor of later I.Q. In J. Osofsky (Ed.), *Handbook of infant development*. John Wiley & Sons, 1979, New York, 707–741.

Meisel, J. A Nationally Organized Collaborative Project to Provide Comprehensive Services for Atypical Infants and their Families: Evaluation Report. Unpublished report. United Cerebral Palsy Associations, Inc., 66 East 34th Street, New York, 1976.

Roger, S. S., D'Eugenio, D., Brown, S., Donovan, C., & Lynch, E. *Early Intervention Developmental Profile*. Ann Arbor: University of Michigan Press, 1977.

Sanford, A. *The Learning Accomplishment Profile*. Winston-Salem: Kaplan Press, 1976.

Simeonsson, R. *The Carolina Record of Infant Behavior*. (Unpublished instrument available from the Frank Porter Graham Child Development Center, Chapel Hill, NC 27514), 1978.

Simeonsson, R., Huntington, G., & Parse, S. Expanding the developmental assessment of young handicapped children. In J. Gallagher (Ed.), *New directions for exceptional children: Young exceptional children*. San Francisco: Jossey-Bass, 1980.

Thomas, H. Psychological Assessment Instruments for use with human infants. *Merrill-Palmer Quarterly of Behavior and Development*, 1970, 2, *16*, 179–223.

Uzgiris, I., & Hunt, J. *Assessment in infancy: Ordinal scales of psychological Development*. Urbana: University of Illinois Press, 1975.

VanderVeer, B., & Schweid, E. Infant assessment: Stability of mental functioning in young retarded children. *American Journal of Mental Deficiency*, 1974, Nov. 79, 1–4.

Vulpe, S. *Vulpe Assessment Battery*. Toronto: National Institute on Mental Retardation, 1977.

Watson, J., & Ramey, C. Reactions to response-contingent stimulation in early stimulation. *Merrill-Palmer Quarterly*, 1972, *18*, 219–227.

Werner, E., Honzik, M., & Smith, R. Prediction of intelligence and achievement at 10 years from 20 months pediatric and psychological examinations. *Child Development*, 1968, *39*, 1063–1075.

White, O., & Haring, N. Evaluating educational programs serving the severely and profoundly handicapped. Unpublished manuscript, University of Washington, Seattle, 1979.

Zelazo, P. Reactivity to perceptual-cognitive events: Application for infant assessment. In R. Kearsley & I. Sigel (Eds.) *Infant at risk: The assessment of cognitive functioning*. Hillsdale, N.J.: Lawrence Erlbaum Associates, 1977.

Chapter 5

THE CENTRAL TENDENCY IN STUDY OF THE HANDICAPPED CHILD

Michael Lewis and Aileen Wehren

In almost all inquiry, the mean or some other measure of the central tendency is used as the primary measure for description, data analysis, and interpretation. The notion that there exists a central tendency and that it is useful in describing individual behavior has been questioned by those interested in an ideographic approach (c.f., Allport, 1940, 1960). Little attention, except in the clinical method, has been paid to approaches that do not utilize some measure of the central tendency and its associated dispersion. This chapter discusses the value of such an approach, in particular when studying and considering the development of handicapped or at-risk children.

In order to explore this issue, it is necessary to consider the broad questions of: 1) the origin of the use of the central tendency, 2) the general problem such an approach generates, and 3) how such an approach affects the study of the handicapped individual. Having accomplished these tasks, it will be necessary also to consider 4) the general conflict within the culture between conformity and individuation and how this affects the problem of central tendency.

ORIGINS OF THE USE OF THE CENTRAL TENDENCY

The exact origin of the use of a central tendency is unknown. Although the use of the mean has a history, there is little information on the origin of the use of the median or mode. This chapter discusses only the statistic of the mean, recognizing that it is the overwhelmingly predominant measure of central tendency both historically as well as contemporarily. For example, tabulation of the data presentation in *Child Development*, 1981, Vol. 52 indicated that 70% of the articles present the mean statistic and only 1 study, or 2%, use a median statistic.

77

The presence of a description of the central tendency for official use and for fiscal negotiations can be traced back into the distant past of Western culture. This measure has been the basis of statistical method and conceptual decisions for at least the past 3 centuries. Initially, this descriptive statistic was used by government officials for practical matters: calculation of population as well as estimates of births, deaths, and disease (Westergaard, 1932). Even then, however, there was recognition that interpretation of the mean required that some measure of the dispersion of the values around the mean be considered. Government officials were aware of and made use of information about the range of values in interpretation of the mean. For instance, 2 to 3 centuries ago in France, the price of land was based upon its value (value being determined by the land's yield over the prior 20 years). Even then, the effect of extreme values on the mean was understood. Rather than use a standard mean, average land yield (and thus sale value) was determined by use of an alpha trimmed mean. In other words, yield for each of the prior 20 years was determined and the year of highest yield and the year of lowest yield were dropped from the calculation (Vail, personal communication).

Not only was the distribution of the individual values that made up the mean considered, but the function of that distribution was explored. The normal distribution was discovered both by Gauss and LaPlace more than 200 years ago (Walker, 1975). At that time, it was felt that this property of normal distribution was inconsequential, its major value being related to determination of odds in gambling. In spite of this prediction, the mean, together with the normal distribution, became the basis of many of our statistics and, consequently, many of the conclusions we draw about child development.

PROBLEMS WITH THE MEAN

It is evident that a measure of the central tendency, in particular the mean, has been used for over 300 years and remains the predominant measure even now. Although the statistical mean and dispersion are useful, there are particular situations in which important and serious errors are correlated with its use. In the following examples such problems are described.

Use of Mean Scales

Of considerable interest is the biasing effect that can occur when we examine a large number of subjects and attempt to find some central tendency to characterize their responses. The type of error that is described is particularly relevant for measures of response that are scaled, but can be applied whenever mean data are used to characterize children's responses. Consider the "stranger approach" situation where children sitting next to their mothers watch a stranger slowly move toward them. For the sake of the example, assume that half of the children are rated on a 5-point scale as "most fearful" (that is, are rated 5). Now consider that half the children are rated 1, that is, "not fearful at all." If their scores are averaged, the result is a rating of 3.0, a value that indicates that children show "sobering" or "wary" behavior. Of course, none of the children exhibited wariness. In fact, half of them showed no fearful behavior at all. Obviously, data presentation is an important consideration. This situation calls for the use

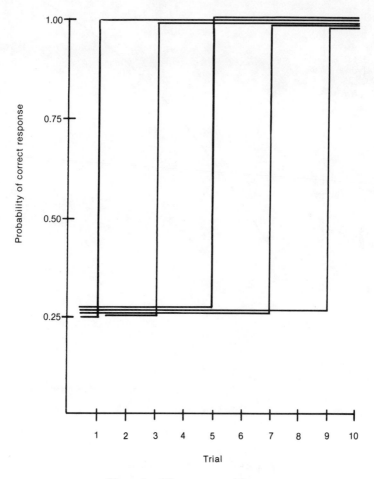

Figure 1.   All or none model.

of the percentage of subjects showing particular emotions and the use of specific behavior rather than mean performance or value on the scales (Campos et al., 1975). Such errors are common and can only serve to distort the phenomenon under investigation.

Learning Curves—Individual versus Group

Another serious distortion is related to the standard learning curve. Recall that the abscissa represents time or number of trials while the ordinate represents the amount of the "thing" to be learned. The learning curve typically found in texts has the function of a positive ex-

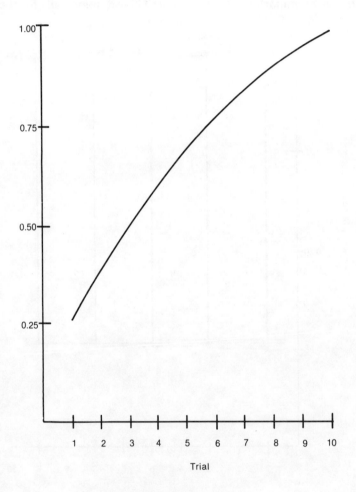

Figure 2.   Continuous model.

ponential function varying in rate of acquisition, slope, and asymptotic level. Such curves suggest that learning takes place as a continuous and gradual acquisition of information or skill. These curves, however, are derived from the mean performance of many individuals. In general, except for physical skills, examination of individual learning curves reveals an entirely different pattern. Individual learning curves can be discrete and sudden. Figure 1 presents a set of individual curves that when averaged together result in the mean curve of Figure 1.

Consideration of the mean curve in Figure 2 suggests that learning acquisition is a gradual process, wherein learning takes place as a function of increased time or total exposure. Consideration of the individual curves in Figure 1 suggests that learning may be an all or nothing process more akin to an "ah ha" event. The use of mean data in this example leads to a model of learning acquisition far different from the process associated with individual learning curves. In fact, research in learning has been dominated by theories of continuous and gradual acquisition instead of theories of discontinuity (Hulse, Deese, & Egeth, 1975).

Attention Studies—Sets of Groups versus Single Group

The mean response for a group of subjects can be shown to: 1) represent the group, or 2) be the composite of markedly different individual curves as seen in Figure 2. An alternative assumption, one that represents some form of compromise, is that for any group of subjects there is neither one central tendency representing that group nor X values (where X equals the number of subjects) representing that group. There exists the possibility that there is more than a single sample mean (e.g., "natural" subgroups). The way to examine such an assumption is through cluster or discriminative function analysis. Such analyses allow for the consideration of more than one central tendency but fewer than the number of subjects.

In studies of attention distribution, such procedures have proved useful. For example, if a group of 5-6-month-olds are presented with a series of redundant stimuli and their visual fixation data are recorded, the mean response over each trial takes the form of a negative exponential function. McCall (1979) found that when cluster analyses are performed on these data, three different habituation and recovery curves emerge. The first curve, shown in Figure 3, is the prototypical habituation curve, with decreasing fixation as the child recognizes the redundance of the stimulus. The second curve reveals a different pattern of information processing, with increasing fixation until trial 4 with an abrupt drop in attention at that point and clear recovery to the

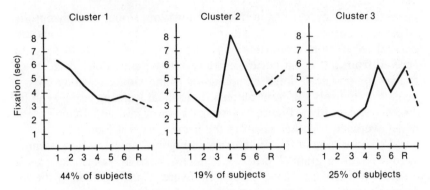

Figure 3. Habituation and recovery clusters (5-month-olds)

novel stimulus. The final curve shows variable attention with neither clear habituation nor clear recovery.

Figure 4 shows the curve that would have resulted if mean data for all subjects combined had been used. The resulting curve does not clearly represent the information processing pattern of any of the three groups of subjects that are portrayed by the other curves. Of course, the usefulness of the generation of three different groups having different central tendencies and dispersions rests on the demonstration that these differences are reliable and that they are related to different information processing strategies. Even so, such analyses have to alert us to the danger of believing that a single mean is necessarily sufficient to describe a groups' or subjects' behavior.

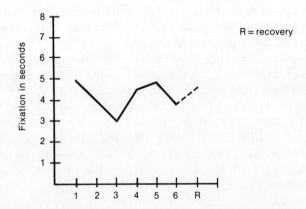

Figure 4. Habituation and recovery: Composite of the Figure 3 clusters.

Difference between the Means:
within versus between Group Differences

When comparing the difference between two means in an attempt to establish whether the groups represented by the means are different from one another, it is necessary to consider the standard deviation or dispersion of each group. If the within group differences are less than the between group differences, assumptions about significant differences between the means of the two groups can be made.

Consider the case where such differences have been shown to exist between two means. It is possible to wash out the differences through the addition of outlying subjects whose score values, although highly discrepant, are in the predicted direction of the mean differences. By adding these additional subjects, and thus increasing the mean difference and the within group variance, it is possible to eliminate the original group differences. By using the mean as a central tendency, the addition of outlying subjects favorable to a group difference hypothesis actually reduces the group difference likelihood because of the associated increase in the group variance. The use of a median measure of central tendency, as well as statistical tests that do not assume a normal distribution of values around a central tendency, can eliminate such problems. A Mann Whitney U-Test, for example, would not produce such a paradox.

These general examples should alert us to the potential difficulties that the use of a central tendency and, in particular, the use of the mean statistic can generate. Such logical and theoretical issues have an impact on the study of handicapped and at-risk children.

THE USE OF THE MEAN IN
RESEARCH WITH HANDICAPPED CHILDREN

The Mean Score of the Individual

The issue of the central tendency can be addressed in terms of the mean performance of a group of subjects as well as the mean score of an individual. An individual's performance can be characterized by a single value such as an IQ score or can be characterized by a set of values representing various capacities. Just as a group of subjects cannot be considered as a single value (central tendency), neither can this be done for the individual. In the case of normal subjects, whose skills tend to covary, the use of a single score may be representative of their performance. This is not the case for the handicapped child, whose skills may vary widely. In the attempt to reduce this variable set of skills to a single overall value, one may lose sight of the individualism of the subject. Although this problem holds true for normal children and infants as well, it is considerably more exaggerated for the handicapped. The incorrelation matrix for a set of skills for the handicapped will be less than that for the normal child. Also, the alpha coefficient (Harman, 1976), the sum of the correlations of each particular item to the total score should vary as a function of the nature of the handicapping condition. For example, a cerebral palsied infant might score high on perceptual items and low on motor items. This would result in: 1) a relatively lower alpha coefficient and 2) a reduction in any overall score when compared to that of a normal child with the same perceptual abilities and better motor skills. From an assessment point of view, total or summary scores do not facilitate the description of the individual nor do they provide the means for developing intervention strategies.

Diagnostic Group as an Average

The use of diagnostic groups to explicate the characteristics of a handicapped individual or a group of handicapped children implies that there is an average or typical set of behaviors and competencies associated with that diagnosis. There is a growing recognition, however, that adages of the type "All children with Down's syndrome are the same" are incorrect. In fact, there is a wide range in competencies among infants having the same handicapping condition. Figure 5 demonstrates this point. This figure shows learning curves for two Down's syndrome infants of the same age in a contingency learning situation. In this situation, either an arm or a leg movement produces a reinforcement. Some children, exemplified by Susan, rapidly differentiate the reinforced from the nonreinforced response, and others, such as George, do not. Both children are Down's syndrome infants, again testifying to the fact that there is no average or prototypical Down's syndrome infant (Brinker & Lewis, 1981).

Generally, diagnostic grouping or etiology is the basis of classification of children for educational purposes. Given the fact, however, that there is no child who can represent all children who fall into a given diagnostic category, this use of diagnosis rather than a skill profile is an error.

A related problem exists in comparisons between normal and handicapped children on a given measure. When testing for or assessing group differences, Group A may be statistically different from Group B. In other words, normal and Down's syndrome infants may be statistically different on a particular dimension. The differences between

Susan: Arm contingency

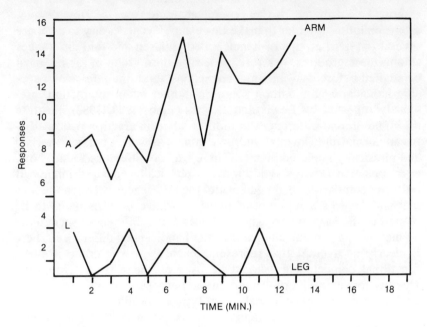

George: Leg contingency

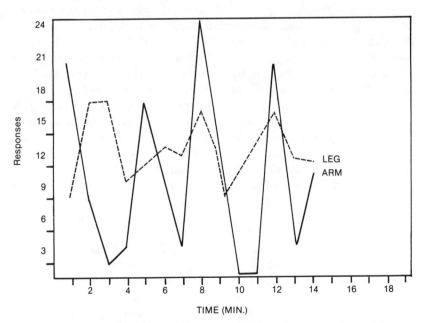

Figure 5.   Response acquisition within one session: Two Down's syndrome infants.

the normal and the Down's syndrome children, however, cannot necessarily be attributed to the general characteristics of Down's syndrome children. In order to make this claim, it is necessary to compare several different groups of handicapped children and find differences among these groups. Therefore, at least a third group of infants must be studied before drawing any conclusions about the effects of a specific handicapping condition. Data on mother-infant interaction, previously reported by Lewis and Brooks-Gunn (1980, 1982) illustrate this. They found differences in mother-infant interaction patterns between normal and Down's syndrome infants as well as between normal and physically impaired infants. There was no difference found, however, between Down's syndrome and physically impaired infants. If only one comparison had been made, the differences between the normal and Down's syndrome infants would have been assumed to be related to the particular diagnosis. Instead, the differences seem to be a function of a general handicapped-nonhandicapped difference. There is clearly no average that represents each diagnostic group. Rather, functional competencies should be used as the basis of groupings, whether for research or for intervention purposes. Such groups can be constructed using cluster analysis of the skill profiles.

The error of a single comparison also arises with regard to premature infants. For example, preterm and term infants show quite different mother-infant interaction patterns, with mothers of preterm infants significantly more interactive relative to their infants than mothers of term infants (Field, 1979; DiVitto & Goldberg, 1979). These preterm-term differences have been attributed, in part, to the effects of prematurity. But, we now know that term and preterm infants differ on a wide set of variables, not just on prematurity per se (Fox & Lewis, 1981). Preterm infants are not only premature, but are often sick (Keller, 1981). In a recent study of 3-month-old preterm healthy infants, preterm sick infants, term healthy infants, and term sick infants, Lewis and Fox (1980) have found that maternal interaction patterns varied as a function of infant sickness rather than prematurity. Although significant differences were found between preterm sick and term healthy infants (the groups usually compared in the prematurity literature), healthy and sick term infants also differed in ways similar to those differences usually reported between preterm and term infants. Additionally, sickness accounted for more variance in maternal interaction patterns than did prematurity. Thus, differences in mother-infant interaction are determined by several, rather than just one, variable. Without several comparison groups, findings may be narrowly interpreted or overdetermined. Here again is the danger of assuming that all preterms are the same; an error caused by trying to look at mean group performance.

The Use of the Mean and P.L. 94-142

The use of a central tendency has implications for the notion of individuality and conformity. In most technological cultures, individuality gives way to conformity. When products were made by hand, it was possible to produce different items. Technological advances produced machines that, in turn, produce items that are the same. Conformity, in this case, leads to cost effectiveness. Thus, more people can have the same things. The advantages of cost are always balanced by the disadvantages of conformity.

In a modern culture such as our own, many items are constructed according to some standard. Extremely tall or heavy people often have difficulty in buying clothes that are not custom made. Steps are almost always 9 inches high even though persons are of varying heights. Because these items are standardized (are constructed for the average person), they may not be available for the aged, infirm, handicapped, or otherwise "different" person. Consider steps as an example. Not only are they constructed to be 9 inches high, but access to many areas is only available by steps (e.g. buildings, buses, subways, etc.), thus excluding people who cannot use them.

Public Law 94-142 affects the issue of individuality in public life by questioning the usefulness of conformity. For our immediate purposes, it addresses the requirement that all people, normal and handicapped, be treated individually. Section 504 of the Rehabilitation Act raises the issue of the elimination of architectural barriers and provides that public facilities have a variety of means of access including steps, ramps, and elevators. The notion that there need be only one way for the "average" person has been revised to include consideration of individual needs.

Individual needs are again addressed in the public law by rejecting the notion of an "average handicapped child." By insisting on individual education programs, the public law returns us to the study and consideration of diversity in curriculum rather than some standard. Each child becomes entitled to an individualized program of instruction based upon an individualized assessment of needs and abilities. Mass education, with its movement toward conformity, is modified to be responsive to the handicapped individual. Whether the premise of the public law will be extended to include all children is unknown; however, it does provide a model for considering the issues of individuality and the pitfalls of conformity.

SUMMARY

The need for a standard and for considering the average person is, in part, a function of modern technology. As machines replaced people in the production of items, it became more cost effective to consider the "average." The future of technological cultures can either be toward more conformity or toward the utilization of the technological process, especially computers, to promote individuality. Nevertheless, the use of a central tendency, although valuable for some forms of abstraction, does not capture (nor is intended to) the individual. To the extent that assessment, diagnosis, and intervention are directed toward the individual, the use of a central tendency produces difficulties that require solution. Our models need to be directed away from the use of a single mean and toward the consideration of techniques that can capture both the individual and the individual in relationship to the group.

REFERENCES

Allport, G. The psychologist's frame of reference. *Psychological Bulletin*, 1940, *37*, 1–28.
Allport, G. *Personality and social encounter*. Boston: Beacon Press, 1960.
Brinker, R., & Lewis, M. Patterns of learning by handicapped infants. Paper presented at the biennial meeting of the Society for Research in Child Development, Boston, April, 1981.
Campos, J., Emde., R., Gaensbauer, T., & Henderson, C. Cardiac and behavioral interrelationships in the reactions of infants to strangers. *Developmental Psychology*, 1975, *11*, 589–601.
DiVitto, B., & Goldberg, S. The effects of newborn medical status on early parent-infant interaction. In T. Field (Ed.), *Infants born at risk: Behavior and development*. New York: S.P. Medical & Scientific Books, 1979.
Field, T. (Ed.) *Infants born at risk: Behavior and development*. New York: S.P. Medical and Scientific Books, 1979.
Fox, N., & Lewis, M. The role of maturation and experience in preterm infant development. In J. J. Gallagher (Ed.), *New directions in special education*. San Francisco: Jossey-Bass, 1981.
Harman, H. *Modern factor analysis* (3rd Ed.). Chicago: University of Chicago Press, 1976.
Hulse, S., Deese, J., & Egeth, H. *The psychology of learning*. New York: McGraw-Hill, 1975.
Keller, C. Epidemiological characteristics of preterm births. In S. Friedman & M. Sigman (Eds.) *Preterm birth and psychological development*. New York: Academic Press, 1981.
Lewis, M., & Brooks-Gunn, J. Logical problems in research with exceptional children. Paper presented at a symposium on Social and Cognitive Development in Down's Syndrome Infants at the International Conference on Infant Studies, New Haven, Conn., April, 1980.
Lewis, M., & Brooks-Gunn, J. Developmental models and assessment issues. In W. Frankenburg (Ed.), *Early identification of children who are at-risk*. Baltimore: University Park Press.
Lewis, M., & Fox, N. Predicting cognitive development from assessments in infancy. In B. Camp (Ed.), *Advances in behavioral pediatrics* (Vol. 1). Greenwich, Conn: JAI Press, 1980.

McCall, R. Individual differences in the pattern of habituation at 5 and 10 months of age. *Developmental Psychology*, 1979, *15*(5), 559–569.

Walker, H. *Studies in the history of statistical method: With special reference to certain education problems*. New York: Arno, 1975.

Westergaard, H. *Contributions to the history of statistics*. The Hague: Mouton Pub., 1969 (Orig. 1932).

Chapter 6

PIAGET, THE NOTION OF ACTION, AND ASSESSING INTELLIGENCE IN HANDICAPPED INFANTS

Gerald Gratch

This chapter concerns the relevance of Piagetian infancy scales to the assessment of handicapped infants. It focuses on two areas. One area is the practicality of that issue. It is argued that such scales can be the occasion for looking at the handicapped infant in profitable ways but that they are no more likely to provide a useful step-by-step way of characterizing handicapped infants than such psychometric instruments as the Bayley. The second area involves the meaning of the notion of activity in Piaget's account of sensorimotor development. The reports on thalidomide children by Decarie (1969) and Kopp and Shaperman (1973) are discussed, and some amplifications of Piaget's ideas are suggested in an attempt to indicate how they might help readers to understand the intellectual development of handicapped infants.

A considerable body of literature exists that suggests that psychometrically oriented infancy schedules, even Piagetian ones, are of equivocal value in making prospective statements about normal infants and differential-diagnostic statements about high-risk and handicapped infants (e.g., Lewis, 1976; McCall, 1979; Meier, 1973; Wachs & DeRemer, 1978). Michael Lewis, during the course of this conference, said that blind infants can see, deaf infants can hear, and that there's more variance within a diagnostic category than there is between diagnostic categories. If one couples this limitation on the study of handicapped infants with the fact that psychometrically oriented tests deal with performance and population categories, then a reasonable conclusion might be, on a practical level, that the issue is a non-question.

Paper prepared for Conference on Handicapped and At-Risk Infants: Research and Application, held at Asilomar, Monterey, California, April 29 to May 2, 1980. The preparation of this paper was supported, in part, by Research Grant 5 RO1 HD 10252 from the National Institute of Child Health and Human Development.

Work with the handicapped should proceed on a case-by-case basis, and in large part, that is what occurs.

Whether work with handicapped infants is done on a single case basis or in terms of qualified assignment to categories of handicap, tests in some form are used. The practical questions do not go away. Assessments of children have to be made, either formally or informally. Programs of intervention have to be developed and assessments made of their impact, and again, tests or their components are used. In terms of practice, the issue does not seem to be whether tests will be used, but for what purpose and in what manner. We should strive to be aware of the assumptions that are inherent in the assessment instruments we use. No matter how standardized are our tests and methods, they always involve adaptation to the particularities of each case or situation. Such adaptations profit from reflection on assumptions and provide the opportunity to learn more about assumptions.[1]

Decarie's study of thalidomide children involves an exemplary adaptation of standard assessment procedures. In her sample of children, the drug had manifestly affected at least limb development, and there was controversy about its impact on intelligence in the literature. In addressing the issue of the young children's intellectual status, she used a number of instruments, one of which was a scale based on Piaget's theory that she had developed for a prior study. That she used a scale derived from Piaget's theory to speak about intelligence is not the key issue; rather, it is how she did it. She made the focus what so often is left implicit in such work. She directly confronted what it means to speak of intelligence in Piaget's terms and how the nature of the thalidomide child might provide information about that theory and vice versa.

She assessed the children's understanding of objects-in-space through a scale that mirrored milestones Piaget has described. As is widely known, Piaget (1954) under the rubrics of object permanence and object concept, has described the development of infants' ability to keep track of hidden objects in terms of a series of stages. The sixth stage culminates in the infant not only being able to search for a hidden object wherever it has been observed to disappear, but to be able, apparently, to infer where it might be when its exact location is in-

---

[1] Even that great apostle of factor analysis as an inductive method for the discovery of abilities, L. L. Thurstone, thought long and hard, although it is not in print, about which items to include in the battery to be analyzed (T. G. Johnson, personal communication) and preceded his factor-analytic work by writing a theoretical book on intelligence (1960) that in many ways anticipated developments in current cognitive psychology. Similar statements could be made about a current apostle of the value of induction and "engineering," namely B. F. Skinner (1964).

determinate—the invisible displacement problem. In Piaget's view, early searching behaviors are continuations of sensorimotor actions, whereas in Stage 6, the infant is able to step out of the sensorimotor stream and plan his or her search on the basis of ideas about where the object might be.

Decarie's focus on the object concept in the case of the thalidomide child was most apt. Whatever one means by intelligence, the ability to keep track of objects in space through making inferences about their location captures one of the meanings of that term. Although attempts to relate performance on object concept scales to later measures of intelligence have led to equivocal results (e.g., Lewis, 1976), it would be hard to imagine calling a normal child intelligent if he or she could not cope with the issues subsumed under the headings of object permanence and object concept. But if overt activity, particularly touch and locomotion, play a central role in solving such problems, how can thalidomide children who cannot touch and locomote in usual ways achieve their solution? This is the paradox that Kopp and Shaperman draw attention to in reporting that a limbless thalidomide child solved such problems on a Stage 6 level. Either action on objects is not necessary for the achievement of Stage 6 object permanence or action has to be redefined.

Decarie discovered that most of the children she studied could solve such problems on a Stage 6 conceptual level when the problems were adapted to their motoric limitations. Decarie points out how these results are not inconsistent with Piaget's theory. She notes how the children substituted alternative limbs and digits, and where such means were not present, came to use unlikely instruments (e.g., nose). As with Fraiberg's (1977) observations of blind infants, the lack of typical avenues of action and experience might pose grave difficulties for the infant, but they need not preclude the possibility of achieving an awareness of a coherent and objective world. Fraiberg, through encouraging reaching for sound-producing objects located in near space, created a basis that some infants could go beyond to develop a "map" of object in space. Decarie indicates how the feet or the nose or . . . can substitute for the hand to form the coordinations with vision that lead the thalidomide child to search on an "ideational" basis.

Thus, both Decarie and Fraiberg believe that Piaget's emphasis on the role of activity in forming ideas about objects in space is supported by their studies. They, like Piaget, seem to identify activity as motoric activity. It is this point that is discussed in this chapter. It is claimed here that this motoric emphasis is not necessary to Piaget's basic notions and that interesting possibilities become apparent if an alternative that Piaget neglected is examined.

At the risk of some simplification, it can be said that Piaget adopted the view that the senses register only proximal or sensory information about the distal object and that touch teaches vision about the distal object (Piaget, 1950). Given that assumption, his view of action neglected the possibility that the visual stimulus provides not only sensory information but also provides direct information about objects-in-space. In other words, it is possible that the infant can come to know about objects through looking even when he or she cannot contact the environment with his or her limbs. Within the framework of the object-permanence and object-concept issue, Bower has vigorously championed this alternative (1977). He reported a number of studies that purport to demonstrate that before infants can effectively locomote toward and grasp objects, they are aware of their presence when they are out of view. For example, he argued that 5-month-olds can find an interesting object when the room lights go out and will look back to the occluding screen to find the missing object if the object they had been expecting disappears and a different object appears.

Bower's facts and interpretations have been a source of controversy (see Gratch, 1975, 1977, 1979a for reviews). There is a domain, however, where the facts have been replicable and the alternative interpretations have been examined, namely Stage 4 in Piaget's account of object concept development. Stage 4 is marked by an anomaly from the adult's point of view. Infants of about 8-9 months of age get interested in a toy, see it covered, and are able to remove the cover and gain the toy. When they observe the toy hidden in a second place, however, they immediately turn away from the new place of hiding and search for the object in the first hiding place. The anomaly stems from the fact that the infants' performance does not seem to involve forgetting in the ordinary-language sense. The infants clearly seem to observe the second place of hiding but seem to act as if the disappearance at that place means that they will find the object at the first place. Piaget interprets this anomalous behavior as evidence that the infants' observations are dominated by their prior actions. In other words, like the child who says, "a hole is to dig," the Stage 4 infant interprets what he or she sees as "the object I-find-at-the-first-place has disappeared." Piaget views the Stage 4 phenomenon as yet one more example of how the infants' perceptions are dominated by egocentric action schemes, and it is not until the infants are in Stage 5 that they will search where they see the object disappear rather than where they have overtly and motorically acted upon it.

Piaget's account raises questions about how the infant manages to succeed at the first place, if prior action is so important, and does not make clear which aspects of the stimulus field bear on the search behavior. Evans (1973) focused on the first issue by varying whether infants searched at the first place or simply watched the object being covered and uncovered and the number of such trials (2 or 5). He found that infants were as likely to search at the first place when the object was hidden at the second place in each of the 4 conditions. In other words, the infants learned something about the "specialness" of the first place through observation as well as through overt search. A number of investigators have begun to explore how the nature of the stimulus field affects the likelihood of error. For example, Acredolo (1978), Bremner (1978), and Butterworth (1975) have pursued the notion that infants orient spatially to their visual world in both egocentric and allocentric ways; that is, they orient to objects in terms of directions centered on their own body and in terms of relations of objects to one another. Thus, Butterworth found that infants are more likely to err when the first hiding place is at the midline than when it is off to the side. Furthermore, by varying the relation between the distinctiveness of the covers and the distinctiveness of the background, the likelihood of error can be varied. In particular, Butterworth et al. (1980) made the following interesting observation. Imagine a table with a green and a black side and two covers, one blue and one white. Infants are as likely to err when (1) the object is hidden on the second trial in the same place under the same distinctive cover but the background colors are reversed and when (2) the cover-background relations are maintained but the object is hidden at the other place on the second trial, but (3) are not likely to err if the object is hidden at the second place but the cover-background relation that marked the first place is reversed on the second trial so that the new place has the same cover-background as the first place of hiding.

Thus, these examples bring out the not surprising fact that the infants' searches are keyed to the stimulus field. The contrast between egocentric and allocentric modes of orientation can be interpreted as an attempt to bring out the idea that the arrangement of the environment can facilitate or impede the search of infants whose understanding of what they see is limited. In one sense, these findings about the importance of perception and its ecology are not at variance with Piaget's notions. Although he did not tend to carefully analyze the stimulus field, he certainly did not neglect the relation between action and perception. Thus, Piaget's analysis of what is entailed in knowing the permanence of objects involves a relatively straightforward set of ideas about the relation of action to perception. He argued that older infants, adults, and children perceive objects as "disappearables" whereas younger infants do not. In other words when adults watch objects in space and do such things as recognize and follow them, they tacitly see them as possibly being occluded and therefore are aware the object exists even when moved behind some other object or barrier. The young infant is at a loss when the object disappears because he or she only sees more or less familiar forms in space. The infant sees things *in* space, but unlike the older infant, does not know space. The space in which the action occurs provides the envelope within which the young infant can appreciate the coherence of objects to some degree, but the older infant carries the envelope in his head as a kind of "map" or "concept." That "map" is constructed from prior actions and permits the percepts, as well as the actions, of the older infant to be different from those of the younger infant.

Most psychologists, like Piaget, have assumed that perception begins with sensation, the registering of physical energies by the sense receptors. The distal object is the source of the physical energies, but the infant is aware of the distal stimulus only when he or she adds something to the sensation or proximal stimulus. The construction of the percept from the sensations has been explained in various ways, for example, associations of sensations, innate categories, some kind of inferential process based on underlying schemes. Piaget developed a model of perceptual development based on the idea that the percept is constructed from the development of both, which energies are registered, and the interpretative schemes. In his view, infants at different stages might be affected by different sensory energies because they might "center" on different facets of the sensory array, and the older infant is more likely to actively scan it. For Piaget, the critical difference lies in the schemes that assimilate the stimulus. The information about events is not in the energies but in the schemes. These schemes develop as a function of the infant's actions on perceived events. For example, the infants do not see the object as solid until they have coordinated the experiences of vision and touch such that they develop a scheme that coordinates these initially disparate schemes. To get to "reality" as opposed to "appearance," one must go beyond perception, no matter how sophisticated is the scheme that determines it. "Reality" is known only through "intelligence," through multiple, systematically organized perspectives on events.

In his analysis, Piaget made two strategic assumptions that he need not have made given the tradition he was elaborating. One was the sharp distinction he made between intelligence and perception. The other was that the "stuff" of perception was sensation. The examples given here from the object permanence literature primarily address the latter point; it is discussed below in a more general form. Then, the intelligence-perception distinction is again discussed.

At least part of the reason Piaget identified the stimulus with sensation was because he could not accept the Gestalt analysis of the stimulus. The Gestalt psychologists saw organization in the stimulus, which involved a one-to-one correspondence between the perceptual field and awareness. For example, closure refers to the fact that we usually see a circle that contains a small gap as a circle rather than a circle-with-a-gap. Piaget saw the Gestalt claim of such organization as implying that the knower need not actively construct his or her understanding of the world. Piaget believed that the Gestalt appeal to an isomorphism between the stimulus and the knower left the problem of explaining how we know the world unanalyzed.

Heider and Simmel (1944) and Michotte (1955), however, provided concrete reasons for believing that the Gestalt line of explanation is not as mysterious as Piaget supposed. They constructed sets of stimuli that in one form lead to the immediate pick up of complex information and do not in other forms. If complex information can be picked up directly, then one need not assume that the perception involves a complex and lengthy process of registering lots of discrete information and interpreting it. Perception of complex events may be as quick and direct as the perception of simple events. The perceiver need only tune into the stimulus invariant that specifies the complex event. A demonstration that the perceiver acts in such a fashion does not explain how the perception occurs, but it does rule out forms of explanation that focus on registering stimulus energies and then going through lengthy and complicated forms of information processing.

The Gibsons (1966, 1977, 1979) elaborated on and extended these ideas into a theory of ecological optics. On the one hand, the Gibsons provided a number of impressive demonstrations that present information about events such as occlusion, shearing, elasticity, etc. A principal point they make is that the stimulus cannot be thought of as a briefly presented scene, but both it and the perceiver must be thought of as time-lined. Information about occlusion is present and directly describable as an event over time, whereas it can only be inferred from a series of "snapshots." In that regard, the Gibsons are at pains to point out that the classical theory of the perception of physical energies assumes a stationary observer whereas the "real-life" situation involves a moving observer whose shifting gaze and moving body leads to different objects being occluded and unoccluded within a larger frame.

To ground such ideas in terms of the prior discussion of how normal and thalidomide infants find hidden objects, consider the following speculation of J. J. Gibson (personal communication). Imagine an infant watching a ball moving toward and behind a screen. Gibson assumes that if the infant is under 6 months of age then it will keep its eye on the ball. As the ball slowly moves behind the screen, the infant will strain to keep seeing the ball, and it will startle when it is completely occluded. The infant's attention is on the ball and not on the ball in relation to the screen. The infant startles because he or she has not seen a ball disappear; rather the ball vanishes or is annihilated. The infants' efforts have been directed to seeing the ball and hence they fail to detect the information about disappearance provided by the gradual occlusion of the ball by the screen. The information is there in the stimulus array and adults and older infants do not startle because they attend to the larger array. Although this author has not system-atically investigated this speculation, it does make sense, and a related phenomenon was noticed. When the object reappears from behind the screen, 6- and 9-month-old infants often will startle whereas infants in the second year of life and adults are highly unlikely to do so. The reappearance, like the disappearance, is specified in the time-lined event, and adults know it with as much certainty as they know that there is a wall behind the sofa in the room (Michotte, 1955). It is hoped that these speculations bring out how the normal or the thalidomide infant need not handle the hidden object in order to make some sense of its comings and goings.

According to the Gibsons, which aspects of the information pres-ent in the stimulus field are detected by organisms depends upon the structures that have evolved to fit them to their particular ecological niches, their level of experiences, and how they deploy their perceptual structures in any given situation. A number of unresolved issues are posed by the Gibsons' theory. It is unclear how the information is picked up, where reasoning fits into the picture, etc., but what the Gibsons clearly point up is that a theory of levels of knowing, such as Piaget's, need not rest its analysis of how intelligence develops on an analysis of the stimulus as a sensory array. Events "out there" provide information about what actions they permit and how events interact with each other. The speculations of the above paragraph indicate how the Gibsons can agree with Piaget, that there might be different levels of awareness of object permanence, but can account for it in terms of which aspect of the stimulus array the infant attends to, rather than in terms of the nature of the infant's organization of schemes.

Thus, this discussion of some aspects of Piaget's analysis of early intellectual development provides a basis for suggesting that the ob-servations of thalidomide infants by Decarie and Kopp and Shaperman need not seem so paradoxical. Disappearances and reappearances are there to be seen, although we presently do not know which aspects of that visual process involve motoric action in an important way. Just as a blind child can learn the language of seeing colors and shapes and not know about important aspects of those events in concrete situations, so too it can be imagined that a child with severe motor restrictions might not know about important facets of events that he or she has observed but not handled. One can dwell on the gaps, but an important point about "blindisms" is that they indicate that a child can come, through alternative routes, to engage a significant aspect of reality in an intelligent manner. Those concerned with handicapped children must be prepared to believe that not all aspects of the course of "normal" development are necessary steps in the route to some goal desired for children, both when the children are deviant or normal. The difficult key issue is how one describes functionally what really is involved in such goals as locomotion or reasoning. To over concretize the goals both distorts them and keeps us from realizing that there may be alternative routes that children can acquire to reach such goals.

The intent of this chapter thus far has not been to explain how the thalidomide infants achieved object permanence nor to diminish the significance of the impressive studies and analyses made by Decarie and Fraiberg. It has not been argued that they and Piaget are wrong in emphasizing the role of action in development. Rather, a more "ecologically" sound basis for Piaget's theory of action is provided. Such a basis would lead us to more carefully evaluate the stimulus field of the infant and thereby would put us in a better position to appreciate how there can be multiple routes to certain intellectual goals.

This "ecological" analysis can be further discussed by considering the second strategic assumption Piaget made, namely that intelligence and perception are sharply distinguishable. Piaget made this distinction when trying to map how the child proceeds from a subjective view of the world in which value and function dominate the awareness of events to a view in which rational analysis permits us to sometimes objectify ourselves and the physical and social world. The distinction served him well as a basis for identifying different levels of awareness of a problematic situation at different levels of development. In Piagetian analyses, there always is a child who is aware of the wrong elements and is resourceless when asked to solve the problem. There are children who are aware of the wrong elements but somehow can grope their way to a solution. Then there are the children who can look at the right elements, can solve the problem, and can reason their way through the complexities of the problem.

The distinction, however, also led Piaget to conjure stages of mental organization that were too tied to formal logic and were too divorced from the pragmatic situation. That is the substance of a number of sympathetic critiques of his ideas about the development of reasoning that began with Vygotsky (1962) and recently have been elaborated upon by such writers as Donaldson (1978), Feldman and Toulmin (1976), Rotman (1978), and Gratch (1979a, 1979b).

In these critiques, there is general agreement on the necessity of describing different levels of the known and different levels of the knower and of the value of formal models in making such descriptions. We devise, and revise, our models of energy and weather systems and industrial organizations and try to mathematize these models because of the clarity and power that such abstractions provide. A major source of the importance of Piaget's observations has been his sensitivity to this aspect of the problem of intelligence. The child has to come to know the "curriculum" as we presently model it, and a most fruitful way of understanding how the child's mind works is by asking him how he or she thinks about and understands central ideas rather than "rote-learned" details. The conservation tasks are the most celebrated examples, and it makes sense to turn to Piagetian-based assessment schedules such as those of Uzgiris and Hunt (1975), Laurendeau and Pinard (1962), and Fischer (1980) because they are composed of items that provide a method for arriving at knowledge in a systematic fashion.

Investigators also try to develop models of the mind and brain. Again formal models can be valuable in marking out the set of events that must be taken into account if certain achievements are to follow. Thus, the mathematical structure, the abelian group, that figures so frequently in Piaget's thought permits one to describe a great number of transformations of events in space such as the many turns of a clock hand or the various routes to objects in a room, and one can use such a mathematical form to model the behavior of a child in the "as if" sense. Lining up what the child does with the model provides a basis for describing the fit with the model. But even if one makes the systematic identification—something Piaget has not really done—one is left with the conclusion that it is "as if" the child's mind has the properties of the group or the child knows and uses group theory. Stone and Day (1980) nicely point out that analog and digital computers may solve the same problem, but their workings are very different. The model helps to structure the field of inquiry but it alone does not describe the mind's workings.

The spirit of these critiques, then, is not that Piaget tries to model structures but that he mistook the model for the modeling process. When Piaget or we model, we arrive at a notion of what *is* through an elaborate "conversation" with "nature" and our colleagues. The "conversation" is an intricate mix of perception, intuition, and systematic reasoning. A metaphor for the process might be the way in which a sculptor re-sees his or her intention in the course of adapting it to the particularities of the material used. The process begins with a tentative model and ends with a more definitive model that then sets the stage for further revising of the model. This process of model revision occurs in a context of "conversations" with relevant others. There must be some kind of "ghost" that underlies the "reasoning machine," and it must have some kind of a root in our evolutionary history. Despite Washoe and fantasies of signing chimp communities, the odds are chimps will not become homologous with humans. The "ghost" has to be less well-formed and more context-bound than the models Piaget conjures. As Vygotsky so presciently saw, Piaget thought of the development of thought as basically a conversation between the child and nature; this despite Piaget's thorough awareness of the fact that we grow up in social groups. In Vygotsky's view, what we look at and talk about and how we do this depends importantly on the "conversations" we have with others—they help form the agendas, supply the tools, fill in gaps, join with us in utilizing and validating the results of our thoughts as well as the process. In particular, Vygotsky pointed out how such conversations bear upon the process of diagnosing and developing levels of intelligence in a way many presently utilize to reinterpret Piagetian findings, for example, Donaldson (1978).

Moreover, Zajonc (1980) and Campos and Stenberg (in press) point to the importance of intuitive knowing, feeling, and value, and its sources in our environment as the base upon which we reason or, more likely, rationalize all through life. Their work signals, in another way, the intimate relation between perception and intelligence. The theme of feeling and value is latent in the Gibsons' notion that we perceive the affordances of things, what they permit us to do. Zajonc, like the Gibsons, believes that we respond directly to the world and that much of what we mean by feeling is a direct response to what we perceive. The hare who freezes at the flight of the hawk does so immediately and does not see a hawk so much as a pattern of movement in the periphery of the visual field. Zajonc emphasizes that there are aspects of situations, "preferents," which we respond to on an immediate basis. The objectification of the event and our feeling may or may not occur but that process occurs at a later stage of the act. The themes of affordance and preferent are latent in Freud's distinction between primary and secondary process.

SUMMARY

This chapter articulates some of the complexities in Piaget's notion of object permanence and suggests how his notions of action and intelligence can be made more "ecologically" valid. His tasks and his concepts are valuable aids that can be used to approach the handicapped child, but using them involves us in the dilemma of habit and thought. In the natural and the behavioral sciences one needs standardized techniques, in other words, habits. But, as indicated above, the use of standardized procedures always entails an element of art (Polanyi, 1964).

The handicapped child poses the dilemma in a particularly pointed way. The child's deviance creates important differences in the "opportunity" field, or niche, for both the child and the parents. Our "standardized" notions and procedures will not do. We have to use our wits; follow the child's lead (and also the lead of their parents). Fraiberg's discovery that reading the blind infant's hands could provide affective information that his eyes could not, is a poignant example. We need notions of ends toward which we want the child to develop, but how we specify those ends and the routes thereto may have to be different. In that sense, what Piaget did in arriving at his conclusions is a model of good practice. He used tasks, often developed by others, as a basis for identifying his notions of intellectual stages, and in his "methode clinique" he worked at making the necessary accommodations of child to task to ideas. He may sometimes be faulted for interpreting a miscommunication as evidence of a difference in "mind" and seeing mental consistencies where context supplies the order. But what makes his observations so interesting is that he reaches his conclusions only after he considers many plausible alternatives and tries to empirically assess their relative value. In their own way, Decarie and Fraiberg acted in kind. And so must we all within our limits. To quote Karl Popper: "What matters is not methods or techniques but a sensitivity to problems, and a consuming passion for them; or as the Greeks said, the gift of wonder" (1963).

ACKNOWLEDGMENTS

I thank Joe Campos for suggesting that I dwell on the studies of thalidomide children. I thank Don Campbell for his repeated attempts to convince me that ideas follow on action, that knowledge is more a matter of "blind-trial-and-error" than reason, that one must have the "faith of a grain of mustard seed."

REFERENCES

Acredolo, L. Development of spatial orientation in infancy. *Developmental Psychology*, 1978, *14*, 224–234.
Bower, T. *A primer of infant development*. San Francisco: Freeman, 1977.
Bremner, G. Egocentric versus allocentric coding in nine-month old infants: Factors influencing the choice of code. *Developmental Psychology*, 1978, *14*, 346–355.

Butterworth, G. Object identity in infancy: The interaction of spatial location codes in determining search errors. *Child Development*, 1975, *46*, 866–870.

Butterworth, G., Jarrett, N., & Hicks, L. Spatio-temporal identity in infancy: Perceptual competence or conceptual deficit? Unpublished manuscript, University of Southampton, England, 1980.

Campos, J., & Stenberg, C. Perception, appraisal, and emotion: The onset of social referencing. In M. Lamb & L. Sherrod (Eds.), *Infant social cognition*. Hillsdale, N.J.: Lawrence Erlbaum Associates, in press.

Decarie, T. A study of the mental and emotional development of the thalidomide child. In B. M. Foss (Ed.), *Determinants of infant behavior* (Vol. 4). London: McThuen, 1969.

Donaldson, M. *Children's minds*. New York: W. W. Norton & Company, 1978.

Evans, W. The stage IV error in Piaget's theory of object concept development: An investigation of the role of activity. Unpublished dissertation, University of Houston, 1973.

Feldman, C., & Toulmin, S. Logic and theory of mind. In J. K. Cole (Ed.), *Nebraska symposium on motivation*. Lincoln: University of Nebraska Press, 1976.

Fischer, K. A theory of cognitive development: The control and construction of hierarchies of skills. *Psychological Review*, 1980, *87*, 477–530.

Fraiberg, S. *Insights from the blind*. New York: Basic Books, 1977.

Gibson, E. The ecological optics of infancy: The differentiation of invariants given by optical motion. Unpublished Presidential Address, Division 3, America Psychological Association, San Francisco, August 29, 1977.

Gibson, J. *The senses considered as perceptual systems*. Boston: Houghton Mifflin, 1966.

Gibson, J. *The ecological approach to visual perception*. Boston: Houghton Mifflin, 1979.

Gratch, G. Recent studies based on Piaget's view of object concept development. In L. B. Cohen & P. Salapatek (Eds.), *Infant perception* (Vol. 2). New York: Academic Press, 1975.

Gratch, G. Review of Piagetian infancy research: Object concept development. In W. Overton & J. McC. Gallagher (Eds.), *Knowledge in development* (Vol. 1). New York: Plenum Publishing Corp., 1977.

Gratch, G. The development of thought and language in infancy. In J. Osofsky (Ed.), *The handbook of infant development*. New York: John Wiley & Sons, 1979(a).

Gratch, G. Some thoughts on object permanence and language development. Talk delivered at the Conference on language behavior in infancy and early childhood, sponsored by Johnson and Johnson Baby Products Company, Santa Barbara, California, 1979(b).

Heider, F., & Simmel, M. An experimental study of apparent behavior. *American Journal of Psychology*, 1944, *57*, 243–259.

Kopp, C., & Shaperinan, J. Cognitive development in the absence of object manipulation during infancy. *Developmental Psychology*, 1973, *9*, 430.

Laurendeau, M., & Pinard, A. *Causal thinking in the child*. New York: International Universities Press, 1962.

Lewis, M. What do we mean when we say "infant intelligence scores?" A sociopolitical question. In M. Lewis (Ed.), *Origins of intelligence*. New York: Plenum Publishing Corp., 1976.

McCall, R. Qualitative transitions in behavioral development in the first two years of life. In M. Borstein & W. Kessen (Eds.), *Psychological development from infancy*. Hillsdale, N.J.: Lawrence Erlbaum Associates, 1979.

Meier, J. Screening and assessment of young children at developmental risk. The President's Committee on Mental Retardation, 1973, DHEW Publication No. (OS) 73–90.

Michotte, A. Perception and cognition. *Acta Psychologica*, 1955, *11*, 69–91.

Piaget, J. *The psychology of intelligence*. New York: Harcourt Brace Jovanovich, 1950.

Piaget, J. *The construction of reality in the child*. New York: Basic Books, 1954.

Polanyi, M. *Personal knowledge*. New York: Harper & Row, 1964.

Popper, K. *Conjectures and refutations*. London: Routledge and Kegan Paul, 1963.

Rotman, B. *Jean Piaget: Psychologist of the real*. Ithaca, N.Y.: Cornell University Press, 1978.

Skinner, B. Behaviorism at fifty. In T. W. Wann (Ed.), *Behaviorism and phenomenology*. Chicago: University of Chicago Press, 1964.

Stone, C., & Day, M. Competence and performance models and the characterization of formal operational skills. *Human Development*, 1980, *23*, 323–353.

Thurstone, L. *The nature of intelligence*. Patterson, N.J.: Littlefield, Adams, 1960.

Uzgiris, I., & Hunt, J. McV. *Assessment in infancy*. Urbana, Illinois: University of Illinois Press, 1975.

Vygotsky, L. *Thought and language*. Cambridge, MA: M.I.T. Press, 1962.

Wachs, T., & DeRemer, P. Adaptive behavior and Uzgiris-Hunt scale performance of young, developmentally disabled children. *American Journal of Mental Deficiency*, 1978, *83*, 175–176.

Zajonc, R. Feeling and thinking: Preferences need no inferences. *American Psychologist*, 1980, *35*, 151–175.

Section III
ASSESSMENT STRATEGIES

Chapter 7

ALTERNATIVE ASSESSMENT PROCEDURES FOR HANDICAPPED INFANTS AND TODDLERS: Theoretical and Practical Issues

Philip R. Zelazo

Many early educators and developmental psychologists have met children with serious developmental delays who somehow conveyed an impression that they were more intelligent and aware than formal assessments of their ability revealed. The practitioners sensed that the children had greater awareness through a variety of behaviors. They may have detected a "brightness" in their eyes, a "knowing" gaze or perhaps an appropriate smile to an unintended discrepancy. The clinical judgment, often developed after years of experience with handicapped children, leaves a haunting feeling that there is something wrong with our traditional methods of intellectual assessment. Many of us have come away from this clinical experience believing that there must be a better way to measure intellectual ability among children with serious developmental handicaps.

The creation of alternative assessment approaches for the handicapped child under 3 years of age is intricately tied to a discussion of theory and assumptions. A review of the limitations inherent in the prevailing procedures invariably leads to a re-examination of the beliefs that influence the choice of procedures and items used in traditional tests. The limitations of our current efforts to assess cognitive abilities in the young child go well beyond the procedures themselves and touch on the assumptions that we hold about infant development. Our beliefs and assumptions have shifted dramatically since the seeds for the traditional tests were planted in the early decades of this century. To be sure, the norms have been updated and even the interpretations have been changed, but the traditional tests remain in widespread use despite our shaken convictions. The time has come to critically reexamine the limitations of current tests, articulate the weaknesses of prevailing assumptions and encourage alternate avenues that researchers and clinicians can explore.

DIFFICULTIES WITH CONVENTIONAL TESTS

It has long been acknowledged that conventional tests have low predictive validity (Bayley, 1966; Lewis & McGurk, 1972; McCall, 1982; Stott & Ball, 1965; Zelazo, 1976a). The failure of performance on infant tests to predict later behavior on generally accepted IQ tests is a serious problem, although its significance is diminished for a variety of reasons including the absence of acceptable alternatives. Because many researchers and clinicians have assumed that infants express their intelligence differently than older children, the poor predictive validity of conventional tests did not diminish their credibility or use irreparably. Moreover, conventional tests of infant development announce normality with high validity as Bayley (1969) argued. Although it is believed widely that tests of infant development predict later intelligence poorly, it is questioned less widely whether tests of infant development measure intellectual ability adequately. Behaviors measured on infant tests may have little direct correspondence to intellectual development. The suggestion that we have measured behaviors that "correlate" with cognitive ability at one point, but need not proceed in direct correspondence with cognitive development at a later point, gains strength from a methodological critique of the traditional tests.

Conventional tests should be standardized on large samples of normal children. It was not anticipated, however, that this apparently sound methodological prerequisite would limit the appropriateness of these conventional tests to normal children. Unfortunately, tests of early development are given usually to handicapped children—children with motor, language, behavior, and emotional disabilities. The use of conventional testing procedures with developmentally disabled children almost invariably places their intellectual status in doubt.

Examination of the Bayley Scales of Infant Development (1969), a highly regarded and widely used test, illustrates at least five limitations. First, gross and fine motor items are measured directly in the Motor Scale. The use of a motor scale is easy to discount as a measure of intellectual ability, but it has not always been that way. The original scales, created in the late 1920s and early 1930s, were predicated on the assumption that intact neuromotor functioning would reflect intact intellectual ability. This is a reasonable inference and seems to be valid in many instances. Conventional neuromotor schedules can announce normal intellectual functioning; the problem is that a poor neuromotor performance need not announce impaired intellectual ability. Today, many researchers and clinicians acknowledge this limitation.

Second, imitation items requiring motor facility of the upper extremities are measured directly on the Mental Scale, with particular emphasis during the second year of life. In fact, Bayley (1969) reported a modest correlation ($r = 0.55$) between the Motor and Mental Scales.

Third, language comprehension items are emphasized on the Mental Scale during the second year also, but it is less obvious to outside observers that language comprehension items require facility of the upper extremities for unambiguous pointing to occur. Fourth, language production items play a dominant role in measures of intelligence from about the beginning of the third year. The ability to talk, a motor component of language becomes virtually essential for the assessment of cognitive ability. Fifth, conventional tests are constructed in a manner that requires compliance with the examiner. Compliance cannot be taken lightly with children in an age range that has achieved recognition as "the terrible two's." A child that will not comply with the examiner's requests is at risk for delayed development as measured by conventional schedules.

This analysis indicates that measures used in the traditional tests of intellectual ability are confounded by many of the handicaps that children display during the early years of life. Unwittingly, children with motor disabilities, productive language delays, emotional and/or behavioral problems are, in some instances, unjustly placed at high risk for intellectual impairment. It is essential to distinguish a deficit in one of these peripheral areas from a deficit in central processing ability in the assessment of developmentally handicapped children. A child with a productive language delay may have normal intelligence even though his or her test scores may be depressed.

Because children with developmental disabilities are evaluated on tests that were standardized on normal children with intact developmental capabilities, the results yield often a depressed estimate of the disabled children's intellectual functioning. As an unintended consequence of this bias, the testing community conveys frequently lowered expectations to the child's parents and teachers derived from tests of questionable validity. Thus, the seeds for iatrogenic retardation—a term used to characterize this phenomenon (see Kearsley, 1979; Zelazo & Kearsley, 1981) are planted in the traditional scales themselves. It is imperative that tests applicable to both normal and disabled children with equal confidence and free from prejudice be developed.

CHALLENGES TO THE
ASSUMPTION OF SENSORIMOTOR INTELLIGENCE

Guiding Assumptions for Conventional Tests

Many of the problems with conventional tests can be traced to the related assumptions of sensorimotor intelligence and cephalo-caudal development (Zelazo, 1976a,b; 1979; 1981). It is assumed widely, although with varying degrees of commitment, that intelligence among infants and toddlers is reflected through gross and fine motor actions.

Existing theories and tests of infant development adhere explicitly or implicitly to the assumption of sensorimotor intelligence. On one extreme, in the case of the neurologist, the integrity of the child's central nervous system as reflected in his or her neuromotor status, is regarded as a direct measure of the child's intellectual status. Questions of intelligence seem to be synonomous with questions of central nervous system functioning. Neuromotor dysfunction as indicated by the reflexive examination is used to infer a lesion or insult to the brain, and brain damage is considered to be indicative of intellectual impairment. Moreover, CNS maturation is believed to follow a cephalo-caudal pathway, thereby dictating the sequencing of items on conventional tests of neuromotor development (see Zelazo, 1976a, 1976b).

These related assumptions influenced psychologists during the early days of test construction. Over the years, psychologists seem to have relaxed their commitment to strict interpretations of sensorimotor intelligence and cephalo-caudal development. However, the traditional tests of infant development—the tools of assessment—continue to reflect the influence of sensorimotor measures. For example, Gottfried and Brody (1975) determined that the Bayley Motor Scale accounted for more variance (between 13% and 36%) in both the Bayley Mental and two Piagetian Scales (The Escalona-Corman Object Permanence Scale, Corman & Escalona, 1969, and the Uzgiris-Hunt Development of Schemes in Relation to Object Scale, 1966) than any other variable examined. Moreover, they found positive moderate (ranging from 0.47 to 0.85) and significant ($p < 0.01$) correlations between the psychometric and Piagetian Scales of sensorimotor intelligence and similar correlation networks for 207 infants (mean age = 11 months). These results imply that the two types of scales are measures of the same construct and establish a clear relation between motoric precocity and advanced sensorimotor development at 11 months of age. In contrast to the finding by Gottfried and Brody that motor facility predicted sensorimotor intelligence, the correlations between motor development and later intelligence are weak for kindergarten, first and second (Dudek, Lester, Goldberg, & Dyer, 1969), and third and sixth grade children (Singer, 1968). The divergent results for infants and older children indicate that tests of sensorimotor intelligence measure different factors than later intelligence tests.

Many clinicians discard the global Mental Developmental Index or Psychomotor Developmental Index and try to correct for the child's disability by overlooking inappropriate items and/or focus on the child's strengths and weaknesses. These strategies reflect a partial corrective for shortcomings of the tests, but most of the scales were not constructed to be used in this manner.

Research on Infant Memory Formation

A major challenge to the assumption of sensorimotor intelligence is inherent in the research on memory formation in infancy. This work, conducted over the past 23 years, indicates that infants can create memories for visual and auditory events through simple exposure and without gross and fine motor involvement. The early and subsequent work on visual preferences (Fagan, 1978, 1979; Fantz, 1958; Fantz & Nevis, 1967; Miranda et al., 1977; Miranda & Fantz, 1974) demonstrated that infants look reliably at a novel stimulus if paired with a familiar one. The preference for the novel stimulus implies that a firm memory was formed for the familiar event. These researchers demonstrated respectable correlations between early performances on tests of visual preference and later intelligence scores. For example, Fagan (1979) found correlation coefficients of 0.37 and 0.66 between infant recognition memory scores and language comprehension scores at 4 and 6 years of age, respectively.

Lewis and Goldberg (1969) demonstrated that infants display habituation to a repeated visual or auditory event followed by dishabituation to the introduction of a transformation of the standard. Dishabituation to a different stimulus strengthens the inference that habituation was produced by the formation of a memory for the standard rather than by effector fatigue or local receptor adaptation. Both the habituation and dishabituation phenomena imply that an internal representation of the standard—a schema or memory—was created. The pattern of habituation-dishabituation has been demonstrated for infants older than 2 months using both visual (McCall & Kagan, 1967; McCall & Melson, 1969) and auditory (Kinney & Kagan, 1976) stimuli. Moreover, habituation and dishabituation effects have been shown for a variety of responses including duration of fixation, length of first fixation, and cardiac deceleration (Cohen, 1972, 1973; McCall & Kagan, 1967; McCall & Melson, 1969; Super et al., 1972).

Research with neonates indicates that the capacity to process visual and auditory events, free from reliance on gross and fine motor performance, may begin within the first few days of life. Engen and Lipsitt (1965) examined breathing patterns in response to olfactory stimuli and demonstrated habituation to a standard and dishabituation to a different stimulus using appropriate counterbalancing procedures. Adkinson and Berg (1976) examined cardiac decelerations to mild intensity colored lights appropriately counterbalanced for order of presentation and demonstrated habituation followed by dishabituation. A recent experiment by Zelazo, Brody, and Chaika (1981) extended the inference of information processing and memory formation among neonates to auditory stimuli using a clearly observable response, head turning to a sound source. Three-day-old infants displayed a criterion level of turning toward the sound source followed by habituation and dishabituation to appropriately counterbalanced rattle sounds. Brody, Zelazo, and Chaika (1982) repeated this result using speech stimuli, namely, the English words *tinder* and *beagle*. Together, these results imply that the newborn infant has the capacity to process and respond to sensory information, hold that information in memory and retrieve it for comparison with dishabituating stimuli at the beginning of the sensorimotor period.

Questions have been raised about the lack of consistency among experiments on habituation-dishabituation effects (Clifton & Nelson, 1976). Additional research can strengthen the data base upon which the inference that children create internal representations in the brain is made. The reliable occurrence, however, of habituation-dishabituation effects in numerous laboratories for different modalities and responses not only indicates a robust finding, but implies that knowledge can be acquired without reliance on gross and fine motor performance during the sensorimotor period.

SHOULD THE ASSUMPTION OF SENSORIMOTOR INTELLIGENCE BE MODIFIED?

The evidence summarized thus far implies that the assumption of sensorimotor intelligence does not account for the data on memory formation in infancy convincingly. The assumption of sensorimotor intelligence itself restricts the approaches available to assess handicapped children. Both the sensorimotor assumption and the procedures dictated by this belief contribute to a strategy that is more likely to yield depressed, rather than inflated, estimates of intellectual ability. These limitations imply that modification of the assumption of sensorimotor intelligence may be desirable.

Perhaps the assumption of sensorimotor intelligence should be modified to include acceptance of subtle motoric responses as evidence from which inferences of memory formation can be made. First, it seems that infants, including newborns, can process visual and auditory information and form memories for internal representations of events, free from reliance on gross and fine motor involvement (Adkinson & Berg, 1976; Engen & Lipsitt, 1965; Zelazo et al., 1981). Additionally, the research on preferences and habituation and dishabituation effects to visual and auditory events implies that the distal receptors (see Walters & Parke, 1965) play a greater role than acknowledged either in theory or conventional assessment procedures. Moreover, it seems that infants not only create memories for events, but display greater sustained attention to moderately discrepant variations from those memories (Kagan, 1971; McCall & Melson, 1969; Super et al., 1972; Kinney & Kagan, 1976; Zelazo, Hopkins, Jacobson, & Kagan, 1974). Thus, stimuli that are moderately discrepant from the information that infants acquire through experience also influence visual and auditory information that they attend to and process during the first year of life.

The evidence that 72-hour-old infants can process and form memories for auditory information despite their grossly immature neuromotor systems implies that sensorimotor intelligence as presently conceived is excessively restrictive. The findings from the habituation-dishabituation research imply that either infants possess the capacity to process information and create memories for visual, olfactory, and auditory events from the first days of life or the habituation-dishabituation paradigm is not a valid indication of the capacity to form internal representations for external events.

A second modification to the assumption of sensorimotor intelligence seems worthy of consideration. A cognitive transition, or metamorphosis, seems to emerge toward the end of the first year announcing a major change in both information processing ability and the capacity to act on the environment (see Kagan, 1971; Zelazo, 1975, 1982). Traditional assessment procedures do not acknowledge that measurement of this cognitive transition may be possible without reliance on gross and fine motor measures as the analysis by Gottfried and Brody (1975) implies. The cognitive transition, occurring between about 9 and 13 months, deserves greater recognition in theory and assessment. A brief description of the qualitative changes occurring in children's free play will illuminate the nature of the cognitive transition.

Zelazo and Kearsley (1980) examined 64 infants between the ages of 9½ and 15½ months during a 15-minute free play period. As shown in Figure 1, the indiscriminate application of stereotypical responses involving banging, waving, mouthing, and fingering of objects was the dominant form of active play at 9½ months. There was a precipitous drop from 87% to 49% in stereotypical activity from 9½ to 11 ½ months and to 31% by 13½ months. The decline in stereotypical object manipulations seems to be linked to the appearances of functional play in which the appropriate uses for objects are displayed and of relational play in which two or more objects are brought together in an idiosyncratic manner. The appropriate use of objects involving both specificity and diversity of function characterizes the nature of the cognitive change occurring during this period. Beginning at about 11½ months and increasing linearly through at least 15½ months, children begin to display specific uses for objects across many different toys. Belsky

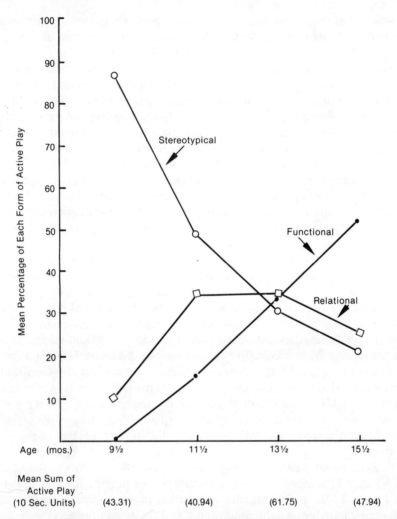

Figure 1.   Mean percentages of stereotypical, relational, and functional play at each of four ages. (From Zelazo, P., & Kearsley, R. The emergence of functional play in infants: Evidence for a major cognitive transition. *Journal of Applied Developmental Psychology*, 1980, *1*, 95–117).

and Most (1981) observed a similar pattern between 9½ and 15½ months and extended the systematic observations of development of symbolic play through 21 months of age.

   The paradoxical increase in both specificity and diversity occurring from about 12 months is consistent with Kagan's (1971) suggestion that children gained the capacity to generate hypotheses toward the end of the first year. An evaluation of play as an index of cognitive ability may be useful for the child with behavior problems who may not comply with the examiner's requests and, in some instances, with children who experienced environmental deficits. The question remains, however, as to how these cognitive skills, including the formation of memories for visual and auditory events and the capacity for diversity and specificity can be measured in children for whom play procedures are inappropriate—children with serious neuromotor disabilities.

THE PROCESSING OF VISUAL AND AUDITORY
INFORMATION: AN ALTERNATIVE ASSESSMENT STRATEGY

The information processing approach used at the Center for Behavioral Pediatrics and Infant Development assesses the speed with which infants create memories for visual and auditory events (see Zelazo, 1979, 1981; Zelazo & Kearsley, 1981, 1982; Kearsley, 1981). Clusters of specified behaviors are used to draw inferences about childrens' capacities to process and respond to the standard sensory information, retain that information in memory and retrieve it for comparison with dishabituating stimuli. The paradigm is similar for both visual and auditory sequences. An event is repeated so that an expectancy can be formed, a moderately discrepant variation of the standard is introduced and repeated, followed by the reappearance of the standard and its repetition. Typically, there are six presentations of the standard, three presentations of the discrepancy and three reappearances of the standard.

Method

In the car-doll sequence, a toy car is released from its resting position at the top of a ramp, allowed to roll down and to tap over a brightly colored styrofoam object upon contact. During the discrepant variation, the car taps the object, but it does not fall. There are six presentations in which the styrofoam object falls when tapped by the car, three presentations in which the object does not fall when tapped and three reappearances of the original event.

The child observes this sequence in a room resembling a puppet theater. The visual events are presented on a brightly lit stage, in front of the child who is seated on the mother's lap. The durations of visual fixation, smiling, vocalizing, and fretting are coded on a button box by an observer on one side of the stage. Anticipatory fixation, pointing or clapping, waving, twisting, and turning to mother are coded on a button box by an observer seated behind the other wing of the stage.

Surface leads attached to the infant's chest are used to produce an electrocardiogram that is converted to a beat-by-beat recording of heart rate using a cardiotachometer. The car sequence was constructed to produce signals indicating when the car was at the top, runway, or bottom segments of the ramp and whether the styrofoam object was erect or down. Thus, the measures of the child's heart rate increases and decreases and selected behaviors are recorded online and time-locked with identifiable portions of the stimulus sequence during the standard, transformation, and return portions of the event.

This information processing approach generates a complex profile of elicited behaviors for both visual and auditory sequences lasting up to about 4 minutes each. Moreover, this approach contains a number of distinct advantages over traditional procedures and the basic research on memory formation in infancy. One distinction from previous research is that sequential rather than static (redundant) stimuli are used. This methodological consideration elicits greater similarity of infant responsiveness to visual and auditory events. A second distinguishing factor is that the perceptual-cognitive procedures described here are appropriate for children between the ages of 6 and 36 months. Most of the basic research on memory formation was conducted with infants younger than 7 months and using static visual stimuli. A third defining characteristic is that subtle elicited responses rather than gross and fine motor behaviors are measured. Rather than appropriate responses to requests, imitation, pointing or naming, less obvious behaviors such as cardiac changes, visual fixation, smiling, and vocalizing are recorded.

A fourth and crucial development that has advanced the dynamic assessment of memory or schemata formation is the use of clusters of behaviors to announce recognition and to infer that an internal representation has been formed in the brain. These clusters (see Zelazo, 1981; Zelazo & Kearsley, 1982), influenced by previous research such as that of Lewis and Goldberg (1969), are defined to include a high level of visual fixation accompanied by a cardiac deceleration that is equal to or greater than 6 beats and one or more of the following behaviors: smiling, vocalizing, laughter, pointing, clapping, turning to mother, and appropriate speech. It is common to see a 32-month-old child point, smile, vocalize, and show a 15-beat cardiac deceleration while watching intently during the third presentation of the car sequence. Through the use of clusters of elicited behaviors, even a quadriplegic child can announce that "he or she's got it." The evidence implies that these elicited behaviors reflect the matching of an external event to an internal representation of that event (see Zelazo & Komer, 1971; Zelazo, 1979).

Clusters of behaviors implying that an internal representation of the event has been formed occur before habituation. Presumably, as an internal representation for an unfamiliar event is created, reactivity is low initially, increases to peak responding and is followed by a decline in expressiveness (see Zelazo, 1972; 1979; Zelazo & Komer, 1971). The perceptual-cognitive procedures described here seem to assess changes in the speed of processing and memory formation over the first 3 years of life. Thus, the perceptual-cognitive procedures assess a dynamic process—the formation and assimilation of "schemata," presumably—rather than the child's static storehouse of previously acquired knowledge.

Results

Infant responsiveness to the information processing procedures reflect broad classifications of ability rather than month-by-month profiles. The summary of results presented here is drawn from both cross-sectional and longitudinal samples of normal children collected in collaboration with Kagan and Kearsley (Kagan, Kearsley, & Zelazo, 1978). Moreover, the utility of these procedures has been explored with children displaying varying handicaps including children with cerebral palsy and Down's syndrome. The principal emphasis and experience has been with children who display developmental delays of unknown etiology. The results of a 4½ year investigation revealed that children with intact as opposed to impaired information processing ability can be identified from a sample of children who display delays on the Bayley Scales of Mental Development. Children with intact information processing ability display improved scores on the Stanford-Binet Test of Intelligence with 10 months of behavioral treatment, whereas children with impaired information processing ability do not (Zelazo & Kearsley, 1981).

Between about 3 and 10 months of age, infants display increased attention and responsiveness to both visual and auditory events. Reactivity, however, is generally disjointed and vocalization in particular declines measurably at about 9½ months. The first appearance of integrated clusters of behaviors occurs at about 11½ months in our samples. By the end of the first year, attention continues to increase, there is evidence of cardiac acceleration during the anticipatory phases of the car sequence and clusters of behaviors including vocalization begin to occur late during the standard and return segments of the sequences.

At about 20 months of age, interest remains high, clusters occur sooner in each sequence and clusters occur more uniformly across the four principal sequences that are used. It is common for clusters to occur to the third or fourth presentation of the standard and to the first or second reappearance of the standard following the discrepancy, but not to the discrepancy itself. At about 30 months of age the discrepant variations of the standards elicit unambiguous clusters of behaviors that imply the rapid formation of an internal representation for the discrepant event. Clusters of responses to the standards and return portions of the sequences are generally, clear, quick, and uniform across the sequences.

Thus, the use of first clear clusters of reactivity implying memory formation occur sooner in the sequence as the child gets older. Moreover, the use of discrepant variations of the standards seem to distinguish normal children at the older ages. These factors combined with the use of fixed numbers of trials imply that the procedures are measuring the speed with which information is processed and memories are formed over the first 3 years of life (Zelazo & Kearsley, 1981, 1982).

Advantages

There are several distinct benefits from the use of this information processing approach. First, the information processing procedures do not require that children possess a disposition to comply with the requests of an examiner. The perceptual-cognitive information itself tends to engage children, and it is not necessary to compel them to watch or listen. The use of sequential rather than static visual and auditory stimuli seems to contribute substantially to the compelling quality of the procedures. Second, the assessment of information processing ability may be a less biased measure of the children's intellectual ability than the use of measures that rely on gross and fine motor development, productive language, and compliance with the examiner. Impaired information processing ability implies that developmental delays are central in origin. Conventional testing approaches cannot distinguish central from peripheral bases for the delays reliably. Many children with productive language delays and delays in functional and symbolic object use who are assessed with conventional procedures are placed at risk for moderate retardation, unwittingly (Zelazo & Kearsley, 1981). Third, and most important, the perceptual-cognitive procedures are not biased against children with neuromotor, productive language, or behavioral handicaps.

Children for whom these perceptual-cognitive procedures offer the clearest advantages with least doubt are those afflicted with neuromotor impairment or delays and who are regarded generally as untestable or unfairly testable using conventional procedures. It has been shown (Crothers & Paine, 1957) that approximately one-third of the children with cerebral palsy eventually go on to display normal intelligence. What might be the incidence of iatrogenic effects on cognitive development among children with cerebral palsy? Early identification of normal information processing ability not only is a badly needed alternative to conventional testing for these children, but may correct for the lowered expectations and diluted demands on their development that occur frequently as a result of their disabilities.

A CASE STUDY

Jay, a child with a diaphragmatic hernia, agenesis of the left diaphragm, and glottic stenosis required repeated surgery and intensive care during the first 380 days of his life to correct these congenital deformities. He required a tracheostomy and gastrostomy during most of that time. An extraordinary effort was made to provide Jay with as nearly normal an environment as possible given the constraints of ventilatory assistance and the need to be in the intensive care unit for the first critical year of his life. Obviously, severe restrictions were placed on the gross and fine motor stimulation that Jay could experience, although his level of social stimulation seemed adequate. His mother visited nearly every day and the nursing staff developed an affectionate relationship with him during his confinement to the intensive care unit.

Jay was tested on three occasions using the perceptual-cognitive procedures following his dismissal from the intensive care unit. He was evaluated at 14.25, 20.25 and 36.5 months of age. He was also administered a standard 15-minute free play sequence at these three ages and again at 17.25 months.

It was considered inappropriate to administer a traditional test of infant development when Jay was first examined and so those scores are not available. At 14.25 months, however, Jay had no words, could not walk, and could not sit without support. When left to his own means, securely propped during the free play sequence, and with toys brought well within his reach, he did not display appropriate uses for the toys. Ninety-seven percent of his play was spent in immature waving, fingering, banging, and mouthing of objects, and there were only two relational acts. Observations of his behavior indicated marked delays in motor development, object manipulations, and the absence of words.

In contrast to the profile presented by Jay's grossly observable behaviors, his performance on the perceptual-cognitive tasks at 14.25 months was clearly age appropriate. The results for the car-doll sequence are presented in Table 1 to illustrate this point. A cluster of behaviors including a 17-beat cardiac deceleration and laughter involving smiling and vocalization while attending vigilantly, occurred on the fourth presentation of the standard implying that Jay formed a

Table 1.   The occurrences of first clear behavioral clusters* to the car-doll sequence at 14.25, 20.25, and 36.5 months of age

Test number and age	Standards	Returns	Transformations
Test 1			
14.25 months	S-4*-5	R-1*-3	(Reduction in laughter, Mechanical problems)
Test 2			
20.25 months	S-2*	R-2*	(First break in fixation)
Test 3			
36.50 months	S-1*	R-1*	T-1*

clear memory and expectation for the event. The introduction of the discrepancy during which the styrofoam object did not tap over, elicited a reduction in laughter and stimulus related cardiac decelerations although attention remained high. When the standard sequence reappeared, however, the cluster of behaviors implying recognition of the original event reoccurred; there was renewed cardiac deceleration and laughter accompanied by vigilence. This result was confirmed in the other sequences implying age-appropriate information processing ability.

The results for the car-doll sequence (summarized in Table 1) showed age-appropriate performances at 20.25 and 36.5 months of age indicating progressively earlier recognition as Jay got older. Scoring of the first assimilative clusters revealed that recognition was announced on the fourth presentation of the standard during the first testing, second presentation during the second testing, and first presentation during the third evaluation. Similarly, despite disruptions during the discrepant portion of the event during the first evaluation, assimilative clusters occurred through the third presentation of the return stimulus at 14.25 months, the second presentation at 20.25 months and the first presentation at 36.50 months. Mechanical difficulties during the transformation phase of the first testing in which the doll fell down inadvertently, seem to have contributed to the earlier appearance of clusters during the return phase.

Recognition clusters were not produced during the transformation trials for either the first or second testings. In fact, the first break in visual fixation to the car-doll sequence occurred during the transformation phase of the second testing. At 36.5 months, recognition clusters occurred during the first presentations of the standard and the reappearance of the standard following the transformation. More importantly, the third testing represented the first time that a behavioral cluster, implying memory formation, occurred to the discrepant portion of the sequence. The immediate response during the transformation phase of the sequence represents the major change anticipated between 20 and 36.5 months of age. The changes in behavioral clusters to the various portions of the car-doll event are similar to those observed with normal children of comparable ages in the samples.

Observations of Jay's free play reflect a different picture during the first two evaluations. The relative percentages of stereotypical, relational, and functional play for each of Jay's four testings are illustrated in Figure 2. Upon initial testing, 97% of Jay's play was ster-

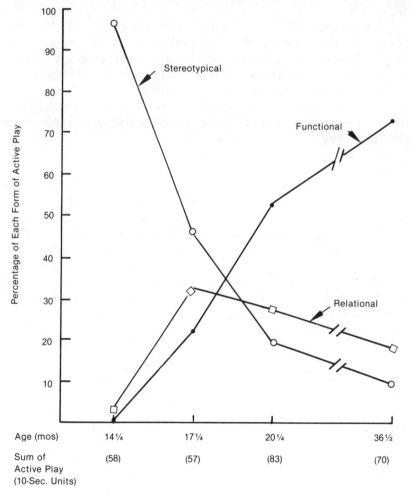

Figure 2.   Percentage of stereotypical, relational, and functional play at each of four ages for a single child. (From Zelazo, P., & Kearsley, R. The emergence of functional play in infants: Evidence for a major cognitive transition. *Journal of Applied Developmental Psychology*, 1980, *1*, 95–117).

eotypical involving mouthing, waving, banging and fingering of objects in contrast to a normal sample of children of the same age who displayed predominately functional play. The combination of age appropriate information processing ability and clearly delayed object use during the first testing resulted in the initiation of a treatment program to facilitate productive language (Zelazo, Kearsley, & Ungerer, 1980) and to encourage functional manipulation of objects (Zelazo & Kearsley, 1980). The productive language program required 12 minutes and the play procedures about 15 minutes of adult-child stimulation per day.

Jay received his second evaluation of free play at 17.25 months of age following 3 months of parent implemented treatment. It can be seen in Figure 2 that stereotypical play decreased, relational play increased and, more importantly, functional play rose from 0% to 22% of the active play to occur during the 15-minute session. Thus, at 17.25 months, Jay displayed a distribution of play that was comparable to the array seen for normal children at approximately 11½ months as shown in Figure 1.

The third evaluation of Jay's play, at 20.25 months of age, revealed continued improvement. Stereotypical and relational play decreased and functional play increased from 22% to 53% to become Jay's dominant form of object use. Comparisons of Figures 1 and 2 reveal that the distribution of Jay's play at 20.25 months of age was comparable to the distribution seen for normal children at 15.5 months. At 36.25 months of age, the vast majority of Jay's play (73%) was functional and symbolic. Moreover, the number of different appropriate uses for the 36 toys in the array rose steadily from 0 to 3 to 8 to 15 over the four testings. These results indicate that increases in the diversity of applications paralleled the improvement in the amount of functional and symbolic object use.

At 37 months of age, the administration of the Stanford-Binet (Form L-M) Test of Intelligence (Terman & Merrill, 1973) revealed that Jay had a mental age of 39 months, corresponding to a low average score. Jay, however, was highly distractible and not fully cooperative during testing, and the examiner reported that his score was "definitely a minimal estimate of his intellectual abilities." The independent examiner concluded that Jay was "developing normally in terms of his intellectual attainments." At this point, Jay spoke in multiple word, complex, grammatically correct sentences and was reading such words as "stop" and "open." By 3 years of age, most signs of Jay's development were within normal limits despite his restricted gross and fine motor experience during the first 380 days of his life.

Implications

There are three important implications from the results of this case study. First, the perceptual-cognitive procedures seem to be able to detect age-appropriate information processing at 14.25 months of age when Jay's overall appearance reflected obvious delays in gross and fine motor development and object manipulation. Second, evaluation with the Stanford-Binet Scales at 37 months revealing a near age-appropriate performance lends validity to the assessments using the perceptual-cognitive procedures. Third, Jay's near normal intellectual ability, despite the absence of gross and fine motor stimulation during the first year, creates difficulties for a strict interpretation of the assumption of sensorimotor intelligence.

A Validation Study: Preliminary Results

The validity of the information processing procedures is most strongly supported by the preliminary results of a recently completed study by Zelazo and Kearsley (1981) of 44 prospective and 10 retrospective children with developmental delays of unknown etiology. Children in the prospective groups were enrolled at either 20 or 32 months of age, had no evidence of congenital or acquired disorders associated with mental or motor retardation and had delays on the Bayley Scales of Infant Development of at least 4 or 5 months, respectively. The perceptual-cognitive procedures were used to discriminate infants whose information processing skills seemed age appropriate from those who showed significant impairment. All groups were given 10 months of parent implemented treatment designed to stimulate productive language and age-appropriate object use and to eliminate maladaptive behaviors (Zelazo, Kearsley, & Ungerer, 1980). Children were reevaluated at the end of active treatment using either the Bayley Scale of Mental Development or the Stanford-Binet Scale of Intelligence. Follow-up evaluations were obtained at 6 and 18 months after the active treatment phase. Ethical considerations precluded the assignment of children to no-treatment control groups during this initial investigation.

In an effort to determine whether developmental delays of unknown etiology undergo spontaneous improvement, two retrospective control groups were recruited. A review of hospital records identified children, either 36 or 48 months of age, who had documented evidence of developmental delays of unknown etiology at 20 or 32 months, respectively. Children in the retrospective control groups received the same evaluation as those in the prospective treatment groups during the follow-up phase. Children in the retrospective samples, however, did not receive active treatment in our program although many were enrolled in early intervention programs. Average delays (chronological age minus mental age) and average rate of mental development (mental age divided by chronological age) were calculated for the two prospective and two retrospective samples, and results for first testings were examined. Analyses revealed that the mean rate of mental development was comparable for all four age groups: 0.62, 0.65, 0.66, and 0.68 at 22, 32, 36, and 48 months, respectively, but that the magnitude of mean delays in mental age increased with age. Mean delays for the four respective age groups were 8.2, 11.1, 12.4, and 15.6 months. Thus, developmental delays of unknown etiology did not undergo spontaneous improvement for this sample of children; on the contrary, children were more likely to display larger delays the older they were.

The capacity of the perceptual-cognitive procedures to discriminate intact from impaired information processing ability among children with delays on conventional tests was examined by comparing conventional test scores upon entry, at the end of the 10-month intervention phase and at the 6-month follow-up evaluation. A Group X Test Interaction was predicted; children whose information processing seemed age appropriate were expected to improve over testings, whereas children with impaired information processing ability were not. The anticipated results were confirmed ($F = 16.08$, 2/44, $p < 0.0001$), not only supporting the validity of the perceptual-cognitive procedures but also demonstrating the effectiveness of the parent implemented treatment procedures. Reductions in delays from about a mean of 8.0 to 3.0 months occurred for the intact group whereas the magnitude of the delays for the impaired group increased from a mean of 15.5 to 24.0 months.

Analysis of the mean rates of mental development revealed statistically significant differences between intact and impaired children also. Intact children displayed progressive increases in mean rate of mental development from 0.70 at the time of entry to 0.92 at the end of the 6-month follow-up testing. In contrast, impaired children showed a mean rate of 0.44 upon entry that increased slightly to 0.47 by the end of the 6-month evaluation.

Of the 44 children in the prospective sample for whom complete data were available through the first 6-month follow-up evaluation, 77% displayed intact information processing ability. This finding deserves emphasis. Three of every four of the children with developmental delays of unknown etiology in our sample displayed intact information processing ability. Moreover, within the intact sample, 45% eliminated their delays on conventional tests and achieved a mental age that was equal to or greater than their chronological age by the 6-month follow-up evaluation. Only six of the intact children failed to show any reduction in the magnitude of their initial delay despite treatment. In contrast, none of the impaired sample improved significantly on standard tests of development despite treatment of comparable intensity. Follow-up evaluations one year later, although incomplete, indicate that this pattern of results continues to hold as children approach the eve of entry to kindergarten and first grade. The perceptual-cognitive procedures identified children whose information processing ability was intact, despite substantial observable delays; the elimination of those delays in a sizable percentage of children lends credibility to their effectiveness.

SUMMARY

The creation of perceptual-cognitive procedures to assess information processing ability offers promise as an alternative to conventional tests of early development. There is evidence that infants can process and create memories for visual, olfactory, and auditory information within the first days of life. The perceptual-cognitive procedures described here permit the assessment of information processing ability to about 36 months of age and seem to distinguish central from peripheral delays. The results from a recent intervention effort indicate that peripheral delays with productive language, appropriate object use and behavior problems that may interfere with development, carry a better prognosis for reversal than delays with central processing ability (see Zelazo & Kearsley, 1981).

Conventional tests pose particularly serious problems for children with developmental disabilities. Traditional procedures contain confoundings between children's handicaps and the measures used to infer intellectual status; however, when restricted to children with intact vision and hearing, the perceptual cognitive procedures described here seem to offer a less biased estimate of central processing ability. The potential contribution of this approach warrants a continued effort to validate and refine the perceptual-cognitive procedures.

Finally, the research on information processing during infancy and the demonstrated effectiveness of the perceptual-cognitive procedures carry major implication for our assumptions about the assessment of intellectual ability during the first 3 years of life. These data imply that the assumptions of sensorimotor intelligence and cephalo-caudal development may need modification to account for recent data. It seems that, although mutually facilitative generally, intellectual and sensorimotor development may proceed independently. The hesitancy to acknowledge this fact in our tests of development seems to have contributed to the handicaps faced by disabled children. The hesitancy to rectify this limitation after it has been brought to light may handicap our credibility as professionals responsible for the assessment and treatment of disabled children. It seems that we cannot turn back; the search for alternative procedures based on the infant's capacity to process information should be pursued with vigor.

REFERENCES

Adkinson, C., & Berg, W. Cardiac deceleration in newborns: Habituation, dishabituation, and offset responses. *Journal of Experimental Child Psychology*, 1976, *21*, 46–60.

Bayley, N. Psychological development of the child, Part III: Mental measurement. In F. Faulkner (Ed.), *Human development*. Philadelphia: Saunders, 1966.

Bayley, N. *Manual for the Bayley Scales of Infant Development*. New York: The Psychological Corporation, 1969.

Belsky, J., & Most, R. From exploration to play: A cross-sectional study of infant free play behavior. *Developmental Psychology*, 1981, *17*, 630–639.

Brody, L., Zelazo, P., & Chaika, H. Habituation and dishabituation to speech in the neonate. In press, 1982.

Cohen, L. Attention-getting and attention-holding processes of infant visual preferences. *Child Development*, 1972, *31*, 869–879.

Cohen, L. A two process model of infant visual attention. *Merrill-Palmer Quarterly*, 1973, *19*, 157–180.

Corman, H., & Escalona, S. Stages of sensorimotor development: A replication study. *Merrill-Palmer Quarterly*, 1969, *15*, 351–361.

Clifton, R., & Nelson, M. Developmental study of habituation in infants: The importance of paradigm, response system, and state. In T. Tighe and R. Leaton (Eds.), *Habituation: Perspectives from child development, animal behavior, and neurophysiology*. Hillsdale, NJ: Lawrence Erlbaum Associates, 1976.

Crothers, B., & Paine, R. *The Natural History of Cerebral Palsy*. Cambridge, MA: Harvard University Press, 1957.

Dudek, S., Lester, E., Goldberg, J., & Dyer, B. Relationship of Piagetian measures to standard intelligence and motor scales. *Perceptual and Motor Skills*, 1969, *28*, 351–362.

Engen, T., & Lipsitt, L. Decrement and recovery of responses to olfactory stimuli in the human neonate. *Journal of Comparative and Physiological Psychology*, 1965, *59*, 312–316.

Fagan, J. Infant recognition memory and early cognitive ability: Empirical, theoretical, and remedial considerations. In F. Minifie & L. Lloyd (Eds.), *Communicative and cognitive abilities–early behavioral assessment*. Baltimore: University Park Press, 1978.

Fagan, J. Infant recognition memory and later intelligence. Paper presented at the Biennial Meeting of the Society for Research in Child Development. San Francisco, March 16, 1979.

Fantz, R. Pattern vision in young infants. *Psychological Record*, 1958, *8*, 43–49.

Fantz, R., & Nevis, S. The predictive value of changes in visual preferences in early infancy. In J. Hellmuth (Ed.), *The exceptional infant*. (Vol. 1). Seattle: Special Child Publications, 1967.

Gottfried, A., & Brody, N. Interrelationships between and correlates of psychometric and Piagetian Scales of sensorimotor intelligence. *Developmental Psychology*, 1975, *11*, 379–387.

Kagan, J., *Change and continuity in infancy*. New York: Wiley, 1971.

Kagan, J., Kearsley, R., & Zelazo, P. *Infancy: Its place in human development*. Cambridge: Harvard University Press, 1978.

Kearsley, R. Iatrogenic retardation: A syndrome of learned incompetence. In R. Kearsley and I. Sigel (Eds.), *Infants at risk: Assessment of cognitive functioning*. Hillsdale, N.J.: Lawrence Erlbaum Associates, 1979.

Kearsley, R. Cognitive assessment of the handicapped infant: The need for an alternative approach. *American Journal of Orthopsychiatry*, 1981, *51*, 43–54.

Kinney, D., & Kagan, J. Infant attention to auditory discrepancy. *Child Development*, 1976, *47*, 155–164.

Lewis, M., & Goldberg, S. The acquisition and violation of expectancy: An experimental paradigm. *Journal of Experimental Child Psychology*, 1969, *7*, 70–80.

Lewis, M., & McGurk, H. Evaluation of infant intelligence: Infant intelligence scores—true or false? *Science*, 1972, *178*, 1174–1177.

McCall, R. Issues in the early development of intelligence and its assessment. In M. Lewis & L. Taft (Eds.), *Developmental disabilities: Theory, assessment and intervention*. Jamaica, N.Y.: S. P. Medical and Scientific Books, 1982.

McCall, R., & Kagan, J. Stimulus-schema discrepancy and attention in the infant. *Journal of Experimental Child Psychology*, 1967, *5*, 381–390.

McCall, R., & Melson, W. Attention in infants as a function of magnitude of discrepancy and habituation rate. *Psychonomic Science*, 1969, *17*, 317–319.

Miranda, S., Hack, M., Fantz, R., Fanaroff, A., & Klaus, M. Neonatal pattern vision: A predictor of future mental performance? *Pediatrics*, 1977, *91*, 642–647.

Miranda, S., & Fantz, R. Recognition memory in Down's Syndrome and normal infants. *Child Development*, 1974, *45*, 651–660.

Singer, R. Interrelationship of physical, perceptual-motor, and academic achievement variables in elementary school children. *Perceptual and Motor Skills*, 1968, *27*, 1323–1332.

Stott, L., & Ball, R. Infant and preschool mental tests: Review and evaluation. *Monographs of the Society for Research in Child Development*, 1965, *30*, (Serial No. 101).

Super, C., Kagan, J., Morrison, F., Haith, M., & Weiffenbach, J. Discrepancy and attention in the five month infant. *Genetic Psychology Monographs*, 1972, *85*, 305–311.

Terman, L., & Merrill, M. *Stanford-Binet Intelligence Scale: Manual for the third revision Form L-M*. Boston: Houghton Mifflin Co., 1973.

Uzgiris, I., & Hunt, J. McV. An instrument of assessing infant psychological development. Unpublished manuscript, University of Illinois, Psychological Development Laboratory, 1966.

Walters, R., & Parke, R. The role of the distance receptors in the development of social responsiveness. In L. Lipsitt and C. Spiker (Eds.), *Advances in child development and behavior*, (Vol. 2). New York: Academic Press, 1965.

Zelazo, P. Smiling and vocalizing: A cognitive emphasis: *Merrill-Palmer Quarterly*, 1972, *18*, 349–365.

Zelazo, P. The year-old infant: A period of major cognitive change. Paper presented at the Conference on Dips in Learning and Development Curves. St. Paul-de-Vence, France, March 24–28, 1975.

Zelazo, P. Comments on genetic determinants of infant development: An overstated case. In L. Lipsitt (Ed.), *Developmental psychobiology*: The *significance of infancy*. Hillsdale, N.J.: Lawrence Erlbaum Associates, 1976 (a).

Zelazo, P. From reflexive to instrumental behavior. In L. Lipsitt (Ed.), *Developmental psychobiology: The significance of infancy.* Hillsdale, N.J.: Lawrence Erlbaum Associates, 1976 (b).

Zelazo, P. Reactivity to perceptual-cognitive events: Application for infant assessment. In R. Kearsley & I. Sigel (Eds.), *Infants at risk: Assessment of cognitive functioning.* Hillsdale, N.J.: Lawrence Erlbaum Associates, 1979.

Zelazo, P. An information processing approach to infant cognitive assessment. In M. Lewis & L. Taft (Eds.), *Developmental disabilities: Theory, assessment, and intervention.* Jamaica, N.Y.: S. P. Medical and Scientific Books, 1981.

Zelazo, P. The year-old-infant: A period of major cognitive change. In T. Bever (Ed.), *Regressions in development: Basic phenomena and theoretical alternatives,* Hillsdale, NJ: Lawrence Erlbaum Associates, 1982.

Zelazo, P., Brody, L., & Chaika, H. Auditory habituation and dishabituation in the newborn. Paper presented at the Annual Meeting of the Eastern Psychological Association, New York, April 25, 1981.

Zelazo, P., Hopkins, J., Jacobson, S., & Kagan, J. Psychological reactivity to discrepant events: Support for the curvilinear hypothesis. *Cognition,* 1974, *2,* 385–393.

Zelazo, P., & Kearsley, R. The emergence of functional play in infants: Evidence for a major cognitive transition. *Journal of Applied Developmental Psychology,* 1980, *1,* 95–117.

Zelazo, P., & Kearsley, R. *Cognitive assessment and intervention in developmentally delayed infants.* Final Report to the Office of Special Education, Grant #G007603979, Educational Resources Information Center, February, 1981.

Zelazo, P., & Kearsley, R. Memory Formation for Visual Sequences: Evidence for Increased Speed of Processing with Age. Paper presented at the International Conference on Infant Studies, Austin, TX., March, 1982.

Zelazo, P., Kearsley, R., & Ungerer, J. *Learning to speak: A manual to aid the acquisition of speech.* Boston: Center for Behavioral Pediatrics and Infant Development, 1980.

Zelazo, P., & Komer, M. Infant smiling to nonsocial stimuli and the recognition hypothesis. *Child Development,* 1971, *42,* 1327–1339.

Chapter 8

PROBLEMS IN THE
ASSESSMENT OF CHANGE IN
ABNORMAL REFLEX BEHAVIOR

Anne Henderson

The motor behavior of infants at birth is structured by a wide range of reflexes. Some reflexes, such as the blink reflex or the knee jerk change very little over the life span. Others, such as the rooting and sucking reflexes, disappear in their primitive form and become integrated into voluntary behavior. This chapter is focused upon a discussion of primitive postural reflexes, which are a class of reflexes of the latter type that become integrated into the child's voluntary motor repertoire if development proceeds without problem. Some of the primitive postural reflexes influence the orientation of the body in space, for example, the labyrinthine righting reflexes orient the head in a vertical position. Other postural reflexes influence the relative postures of body parts. Examples of the latter are: 1) the neck righting reflexes that orient the body in a position of alignment with the head, and 2) the tonic neck reflexes in which head movement alters the postures of the arms and legs.

The development of normal motor abilities in the infant depends upon the appearance of primitive postural reflexes, their subsequent integration into more complex automatic responses and their eventual integration into voluntary motor behavior. Furthermore, these reflexes continue to be a substrate of motor function throughout life. Although the overt manifestations of these reflexes can be seen only in children, changes in muscle tone can be demonstrated to be universally present in adults (Hellebrandt, Schode, & Carns, 1962). These postural reflex mechanisms continue to contribute to the orientation of the body in space and of the interrelationships of body parts in all purposeful movement.

NEURODEVELOPMENTAL TREATMENT (NDT)

When, as a result of central nervous system damage, the integration of a reflex into voluntary motor behavior is only partial, the stereotyped nature of the reflex becomes an obstacle to the development of normal movement. The reflex is obligatory, that is, the child is unable to move out of the characteristic reflex pattern. The disabling effects of exaggerated obligatory primitive reflexes have been known clinically for many years (Bobath, 1966; Paine, 1964; Twitchell, 1951) and recent studies confirm the earlier reports that some motor functions do not develop in their presence (Bleck, 1975; Capute et al., 1978a; Molnar & Gordon, 1976). Therefore, occupational therapy and physical therapy treatment techniques for neurologically impaired children have as an important goal the modulation of the effects of abnormal postural reflexes and the normalization of motor activity (Bobath, 1967; Stockmeyer, 1967). This goal has been emphasized in the plan of therapy developed by Berta and Karl Bobath over a period of more than 20 years. The plan of therapy, called Neurodevelopmental Treatment (NDT), has become the most commonly used approach to the treatment of the motor disabilities of cerebral palsied children. NDT is based on sound principles derived in part from research in neurophysiology and in motor development, but principally the techniques arise from careful and extensive clinical observations. Although widely used, the theory and practice of NDT, including reflex modulation, has been subjected to little experimental verification. Only three studies have been done of the Bobath plan of treatment as a whole, and only one of those included change in reflex status as a dependent variable. In two studies, a greater mean change in the motor development of children in the experimental groups was found (Carlsen, 1975; Scherzer, Mike, & Ilson, 1976). The third study that attempted to assess change in reflex status as well as in motor development found no differences in treated and untreated groups in reflex status and differences in motor development only in quadraplegic children (Wright & Nicholson, 1973). These studies provide some support for the value of the NDT approach to therapy, but they do not indicate that changes occurred in the reflex status of the cerebral palsied children who were studied.

The formal evaluation of the effectiveness of techniques directed toward the modulation of primitive reflexes is severely limited by the lack of quantitative procedures for measuring developmental changes in reflex activity. The research study mentioned above (Wright & Nicholson, 1973), used the classic diagnostic technique of assessing a reflex as being either present or absent. This present/absent dichotomy is found neither in normal development nor in the development of children with central nervous system dysfunction. Reflexes occur on a continuum from normally transient to abnormally obligatory. In the former, the reflex may be manifested in a change in muscle tone or a tendency to assume the reflex posture, and not disrupt active movement. The abnormally obligatory reflex on the other hand, prevents voluntary movement.

Developmental studies have determined that reflexes do not suddenly appear and then later suddenly disappear; but that the strength of the responses gradually decreases over time (Byers, 1938; Gesell, 1938; Paine, 1964). The same observation has been made of children with cerebral palsy. Some of these children show an obligatory response in infancy but relatively mild signs at 1 or 2 years of age (Molnar & Gordon, 1976). It should also be noted that the voluntary control of some reflex responses in normal children has been shown to be immature up to the age of 8 years (Parmenter, 1975; Parr et al., 1974; Silver, 1952), even though primitive reflexes as tested clinically are not observed in normal children after the age of 6 months.

The classic method of assessment of reflexes was developed in order to detect the presence of central nervous system damage. The procedures have been refined over the years through medical practice, and studies have established the age limits beyond which manifestations of the reflexes are abnormal. Because of their availability and the lack of alternatives, these diagnostic procedures have been used for a variety of purposes for which they were not intended. The procedures were not designed for and not valid for the assessment of change either in normal infants or in children with central nervous system dysfunction.

The need for more discrete measures of reflex activity has been recognized and has led to the development of a number of scales (Carter & Campbell, 1975; Hoskins & Squires, 1973; Mayberry, 1974). The most comprehensive quantitative assessment is being developed by Capute et al. (1978b). Primitive reflexes are graded on a 5 point scale, which ranges from no response, through an increase in muscle tone alone, to an obligatory response. Extensive studies are being conducted, and when they are completed, the scales should provide a greatly improved assessment of developmental changes as well as a better measure of the effectiveness of therapy.

ASYMMETRICAL TONIC NECK REFLEX (ATNR)

The purpose of the research being conducted by Jane Coryell and this author is the same as that of other researchers concerned with the evaluation of treatment for children with motor disabilities resulting from central nervous system dysfunction. The long range goal is the development of methods of measurement that can be used to evaluate the effects of intervention. The goal includes the development of a quantitative scale measuring small increments of change. The approach to the problem, however, has been somewhat different from other researchers concerned with the problem. In developing quantitative scales, researchers have used the classic methods of eliciting the reflex, and focused on techniques of rating the response. Developmental research literature led to the question of whether there might be better ways of eliciting a reflex. This questioning has led to examining some alternative methods. The purpose of the study completed was to specify some of the parameters of the Asymmetrical Tonic Neck Reflex (ATNR), the most extensively studied of the primitive reflexes (Coryell, Henderson, and Liederman, in press).

The ATNR is one of the best known of the postural reflexes, and is considered to be one of the most important in early diagnosis of neurological abnormalities (Paine, 1964). The reflex is elicited when the infant's head is turned to one side. The response is defined by extension of the arm and leg on the side toward which the head is turned, that is the face side, and flexion of the contralateral limbs, those on the skull side.

When, as a result of central nervous system damage, the reflex is strong and obligatory, it is extremely disabling. For example, a child will not be able to bring a hand to his or her face for feeding if he or she turns the head away from midline as the hand holding the spoon approaches. Even when the reflex is at the peak of its strength, it is never completely obligatory in a normal child; hence its diagnostic value.

The ATNR is evaluated clinically as follows. The child is placed supine. The head is passively turned to 90 degrees so that the chin is over the shoulder, and held in that position for lengths of time, which have not been standardized. The reflex is graded as being present or absent, with present being indicated only when the reflex is more or less obligatory. The reflex is considered abnormal if it continues to be obligatory past the age of 6 months. The test is carried out with the head to the left and to the right and a difference in response between left and right turn is considered to be abnormal.

This classic measurement technique has a major limitation—it is graded dichotomously. Another limitation is that the span of normal development in which the reflex is manifested is very small. Experimental literature indicates that alternate methods of eliciting the reflex result in different findings as to the developmental course. The differences between responses to active versus passive head turning was a point of interest.

In the clinical evaluation of the ATNR the head is usually passively turned and held by the examiner. Early reports indicated that active and passive head turning elicited identical reflex patterns (Magnus,

1924/1953; Peiper, 1963). Later studies of normal infants showed, however, that the reflex can also be observed when the child spontaneously turns his or her head (Coryell & Cardinali, 1979; Gesell, 1938; Touwen, 1976), and that the developmental course of the reflex is quite different under these two conditions. When passive head turning is used, the reflex is not observed in normal neonates. It is observed in the majority of infants in the second and third month of life. It is seldom observed after the third month (Prechtl & Beintema, 1964; Paine et al., 1964) in normally developing infants.

When spontaneous head turning is the stimulus, the reflex has been found to be present in all newborns, and to continue through 6 months of age (Touwen, 1976). Furthermore, a few infants with cerebral palsy have been found to actively assume the ATNR posture even when the pattern could not be elicited by passive rotation (Paine et al., 1964; Byers, 1938). One possible reason for the difference between spontaneous and passive head turning is that forced turning and holding of the head may arouse resistance reactions that override the change in posture induced by the reflex (Gesell, 1938; Vassella & Karlsson, 1962).

The observation of spontaneous head turning is a time-consuming procedure. A third method, however, has been cited in the literature. This method uses visual or auditory stimuli to induce head turning. Such a procedure was found to be superior to passive rotation for the elicitation of the ATNR in some children with cerebral palsy (Byers, 1938) and was recommended by Cupps, Plescia, and Houser (1976) in their discussion of the Landau reflex.

Therefore, one of the variables chosen for study was response to active and passive head turning. Twenty infants between the ages of 4 and 10 weeks of age were tested using time sampling to quantify the behavior. The child's head was turned for a 40-second period and the arm postures were noted at 2-second intervals during that period. Active head turning was induced by the presentation of a visual stimulus. It was found that, although the percent of time that active head turning elicited the ATNR was greater than that of passive head turning, the difference was not significant. Ten of the infants showed a higher percentage of ATNR in the active than in the passive condition, only four showed a higher percentage in the passive condition, and the other six showed no difference between the two conditions. Active head turning is clearly at least as effective in eliciting the ATNR as passive head turning during this age span. The active eliciting method has one disadvantage. Inducing active turns of the head requires the capture and holding of the attention of the infant, and so requires more time and patience for testing. Passive head turning must, of course, be used with children who show no awareness of their environment. With responsive children, however, passive head turning not infrequently causes crying, resistance or struggling, which contaminates the response. Furthermore, if induced head turning elicits the reflex to the same degree as spontaneous head turning, the developmental course should be extended beyond that described for passive head turning. It was concluded that active head turning is the better technique because it is less adversive and promises to be useful over a longer developmental span.

A second question that was raised by the comparison of techniques used clinically and in developmental studies was the degree to which the head needs to be turned to elicit a response. The classic measurement technique requires a turn 90 degrees from midline so that the chin is over the shoulder. Gesell (1938) reported that ATNR responses could be elicited by passing an object slowly back and forth across the infant's field of vision. In normal adults, changes in muscle tone begin to occur as soon as the head begins to be rotated (Tokizane et al., 1951). It was reasoned that if moderate rotation of the head elicits the reflex to the same degree as full rotation, then the response could be obtained more easily and with less discomfort for the child. Therefore, partial and full head turning was compared. The findings clearly indicate that the partial head turn was less effective in eliciting the ATNR than the full head turn, because the difference was highly significant. A full head turn should be induced for maximum stimulation.

The third parameter studied was selected because of discrepant findings in the research literature. The ATNR in infants has generally been found to be comparable for left and right turns (Paine et al., 1964; Vassella & Karlsson, 1962). In older children, one study found the reflex to be stronger when the head was turned to the left (Parmenter, 1975) and another found no differences between directions of turn (Parr et al., 1974). The responses to left and right head turning in the population of 20 infants were found to be different. Left head turning elicited a significantly higher percentage of ATNR positions than did right head turning.

It seems that more attention should be paid to the direction of head turn in establishing the range of ages at which the reflex is overtly elicited. The reflex has been considered to be equal on the left and the right, and differences in strength on the left and right have been considered to be pathological. If the difference is great, pathology would be indicated, but slight left-right differences in the degree to which the reflex can be inhibited seem to be normal as the child gets older.

The conclusion from this initial study is that active movement through the full range of head rotation is the method of choice and that left and right-turning need to be examined separately. Having specified these parameters of the ATNR, the next step is to experiment with stimuli for inducing head turning with consistency and determining the best method for quantifying the strength of the reflex. The resulting procedure will then be tested for its ability to detect change in the normal and abnormal child.

VOLUNTARY MOVEMENT AND CHANGES IN REFLEX STATUS

There is another factor in reflex activity that is important to the methods by which reflexes are measured and is of theoretical interest. This is the relationship between voluntary movement and changes in reflex status. As has been noted, some motor abilities do not develop in the presence of obligatory reflexes. Byers (1938) noted, in cerebral palsied children, that the disappearance of primitive reflexes seemed to coincide with a gradually increasing effectiveness of voluntary movement. Furthermore, reflex changes that occur in recovery from hemiplegia following cerebral vascular accident in adults, correspond to an increase in voluntary motor ability (Twitchell, 1951). Where there is pathology, reflex and voluntary motor activity are closely related.

It is possible that the disappearance of reflexes in their overt form is entirely a maturational process that must occur before voluntary activity can develop. An alternate possibility is that voluntary activity plays a part in the gradual suppression of a reflex. At present, the weight of evidence is toward the maturational explanation. In a study of retarded infants, Molnar (1978) found a temporal disassociation between the loss of primitive reflexes and the attainment of motor milestones. The late acquisition of motor skills seemed not to be related to the disappearance of primitive reflexes but rather to the delay in appearance of propping (e.g., automatic arm extension with loss of balance) and equilibrium (e.g., automatic movement to maintain the body center of gravity over the base of support) reactions. Touwen (1971) found no relationship between the loss of the grasp reflex and the onset of voluntary grasp.

Whether voluntary movement influences the development of reflex integration is unclear, but it is clear that reflexes such as the ATNR come increasingly under voluntary control. The normal infant can inhibit the ATNR posture from the day of birth, but it is difficult with current measurement techniques to show developmental changes in the degree of inhibition. Developmental differences, however, in the ability to inhibit the posture can be demonstrated in the preschool and school-age years. When children rotate their heads while supporting themselves on their hands and knees, flexion in their skull arm is a natural response. Older children can inhibit this response at will, but younger children flex even when their attention is directed toward their arm. The ability to inhibit flexion in the skull arm increases gradually between the ages of 3 and 8 years (Parr et al., 1974; Parmenter, 1975).

It is possible that voluntary movement plays a part in the development of the ability to inhibit the residual effect of the ATNR, the effect that is a normal aspect of mature motor function. This could explain the left-right differences found in the study of infants and in Parmenter's study of first and second grade children. The greater use of the right or dominant hand may result in earlier inhibition of the reflex pattern on the dominant side.

SUMMARY

This chapter touches upon a few of the factors important to the development of measures of reflex activity. Although there is a considerable literature describing primitive reflexes, there is little information on the evolution of reflex patterns in infants and young children. Acquisition of information is severely hindered at present by methodological problems. Attention to this problem is essential to subsequent progress. In addition, longitudinal studies are needed to examine the changes occurring throughout the early years of the normal child and of the child with central nervous system dysfunction. Experimental studies are needed to enhance our understanding of the mechanisms influencing reflex integration. Growth in our knowledge should result in the development of tools that determine which intervention techniques are most effective in fostering the development of the handicapped infant.

REFERENCES

Bleck, E. Locomotor prognosis in cerebral palsy. *Developmental Medicine and Child Neurology*, 1975, *17*, 18–25.

Bobath, K. *The motor deficit in patients with cerebral palsy*, Clinics in Developmental Medicine, No. 23, The National Spastics Society in Medical Education and Information, Unit in association with William Heinemann Medical Books Ltd., London, 1966.

Bobath, B. The very early treatment of cerebral palsy. *Developmental Medicine and Child Neurology*, 1967, *9*, 373–390.

Byers, R. Tonic neck reflexes in children. *American Journal of Diseases of Children*, 1938, *55*, 696–742.

Caputo, A., Accardo, P., Vining, E., Rubenstein, J., Walcher, J., Harryman, S., & Ross, A. Primitive Reflex Profile, *Physical Therapy*, 1978, *9*, 1061–1065 (a).

Caputo, A., Accardo, P., Vining, E., Rubenstein, J., & Harryman, S. *Primitive Reflex Profile*. Baltimore: University Park Press, 1978 (b).

Carlsen, P. Comparison of two occupational therapy approaches for treating the young cerebral palsied child. *American Journal of Occupational Therapy*, 1975, *29*, 267–272.

Carter, R., & Campbell, S. Early neuromuscular development of the premature infant. *Physical Therapy*, 1975, *55*, 1332–1340.

Coryell, J., & Cardinali, N. The asymmetrical tonic neck reflex in normal full term infants. *Physical Therapy*, 1979, *59*, 747–753.

Coryell, J., Henderson, A., & Liederman, J. Factors influencing the asymmetrical tonic neck reflex in normal infants. Physical and Occupational Therapy in Pediatrics. In press.

Cupps, C., Plescia, M., & Houser, C., The Landau reaction, a clinical and electromyographic analysis. *Developmental Medicine and Child Neurology*, 1976, *18*, 41–53.

Gesell, A. The tonic neck reflex in the human infant. *Journal of Pediatrics*, 1938, *13*, 455–464.

Hellebrandt, F., Schode, M., & Carns, M. Methods of evoking the tonic neck reflexes in normal human subjects. *American Journal Physical Medicine*, 1962, *41*, 90–139.

Hoskins, T., & Squires, J. Developmental assessment: A test for gross motor and reflex development. *Physical Therapy*, 1973, *53*, 117–126.

Magnus, R. *Korperstellung*. (S. Brunnstrom, abstractor and translator) *Physical Therapy Review*, 1953, *33*, 281–290 (Originally published, 1924).

Mayberry, W. A preliminary report: developing infant predictors for sensory integrative dysfunction. *American Journal Occupational Therapy*, 1974, *28*, 141–143.

Molnar, G. Analysis of motor disorder in retarded infants and young children. *American Journal of Mental Deficiency*, 1978, *83*, 213–222.

Molnar, G., & Gordon, S. Cerebral palsy: predictive value of selected clinical signs for early prognostication of motor function. *Archives of Physical Medicine and Rehabilitation*, 1976, *57*, 153–158.

Paine, R. The evolution of infantile postural reflexes in the presence of chronic brain syndromes. *Developmental Medicine and Child Neurology*, 1964, *6*, 345–361.

Paine, R., Brazelton, T., Donovan, D., Drorbaugh, J., Hubbell, J., & Sears, E. Evolution of postural reflexes in normal infants and in the presence of chronic brain syndromes. *Neurology*, 1964, *14*, 1036–1048.

Parmenter, C. The asymmetrical tonic neck reflex in normal first and third grade children. *American Journal of Occupational Therapy*, 1975, *29*, 463–468.

Parr, C., Routh, D., Byrd, M., & McMillan, J. A developmental study of the asymmetrical tonic neck reflex. *Developmental Medicine and Child Neurology*, 1974, *16*, 329–335.

Peiper, A. *Cerebral Function in Infancy and Childhood*. New York: Consultants Bureau, 1963.

Prechtl, J., & Beintema, D. *The Neurological Examination of the Full-Term Newborn Infant*. Little Club Clinics in Developmental Medicine, No. 12. The National Spastics Society Medical Education and Information Unit in association with William Heinemann Medical Books Ltd., London, 1964.

Scherzer, A., Mike, V., & Ilson, J. Physical therapy as a determinant of change in the cerebral palsied infant. *Pediatrics*, 1976, *58*, 47–52.

Silver, S. Psychologic aspects of pediatrics: postural and righting responses in children. *Pediatrics*, 1952, *41*, 493–498.

Stockmeyer, S. An interpretation of the approach of Rood to the treatment of neuromuscular dysfunction. *American Journal of Physical Medicine*, 1967, *46*, 900–956.

Tokizane, T., Murao, M., Ogata, T., & Kondo, T. Electromyographic studies on tonic neck, lumbar and labyrinthine reflexes in normal persons. *Japanese Journal of Physiology*, 1951, *2*, 130–146.

Touwen, B. A study of the development of some motor phenomena in infancy. *Developmental Medicine and Child Neurology*, 1971, *13*, 335–446.

Touwen, B. *Neurological Development in Infancy*. London: Lavenham Press, 1976.

Twitchell, T. The restoration of motor recovery following hemiplegia in man. *Brain*, 1951, *74*, 443–480.

Vassella, F., & Karlsson, B. Asymmetrical tonic neck reflex: A review of the literature and a study of its presence in the neonatal period. *Developmental Medicine and Child Neurology*, 1962, *4*, 363–369.

Wright, T., & Nicholson, J. Physiotherapy for the spastic child: an evaluation. *Developmental Medicine and Child Neurology*, 1973, *15*, 146–163.

Section IV
ENVIRONMENTAL CONTEXT

Chapter 9

THE ENVIRONMENTAL CONTEXT
OF DEVELOPMENTAL DISABILITIES

Arnold J. Sameroff

Context has become a major concern in recent years in research efforts aimed at understanding and remediating developmental disabilities. The importance of context has been twofold. It has affected the situations in which scientists have found themselves employed and also the situations in which scientists have found it necessary to do their research. In the first instance the reduction in available academic positions for graduates of research training programs has moved many to take positions in what have typically been called applied settings. At the same time academic researchers have found that the cognitive, emotional, and social problems that typify developmental disabilities cannot be understood outside of the actual "applied" living circumstances of the developing child. These two developments have come together to provide a talented research force working in the settings most conducive to the investigation of children's problems at the appropriate level of analysis.

One might ask "How is it possible to move from the controlled conditions of the laboratory to the uncontrolled hodge-podge of the real world and be able to do better research?" The answer lies in the recognition that research questions being asked currently relate to real-world and not laboratory functioning. When we ask what will be the developmental outcome for a child with poor genes, poor gestation, or poor birth we are not asking if he or she will still have those genes, or birth complications, or biological handicaps but whether those early conditions will affect the child's later cognitive, emotional, and social functioning. Because this later functioning is related to the educational, family, and cultural environment of the child, developmental scientists are required to incorporate these variables into their research designs. As a consequence it is no longer sufficient for one in this area to know only a single discipline. One must know sociology, anthropology, and even political science in addition to psychology and education to make sense out of the developmental process.

CARETAKING CASUALTY

In 1975, Chandler and this author were asked to write a review of the role of perinatal factors in developmental deviancy. This task was of interest because of our involvement in a research project that was attempting to find the roots of serious mental disturbances in the perinatal period. Both the research and the review were initiated with the expectation of finding clear indicators from early assessments that would show straightforward linkages with later disorders. It was quite a surprise to find that these indicators were neither evident in the review of past research (Sameroff & Chandler, 1975) nor in our own ongoing work (Sameroff & Seifer, 1981).

Whenever a perinatal risk factor was hypothesized to be related to later dysfunction, prospective studies found no greater incidence of disorder in the risk population than in control populations without the risk factor. Whether the risk was related to preterm birth, low birth weight, anoxia, or neurological signs, few causal chains were found when appropriate control populations were studied. The most important variable that needed to be controlled was socioeconomic status. Where later deficits were associated with perinatal factors, it was generally in combination with an economically deprived environment. Where birth status showed little relation to later outcome, it was generally in combination with a better economic situation. The reason that birth complications are thought to be important is that high percentages of infants with reproductive problems have poor intellectual outcomes. The confounding factor is that most children who have these complications, however, are from the poorer segments of society (Birch & Gussow, 1970). These findings led to proposing a *continuum of caretaking casualty* (Sameroff & Chandler, 1975). At one end of the continuum the caretaking environment was sufficiently supportive and adaptive to compensate for almost any biological risk factor so that it was not transformed into later intellectual or emotional problems. At the other end of the continuum, the caretaking environment had neither the educational, emotional, nor economic resources to deal with even minor perinatal problems. Thus, the child, if allowed to survive, would maintain deficits into later stages of intellectual and emotional growth.

At the conclusion of the paper three models that could be used to explain the relation between early risk factors and poor developmental outcomes were identified.

The simplest version was a *single-factor* model that emphasized either constitutional or environmental determinants of development. A more complex version was an *interactional* model in which constitutional risk factors combined additively with environmental supports so that the effects of the risk would be reduced or augmented by better or worse environments. The static quality of these two models, however, in which neither constitution nor environment were seen in dynamic terms, led to proposing a *transactional* model in which development was believed to result from a continual interplay between a changing organism and a changing environment. From this perspective, an early deviancy would be maintained into later life only if it were perpetuated by a frozen relationship between the child and his or her environment. Developmental continuities as well as discontinuities were to be sought in the organism-environment relationship rather than in either component taken alone.

The original conceptualization of the transactional model was heavily based on temperament data from the New York Longitudinal study reported by Thomas et al. (1963). It seems now that the original emphasis on temperament as a major long-term determinant of the character of observable caregiver-child interactions may have been an overstatement. Children with difficult temperaments may have more contemporaneous adjustment problems in childhood, but the passage of time can wipe out or compensate many of these early differences. As children move into new areas of behavior, temperamental style becomes less important than the actual content of their behavior.

Similarly, studies of caregiver-infant interactions have shown that both partners are sensitive to the other's characteristics in the immediacy of their interchanges, but these studies have had difficulty in demonstrating long-term intellectual consequences from differences in early interactions.

The disappearance of early deviancies has been attributed to analogies of the self-righting tendencies that Waddington (1966) hypothesized in embryological development. Self-righting tendencies, however, that maintain a canalized path of ontogeny cannot be treated as some magical property. They must be given psychological and behavioral reality and therefore it becomes important to determine what are the self-righting tendencies in child development.

SELF-RIGHTING TENDENCIES

These tendencies can be divided into two categories, those from the child's side and those from the caregiver's side. The best examples on the child's side arise in the area of developmental disabilities. When one examines the development of behavior in a handicapped child, one is struck by performances that are discontinuous with the handicap. Although blind children may remain blind and deaf children remain deaf, they can achieve a normal level of thinking permitting them to go on to learn language and engage in adequate social interchanges.

A dramatic description of this process can be found in the observations of Decarie (1969) on the development of thalidomide babies. Despite the lack of two or even four limbs, which precluded typical hand-eye coordination, these infants achieved their cognitive development through the coordination of whatever was available, whether it was toes, feet or hips. The retardation found in these infants was correlated less with their degree of handicap than with their degree of social isolation. Retardation in language behavior, for example, was more highly correlated with amount of social interaction than with degree of handicap.

The most pervasive self-righting tendencies, however, are found in the caregiving environment, which can compensate for not only the individual differences of temperament but also the qualitative differences in the performance of handicapped children.

Some of these self-righting variables have been emphasized in the recent work on attribution theory in social psychology. Individuals filter their experience through a net of expectations and attributions such that similar events are reported as being different by people with different cognitive sets. Baldwin (1967) has elaborated a theory of "naive psychology" originally formulated by Heider (1958) in which each individual is seen as having his or her own interpretation of reality. Goodnow (1979) has raised serious questions about the adequacy of research that does not take into account how cross-cultural contexts have an impact on these interpretations that filter parents' understandings of developmental processes. Even within a single culture it is difficult to interpret observations of actual parental behavior when the parents' knowledge, attitudes, and perceptions are ignored (Parke & Sawin, 1977).

Attitudes and personal and social norms generally do not exist in isolation but tend to be organized. The most clear evidence of organization can be seen in social norms. Each culture is an organized system of behavior and values that influences the behavior of individuals living in that culture. Within cultures social classes differ in norms and expectations. Kohn (1969), for example, found strong differences in child rearing value systems in comparisons between high and low social classes in the United States and Italy. Working class parents valued conformity and highly rated neatness and good manners as child rearing goals. Upper class parents tried to instill self-direction in their children by emphasizing curiosity and self-control as developmental goals. Kohn found that these differences in values were reflected in social class differences in child rearing behavior and life experiences.

Another approach to understanding the organization of parental thinking is to analyze the level of abstraction used to understand development. Research on the cognitive development of the child has shown that the infant must go through a number of stages before achieving the logical thought processes that characterize adulthood (Piaget, 1950). Similarly, parents may use different levels in thinking about their relationship to their child. Parents whose understanding of the child is restricted to more primitive levels may have difficulty in dealing with what they consider to be deviant children (Sameroff, 1975).

Stages in Parent's Perspective on Child Development

Our attempt to formulate stages in the parent's perspective on child development was made at four levels analogous to Piaget's sensori-motor, pre-operational, concrete operational, and formal operational stages. These hypothesized levels are 1) the symbiotic, 2) the categorical, 3) the compensating, and 4) the perspectivistic.

At the *symbiotic* level, the mother is concerned primarily with her immediate relationship to the child. She responds in a here-and-now fashion to the child's behavior. Her emotional response is directly related to how successful she is at ministering to the child. In a sense she does not see herself as separate from the child because she interprets the child's behavior as being directly tied to her own activity.

At the second level, the *categorical* level, parents are able to see their children and themselves as separate entities, such that the children's actions can be viewed as being intrinsic characteristics of the child and not only the result of the parent's activity. The mother who has had a successful experience with her child assigns positive labels, for example, the good child, or the bright child. Once these labels are assigned, however, they are thought to inhere in the child. This device can be very adaptive, for when the good child occasionally acts badly, such as crying too much, or breaking a dish, the mother will still think of her child as the good one. On the other hand, such categorization can be maladaptive as in the case where the mother, because of negative early experiences, comes to label the child as difficult or deviant. Even though this child may outgrow the behavior that caused him or her to be labelled as deviant in the first place, the perceptions and reactions of the parent restricted to the categorical level may be dominated by the original classification.

Another consequence of categorization of the child's behavior is that it leads to parents restricting their explanations to single variables. A behavior may be thought to have constitutional roots in that the child "was born that way" or environmental roots in that the child was "spoiled." Such categorical explanations of behavior restrict the opportunities for the parent to engage in therapeutic or remedial activities with the child.

At the third level, the *compensating* level, the parents view the child as having an existence not only apart from their activities (e.g., the symbiotic level), but also apart from the labels they assigned to the child (e.g., the categorical level). At the compensating level no single label can typify the entire range of the child's behavior.

Additional context is provided for parents who view their child from the fourth level, the *perspectivistic* level. At this level a particular child and a particular care situation can be placed in a hypothetical context of any child in any care situation. The concrete situation at hand is only one of a multitude of possibilities. Parents are able to see children's behavior as stemming from individual experiences with specific environments. If those experiences had been different, the children's characteristics would be different. At this level deviancies in the child are perceived as being deviancies in the relation of a particular child to a particular environment, rather than as concrete expressions of the essential nature of the child. Remediation can be proposed by altering the experience of the child through environmental changes. Achievement of the perspectivistic level frees both elements in the child-caretaker system from their concrete context and places them into a generalized hypothetical structure.

To determine if the validity of this conceptualization of parental perspectives on development, a questionnaire was devised and administered to a sample of English and American mothers who varied in social status (Sameroff & Feil, 1981). In general, the data supported the hypothesis that higher social status is related to higher levels of understanding development. The English were generally more categorical than the Americans except for one interesting exception. The English upper social status group was more categorical than any of the other groups, reflecting the upper class English emphasis on inherited constitutional differences as explanations for class distinctions in achievement.

In a second study (Sameroff, Barocas, & Seifer, 1980), the adaptational and attentional behavior of 4-year-old children were found to relate to parents' concepts of development as well as Kohn's parental values (Kohn, 1969). Those parents who scored as being more categorical on our scales and more conforming on Kohn's values did more poorly in both behavioral domains than those parents who were more perspectivistic and self-directing.

What restricts parents in their understanding of development? The major factors seem to be lack of education and/or experience. For example, in the case of teenage mothers from lower social economic groups, lack of education would be a major factor. Of more interest here is the mother with substantial education and experience with normal development but who is faced with a handicapped or exceptional child. Such parents may have no compensatory model for incorporating the child into their development scheme.

Roskies (1972) in her absorbing book on the development of a Canadian sample of thalidomide babies reports on the conflict parents faced in deciding whether their children were normal or abnormal. Despite the lack of limbs, an abnormal characteristic, if the parents were able to engage in eye-to-eye contact or mutual smiling with the child, they became convinced that the child was normal. Conversely, Klaus Minde (personal communication) in a study of children from an intensive care unit reported how the same behaviors that parents viewed as quite normal became suspect after the parents were informed that there might be something wrong with their child.

Such redefinitions of the child who is, or is thought to be atypical can be of two forms, one based on individual differences interpreted within the family system, and the second based on developmental milestones defined within a cultural system. Examples of the former were the colicky child who is redefined as being difficult or the hypoactive child who is redefined as fragile. Redefinitions related to individual differences have developmental significance only in those families in which the parents are restricted to a categorical understanding of development. For those parents at the higher compensating level, the culturally-defined developmental milestones are far more significant in altering their behavior.

For parents at the *symbiotic* level, developmental progressions can come as a welcome or unwelcome surprise. Frequent clinical observations have been made of an emotionally immature mother who thrives with a dependent responsive infant. Observers would note all the ingredients of a finely tuned, positively interacting mother. As the child begins walking and seeking autonomy, however, these mothers tend to resist this developing independence and a period of abuse ensues that frequently ends with the child in a foster home.

With other mothers the development of autonomous functioning, locomotion, and speech are hallmarks that the child has matured enough to be considered a human. Observation of early mother-child interactions would have found a cool distant mother who only engaged her child while caretaking and who minimized affectional bonds. After evidence of the child's autonomy the parent changes and becomes an accepting approving parent, actively fostering the further development of the child.

Another factor limiting the parents' concepts of development is the level at which their particular culture views development. If the society functions categorically, as nomadic tribes do in destroying sets of twins because they are considered evil, then it is difficult for individual members of that society to function at higher levels.

To summarize, the way a parent interprets the behavior of his or her child is related to the level at which parents view development. At progressively higher levels, parents are able to place the elements of the interaction into an increasingly broader context, from the most simple level of here-and-now interaction with the child, to being able to separate the child from their labels, and eventually to being able to take perspective and separate the child from the particular environment in which he or she was raised. If that environment had been or would become different, a child with different characteristics would be produced.

The parents' abilities to place a child in a developmental context, as described above, however, is only one facet of the matrix necessary to conceptualize a child's environment. Other facets include 1) the parents' developmental models, 2) sociocultural norms, 3) the parents' personalities, and 4) the parents' interactional resources. These categories are intertwined and must be understood in their interconnectedness if individual developmental predictions are to be successful.

A curious fact is that most children grow up to think, speak, and act like human adults. These are complex achievements. How can children continue to reach mature adulthood without scientists and educators understanding how they do it? The simple answer is that although we as scientists tinker with bits and pieces of the system over short periods of time, society as a whole has spent eons evolving the system. It is a common biological characteristic of surviving species that they must have a developmental agenda that produces adults. This agenda need not be planned nor reflected upon by the individual for it evolved over generations in which the changes in rearing strategies always had to produce a viable endproduct. It is with these historic processes that scientists and educators have had to grapple. An intervention or even a deprivation is usually only a nuance in the grand developmental scheme of the human species. It is only the concern with individual differences that converts these nuances into the central theme of educational accountability. Educational systems have not been evaluated on the basis of whether they produce viable adults, but rather, whether these adult products are better than the adult product of other educational systems. The production of a better product is not to be depreciated, especially in a society where individual achievement is so highly valued. If one desires ultimately to understand human development, however, one should not and cannot view these differences in performance as reflecting basic differences in psychological competencies.

TRANSACTIONS DEFINED

The initial description of the transactional model emphasized the dynamic mutual interactive organism-environment system in contrast with the earlier emphasis on the search for static risk factors in the hope of predicting later development. The dynamic character of growth is now generally accepted by developmentalists, leading to a need for a more explicit definition of transactions. From a sociobiological perspective each culture has a system of child rearing organized to reproduce the culture. That system is keyed in part to the changing characteristics of the child and in part to the age of the child. Transactions in development refer to points when the system changes and the participant places a new meaning on his or her experience. That the child has an influence on its caregiver has been documented, but less attention has been paid to whether that influence is transactional; that is, does the child change the caregiver's interpretation of the situation. For example, in a study of East African cultures, deVries and Sameroff (1979) found that estimates of infant competence were tied to the initiation of education. Members of the Digo tribe believed that infants were competent at birth and began early sensorimotor training such that toilet-training was frequently completed in four months and their children were walking soon after. The Kikuyu tribe of the same genetic origins believed that children were incompetent until one year of age and backpacked the swaddled infants until after their first birthday.

In our own culture, schooling has been tied to estimates of when the child is prepared to learn. These estimates have stabilized over generations in which it was found that 6 years of age was a good point at which to begin formal education regardless of the condition of any individual child. Puberty rites and Bar-Mitzvahs are examples of other such age-keyed transactions. Commonly recognized early milestones are crawling, walking, and talking. Each of these changes entail a shift in the behavior of the caregivers to allow for the new competencies of the child. The shifts engendered by these developmental milestones create discontinuities in the parent-child interaction that are not predictable without knowing the social context.

From our modern empirical perspective, the child's behavior develops sequentially in an organized fashion whether one follows the teachings of Gesell or Piaget. The newborn is currently viewed as competent to make perceptual discriminations and even exhibit evidence of learning capacities. The environment can ignore these characteristics, however, until they are necessitated by the normative developmental course of that culture. It is amazing that until fairly recently there were obstetricians and pediatricians who believed that newborns were deaf and blind. When society was ready for infants to see and hear, then these characteristics were identified and utilized. Before that time they were irrelevant.

With this background we can return to the identification of self-righting tendencies in development. Self-righting implies a buffered system. Evolution has ensured that the species should survive. The biological development of the child takes place in an insulated fluid environment that maintains a buffered biochemical milieu despite environmental perturbation. Waddington's self-righting tendencies in embryology are called into play when deviancies at one level of the developing system are detected by monitors at a higher level of organization which then initiate compensatory biochemical changes. Similarly, cultures provide a buffered system in which perturbations are minimized. When a child's behavior produces a transactional redefinition, the parent must be able to put that redefinition into some larger context. To the extent that a larger context is available with alternative caretaking strategies to compensate for deviancies in the child, self-righting of the system will occur. To the extent that such alternatives are unavailable to the parent, the deviancy may be expected to continue or the child will be aborted.

Although the necessity of a dynamic transactional model to understand development has been stressed, the environmental restrictions in any given situation could produce effects that would fit a single-factor or interactional model. The treatment of birth defects is a good example. When children born with Down's syndrome or other anomalies are institutionalized, it is possible to make some predictions as to developmental outcomes. Institutionalization automatically defines the child as different from other human beings with the expectation that normal outcomes are impossible. With such expectations built into the system there is no point in developing programs to attempt to counter the effects of the deviancy thereby guaranteeing an abnormal outcome. If we hypothesize a universe in which language and communication only occur in the visual modality, a blind child will not learn language in any environment within that universe. In that universe, blindness will be a single risk factor that will predict later intellectual deficits. Within our own universe, where there are communication channels other than visual, blindness need not be linearly related to later cognitive deficit.

If we hypothesize a universe where the only communication is vocal, deafness will be seen to have an additive interactive effect with environment. Deaf children raised in supportive environments where lip reading is taught, will do better intellectually than deaf children without such training. But in all such communicative settings, the deaf children will do more poorly than hearing children in the same environment. In our own universe, language can be gestural as well as vocal. Deaf children reared in environments where signing is encouraged and accepted need show no intellectual deficits in comparisons with hearing children reared in the same environments.

In short, a transactional model is needed to explain development in environments that are sensitive to and can compensate for early deviancies so that they are not transformed into later deficits. When the range of environments is restricted, however, either through ignorance or choice, outcomes can be found that appear to be additive or produced by single risk factors taken alone.

SUMMARY

It has become increasingly clear that what we have previously thought to be characteristics of the child that are independent of child rearing context are inextricably tied to the experiential environment. Only the most extreme cases of brain damage still present us with immutable children. For every other category of handicap, there has been clear evidence that variations in experience produce variation in outcome. More importantly, the relation between the child's characteristics and the characteristics of the environment should not be seen as additive. There are many handicaps, especially in the sensory domain, for which the human outcome is no different than for children without those handicaps. A child may remain deaf or blind but reach high levels of intellectual and social adjustment and achievement.

What we have learned from our intervention efforts in the past is that the limits of human plasticity have not yet been reached. What is also clear, however, is that this individual plasticity is a consequence of contextual plasticity, that is, the ability of caregivers to adapt to the needs of the developing child. As those needs become better studied, our interventions efforts will also improve. Development is an organized system (Sameroff, 1982). Its complexity is also its virtue. The many paths to happiness in life offer us as many opportunities for education and remediation.

REFERENCES

Baldwin, A. *Theories of child development.* New York: John Wiley, 1967.
Birch, H., & Gussow, G. *Disadvantaged children.* New York: Grune & Stratton, 1970.
Decarie, T. A study of the mental and emotional development of the thali-

domide child. In B. Foss (Ed.), *Determinants of infant behavior*. (Vol. 4). London: Methuen, 1969.

deVries, M., & Sameroff, A. Cultural and modernization influences in infant temperament in East Africa. Unpublished manuscript, 1979.

Goodnow, J. Conventional wisdom: Everyday models of development. In L. Eckensberger, W. Lonner, & Y. Pourtinga (Eds.), *Crosscultural contribution to psychology*. Amsterdam: Swets and Zeitlinger, 1979.

Heider, F. *The psychology of interpersonal relations*. New York: John Wiley, 1958.

Kohn, M. *Class and conformity*. Homewood, IL: Dorsey, 1969.

Parke, R., & Sawin, D. The family in early infancy: Social interactional and attitudinal analyses. Paper presented at the meeting of the Society for Research in Child Development, New Orleans, 1977.

Piaget, J. *Psychology of intelligence*. New York: Harcourt Brace Jovanovich, 1950.

Roskies, E. *Abnormality and normality: The mothering of thalidomide children*. Ithaca, N.Y.: Cornell University Press, 1972.

Sameroff, A. Transactional models in early social relations. *Human Development*, 1975, *18*, 65–79.

Sameroff, A. Development and the dialectic: The need for a systems approach. In A. Collins (Ed.), *Minnesota Symposium on Child Development* (Vol. 15). Hillsdale, N.J.: Lawrence Erlbaum Associates, 1982.

Sameroff, A., Barocas, R., & Seifer, R. Humility and the high-risk researcher: Confounded variables in the study of schizophrenia. Paper presented at the Risk Research Consortium Plenary Conference, San Juan, Puerto Rico, March, 1980.

Sameroff, A., & Chandler, M. Reproductive risk and the continuum of caretaking casualty. In F. Horowitz, M. Hetherington, S. Scarr-Salapatek, & G. Siegel (Eds.), *Review of child development research* (Vol. 4). Chicago: SRCD, 1975.

Sameroff, A., & Feil, L. Parental Perspectives on Development. Paper presented at the meeting of the Society for Research in Child Development, Boston, 1981.

Sameroff, A., & Seifer, R. The transmission of incompetence: The offspring of mentally ill women. In M. Lewis & L. Rosenblum (Eds.), *The uncommon child*. New York: Plenum Publishing Corp., 1981.

Thomas, A., Chess, S., Birch, H., Hertzig, M., & Korn, S. *Behavioral individuality in early childhood*. London: University of London, 1963.

Waddington, C. *Principles of development and differentiation*. New York: Macmillan Publishing Company, 1966.

Chapter 10

THE EARLY ENVIRONMENT
OF THE AT-RISK INFANT:
Expanding the Social Context

Ross D. Parke and Barbara R. Tinsley

Conceptualizations of the factors mediating the development of at-risk infants have been revised in recent years to reflect a shift in emphasis from reproductive casualty to consideration of caregiving casualty as well (Sameroff & Chandler, 1975). Our understanding, however, of the effects of the caregiving environment on development in at-risk populations is very incomplete. In this chapter, it is argued that an exclusive focus on mother-infant interaction as a predictor of infant outcome is too narrow, and an alternative approach in which multiple levels of social context are considered is advocated.

THE IMPACT OF PREMATURITY ON THE FAMILY AND INFANT

Until recently researchers have focused on the mother-infant dyad as the preferred unit of analysis in attempts to understand the role of the social environment in the development of the at-risk infant. Increasingly, models that recognize the embeddedness of the mother-infant dyad in a variety of other social systems are guiding both research and intervention (Bronfenbrenner, 1979; Garbarino & Gilliam, 1980; Parke, 1977). Included in the other social systems that are recognized in these models are: 1) the mother-father-child family system (Belsky, 1981; Lewis & Feiring, 1981; Parke, Power, & Gottman, 1979; Pedersen, 1980); 2) the role of formal and informal support systems (Bronfenbrenner, 1979; Cochran & Brassard, 1979; Garbarino & Gilliam, 1980; Parke, 1977); and finally, 3) the role of the cultural system (LeVine,

This chapter was written during the first author's tenure as a Belding Scholar at the Foundation for Child Development. Preparation of the chapter and some of the research reported was supported by NICHD Grant HEW PHS 05951, NICHD Training Grant HDO 7205-01, and The National Foundation March of Dimes.

1977; Parke, Grossman, & Tinsley, 1981). It is hypothesized that the family's ability to adapt to a stressful event such as the birth of a premature infant or other similar stressful situations (e.g., divorce, residence change, unemployment, death of a family member (Elder & Rockwell, 1979; Garbarino & Gilliam, 1980; Hetherington, Cox, & Cox, 1978)) is in part mediated by its position within these various levels of social organization, and its access to and utilization of various social supports (Parke & Lewis, 1981). These models suggest an increasing recognition of the reciprocity of families as socializing agents embedded in social networks, both directly and indirectly influencing and being influenced by interactions within and outside the family (see Figure 1).

THE BIRTH OF A PREMATURE INFANT: A FAMILY STRESSOR

Although a variety of factors may place an infant at risk, this chapter focuses on the premature infant. The birth of a premature infant is indeed a stressful event, as evidenced by descriptions portraying parents with infants in at-risk nurseries as shocked, angry, and otherwise emotionally distraught (Kennedy, 1973; Kopf & McFadden, 1974; Slade, Redl, & Manguten, 1977). Furthermore, reactions to the birth of a premature infant are unlikely to be similar across families. The degree of stress associated with this event is determined, in part, by the parents' subjective perceptions of the event. In turn, it is assumed that their perceptions will influence their interactions with their infants. This cognitive-mediational approach suggests that parental knowledge, expectations, and labeling must be considered in order to understand the degree of stress as well as the parents' treatment of their infant (Parke, 1978).

The survival rate of the low birth weight infant has increased greatly in recent years due to advances in medical care and technology (Klaus & Fanaroff, 1979). Many of these "new" survivors often have serious medical difficulties as well as a higher rate of short-term and long-term developmental problems than term infants. Caputo and Mandell (1970) pointed out a number of outcomes that may make the low birth weight infant at risk for possible parental maltreatment. It should be noted that some of the outcomes may alter the parent-child relationship in the early postpartum months, while others may not affect the parent-child dyad until the child is beyond infancy. Disturbances in early parent-child interaction may, in fact, be important contributors to disturbances in later years.

In addition to the disequilibrium initiated by the birth of any infant (e.g., additional tasks associated with caregiving, modifications of schedules and activities, readjustment of the marital relationship,

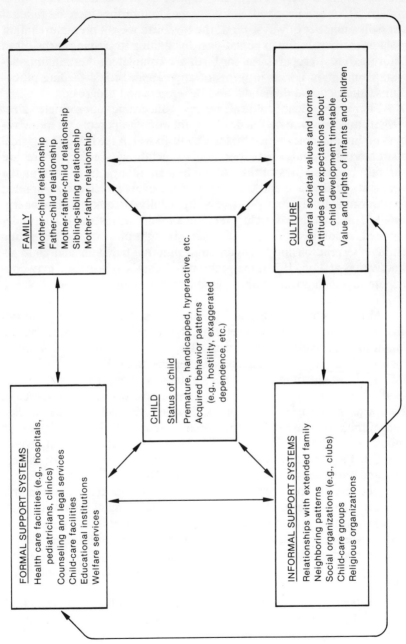

Figure 1.   The social network of the preterm child.

(Bakan, 1971; Ryder, 1973)), the birth of an at-risk infant (e.g., premature, ill, or handicapped) has outcomes that further increase familial stress in a number of ways. First, the low birth weight premature infant violates many parental expectations. In addition to arriving early, often before parental preparations for birth are completed, these infants deviate from infant norms in terms of appearance, cries, feeding procedures, interactional demands, and developmental progress.

There are clear cultural norms concerning appropriate size, weight, and appearance for newborn infants; the parents' responsiveness is, in part, determined by the extent to which the infant's physical characteristics conform to parental expectations. In fact, there are certain characteristics of the normal human infant's face, such as the concavity of the face and the height of the eyes, which are responded to discriminatively and positively by adults (Brooks & Hochberg, 1960). The low birth weight premature infant seems small and undeveloped in contrast to the term infant. In light of evidence suggesting an inverse relationship between adult punitive behavior and child attractiveness (Dion, 1974), the premature infant's appearance may contribute to a higher rate of abuse among preterm infants (Klein & Stern, 1971).

More recently Frodi and her colleagues documented that in addition to the appearance of preterms, the cry patterns of the premature infant may be aversive for parents. The cry of the premature infant is high-pitched and potentially more aversive than the cry of the term infant. Using videotaped sequences of infants, these researchers (Frodi et al., 1978) compared parental reactions to the cry and appearance of both a term and premature infant. Through the use of sound tracks, half of the terms and half of the preterms 'emitted' the cry of the term infant; the other half emitted the cry of the preterm infant, which permitted assessment of the separate and combined impact of the appearance and sound of term and preterm infants. Results confirmed that the cry of the premature infant resulted in greater autonomic arousal than the term cry as well as parental rating of greater disturbance, irritation, and annoyance. The arousal effects were particularly pronounced when the parents were exposed to both the sight and cry of a premature infant. In addition, the parents reported that they were less eager to interact with the premature infant whom they found less pleasant.

Preterm infants place greater demands on their parents than term infants. For example, feeding disturbances are more common among low birth weight infants. Because of their low weight, these infants must be fed more often, and, especially in the case of very low birth weight infants, special feeding techniques may be necessary (Klaus

& Fanaroff, 1979). In addition, premature infants may cry more and be more irritable (Elmer, 1976). In part, these difficulties may stem from the fact that medical problems are often associated with prematurity and low birth weight. For example, Klein and Stern (1971) reported that 9 of their 12 low birth weight infants had major neonatal problems (e.g., exchange transfusion, pneumonia, birth asphyxia). In contrast, only 15 out of the 39 normal birth weight infants had medical or developmental complications. The profound impact that these problems can have on parent-infant relationships is illustrated by a recent British study (Lynch, 1976). Although 60 percent of the abused infants in this sample were ill, with problems ranging from relatively minor conditions such as eczema, colic, and vomiting to major problems such as pyloric stenosis and severe cleft palate, less than 10% of the nonabused siblings in these same families were ill during the first year. Low birth weight infants (who have a higher probability of health problems) make more demands on their parents and caregiving becomes a more difficult task for these families.

Recent observational studies of the interaction patterns between parents and their premature infants suggest that these parents have to expand more effort to maintain ongoing social interaction during feeding. Premature infants are behaviorally different than their term peers; as Goldberg and her colleagues (1979) reported, premature infants spend less time alert, are more difficult to keep in alert states, are less responsive to sights and sounds than term infants, and provide fewer distinctive cues to guide parental treatment. In view of these behavioral characteristics, it is not surprising that parents have to work "harder" when interacting with a premature infant. Brown and Bakeman (1980) documented that preterm infants are more difficult and less satisfying to feed than term infants; during feeding interactions, preterms contributed less to maintenance of the interactive flow than term infants, and the burden of maintaining the interaction fell disproportionately on the mothers of these preterms.

Parents of preterm infants may have unrealistic expectations concerning the developmental timetable that these infants are likely to follow; preterm infants may continue to violate their parents' expectations, because their developmental progress in motor, social, and cognitive spheres is often slower than term infants during at least the first 2 years (Field et al., 1979). This discrepancy between parental expectations and child behavior may be another source of stress for the family, especially in light of research findings that suggest that lack of accurate knowledge of developmental timetables may be a factor in child abuse (Egeland & Brunnquell, 1979), a finding that provides further support for a cognitive mediational analysis (Parke, 1978).

EARLY MATERNAL-INFANT SEPARATION

There are other factors that may be additional stressors on families of
the low birth weight preterm infant. Often the preterm infant, particularly the sick preterm, is separated from his or her mother during the
early post-partum period. This may occur for a number of reasons,
such as the necessity of isolating the infant in an intensive care nursery
which, in turn, may initially limit the amount of mother-infant contact.
Second, in cases where the infant has been transported to a central
regional neonatal facility, the mother and infant may be in separate
hospitals. Finally, even after the mother is discharged, the preterm
infant may often remain hospitalized. In view of the significance that
the early post-partum period may have for the development of parent-
infant attachment (Klaus & Kennell, 1981), the separation that often
characterizes parents and their preterm infants assumes greater
importance.

Evidence in support of this general view that early and prolonged
contact may facilitate mother-infant attachment has been marshalled
by Klaus and Kennell (1981). Other investigations (O'Connor et al.,
1980) have demonstrated that "rooming-in" during the mother's post-
partum hospitalization is associated with fewer incidences of parenting
inadequacy. The evidence for this link between early contact and maternal-infant attachment, however, is not consistent across all studies
and some recent investigations have failed to find significant effects
(Pannabecker & Emde, 1977). In fact, Klaus and Kennell (1981) recently retreated from their emphasis on the immediate post-partum
period as *critical* for mother-infant bonding. Nevertheless, a significant
number of studies have found a relationship between parenting disorders and neonatal hospitalization (Hunter et al., 1978; Klein & Stern,
1971; Lynch & Roberts, 1977). As Penticuff (1980) suggested, however,
it is unclear whether to primarily attribute this relationship to the stress
associated with neonatal hospitalization or the separation resulting
from the infant's stay in an at-risk nursery. Results from a recent
Canadian study (Minde et al., 1980) suggest that mothers' behavior
with their at-risk infants in the neonatal nursery was most related to
maternal background variables (i.e., her life experiences and relationships with her mother and the infant's father), in comparison with the
predictive value of prenatal or perinatal medical conditions for parenting behavior. This suggests that the stress involved in the hospitalization of the preterm newborn may adversely affect those least able
to withstand prolonged strain (i.e., mothers with problematic childhood
histories or unsatisfying familial relationships), thus contributing to the
likelihood of less than optimal parenting. Identification of the set of
critical features associated with hospitalization of preterm infants that

may account for later parenting disorders is still incomplete. As our review suggests, multivariate models are clearly necessary to incorporate the many factors that contribute to the stressful impact of premature infants on their caregivers.

BEYOND THE MOTHER-INFANT DYAD: THE FATHER-INFANT DYAD AND THE FAMILY TRIAD AS CONTEXTS FOR THE DEVELOPMENT OF THE AT-RISK INFANT

Father-Infant Dyad

In recent years, the father's important role in infancy has been acknowledged (Parke, 1981, 1982a; Lamb, 1976). Fathers are active and interested participants in early infancy and competent in their execution of early caregiving tasks such as feeding (Parke & Sawin, 1976). Although the majority of studies have involved fathers with their term infants, a number of researchers have begun to recognize the special role that the father may play in the family when an infant is born prematurely.

In a recent investigation, Marton, Minde, and Perrotta (1981) examined the interaction patterns of fathers as well as mothers with their premature infants in the hospital and at home. Fathers were active and interested interactants and in this sample visited an average of 2.5 times prior to the mother's first visit with the infant. Particularly in transport situations, where the infant may be moved to an intensive care nursery at a centralized perinatal unit without the mother, the father may often have the earliest contact with the infant (Parke & Collmer, 1975). Father involvement, however, as indexed by the visitation patterns, did not diminish after mother visitation became possible. Both parents visited an average of three to four times each week during the infants' average 6–7 week hospital stay. Just as others (Parke & O'Leary, 1976; Parke & Sawin, 1980) have observed in the case for term infants, in the hospital the behaviors of mothers and fathers with their infants were similar; however, mothers talked to their preterm infants more than fathers.

At home, 3 months after discharge, a 5-minute face-to-face play segment again revealed a high degree of similarity between mothers and fathers in all but one category of behavior. Mothers engaged significantly more in instrumental touching than fathers, which indicated that mothers were more likely to engage in some form of caregiving even during play. Although there was no comparison group of term infants in this study, other studies of term infants indicate clear differences in the style of mother and father play in face-to-face situations (see Parke, 1979). Specifically, fathers engage in more physical play.

Perhaps fathers of preterm infants perceive their infants as too fragile and incapable of robust, physical interaction. Regardless of the reason, this finding of similarity in play patterns of mothers and fathers underscores the difference in social environment that parents provide for preterm, in contrast to term infants. Finally, Marton et al. (1981) found that fathers contributed significantly less to routine caregiving (feeding, bathing, diapering, comforting) than mothers—a finding consistent with other data for parents of term infants.

One of the important implications of these findings is that the father could play an important role in reducing some of the detrimental effects of the social isolation that is often associated with the hospitalization of the premature infant. The father may be available as a social interactant before the mother, particularly in the case of at-risk infants who are often transported and being cared for at a central at-risk nursery.

Although Marton el al. (1981) did not directly compare fathers of preterm and term infants, other investigators suggest that the degree of father involvement may be higher in the case of the preterm infant. In a U.S. sample, Yogman (1981) found that fathers of premature infants exhibit higher levels of caregiving involvement (e.g., bathing, diapering) than fathers of term infants. These patterns of heightened father involvement with preterms may, in part, be attributable to the difficulties associated with the care of the preterm infant. Prematurity may elicit greater father involvement in caregiving at least partially because of the father's desire to relieve the mother of full responsibility for the extra time and skill required for caring for these infants. It is clear that an exclusive focus on either the mother-infant or father-infant dyad alone is inadequate.

The Family Triad

Models that limit examination of the effects of interaction patterns to only the father-infant and mother-infant dyads and the direct effects of one individual on another are inadequate for understanding the impact of social interaction patterns in families and especially in families with at-risk infants (Lewis & Feiring, 1981; Parke, Power, & Gottman, 1979). The full family group must be considered. Second, parents influence their infants indirectly as well. A parent may influence a child through the mediation of another family member's impact (e.g., a father may contribute to the mother's positive affect toward her child by praising her caregiving ability). Another way in which one parent may indirectly influence the child's treatment by other agents is by modifying the infant's behavior. Child behavior patterns that develop as a result of parent-child interaction, may, in turn, affect the child's treatment by other social agents. For example, irritable infant patterns induced by an insensitive and impatient mother may, in turn, make the infant more difficult for the father to handle and pacify. Thus, patterns developed in interaction with one parent may alter interaction patterns with another caregiver. In larger families, siblings can play a similar mediating role.

The importance of the relationship between family characteristics and infant status should also be emphasized. The development of at-risk infants has been demonstrated to be signficantly affected by the infants' ordinal position, family background factors, parent-infant interaction patterns, and other socioeconomic factors (Caputo, Goldstein, & Taub, 1981; Drillien, 1964; Sigman et al., 1981). Parents have been shown to behave differently when alone with their infant than when interacting with the infant in the presence of the other parent. In two of our earlier studies (Parke & O'Leary, 1976) the father was a highly involved participant in the triad context, equalling or excelling the mother in stimulating and nurturing the infant. Furthermore, the presence of the other parent significantly altered the behavior of the partner; specifically, each expressed more positive affect (smiling) toward their infant and showed a higher level of exploration when the other parent was present. The family context seemed to elicit greater affective and exploratory behavior on the part of both parents. These results indicate that parent-infant interaction cannot be understood by focusing solely on parent-infant dyads.

Other recent investigations emphasize the importance of studying the family triad in terms of the impact of the husband-wife relationship on the parent-infant interaction process and the influence of the birth of an at-risk infant on the cohesiveness of the family. Pedersen (1975) assessed the influence of the husband-wife relationship on the mother-infant interaction in a feeding context. Ratings were made of the quality of the mother-infant relationship in connection with two time-sampling home observations when the infants were 4 weeks old. Of particular interest were the ratings of "feeding competence," which refers to the appropriateness of the mother in managing feeding. "Mothers rated high are able to pace the feeding well, intersperse feeding and burping without disrupting the baby and seem sensitive to the baby's needs for either stimulation of feeding or brief rest periods during the course of feedings" (Pedersen, 1975, p. 4). In addition, the husband-wife relationship was assessed through an interview; and finally, neonatal assessments (Brazelton, 1973) were available. Pedersen found that:

> When the father was more supportive of the mother, that is, evaluated her maternal skills more positively, she was more effective in feeding the baby. Then again, maybe competent mothers elicit more positive eval-

uations from their husbands. The reverse holds for marital discord. High tension and conflict in the marriage was associated with more inept feeding on the part of the mother (1975, p. 6).

The status and well being of the infant, assessed by Brazelton scores of alertness and motor maturity, were also related to the marital relationship. With an alert baby, the father evaluated the mother more positively; with a motorically mature baby, there seemed to be less tension and conflict in the marriage. In Pedersen's (1975) view "a good baby and a good marriage go together."

Both the Parke and O'Leary (1976) and Pedersen (1975) investigations studied families with healthy, term infants. One would expect, however, that the impact of an at-risk infant would have an even more profound impact on family interaction patterns. Of relevance to this issue is the work of Leiderman (Leiderman & Seashore, 1975; Leifer et al., 1972). These investigators examined the impact of the separation that often occurs between parents and premature infants on subsequent mother-infant interaction and family functioning. Although these studies demonstrate the importance of contact for the development of the mother-infant relationship, a finding of particular relevance concerned the impact of the premature infant on family cohesiveness. In the investigators' original sample of 66 families, 8 divorces had occurred by the time the infants were 21 months old: five divorces occurred in the families of the separated group, two in the contact group, and one in the term group. Leiderman and Seashore suggest "that separation in the newborn period does have an effect, albeit nonspecific, by acting through the family as a stress that creates disequilibrium in the nuclear family structure" (1975, pp. 229–230). Although the Leiderman et al. study provides further support for considering the family unit, the specific ways in which the birth of a preterm infant affects relationships among family members remains unclear.

Recent studies indicate the importance of the father as a support figure for the mother when the infant is born prematurely. Paternal support can take a variety of forms such as providing nurturance and emotional support for the mother as well as providing instrumental support by increased involvement in caregiving. In an interview study of more than 100 families with premature infants, Herzog (1979) found that the most important function of fathers of premature infants was to provide support for the mother to facilitate her caregiving role and her positive feelings toward the infant. Further support for this position comes from a study of parental visiting patterns in an English at-risk nursery (Hawthorne, Richards, & Callon, 1978). These investigators found that mothers of premature infants were helped by fathers who became highly involved in caring for the infant. While these studies indicate that fathers assume a more active supportive role in the case of a premature infant, neither the factors that promote differential degrees of paternal involvement nor the subsequent impact of this involvement for either the a) husband-wife relationship; b) the mother-infant relationship; or c) the father-infant relationship have been specified.

A further clue concerning these issues comes from a recent study by Minde et al. (1977) who recently reported that the frequency with which mothers visited their hospitalized premature infants was related to the quality of the husband-wife relationship; visitation was less frequent in distressed marriages than in nondistressed families. In light of the relationship between visitation patterns and parenting disorders such as child abuse (Fanaroff, Kennell, & Klaus, 1972), and considered in combination with the findings of Minde et al. (1980) discussed above, relating maternal-infant behavior and familial relationships such as that of the mother and the infant's father, these findings assume more significance. Although low frequencies of visitation by mothers may contribute to later problems due to the lack of opportunity for the development of a strong mother-infant relationship, it is possible that the poor husband-wife relationship may be a factor in both low involvement (visitation) and subsequent parenting disorders. For example, infant or child abuse can be an outcome of husband-wife quarrels. Alternatively, the husband in a poor marriage may not share in the caregiving activities, which may increase the likelihood of stress-related abuse of infants by mothers (Parke, 1977; Parke & Collmer, 1975). Further support for this hypothesis comes from a study of maternal adjustment to having a handicapped child (Friedrich, 1979). Marital satisfaction was found to be the best predictor of maternal coping behavior.

The importance of these findings is clear: in order to understand either the mother-infant or father-infant relationship, the total set of relationships among the members of the family needs to be assessed. Although interviews are helpful, they are not sufficient; rather, direct observations of both mother *and* father alone with their infants as well as the mother, father, and infant together are necessary to understand the effects of prematurity on the family and the infant.

THE ROLE OF THE COMMUNITY IN MODIFYING FAMILY INTERACTION PATTERNS: AN ECOLOGICAL ANALYSIS

A further extension of our theoretical framework—from the dyad to the triad to the family in its ecological context—is needed to better understand the development of the at-risk infant. Families do not exist as units independent of other social organizations within society. Thus, as outlined in our earlier theoretical scheme, families need to be viewed within their social context; and recognition of the role of the community as a modifier of family modes of interaction is necessary for an adequate theory of early development.

Recognition of the embeddedness of families in a set of broader social systems such as community and culture or in Brim's (1975) terms in the meso and macro systems is only a first step. The next important task is to begin a) to articulate the ways in which these other levels of social organization affect family functioning, and b) to explore the ways in which these processes take place. It should be noted that community influence, regardless of its form, can be either positive or negative; this view stands in contrast to the view that high degree of connectedness with community resources is, *ipso facto,* necessarily positive. In addition, it is assumed that the relationship between communities and families is bidirectional with the influence moving in both directions. It is assumed that both the ways in which communities and families are related will vary across the developmental span. Moreover, the influence of support systems on families may either be direct or indirect in its effects. Finally, both availability and utilization need to be separately considered. Families may have friends, relatives, and neighbors available, but fail to utilize these members of their informal social network in times of stress or crises.

The functions that extra familial support systems play in modulating intrafamily interaction patterns flow from our theoretical analyses. As noted above, premature infants may be at risk as a result of a) limited knowledge of development on the part of parents, b) inappropriate infant care skills and/or c) the stress associated with the care and rearing of a preterm infant. Extrafamilial support systems can function to alleviate these problems a) by providing accurate timetables for the development of premature infants as well as the term infants, b) by monitoring current infant care practices and providing corrective feedback in order to improve infant care skills, and c) by providing relief from stress associated with the birth and care of the preterm infant.

Communities may alter the social environment of the preterm infant by education, by monitoring of child-care practices and by the alleviation of stress. Following are some of the *mechanisms* through which these extrafamilial influences operate to modify family interaction patterns.

INFORMAL AND FORMAL SUPPORT SYSTEMS

To explore the mechanisms by which community influence is transmitted to the family, two kinds of support systems need to be distinguished: informal and formal.

Informal Support Systems

Informal support systems refer to: 1) unstructured social networks, which consist of a person's relatives, friends, neighbors, co-workers, and other acquaintances who interact with the person; and 2) structured social support systems, which include a variety of neighborhood or community-based organizations or groups that are generally not officially generated, controlled, or funded by local or other government officials (Cochran & Brassard, 1979). Both of these types of social support systems can help families adapt to stressful change such as the birth of a premature infant, in a variety of ways: providing instrumental physical and financial support; providing emotional/social support; and providing informational support (Unger & Powell, 1980).

In the past, the primary informal support system was the extended family, which more often resided with or near the young nuclear family. In modern society there has been a general shift in the structure of living arrangements from an extended family to a self-contained nuclear family. For example, 50 years ago, 50 percent of the households in Massachusetts included at least one adult besides the parents, in contrast to 4 percent in 1974 (Bronfenbrenner, 1974). Furthermore, because of greater mobility, the contemporary nuclear family is often removed from its original community and established family ties.

In the past, the extended family may have functioned in various ways as a social support system for the young and newly formed nuclear family. First, the stress often associated with child care may have been alleviated by other family members' assistance. Second, the novice mother may have had an experienced model available from whom to acquire mothering skills. At the same time, an older caregiver may have been available to modify "inappropriate" and ineffective child care tactics. The extent to which extended families function as social support for young nuclear families today is as yet unexplored. It can probably be assumed, however, that with the demise of the extended family living arrangement, these social support roles may be played by the community informal social support systems to a greater degree. Patterns of use of different parts of informal social networks—unstructured and structured—varies considerably across ethnic groups, income, and educational levels, and the type of stressor that the family is experiencing (Unger & Powell, 1980). These patterns of utilization, however, are poorly understood.

In the case of some crises that involve social stigma such as alcoholism or, of more direct relevance, the birth of a handicapped or retarded infant, families may often avoid or be unable to make social contacts with friends and relatives. Instead, formal community support systems such as medical, government, and educational institutions may play an even more important role in the case of these families.

Formal Support Systems

Two types of formal support systems need to be distinguished: 1) general and 2) specific to at-risk infants and families. *General* support systems refer to the types of formal support systems that are available to all members of the community, including such support agencies as: health care facilities for both adults and children; counseling services for individuals and families; employment agencies; educational opportunities; social work services to facilitate adoption and placement of infants and children; housing assistance; welfare assistance; and recreational facilities.

There are a variety of support systems of special relevance to at-risk infants and families. These programs serve both the educational function of providing child care information as well as alleviating stress associated with premature or ill infants. Support systems that serve an educational function include: hospital-based courses in child care and child-rearing; nurse visiting programs; well-baby clinics; follow-up programs; and parent discussion groups. Some other supportive programs that offer stress relief are: family and group day care facilities; baby-sitting services; mother's helpers; homemaker and housekeeping services; drop-off centers, crisis nurseries, and hot lines.

Evidence in support of the role of informal and formal support systems in regulating family ability to cope with at-risk infants is limited. In this section some illustrative studies of the role of support systems in modifying family management of infant care and development are reviewed. Although some recent studies involve informal social support systems, many of the studies have primarily involved modification of the formal support systems available to families. Finally, in some cases, informal and formal support are provided together, which underlines the interconnectedness of these two levels of social support for families.

Relationship between Informal Social
Support Systems and Family Interaction Patterns

A number of studies have suggested that there is a positive relationship between informal social networks and a family's adaptation to stress. Specifically, interaction patterns among family members are influenced by the availability and utilization of informal social networks (Cochran & Brassard, 1979). In studies of abusive families, it has been found that these families are often socially isolated and lack adequate social support systems (Garbarino & Gilliam, 1980; Parke, 1982b; Parke & Collmer, 1975). Similarly, in their study of divorce, Hetherington et al. (1978) found that the adequacy of the mother's social support network was positively related to her effectiveness with her children. Of more direct relevance are two recent studies of the relationship between social networks and mother-child interaction.

Unger (1979) examined the influence of social networks on mother-infant interaction in a small sample of white low-income mothers and their young infants (under 6 months). Using the HOME Scale (Elardo, Bradley, & Caldwell, 1975) to assess interaction, Unger found that mothers who experienced high levels of stress were found to be more actively involved with their infants when they had weekly contact with friends than when they were infrequently in contact. Parents also seemed more responsive to their infants if they were receiving material resources from their network members. In a related study that also employed the HOME Scale, Pascoe et al. (1981) found a positive relationship between the level of maternal social support and selected subscales from the HOME Scale in a group of families with 3-year-old children. Unfortunately, Pascoe et al. did not examine both intrafamilial (i.e., spouse support) and extrafamilial social support separately, which does not permit an evaluation of the relative importance of differing sources of support. These two studies of Pascoe et al. and Unger and Powell, however, are important in view of the previously established positive relationship between the HOME Scale and mental test performance (Bradley & Caldwell, 1976). These investigations suggest that social support may affect infant and child developmental outcomes indirectly, through modifying the nature of parent-child interaction patterns.

These studies, however, are only suggestive and leave unanswered a variety of questions. First, previous studies have not examined the comparative role of social networks in families of preterm and term infants. It is assumed that social networks will be more important in the families of preterm infants who are under greater initial stress than families of term infants. Many of the children in the Pascoe et al. study were either born prematurely or were ill as infants; however, no assessments were made of the social networks of these families when their children were infants. Nor were there comparisons between families of term and preterm infants. Second, there is no direct observational data available that describes in detail the ways in which parent-infant interaction patterns are altered by the availability of social networks (for a recent exception, see Crockenberg, 1981). Third, the ways in which the relationships between social networks and parent-infant interaction shift across developmental levels of the infant have not been explored. Fourth, the relationships between parent-infant interaction and social support have been restricted to mothers; no data concerning these relationships for fathers is yet available. Nor have there been any investigations that have simultaneously assessed the assumed linkages among social support, parent-infant interaction, and infant cognitive and social outcomes. Nevertheless these studies do underscore the value of expanding our conceptual framework to include the links between the family and external social networks that can function as support systems for families.

Relationship between Formal Social
Support Systems and Family Interaction Patterns

In recent years, a number of investigators have used the hospital to provide social support for parents and, in particular, the post-partum period as a convenient time-point for initiating supportive services for parents of infants. Parents are accessible at this point and often motivation for learning about infant development and caregiving skills is high during this time.

The value of hospital-based programs for parents is illustrated in the work of Badger, Burns, and Vietze (1981). Teenage mothers who were assumed to be at-risk for later parenting problems were recruited in the hospital during the post-partum period and given a series of weekly classes that were the vehicle for a variety of supportive services. In addition to information and instruction in how to stimulate their infant's social and cognitive skills provided in group classes, the young mothers received information about infant nutrition, family planning, and health care. Further institutional support was available from a clinic doctor of a health service team during the class sessions. Results indicated that young teenage mothers (16 years or younger) and their infants profited from this intervention effort. Specifically, the infants of high-risk mothers who attended classes had normal Bayley scores at 1 year in contrast to a comparison group who had significantly lower Bayley mental scores, emphasizing that social support can indirectly as well as directly affect family members. Furthermore, the mothers who attended the classes were more physically and emotionally responsive to their infants than mothers in the comparison samples. Unfortunately, the relative contribution of the components that may account for the observed differences in infant functioning are unclear.

This early postpartum period can be effectively used to provide support for fathers as well. This is demonstrated by a recent hospital-based study (Parke et al., 1980). During the mother's post-partum hospitalization, one group of fathers was shown a short videotape that modeled positive father-infant interaction and caregiving involvement with young infants. In comparison to a control group of fathers who saw no videotape, fathers who viewed the film in the hospital increased their knowledge about infant perceptual abilities, believed more strongly that infants need stimulation, and were more responsive to their infants during feeding and play in comparison to fathers who were not exposed to the film. Based on diary reports of caregiving activities in the home at 3 months, fathers of boys who saw the film were more likely to diaper and feed their infants than fathers in the no-film control group. In summary, the film intervention significantly modified selected aspects of father behavior and attitudes both in the hospital and through the first 3 months of their infants' lives. In a related study, Parke et al. (1981) directly addressed this issue through the use of a film that stressed the importance of spouses providing mutual support for one another. The level of husband-wife assistance in child care was, during the post-partum period, increased through this hospital-based intervention. Furthermore, mothers whose partners had seen a film emphasizing parental cooperation and assistance in caregiving stimulated their infants more in the hospital and the home and tended to help the fathers feed the infants more frequently in the home.

Other studies (Dickie & Carnahan, 1979; Zelazo et al., 1977) show that these types of supportive interventions for increasing paternal involvement need not be restricted to the early post-partum period or to young infants. Parental behavior can be modified at a variety of time points. The capacity of both parents and infants for continual adaptation to shifting circumstances probably overrides the paramount importance of any single time period for the formation of social relationships (Cairns, 1977).

Another set of studies illustrates the potential of health care providers, such as pediatricians, to play a supportive role for parents of young children. Chamberlin (1979) reported that mothers who participated in an educational program concerning child development during pediatric well-baby visits increased in their knowledge of child development and perceptions of being supported in the caregiving role. A second study (Whitt & Casey, 1979) suggests that mothers who were provided with an office-based pediatric intervention program, emphasizing physical and preventive child care, developmental norms, and information on infant communication abilities during well-baby exams, demonstrated a more positive relationship with their infants.

Together, these intervention studies illustrate the ways in which formal institutions such as hospitals and other health care facilities can potentially affect infants through the modification of the skills of mother, father or both parents. Although the infants in these studies were all term, the results have implications for families of preterm infants. Specifically, these same techniques could be profitably applied to supporting fathers and mothers of preterm infants.

Relationship between Informal and Formal Support Systems

Although informal and formal support systems can make independent contributions to family functioning, a number of recent studies have shown that these two types of support systems can work in concert in supporting families. Links between formal and informal support systems can assume a variety of forms, such as: 1) strengthening the informal network through formal intervention (Powell, 1979); 2) mobilizing existing social networks in times of stress (Rueveni, 1979); and 3) using informal network members to help individuals utilize formal support services (Olds, 1981).

Minde and his colleagues (Minde et al., 1980; Minde, Shosenberg, & Marton, 1981) have recently developed a program of self-help groups for mothers of premature infants, which illustrates the interplay between formal and informal systems, and the direct and indirect effects of these supportive systems. Moreover, because this program involves mothers of preterm infants, it is of particular relevance to this discussion. Each group met weekly with an experienced neonatal nurse and a mother for 7–12 weeks following the birth of their infant. The groups provided a variety of services including opportunities to share feelings, information about the developmental and medical needs of premature infants, assistance with a variety of daily tasks such as babysitting accommodations and unemployment benefits, and familiarization with local community resources for family support.

In contrast to a control group, these mothers visited their infants significantly more in the hospital, and touched, talked, and looked at their infants more, and expressed more confidence in their caregiving abilities. At 3 months after discharge, group mothers continued to show involvement with their babies during feedings and were more concerned about their general development. At one year, they gave their infants more general freedom and stimulation and judged their competence more appropriately to their biological abilities in contrast to mothers in the control group. In turn, the infants whose mothers participated in the intervention group showed more social and independent behaviors such as general playing, food sharing, and self-feeding.

Although the mechanisms through which these positive outcomes were achieved were not determined by this study, some of the possible factors were isolated by subsequent analyses. Of special interest was the finding that more mothers in the support groups reported that their relationships with one or more significant persons in their life improved. In turn, one would expect that these mothers more effectively were able to use these significant others for support. These mothers were viewed as more autonomous—a construct reflecting the degree of perceived control and alternatives that the mothers felt they had over their lives. Again the specifics of how this program "worked" remain to be determined; however, the project demonstrates the value of intervening at multiple levels and provides further support for the necessity of expanding our views of the critical social contexts for the development of the preterm infant. Finally, as an illustration of the ways in which formal and informal support systems interact, it should be noted that the "self-support" groups in this study are now being run as an independent organization, by the parents themselves.

The Prenatal/Early Infancy Project developed by Olds (1981) provides a final illustration of how formal and informal support can perform together. This investigation has developed a model in which the professionals (formal system) identify and train members of the parent's informal social network (informal system) to assist at-risk families.

Specifically, a nurse/home visitor provides home-based education for improving pregnancy management and early infant development by involving "significant others" who participate in the home visits with the mothers in order to create a supportive informal environment for behavioral change on the part of the parents. Finally, the nurse visitor links families with other health and support services in the community. A serious attempt is made to better understand the process through which the program's effects are mediated, by assessing maternal health habits and childrearing practices as well as the availability and utilization of informal supports and formal community services. Preliminary results from the pregnancy phase indicate that mothers who had the nurse/visitor were aware of more formal community services and a larger number (65 percent) were enrolled in childbirth education classes than mothers who were not followed by a nurse (50 percent). In the area of informal support, mothers in the nurse/visitor group were accompanied by a support person to childbirth education classes more often than non–nurse-visited mothers. Similarly, nurse-visited mothers experienced support more frequently during labor from a friend or relative. This is of particular significance in light of the recent findings of Kennell et al. (1981) that the presence of a supportive other is associated with a shorter labor and less complications in childbirth. The results to date are promising and indicate further the value of a multi-level intervention. Although our emphasis has been on supportive intervention, the Olds project underlines the fact that the same model has implications for prevention as well (Parke, 1982b), by improving pregnancy outcomes and thereby preventing some preterm births.

These studies illustrate the role that informal and formal social networks together can play in aiding families to adapt to stressful change. The details of the puzzle are only partially clear, however, and the specific direct and indirect ways in which different types of informal and formal supportive intervention alter different aspects of family interaction and, in turn, infant development, are not yet well understood. Descriptive studies of how families spontaneously use and profit from available formal and informal network resources as well as experimental interventions in which the contributions of specific parts of the network are manipulated are both useful strategies for future research.

SUMMARY

The social environment of the at-risk infant needs to be expanded beyond the mother-infant dyad. In addition to the inclusion of the father-infant relationship, an understanding of the full set of relationships among mother-father and infant who are recognized as part of a family system is of particular importance. In addition, recognition of the embeddedness of the family in formal and informal social networks as well as the specific direct and indirect ways in which these extrafamilial social systems can alter family functioning are necessary to improve our understanding of the social world of the at-risk infant. By expanding our conceptual framework, our theories of development may begin to match the complexity of development. Finally, this framework can yield guidelines as to the ways in which the early social environment of the at-risk infant can be modified to minimize the impact of perinatal problems on the infant's subsequent social and cognitive development.

ACKNOWLEDGMENTS

Thanks to Eileen Posluszny and Freda Weiner for their assistance in the preparation of this manuscript. Also, we are grateful to Elaine Fleming for library research.

REFERENCES

Badger, E., Burns, D., & Vietze, P. Maternal risk factors as predictors of developmental outcome in early childhood. *Infant Mental Health Journal*, 1981, *2*, 33–43.
Bakan, D. *Slaughter of the innocents*. San Francisco: Jossey-Bass, 1971.
Belsky, J. Early human experience: A family perspective. *Developmental Psychology, 1981, 17*, 3–23.
Bradley, R. H., & Caldwell, B. M. Early home environment and changes in mental test performance in children from 6 to 36 months. *Developmental Psychology*, 1976, *12*, 93–97.
Brazelton, T. B. *Neonatal behavioral assessment scale*. London: Heineman (National Spastics Society Monograph), 1973.
Brim, O. G. Macro-structural influences on child development and the need

for childhood social indicators. *American Journal of Orthopsychiatry*, 1975, *45*, 516–524.

Bronfenbrenner, U. Origins of alienation. *Scientific American*, 1974, *231*, 53–61.

Bronfenbrenner, U. *The ecology of human development*. Cambridge: Harvard University Press, 1979.

Brooks, V., & Hochberg, J. A psychological study of "cuteness." *Perceptual and Motor Skills*, 1960, *11*, 205.

Brown, J. V., & Bakeman, R. Relationships of human mothers with their infants during the first year of life: Effects of prematurity. In R. W. Bell & W. P. Smotherman (Eds.), *Maternal influences and early behavior*. Holliswood, N.Y.: Spectrum, 1980.

Cairns, R. B. Beyond social attachment: The dynamics of interactional development. In T. A. Alloway, P. Pliner, & L. Krames (Eds.), *Attachment Behavior*. New York: Plenum Publishing Corp., 1977.

Caputo, D. U., Goldstein, K. M., & Taub, H. B. Neonatal compromise and later psychological development: A ten-year longitudinal study. In S. L. Friedman & M. Sigman (Eds.), *Preterm birth and psychological development*. New York: Academic Press, 1981.

Caputo, D. V., & Mandell, W. Consequences of low birth weight. *Developmental Psychology*, 1970, *3*, 363–383.

Chamberlin, R. W. Effects of educating mothers about child development in physicians offices on mother and child functioning over time. Paper presented at the American Psychological Association, New York City, 1979.

Cochran, M. M., & Brassard, J. A. Child development and personal social networks. *Child Development*, 1979, *50*, 601–616.

Crockenberg, S. B. Infant irritability, mother responsiveness, and support influences on the security of infant-mother attachment. *Child Development*, 1981, *52*, 857–865.

Dickie, J., & Carnahan, S. Training in social competence: The effect on mothers, fathers and infants. Paper presented at the biennial meeting of the Society for Research in Child Development, San Francisco, 1979.

Dion, K. K. Children's physical attractiveness and sex as determinants of adult punitiveness. *Developmental Psychology*, 1974, *10*, 772–778.

Drillien, C. M. *The growth and development of the prematurely born infant*. Baltimore: The Williams & Wilkins Co., 1964.

Egeland, B., & Brunnquell, D. An at-risk approach to the study of child abuse: Some preliminary findings. *Journal of the American Academy of Psychiatry*, 1979, *18*, 219–235.

Elardo, R., Bradley, R., & Caldwell, B. The relation of infants' home environments to mental test performance from six to thirty-six months: A longitudinal analysis. *Child Development*, 1975, *46*, 71–76.

Elder, G., & Rockwell, R. The life-course and human development: An ecological perspective. *International Journal of Behavioral Development*, 1979, *2*, 1–21.

Elmer, E. *Children in jeopardy: A study of abused minors and their families*. Pittsburgh: University of Pittsburgh Press, 1976.

Fanaroff, A., Kennell, J., & Klaus, M. Follow up of low birthweight infants— the predictive value of maternal visiting patterns. *Pediatrics*, 1972, *49*, 287–290.

Field, T. M., Sostek, A. M., Goldberg, S., & Shuman, H. H. (Eds.), *Infants born at risk: Behavior and development*. New York: SP Medical and Scientific Books, 1979.

Friedrich, W. N. Predictors of the coping behavior of mothers of handicapped children. *Journal of Consulting and Clinical Psychology*, 1979, *47*, 1140–1141.

Frodi, A. M., Lamb, M. E., Leavitt, L. A., Donovan, W. L., Neff, C., & Sherry, D. Fathers' and mothers' responses to the faces and cries of normal and premature infants. *Developmental Psychology*, 1978, *14*, 490–498.

Garbarino, J., & Gilliam, G. *Understanding abusive families*. Lexington, MA: Heath, 1980.

Goldberg, S. Premature birth: Consequences for the parent-infant relationship. *American Scientist*, 1979, *67*, 214–220.

Hawthorne, J. T., Richards, M. P. M., & Callon, M. A study of parental visiting of babies in a special care unit. In F. S. W. Briblecombe, M. P. M. Richards, & N. R. C. Roberton (Eds.), *Early separation and special care nurseries*. Clinics in Developmental Medicine. London: SIMP/Heinemann Medical Books, 1978.

Herzog, J. M. Disturbances in parenting high-risk infants: Clinical impressions and hypotheses. In T. M. Field (Ed.), *Infants born at risk: Behavior and development*. New York: SP Medical and Scientific Books, 1979.

Hetherington, E. M., Cox, M., & Cox, R. The aftermath of divorce. In J. H. Stevens, Jr. & M. Matthew (Eds.), *Mother-child, father-child relations*. Washington, D.C.: National Association for the Education of Young Children, 1978.

Hunter, R. S., Kilstrom, N., Kraybill, E. N., & Loda, F. Antecedents of child abuse and neglect in premature infants: A prospective study in a newborn intensive care unit. *Pediatrics*, 1978, *61*, 629–635.

Kennedy, J. The high risk maternal infant acquaintance process. *Nursing Clinics of North America*, 1973, *8*, 549–556.

Kennell, J., Klaus, M., Robertson, S., & Sosa, R. The effect of a supportive companion on perinatal problems, length of labor, and mother-infant interaction. Paper presented at the biennial meeting of the Society for Research in Child Development, Boston, April, 1981.

Klaus, M. H., & Fanaroff, A. A. *Care of the high-risk neonate* (2nd Ed). Philadelphia: Saunders, 1979.

Klaus, M. H., & Kennell, J. H. *Parent-infant bonding* (2nd Ed). St. Louis: C. V. Mosby Company, 1981.

Klein, M., & Stern, L. Low birth weight and the battered-child syndrome. *American Journal of Diseases of Childhood*, 1971, *122*, 15–18.

Kopf, R. C., & McFadden, E. L. Nursing intervention in the crisis of newborn illness. *Journal of Nursing Midwifery*, 1974, *16*, 629–636.

Lamb, M. E. *The role of the father in child development*. New York: John Wiley & Sons, 1976.

Leiderman, P. H., & Seashore, M. J. Mother-infant separation: Some delayed consequences. Parent-infant interaction. CIBA Foundation Symposium 33. Amsterdam: Elsevier North Holland Publishing Company, 1975.

Leifer, A. D., Leiderman, P. H., Barnett, C. R., & Williams, J. A. Effects of mother-infant separation on maternal attachment behavior. *Child Development*, 1972, *43*, 1203–1218.

LeVine, R. A. Child rearing as cultural adaptation. In P. H. Leiderman, S. R. Tulkin, & A. Rosenfeld (Eds.), *Culture and infancy: Variations in the human experience*. New York: Academic Press, 1977.

Lewis, M., & Feiring, C. Direct and indirect interactions in social relationships. In L. Lipsitt (Ed.), *Advances in infancy research* (Vol. 1). New York: Ablex Publishing Corp., 1981.

Lynch, M. A. Risk factors in the child: A study of abused children and their siblings. In H. P. Martin (Ed.), *The abused child: A multi-disciplinary approach to developmental issues and treatment.* Cambridge: Ballinger, 1976.

Lynch, M. A., & Roberts, J. Predicting child abuse: Signs of bonding failure in the maternity hospital. *British Medical Journal,* 1977, *60,* 624–626.

Marton, P., Minde, K., & Perrotta, M. The role of the father for the infant at risk. *American Journal of Orthopsychiatry,* 1981, *51,* 672–679.

Minde, K. K., Marton, P., Manning, D., & Hines, B. Some determinants of mother-infant interaction in the premature nursery. *American Academy of Child Psychiatry Journal,* 1980, *19,* 1–21.

Minde, K., Shosenberg, N. E., & Marton, P. L. The effects of self-help groups in a premature nursery on maternal autonomy and caretaking style one year later. Unpublished manuscript. University of Toronto, 1981.

Minde, K., Shosenberg, N. E., Marton, P., Thompson, J., Ripley, J., & Burns, S. Self-help groups in a premature nursery—a controlled evaluation. *The Journal of Pediatrics,* 1980, *96,* 933–940.

Minde, K., Trehub, S., Corter, C., Boukydis, C., Celhoffer, B., & Marton, P. Mother-child relationships in the premature nursery—an observational study. Unpublished manuscript, Department of Psychiatry, The Hospital for Sick Children, Toronto, Canada, 1977.

O'Connor, S., Vietze, P. M., Sherrod, K. B., Sandler, H. M., & Altemeier, W. A. Reduced incidence of parenting inadequacy following rooming-in. *Pediatrics,* 1980, *66,* 176–182.

Olds, D. L. The Prenatal/Early Infancy Project: An ecological approach to prevention. In J. Belsky (Ed.), *In the beginning: Readings in infancy.* New York: Columbia University Press, 1981.

Pannabecker, B. J., & Emde, R. The effect of extended contact on father-newborn interaction. Paper presented at the Western Society for Research in Nursing, Denver, Colorado, May, 1977.

Parke, R. D. Socialization into child abuse: A social interactional perspective. In J. L. Tapp & P. J. Levine (Eds.) *Law, justice and the individual in society: Psychological & legal issues.* New York: Holt, Rinehart & Winston, 1977.

Parke, R. D. Parent-infant interaction: Progress, paradigms and problems. In G. P. Sackett (Ed.), *Observing behavior (Vol. 1): Theory and applications in mental retardation.* Baltimore: University Park Press, 1978.

Parke, R. D. Perspectives on father-infant interaction. In J. Osofsky (Ed.), *Handbook of infant development.* New York: John Wiley & Sons, 1979.

Parke, R. D. *Fathers.* Cambridge: Harvard University Press, 1981.

Parke, R. D. Father-infant interaction in a family perspective. In P. Berman (Ed.), *Women: A developmental perspective.* Washington, D.C.: U.S. Government Printing Office, 1982(a).

Parke, R. D. On prediction of child abuse: Theoretical considerations. In R. Starr (Ed.), *Prediction of abuse.* Philadelphia: Ballinger, 1982(b).

Parke, R. D., & Collmer, C. W. Child abuse: An interdisciplinary analysis. In E. M. Hetherington (Ed.), *Review of child development research,* Vol. 5. Chicago: University of Chicago Press, 1975.

Parke, R. D., Grossman, K., & Tinsley, B. R. Father-mother-infant interaction in the newborn period: A German-American comparison. In T. Field (Ed.), *Culture and early interactions.* Hillsdale, N.J.: Lawrence Erlbaum, 1981.

Parke, R. D., Hymel, S., Power, T. G., & Tinsley, B. R. Fathers and risk: A hospital based model of intervention. In D. B. Sawin, R. C. Hawkins, L. O. Walker & J. H. Penticuff (Eds.), *Psychosocial risks in infant-environment transactions,* New York: Brunner/Mazel, 1980.

Parke, R. D., Hymel, S., Power, T. G., & Tinsley, B. R. Parent-infant inter-action: Assessment and modification. Unpublished manuscript, 1981.

Parke, R. D., & Lewis, N. G. The family in context: A multi-level interactional analysis of child abuse. In R. W. Henderson (Ed.), *Parent-child interaction: Theory, research and prospect.* New York: Academic Press, 1981.

Parke, R. D., & O'Leary, S. E. Father-mother-infant interaction in the new-born period: Some findings, some observations and some unresolved issues. In K. Riegel & J. Meacham (Eds.), *The developing individual in a changing world* (Vol. II), *Social and environmental issues.* The Hague: Mouton, 1976.

Parke, R. D., Power, T. G., & Gottman, J. M. Conceptualizing and quantifying influence patterns in the family triad. In M. E. Lamb, S. J. Suomi & G. R. Stephenson (Eds.) *Social interaction analysis; methodological issues:* Madison: The University of Wisconsin Press, 1979.

Parke, R. D., & Sawin, D. B. The father's role in infancy: A re-evaluation. *The Family Co-ordinator,* 1976, *25,* 365–371.

Parke, R. D., & Sawin, D. B. The family in early infancy: Social interactional and attitudinal analyses. In F. A. Pedersen (Ed.), *The father-infant relationship: Observational studies in the family setting.* New York: Praeger Special Studies, 1980.

Pascoe, J. M., Loda, F. A., Jeffries, V., & Earp, J. A. The association between mothers' social support and provision of stimulation to their children. *Developmental and Behavioral Pediatrics,* 1981, *2,* 15–19.

Pedersen, F. A. Mother, father, and infant as an interactive system. Paper presented to the American Psychological Association, Chicago, 1975.

Pedersen, F. A. (Ed.), *The father-infant relationship: Observational studies in the family setting.* New York: Praeger Special Studies, 1980.

Penticuff, J. H. Disruption of attachment formation due to reproductive cas-ualty and early separation. In D. B. Sawin, R. C. Hawkins, L. O. Walker, & J. H. Penticuff (Eds.), *Exceptional infant* (Vol. 4). *Psychosocial risks in infant-environment transactions.* New York: Brunner/Mazel, 1980.

Powell, D. R. Family-environment relations and early child-rearing: The role of social networks and neighborhoods. *Journal of Research and Development in Education,* 1979, *13,* 1–11.

Rueveni, U. *Networking families in crisis.* New York: Human Services Press, 1979.

Ryder, R. G. Longitudinal data relating marriage satisfaction and having a child. *Journal of Marriage and the Family,* 1973, *35,* 604–606.

Sameroff, A. J., & Chandler, M. J. Reproductive risk and the continuum of caretaking casualty. In F. D. Horowitz (Ed.), *Review of child development research* (Vol. 4). Chicago: The University of Chicago Press, 1975.

Sigman, M., Cohen, S. E., Beckwith, L., & Parmelee, A. H., Social and familial influences on the development of preterm infants. *Journal of Pediatric Psychology,* 1981, *6,* 1–13.

Slade, C. I., Redl, O. J., & Manguten, H. H. Working with parents of high-risk newborns. *Journal of Obstetric and Gynecologic Nursing,* 1977, *6,* 21–26.

Unger, D. G. An ecological approach to the family: The role of social networks, social stress and mother-child interaction. Unpublished masters thesis, Merrill-Palmer Institute, 1979.

Unger, D. G., & Powell, D. R. Supporting families under stress: The role of social networks. *Family Relations,* 1980, *29,* 566–574.

Whitt, J. K., & Casey, P. H. Mother-infant relationship and infant development: The effect of pediatric intervention. Paper presented at the American Psychological Association, New York City, 1979.

Yogman, M. W. Development of the father-infant relationship. In H. Fitzgerald, B. Lester, & M. W. Yogman (Eds.), *Theory and research in behavioral pediatrics* (Vol. 1). New York: Plenum Press, 1981.

Zelazo, P. R., Kotelchuck, M., Barber, L., & David, J. Fathers and sons: An experimental facilitation of attachment behaviors. Paper presented at the meetings of the Society for Research in Child Development, New Orleans, March, 1977.

Section V
SOCIAL AND DEVELOPMENTAL ISSUES

Chapter 11

FUNCTIONAL CATEGORIES IN EARLY LANGUAGE

Jill G. de Villiers

Language acquisition research has moved from a concern with syntax or form, to a concern with semantics or meaning, and finally to a preoccupation with pragmatics or function (de Villiers & de Villiers, 1978; Bates et al., in press). The emphasis changed as it became recognized that language learning does not proceed in a physical or social vacuum: that it emerges first and foremost as a communications system designed to achieve particular goals for the infant. It was not just that researchers felt the need to broaden the perspective on language, however, but that investigation of the meanings and the functions of early speech might illuminate the means by which a young child could bootstrap his or her way to the learning of grammar. There were two hopes implicit in the research. First, the way the child acquired prelinguistic communication (e.g., joint referencing) might lay the groundwork for later linguistic achievements of the same kind, and second, analysis of preverbal communication could provide data on the motivation for a child to acquire linguistic forms (Bruner, 1975).

The purpose of this chapter is not to review the vast literature that has accumulated in the last 10 years on the transition from preverbal to verbal communication. The coverage here is narrower: the problem of the assignment of functional descriptions to early child speech.

The focus of this chapter is on methodological concerns rather than a review of the field of pragmatics for investigators working in applied settings. Because the field of pragmatics is so new and the research requires longitudinal sampling, information about normal acquisition is accumulating at a rather slow rate. As a consequence, we lack a clear picture of the range of individual differences in the area of pragmatic development (Nelson, 1978). The particular issues discussed in this chapter are: the beginnings of intentional communication; the categories of analysis; the order of emergence of these functional categories; and the relationship of form and function in child speech. In each of these, individual variation is highly likely, and we will need to relate such variation to differences in mother-child interaction, age of onset of language, cognitive stage, and so forth. It is argued here that variations will only become apparent and interpretable if researchers reach consensus about the methodology and the questions that need to be asked. It is important that researchers working with handicapped infants begin from certain basic principles rather than adopting wholesale a classification scheme developed by a single investigator. If such data were merely assigned to predetermined categories, any interesting and important variations, limitations, or extensions in early uses of language would be lost. For this reason, methodological pitfalls are the topic here; not out of pessimism for the field but out of a hope that future studies will reflect the same principles.

THE PROBLEM OF INTENTION

The first issue to be dealt with by researchers interested in a pragmatic analysis of child speech is the point at which a child intends to communicate a message. It has been reported that parents typically interpret even the earliest infant vocalizations as communicative (Wolff, 1969), although it is likely that the baby is responding to noxious or pleasant stimulation with no intent to communicate. The adult acts as though the infant were trying to communicate, and even if the interpretation is wrong, the infant will presumably learn something about the effect of a certain kind of behavior. At a later stage, the child seems to use behavior, either vocalization or gesture, expressly to achieve a desired action on the part of the listener. Because an adult listener is likely to behave consistently all along, how can one identify the point at which the child's behavior becomes intentionally communicative?

An analogy can be drawn with the study of animal communication (Bates, 1976). Writers in that field have struggled in a similar way with how to define a communicative signal. If communication is given a very broad definition, such as "any information passed from a sender to a receiver that influences the receiver's behavior," then it is over-inclusive. This definition does not rule out the sound of a stampeding herd "influencing" a particular zebra to run, or the sight of a bird taking flight causing another to do likewise. Obviously organisms pay attention to each other's behavior, but not all of that is communication. Introducing the notion of "intention" in discussing animal communication is as tricky as it is in talking about infants, but some ethologists have developed an interesting way to finesse it (e.g., Smith, 1977). They talk of behavior specialized for the purpose of conveying information; that is, the behavior has undergone a process of formalization to accentuate its signal value. In some species, the behavior that was a precursor to a particular act has become exaggerated to signal the likelihood of that act, for example, the dog's baring of teeth as a signal of attack, or elaborate neck-stretching and wing extension as a signal of impending flight in some species of birds. The act has become abbreviated or redirected so that it does not serve its original function but rather is only a signal. The process by which these behaviors came to serve as signals lies in the past history of the species, and can occasionally be reconstructed by studying related species (e.g., the dance fly (Kessel, 1955)). In the human infant, the claim is made that a similar process is occurring in ontogeny; that is, certain behaviors become ritualized to serve a signal function over the first year of life. For instance, Bates, Camaioni, and Volterra (1975) described infants trying to reach a desired object. At 6 months, the infant would grunt, whimper, and reach out toward an object. Often a watching adult would interpret these behaviors as a demand and hand the child the object. In contrast, a 9-month-old makes an abbreviated reach in the direction of the object, looks at the adult and vocalizes, sometimes glancing back and forth between object and adult. In this context the behavior of reaching seems to have purely signal value for the child. A similar possibility occurs in the ontogenesis of the head shake as a signal of rejection, which may originate in turning away from the rejected object (Darwin, 1872). One approach to the transition from nonintentional to intentional communication is to study how particular behaviors become ritualized to serve particular functions. A clear demarcation of stages in this development is unlikely, as in the differentiation of signals in animal communication.

An alternative but related proposal made by several writers (Sugarman, 1978; Bates et al., 1975; Bricker & Carlson, this volume) is to study the child's coordination of object-oriented and social-oriented behaviors. In the above example of the child reaching, the key feature is not the abbreviation of the reach, but the eye contact with the adult while reaching. The 6-month-old does not include the listener in his or her scheme for getting the object, but the typical 9-month-old does, by eye contact, looking back-and-forth between object and adult, or by touching the adult. The realization of this new signaling capacity is unlikely to be either sudden or across-the-board. Rather, the new mode of behaving should emerge gradually over the second half of the first year for different objects, circumstances, and interactions.

METHODOLOGICAL ISSUES IN THE ASSIGNMENT OF FUNCTIONS

Moving from the general question of when a child's behavior becomes intentionally communicative, we turn to the narrower question of how one can determine the child's intention on any particular occasion. There are two issues that need to be separated. First, how should the adult in interaction with the child, or the researcher studying a video-tape, arrive at an interpretation of the child's communication? What was the child using the signal *for*—as a request, a label, or a query? Although the adult can arrive at an interpretation and act accordingly with little hesitation, what cues were being used, and did the child control those cues or were they in the context? The second issue is more perplexing. Given that the observer decides what the child intended on a particular occasion, how should that be described? Clearly one can not accumulate an infinite series of descriptions of particular communicative acts in context. The researcher must arrive at a classification scheme for those diverse acts. Which classification scheme is appropriate? The two issues—reading the child's specific intent, and classifying it—are obviously related, but it will be helpful to deal with each in turn.

It would be a great convenience if infants were observed to use linguistic markers to differentiate among their speech acts, for instance, rising intonation for queries, falling intonation for statements. Unfortunately the evidence is weak that children use systematic intonation patterns for different speech acts even at the two-word stage (Bloom, 1973; Crystal, 1978). Neither is the young child capable of using any other of the linguistic forms that differentiate the canonical form of speech acts in adult speech, such as subject-aux inversion in questions, Wh-words, or politeness markers. Researchers concerned with the beginnings of speech must content themselves with less formal cues. What is the adult's response? How does the child react to the adult's interpretation? Does the child persist, suggesting that the adult misinterpreted his or her intent? Are there reliably associated gestures? All of these cues are used to code the child's intention in a particular situation, and independent judges can reach acceptable levels of agreement about how the response should be classified into a predetermined classification scheme (Bates, 1976; Carter, 1979; Dale, 1980).

The determination of an appropriate set of functional categories is the central issue in the field of pragmatics, paralleling the difficulty researchers have had in agreeing on the semantic description of children's utterances (Bowerman, 1976). In both domains it is difficult to determine how finely the categories should be sliced. How can one determine which level of description is the psychologically real one for the child? Or perhaps a little more tractable: which level of description will be most revealing about the process of language acquisition?

At one extreme, each utterance serves a distinct function, as the circumstances or discourse participants are rarely identical. Which features can be collapsed together to form more inclusive categories? It is difficult not to be adult-centered in this problem. For instance, we tend to assume that in all acts in which an adult gives something to the child, all adults and all objects can be regarded as equivalent. Without realizing it, we have then begged the question of how the child recognizes the abstract similarity among all these distinct occasions. Before returning to this problem, various classification schemes that have been applied to early child speech will be reviewed.

Halliday (1975) developed a general classification scheme of "ideational," "interpersonal," and "textual" functions, coinciding roughly with Bühler's (1934) division of utterances into:

a.   those that express emotions or attitudes
b.   those that affect the behavior of others
c.   those that represent and convey information

Halliday, however, used a more extensive set of categories in describing his own subject's earliest utterances. Two broad categories of pragmatic versus mathetic or referential functions were described, each of which was further subdivided. Pragmatic functions were regulatory, instrumental, interactional, and personal; mathetic functions included heuristic, imaginative, and informative. Halliday supplies examples of each, but no criteria for deciding which category an utterance falls under (see critique by Francis, 1979). The scheme thus may not be easily adapted by other researchers attempting to replicate his interesting results.

Dale (1980) reviewed the studies of early pragmatic development and extracted those categories that appear in most, thus using consensus among researchers as the basis for initial selection of the set of functions. These functions were: naming; greetings and ritualized forms; attributes; comments; attention-seeking; requests for present objects, actions or permission; affirmation; denial; reference to past or future; requests for absent objects; requests for information; non-existence; and rejection of object or action. One can see in this list some decisions being made about what to group and what to ignore. For example, why separate absent and present objects? Why ignore the distinction between actions and objects as the goal of a request or a rejection? Presumably the list evolved through practical concerns of what was possible to do, as well as the theoretical interests of the various researchers. Dale demonstrated that given this list, observers could score the functions reliably (88% agreement) from videotapes of mother-child interaction. Dale worked with very young children while Wells (1973) and Dore, Gearhart, and Newman (1978) proposed more extensive schemes for the description of the functions found in conversations of preschool children. In both of these latter studies there is a hierarchical structure to the scheme, such that three broad conversational functions—convey content, regulate conversation, and express attitude—are subdivided into narrower classes such as requestives and assertives. Each of these in turn incorporates a group of particular conversational acts, for example, solicit action and solicit information, both of which are requestives. Although observers can be trained to use the classification schemes reliably, it is not clear that the proposed categories have psychological reality for the child, rather than reflecting only the consensus among adults in assigning intentions to another's actions. To steal a phrase from Menn (1976), we can only tell what the child *conveys* to those around him, not what he *intends*.

There have been a number of proposals about approaching the psychologically real level of functioning in the young child although few investigators seem to take the issue seriously. Data continue to be collected with observer reliability as the only criterion for the validity of the classification scheme. What demonstration would suffice to show that the child makes the same functional classifications of speech acts as does the adult observer? Let me propose the following:

a. The child should differentiate, vocally or gesturally, between circumstances that the adult observers score as different.
b. The child should act, vocally or gesturally, similarly in circumstances that the adult observers score as equivalent.

Let us deal first with the problems posed by requirement a. The least ambiguous case would involve a child using different utterances in different classes of circumstances, for example, "Here" whenever the child hands something to someone, and "Thank you" whenever the child receives something from someone. An adult observer would classify these circumstances as "giving" and "receiving," and the child's speech reflects the same broad distinction, neutral with respect to the object given or participant in the act.

Now imagine a more difficult case. A child uses a particular word, or more likely a vocable, such as "ta." He or she is observed to use it under two clearly different circumstances, when the mother places a toy into the child's outstretched hand, and when the child holds out a spoon to his or her mother, who takes it. Adult observers would probably reach a high level of agreement about the difference between these two acts. One is giving, one is receiving, there is no ambiguity. But does the word *ta* encompass two distinct functions? To argue that would require evidence that the child differentiates the two classes of situations in some aspect of his or her communicative behavior. For instance, is there a systematic difference in the intonation or timing of the word *ta* on the occasions of giving versus receiving? Then the child would be said to mark the difference in speech. Alternatively, does the child have different gestures associated with a vocally identical *ta*? Carter (1978) reported such evidence for her subject, David, who only later differentiated the vocables accompanying the gestures.

In current literature it is rare for researchers to seek this level of differentiation on the child's part; rather, they use rich interpretation of the context alone. If a concerted effort were made to seek variations in the vocal or gestural behavior in the different circumstances, it would need to be assessed against the variability that exists in that behavior when it is repeated in the *same* circumstances.

Turning to requirement b, let us again consider a clear case first. A child says "ta" under all circumstances of giving, and there are no systematic variations when the objects or actors change. The similarity across the different contexts is then reflected in the child's linguistic system.

Suppose, however, the child says "ta" only in circumstances where the mother is the agent of giving, not when other persons occupy that role. Suppose also that the child behaves appropriately toward other givers, but does not use the word in these circumstances. The situation is analogous to *underextension* in the semantic domain (Anglin, 1977); that is, the child's use of the word is more limited than the corresponding adult use, although it may be perfectly correct. Underextension is less evident to the observer than overextension (Anglin, 1977) but in the description of functional categories it is an essential observation. Underextension suggests that there are contextual limitations on the use of a term, and the term's pragmatic description should be appropriately narrow.

Consider an equally difficult case: the child does not have a single morpheme such as *ta* that is used in all acts of giving, but rather the giver's name is used (Mommy, Daddy, Granny, and so forth). Can one then ascribe to these utterances a broad functional category for acts of giving/receiving despite the variability in form? To be strict in applying the criteria, there should only be certain conditions under which this is done. The child must accompany each word with the same distinctive gesture or intonation pattern *not* seen in uses of the words in other circumstances.

It is valid to ask whether the child's general behavior can be used as a guide to the classification scheme. For instance, suppose the child behaves in a common manner in all acts of giving, even though his or her speech or gestures are highly variable. Could the child's behavior indicate the appropriate level of categorization for his or her language? This is a dangerous barrier to cross. As Schlesinger (1977) has pointed out for the field of semantics, we can make many conceptual distinctions for which our language has no use, such as the difference between alienable and inalienable possessives for an English speaker. In the domain of pragmatics, it becomes especially troublesome to distinguish the child's general knowledge of the world from his or her developing linguistic system, but if it is the latter that we are attempting to describe, then it is *within* that system that we should look for functional categories.

Up to this point, only distinctive gestures, vocables, or prosody have been discussed as evidence for functional categories, but another criterion proposed by several authors (Schlesinger, 1974; de Villiers & de Villiers, 1978) is the time of emergence of the expressions and their functions. Barrett (1980) explored this possibility in his data from two children studied longitudinally. His example is the one I have borrowed. A child is observed to use *ta* in acts of giving and receiving. Is this one word used for two functions, or is there only one function, perhaps a label for that general activity? Barrett argued that one way to tell is to look at the developmental time course of the expression. If it occurs in both types of situation from the start and disappears or gets replaced for both simultaneously, then one could argue that the child is treating the situations equivalently in his or her language. If *ta* is used initially only with giving, however, and with receiving only later, perhaps it is one form used for two distinct functions. Alternatively, it may disappear first for one class of situation, showing that by then at least, the child discriminated between the two linguistically.

Intuitively this is an appealing solution; however, Dale (1980) has some criticisms of it in practice. He points out that some functions might appear at the same point in time yet no one would want to group them together because they are clearly distinct. Surely the guideline of simultaneous emergence need only be invoked when other criteria-vocal and gestural differentiation are ambiguous, as in the *ta* illustration.

Second, Dale points out that differences in time of emergence of different functions for the same word might be due to sampling error rather than true changes in the child's knowledge. Barrett acknowledges that difficulty, and given the rapidity of early development the only reasonable solution is extensive sampling by investigators of their own children's speech. This time-honored method is still the source of a great deal of data on early child language.

Arguments about the assignment of functional descriptions to early child speech are not without implications. In particular, two of Halliday's most interesting claims about pragmatic development are that:

a. there is a partial order to the emergence of certain functions in child speech
b. at least some children may begin with a limited mapping between form and function that is later broadened.

It is important to explore the implications of the choice of a classification scheme for these claims.

ORDER OF EMERGENCE OF FUNCTIONS

Halliday proposed that the seven functions of early child speech might emerge in the order: instrumental, regulatory, interactional, personal, heuristic, imaginative, and informative. In his own study, he found only that the first four emerged before the rest, and the informative function was the last to develop. Barrett (1980) described data from two subjects that seemed to support this partial ordering. In his subjects also, instrumental, regulatory, interactional, and personal functions were observed from the outset, but imaginative and heuristic functions were observed later. Barrett recorded *no* instances of unambiguous use of the informative function in the 8-month period of study beginning when the children were approximately 1.5 years old. This seems surprising at first, but the informative function in Halliday's scheme is defined as the child's spontaneously providing information to a listener who does not know it. In the day-to-day interactions with a knowing adult, it is hard for such occasions to arise. The child could report on her internal state (e.g., "pee pee" for the need to go to the bathroom), but then the researchers would probably count the utterance as something else, such as regulatory (e.g., requests action from other people). In contrast to Halliday and Barrett, Dale (1980) found no consistent order of emergence in his study, but his design was cross-sectional rather than longitudinal. More critically, his functional categories were more narrowly differentiated and the sequence may only be true at a more general level of analysis (Barrett, 1980). Pea (1979) analyzed several functions of the negative, and claimed there is an order of emergence to these functions. In his longitudinal study of three subjects, the order is: rejection, then disappearance, then truth-functional negation (roughly: denial). I reviewed all the evidence for order of emergence for negative and interrogative functions in early child speech (de Villiers, in press), and concluded that the evidence at present is equivocal. Thus it is not clear whether these mixed findings reflect real individual differences among the children, or whether as Barrett suggests, the ordering is only revealed at one particular level of analysis. Unfortunately, the level that reveals the orderliness is probably the least well grounded methodologically (Francis, 1979).

FORM-FUNCTION MAPPING

The second important observation noted by Halliday was that some of his subject's earliest expressions were used for specific purposes, that is, served limited functions at first. For instance, Nigel's word *syrup* meant only "I want my syrup," and his word *cat* meant something like "Hello, cat." Even his first phrases had this quality of being reserved for particular functions. Halliday argued that only later did such expressions broaden in use to become free of particular functions and hence acquire true symbolic status. Perhaps only human communication has this property of diverse form-function mapping, with one form serving many functions, and one function served by a multitude of forms. Halliday suggested that some children may begin with a more limited form-function mapping, and it is important to test the generality of this claim.

There are several levels at which the claim might have validity: 1) individual words might enter the child's speech having restricted functions, and be relearned for alternative functions. In *Verbal Behavior* Skinner (1957) made this suggestion for the two classes of verbal behavior he called "mands"—roughly, demands and commands—and versus "tacts"—labeling and making reference. His example was a child learning the word *milk* as a mand, and only later as a tact. There are few reports of early word learning that have considered this possibility (but see Svachkin, 1973; Johnson, 1980) and it would be interesting to know whether this stage occurs generally or only in some individuals, for some words but not others, or only if the child learns words at an early cognitive stage, for example. No research has focused on the possibility that the verbal input to the child contains examples of limited form-function mapping for individual words. 2) Some forms of expression may be preferentially or exclusively used for certain functions. For instance, de Villiers and de Villiers (1979) report work on negative forms in three subjects, all of whom showed preferences for using different kinds of expressions for denial versus rejection negatives. The likelihood exists, therefore, that more complex forms will be acquired to serve particular functions, and only later become flexible in use. At this level there has been some work on the nature of the input (see Shatz, 1979) but much more is needed. Exploring the question of form-function mapping requires attention to the issues discussed previously. In particular, the development of a suitable classification scheme for pragmatic functions, such that different individuals could be compared, and in particular the similarities or differences in the basis for classification between infant and adult speech could be specified.

SUMMARY

The field of pragmatics is rich in its potential for application to research on the handicapped child, focusing as it does on achievements within the first year or two of life that represent a culmination of social and sensorimotor developments. The approach recognizes that use of language begins in social interactions, and there are several interesting proposals about the way that use broadens, and how forms and function interact in early speech. Nevertheless the methodological problems are pervasive and until consensus is reached, meaningful comparisons across studies are very difficult to make. Undoubtedly a hierarchical scheme of classification such as that proposed by Dore et al. (1978) is a more useful approach than single-level schemes such as Halliday's, because hierarchical schemes pay attention to different levels of inclusiveness. The validity of even hierarchical schemes, however, depends crucially upon the basis for classification. If the scheme is meant to be a linguistic description, the basis for classification should be the child's linguistic behavior, rather than the context or nonlinguistic actions alone.

REFERENCES

Anglin, J. *Word, object and conceptual development*. New York: W. W. Norton & Company, 1977.

Barrett, M. Early pragmatic development. Paper presented to the British Psychological Society Developmental Section Annual Conference, Edinburgh, September, 1980.

Bates, E. *Language and context*. New York: Academic Press, 1976.

Bates, E., Bretherton, I., Beeghly-Smith, M., & McNew, S. Social bases of language development: a reassessment. In H. Reese & L. Lipsitt (Eds.), *Advances in child development and behavior* (Vol 16). New York: Academic Press, in press.

Bates, E., Camaioni, L., & Volterra, V. The acquisition of performatives prior to speech. *Merrill-Palmer Quarterly*, 1975, *21*, 205–226.

Bloom, L. *One word at a time: The use of single word utterances before syntax*. The Hague: Mouton, 1973.

Bowerman, M. Semantic factors in the acquisition of rules for word use and sentence construction. In D. Morehead & A. Morehead (Eds.), *Directions in normal and deficient child language*. Baltimore: University Park Press, 1976.

Bruner, J. From communication to language—A psychological perspective. *Cognition*, 1975, *3*, 255–287.

Bühler, K. *Sprachtheorie: die Darstellungsfuncktion der Sprache*. Jena: Gustan Fischer. 1934.

Carter, A. The development of systematic vocalizations prior to words: a case study. In N. Waterson & C. Snow (Eds.), *Development of communication*. New York: John Wiley & Sons, 1978.

192   de Villiers

Carter, A. Prespeech meaning relations: An outline of one infant's sensori-motor morpheme development. In P. Fletcher & M. Garman (Eds.), *Language acquisition*. Cambridge: Cambridge University Press, 1979.

Crystal, D. The analysis of intonation in young children. In D. Minifie & L. Lloyd (Eds.), *Communicative and cognitive abilities: Early behavioral assessment*. Baltimore: University Park Press, 1978.

Dale, P. Is early pragmatic development measurable? *Journal of Child Language*, 1980, 7, 1–12.

Darwin, C. *The expression of the emotions in man and animals*. New York: The Philosophical Library, 1955 (Original in 1872).

de Villiers, J. Form and force interactions: The development of negatives and questions. In R. Schiefelbusch & J. Pickar (Eds.), *Communicative competence: Acquisition and intervention*. Baltimore: University Park Press, in press.

de Villiers, J., & de Villiers, P. Semantics and syntax in the first two years: The output of form and function and the form and function of the input. In F. Minifie & L. Lloyd, (Eds.), *Communicative and cognitive abilities: Early behavioral assessment*. Baltimore: University Park Press, 1978.

de Villiers, P., & de Villiers, J. Form and function in the development of sentence negation. *Papers and Reports on Child Language* (Stanford University), 1979, 17, 56–64.

Dore, J., Gearhart, M., & Newman, D. The structure of nursery-school conversation. In K. Nelson (Ed.), *Children's language* (Vol. 1). New York: Gardner Press, 1978.

Francis, H. What does the child mean? A critique of the 'functional' approach to language acquisition. *Journal of Child Language*, 1979, 6, 201–210.

Halliday, M. *Learning how to mean: Explorations in the development of language*. London: Edward Arnold, 1975.

Johnson, C. The ontogenesis of question words in children's language. Paper presented at the Fifth Annual Boston University conference on language acquisition, October, 1980.

Kessel, E. The mating activities of balloon flies. *Systematic Zoology*, 1955, 4, 97–104.

Menn, L. Pattern, control and contrast in beginning speech: a case study in the development of word form and word function. Doctoral thesis, University of Illinois at Urbana-Champaign, 1976.

Nelson, K. Early speech in its communicative context. In F. Minifie & L. Lloyd (Eds.), *Communicative and cognitive abilities—Early behavioral assessment*. Baltimore: University Park Press, 1978.

Pea, R. The development of negation in early child language. In D. Olson (Ed.), *The social foundations of language and thought: Essays in honor of Jerome S. Bruner*. New York: W. W. Norton & Company: New York, 1979.

Schlesinger, I. Relational concepts underlying language. In R. Schiefelbusch & L. Lloyd (Eds.), *Language perspectives: Acquisition, retardation and intervention*. Baltimore, MD: University Park Press, 1974.

Schlesinger, I. The role of cognitive development and linguistic input in language acquisition. *Journal of Child Language*, 1977, 4, 153–169.

Shatz, M. How to do things by asking: form-function pairings in mother's questions and their relation to children's responses. *Child Development*, 1979, 50, 1093–1099.

Skinner, B. *Verbal behavior*. New York: Appleton-Century-Crofts, 1957.

Smith, W. *The behavior of communicating*. Cambridge: Harvard University Press, 1977.

Sugarman, S. Some organizational aspects of pre-verbal communication. In I. Markova (Ed.), *Social context of language*. New York: John Wiley & Sons, 1978.

Svachkin, N. The development of phonemic speech perception in early childhood. In C. Ferguson & D. Slobin (Eds.), *Studies of child language development*. New York: Holt, Rinehart & Winston, 1973.

Wells, G. *Coding manual for the descriptions of child speech*. University of Bristol School of Education, 1973.

Wolff, P. The natural history of crying and other vocalizations in early infancy. In B. Foss (Ed.), *Determinants of infant behavior* (Vol. 4). London-Methuen, 1969.

Chapter 12

THE EMERGENCE OF SELF-PRODUCED LOCOMOTION: Its Importance for Psychological Development in Infancy

Joseph J. Campos, Marilyn J. Svejda, Rosemary G. Campos, and Bennett Bertenthal

The central thesis of this chapter is that the emergence of self-produced locomotion has major consequences for the infant's cognitive, emotional, and social development, and that many of these consequences may be intimately related to changes in spatial understanding that occur when the child begins to move about independently. Recent studies from our laboratory and those of others are providing consistent evidence that self-produced movement has a fundamental role in the onset of the child's wariness of heights, in the extraction of the invariance of a form from fluctuating displays, and possibly even in the child's growing ability to use environmental landmarks to understand the relationship between two or more environmental objects or events. This chapter suggests a number of studies that need to be carried out in order to elucidate the generality of the effects of self-produced movement, and to specify some of the mechanisms by which locomotion may produce its effects. The chapter concludes with a description of some potentially adverse consequences of locomotor impediment for the psychological development of the infant and toddler.

WHY STUDY SELF-PRODUCED MOVEMENT IN THE HUMAN INFANT?

There is a puzzling neglect in our recent conceptualization of infant behavior. Although there is a wealth of evidence from studies of the perceptuo-motor development of infant animals demonstrating that

This chapter describes research supported by NIMH grant NIMH-23556 to the senior author. Ms. Campos and Ms. Svejda were supported by NIH Nursing Research Fellowships number 5F31NV0538402 and 2F31NU0505904, respectively.

self-produced movement is critically important for sensorimotor development, the implications of this research for understanding the psychological development of human infants has been ignored. To date,
there has been no systematic experimental work or naturalistic observation of intact or motorically impaired human infants designed to
confirm or disconfirm the applicability of the findings obtained with
infant animals to the development of the baby's perceptual and cognitive world.

The neglect of the study of self-produced movement with human
infants is not due to any inconsistency or methodological inadequacy
that renders the conclusions of the animal studies suspect. The animal
work has been strikingly consistent in demonstrating that self-produced
movement is somehow necessary for normal sensorimotor behavior, and has used some of the most ingenious experimental designs
in the history of experimental psychology. Probably the strongest evidence for the role of self-produced locomotion comes from a series
of studies of kittens and monkeys carried out by Held, Hein, and their
collaborators at the Massachusetts Institute of Technology using an
apparatus called the "kitten carousel" (Held & Hein, 1963; Hein, 1972;
Hein, Held, & Gower, 1970). These investigators equated as closely
as possible the type of visual experience that two kitten littermates
have, and systematically manipulated self-produced movement in one
kitten but not the other. This was accomplished by placing the passively-moved kitten in a gondola that is attached by means of a complex
mechanical linkage to the actively-moving kitten. Both kittens then
move about inside the confines of a vertically-striped drum. The studies
with the kitten carousel have generated clear and consistent findings:
kittens that move about actively in the carousel show normal sensorimotor behavior. They avoid the deep side of a visual cliff, they place
their paws correctly in preparation for contact with a solid surface to
which they are being lowered, and they blink in anticipation of contact
with an approaching object. By contrast, the passively-moved kittens
show none of these behaviors (Held & Hein, 1963).

In order to rule out the possibility that the results of the kitten
carousel investigations were attributable to motoric retardation in the
passive kitten, possibly resulting from their motoric restraint in the
gondola, Hein et al. (1970) performed a follow-up study using each
animal as its own control. Using dark-reared kittens, the investigators
alternately covered one eye, placed the animal in the carousel and
allowed it to move about actively, or covered the other eye and allowed
the kitten to move about passively. Hein et al. reported that when
tested with the "active" eye, the kittens avoided the visual cliff, placed
appropriately, and blinked. When tested with the "passive eye," the

kittens did none of these. The effects of the self-produced movement thus seemed to be specific to the eye that was able to note the visual consequences of the self-produced movement.

These classic investigations have led to other important studies designed to demonstrate the significance of self-produced movement for reaching and for movement in space. If a kitten or a monkey is deprived of the opportunity to note visually the consequences of self-produced movement of its paws, it will be deficient in what Held and Bauer (1967) called visually-directed reaching; that is, although the approach of a horizontal surface will trigger an extension of the fore-limbs in animals even without visual experience, the extension will not be voluntarily guided to the solid part of a surface. For instance, if the surface is slotted, the animal deprived of the opportunity to note the consequences of its movements will just as likely stretch its paws toward the empty part of the slotted surface as toward the solid part. These findings are obtained even though during the reaching test both the slotted surface and the forelimbs are in the same visual field.

Most recently, Hein investigated the importance of eye move-ments for visuo-motor development in the kitten (Hein et al., 1979). Kittens whose eyes were surgically immobilized before exposure to light did not acquire the ability to visually direct their behavior toward a target, nor did they succeed in avoiding obstacles as they moved about. On the other hand, animals of the same age whose eyes were immobilized after light rearing showed none of these deficiencies. Hein et al. thus concluded that self-produced eye movements were of critical importance for the establishment (although perhaps not for the main-tenance) of a representation of visual space.

Why should self-produced movement, whether of the eyes, the limbs, or the whole body, be so important for the development of spatial sensorimotor behavior such as that shown by kittens on the visual cliff? One important reason seems to be the much greater power of self-produced movements to provide information that differentiates movements of the *self* from movements of the *world*. For instance, an observer who notices that the entire visual field has moved across the retina cannot tell for certain whether the movement resulted from the displacement of the entire visual world, or from the movement of his body in a direction opposite to that of the retinal image. There is good evidence that passive movement is not as effective as motor commands from the brain to the peripheral musculature as a source of information about whether the body moved or not. To demonstrate this point, try the following: close one eye and press against the partly closed lid of the open eye with your finger. You will note that the *world* will seem to have moved, rather than your eye, despite your obvious awareness that it was your finger that displaced the eye. On the other hand, if you voluntarily command your eye to move in exactly the same way as when you passively moved it, you clearly perceive the world to remain stationary and the eye to have moved.

An even more impressive demonstration of the importance of motor commands for determining what has moved and what has not comes from studies of subjects whose eye muscles have been paralyzed, and hence are not responsive to motor commands from the brain. When those subjects voluntarily direct their eyes to move to the right, they perceive the entire world to move to the right. In other words, the combination of a stationary retinal image, together with a command to the eyes to move right, is resolved perceptually as a movement of the world in the same direction and to the same degree as the command to the eyes. Self-produced, voluntary activity, thus seems to be critical for understanding the position of the world relative to one's own body. In the absence of experience with self-produced movement, then, the kittens and monkeys had trouble placing their bodies and physical objects within the same representation of space.

There is a second reason why self-produced movement is important for the development of an understanding of spatial relationships. Such movement may be important for calibration of distances between one's own body and outside objects. Controversy has occurred over whether the human infant can perceive depth innately, or whether experience is necessary for the perception of the third dimension. In recent years, however, an important conceptual clarification has been emphasized by several theorists (e.g., Gogel, 1977; Kaufman, 1979; Bower, 1974), who point out that there is a major distinction between relative distance perception (i.e., the realization that one object is in front of, or behind another object) and absolute distance perception (the ability to gauge precisely how much distance separates one object from another, or an object from oneself). We are persuaded that even if infants were to possess excellent relative distance perception provided by innate mechanisms, they may require experience in reaching or locomoting to objects in order to have a better appreciation of the absolute distance of an object from the body (Kaufman, 1979).

In order to illustrate this point, consider a few of the variables that specify depth and see how the distinction between relative and absolute distance perception applies. First, some of the variables that specify depth to a perceiver only specify the *ordinal* position of objects in space. Interposition, for instance, can only tell the perceiver that one object is in front of another, but alone cannot tell either by how much the occluding object is in front of another, nor how far away either object is from the perceiver. Other variables, such as texture gradients or linear perspective, can specify the *relative distances* of objects from one another (e.g., by taking into account in perception the number and spacing of texture elements between objects). Texture gradients, however, cannot tell the perceiver how far, in absolute terms, an object is from the perceiver unless the perceiver knows the scale of the texture—that is, how large or small the texture grains are initially. Thus, if one knows that the texture elements are 3 inches in diameter, an object that is 10 elements away from us must be 30 inches away. Without knowledge of the size of the element, however, absolute distance cannot be judged with exactness.

A few depth specifiers can theoretically provide the perceiver with information about the *absolute distance* of an object from one's own body, but the processing of this information makes enormously complex task demands on the infant's information processing abilities. One of the depth specifiers that can potentially provide absolute distance information is binocular convergence, which refers to the angle made by the intersection of imaginary lines projecting from the fovea of each eye when focusing on an object. The angle of convergence varies inversely with the physical distance of an object from the body. So, for instance, if an object is very close, the convergence angle is great. If it is far away, the convergence angle is quite small. Note that changes in convergence angle per se clearly give relative distance information. For convergence to provide the absolute distance of an object from the body, however, at least three assumptions need to be met. First, the brain must know the distance between the two eyes. It must also be aware of the convergence angle of the eyes. Third, it must possess a pre-wired "trigonometric" program to reckon distance between eyes and object given the other two values.

Motion parallax is another depth specifier that can provide the brain with information about both the relative and absolute distances of objects. Motion parallax refers to the tendency for objects to seem to move more slowly the farther away they are if one moves one's head while the eyes are fixating on the horizon. The specification of relative distance is straightforward: the slower the object moves, the farther it must be from oneself. But how far? To determine this, the brain must know exactly how far and how fast the head moved. This can be specified proprioceptively by the brain's taking into account the amount of vestibular or kinesthetic activity. It can also be specified visually by noting the rate of movement of the *nose*. As J. J. Gibson (1979) has pointed out, the nose can provide purely visual information about how far and how fast the head moved by virtue of its constant position in the periphery of the visual field of each eye. Accordingly, the nose can provide an "absolute maximum" of apparent movement of objects across the retina. By comparing the relative rates of speed of an object to the apparent rate of movement of the nose, the brain theoretically can compute absolute distance of an object from the body.

The purpose of this analysis has been to demonstrate how much more complex the processing of absolute distance information is for the young infant than is the processing of ordinal or relative distance information. Because of these complexities we find it difficult to believe that the human infant is pre-wired to perceive absolute distances. Bower (1974) pointed out that the infant's interocular distance, which is a crucial parameter for the binocular estimation of absolute distance, steadily changes with growth. So, even if interocular distance were to be specified at birth, it would lead to increasing errors in estimation of absolute distance as the child grows older unless there is some mechanism for recalibration. It is difficult to conceive of avenues of information available to the infant about interocular distance that would allow the child to "update" the information. Consequently, something else may be needed besides binocular convergence for the child to perceive absolute distance in infancy. It is our thesis that experience with locomotion may be one essential factor.

A different problem besets the use of motion parallax to determine absolute distances. Although Gibson's analysis about the position of the nose as a constant in the visual field is correct, there is no assurance that the infant notices its constant presence, or that the infant can take into account the fact that the movement of the nose is generally op-posite in direction to the relative motion of environmental objects. If either or both of these assumptions fail, as seems likely to us, then motion parallax can provide only relative distance information. Some-thing else is required to provide the organism with the ability to estimate absolute distances. Again, self-produced movement seems to be a plau-sible mediator of absolute distance perception.

The precise mechanism by which self-produced locomotion can calibrate distance of an object from the body has been suggested by Kaufman (1979). According to his analysis, self-produced movements produce changes in the visual angle of an object in the environment. The greater the movement, the greater the change in the visual angle. If one knows how much one moves, the visual system can estimate the distance between the self and the object by noting the change in the visual angle produced by the movement.

In summary then, both the empirical research on the manipulation of self-produced locomotion in the kitten and the theoretical analyses of how absolute distance perception is attained suggest the importance of exploring the relationship between self-produced locomotion and the development of sensorimotor behavior in the human infant.

IS SELF-PRODUCED LOCOMOTION RELATED TO
VISUAL CLIFF PERFORMANCE IN HUMAN INFANTS?

There has been a widespread belief that human infants are innately afraid of heights, even though such a conclusion is not consistent with the kitten carousel research cited above. Two arguments are invariably offered in support of the innateness of fear of heights. First, height is a "natural clue" to danger (Bowlby, 1973; Ainsworth et al., 1978); the avoidance of heights from the earliest opportunity thus has potential biological adaptive value. Second, an impressive body of evidence has suggested that avoidance of heights is evident as soon as an infant animal is able to locomote (Walk & Gibson, 1961; Walk, 1966). Extrapolating from these data, many theorists have concluded that human infants too are innately afraid of heights.

Fear of heights is not innate in human infants, however, as Scarr and Salapatek pointed out in 1970. Indeed, infants do not show much avoidance of heights for a brief period even *after* they have begun to move about on their own. Moreover, studies that contrast the visual cliff performance of human infants of the same age have consistently revealed that it is the locomoting infants who show wariness of heights, and prelocomotor ones generally do not. Finally, there is experimental evidence to indicate that "artificial" self-produced locomotor activity can induce or facilitate the emergence of wariness even in infants who are otherwise not locomotor.

Studies that have tested prelocomotor infants on the visual cliff have consistently failed to find any evidence of fearfulness. For instance, Scarr and Salapatek (1970) placed prelocomotor infants on a "crawligator" and dragged the infants across the deep side, but observed no behavioral indication that the infants were afraid of the deep side. A different testing procedure was used in our laboratory and led to similar conclusions. We placed prelocomotor infants directly atop the deep or the shallow side of the visual cliff and measured the infant's heart rate responses. We expected heart rate to accelerate if the infant were wary, to decelerate if the infant were attentive but nonfearful, and not to change if the infant was disinterested in the stimulus (Campos, 1976). The direct placement procedure does not require locomotor skills on the part of the infant and hence allows one to test infants as young as neonates. Several studies from our lab have consistently shown that infants *decelerate* on the deep side of the cliff between 2 and 5 months of age, and show no significant cardiac response on the shallow side (Campos, Langer, & Krowitz, 1970; Campos & Langer, 1971; Campos, 1976). The infants are thus discriminating the two sides of the cliff, but not because they are afraid of the deep side. With this procedure, heart rate responses indicative of fear were first evident in a study comparing the direct placement reactions of 5- and 9-month-olds (Schwartz, Campos, & Baisel, 1973). Five-month-olds showed decelerative responses, as had younger infants, but 9-month-olds showed consistent cardiac accelerations. These studies thus suggested that the wariness of heights emerges between 5 and 9 months of age.

A second indication that infants are not innately wary of heights comes from maternal reports. Mothers consistently have told us that there is a period after the onset of locomotion when their babies seem unconcerned about the consequences of falling. They note that their infants would easily go over a changing table, bed, sofa, or other high place if the mother did not prevent an actual fall. At later ages, they report, avoidance of heights is well established and falls occur primarily because of clumsiness by the infants.

This observation by mothers has been confirmed with studies of infants on the visual cliff (Campos et al., 1978). These studies have used the standard locomotor crossing method initially used by Walk and Gibson (1961)—the method that has been widely but erroneously cited as proving that human infants are afraid to cross the cliff to their mothers as soon as they can locomote. We asked mothers to notify us when their infants had begun to move about on their own, by whatever means, and to bring them into our laboratory for longitudinal testing on the visual cliff. Subjects' ages when first brought to the lab ranged from 6.3 to 8.3 months. The mother and infant continued to come to the laboratory every 10 to 14 days until the infant showed evidence of avoiding the deep side of the cliff. We obtained striking confirmation of the maternal reports of the existence of a brief period following locomotion onset when the infant is minimally afraid of heights, a period that ends with the emergence of reliable wariness of heights. All 15 infants in this study crossed to the mother over the deep side of the cliff on at least one of the first two testing occasions. Within a month on the average, however, all the infants were showing clear-cut hesitation to cross the deep side. Six of the infants flatly refused to cross at all, despite their previous experience with the solidity of the surface covering the deep side of the cliff table. The remaining nine infants crossed to the mother with a curious "detour" behavior on the deep side. These infants no longer crossed on a beeline or straight diagonal to the mother as they had before. Rather, they traced an "L"-shaped path, moving as closely as possible to the mother on the shallow side and then either "hitching" along the cliff table wall to the mother or else venturing onto the glass as little as possible.

In addition to confirming the emergence of wariness, this study also hinted that the amount of self-produced locomotor experience the infants had on their first test in the lab may have accounted for some of the variance we saw in infants' crossing behavior on the very first testing opportunity. Subjects who had the briefest experience crawling by maternal report (less than 7 days) had the least difference in latency to reach the mother over the deep and the shallow sides. Subjects of the same age, but who had more locomotor experience before they were initially tested in the laboratory (about 21 days), had more substantial differences, with crossing to the mother over the shallow side being some 20 seconds quicker than over the deep.

In a longitudinal study of this sort, it is possible that the development of wariness of heights is the result of age (and possibly maturation) rather than experience locomoting. Consequently, we engaged in a study in which age was held constant (at 7.3 months), but locomotor experience differed among infants. So we tested 92 infants, half locomoting, half not yet moving about on their own, with a variant of the direct placement procedure. We call it the "descent" paradigm, because heart rate reactions are assessed *before* the infant touches the glass surface of the cliff, that is, during the descent period. One of us had noted that lowering an infant toward the cliff table was often associated with a marked tensing of the infant's muscles, though only as he was being lowered. Moreover, the tensing was evident only on deep trials, not on shallow ones. Because muscle tension is closely associated with heart rate accelerations, we decided to measure heart rate as the infant was lowered to the deep and shallow sides, in order to test whether heart rate changes were a function of locomotor experience or not. Moreover, since heart rate changes are measured *before* any overt locomotor activity took place, the descent paradigm controls for the possibility that heart rate changes are merely secondary to actually moving around.[1]

The results of this study again supported the importance of self-produced locomotion in accounting for the wariness of heights. The cardiac response of the prelocomotor infants during the 3-second descent period and the first second of contact with the cliff table was minimal and nonsignificant for both deep and shallow descent trials, whereas the cardiac responses of the locomoting infants of the same age showed marked and highly significant accelerations, but, as expected, *only* on the deep side (Svejda & Schmid, 1979).

The most recent study of this series of investigations of the emergence of wariness of heights provides the most direct evidence for the importance of self-produced locomotion as a determinant of negative

---

[1] It is interesting to note that Richards and Rader (1981a) recently compared reactions of the same infants in the descent and the locomotor crossing paradigms and reported that infants who show cardiac acceleration on descent as we define it show avoidance of crossing the deep side. Those who do not accelerate do not tend to avoid crossing to the mother.

reactions of human infants to heights. Age-held-constant studies such as that by Svejda and Schmid (1979) do not rule out the possibility that a common maturational factor accounts for *both* the emergence of wariness to the deep side, *and* the earlier manifestation of locomotion. Only a study that experimentally manipulates locomotor experience allows one to infer that self-produced locomotion is a determinant, rather than a correlate, of the emergence of wariness.

We engaged in such an experimental study by providing walkers to infants at 5.5 months of age, and subsequently tested the infants when they had acquired 40 hours of forward motion walker experience (Campos et al., 1981). Control subjects had no walker experience of any sort, and were matched for age and sex. Some of the infants given walkers began to crawl spontaneously just before being brought to the laboratory for testing. The data from these infants were dealt with separately from prelocomotor infants with walker experience, and we thus had to obtain another group of control infants matched not only for age and sex, but also for duration of spontaneous locomotor experience. This resulted in obtaining data on four groups of infants:

1. Prelocomotor walkers (Experimental subjects who at testing could not crawl), $N = 18$
2. Control prelocomotors, $N = 18$
3. Locomotor walkers (Experimental subjects who had less than one week of spontaneous self-produced locomotion), $N = 16$
4. Control locomotors, $N = 16$

Two trials were administered on the deep side while the mother watched from an adjacent room (an important methodological feature because considerable evidence suggests that the mother's presence can cancel acceleratory heart rate reactions, Campos et al., 1975). No shallow trials were attempted in this study because heart rate on the shallow side has been unremarkable in previous studies, and because the more trials administered to potentially fussy infants, the more likelihood of subject attrition. Such attrition was particularly to be avoided in this study because of the investment of training time for experimental subjects.

The results of this study are presented in Figure 1, which clearly documents the separate effects of experimentally produced (i.e., "walker") locomotor experience, and of spontaneously achieved locomotor experience. A planned comparison (Kirk, 1968) that contrasted the heart rate responses of all walker infants with those of all control infants was highly significant ($t = 3.23$, $p < 0.008$). A similar planned comparison of all spontaneously locomoting infants with all prelocomotor infants was also significant ($t = 2.99$, $p < 0.01$). More-

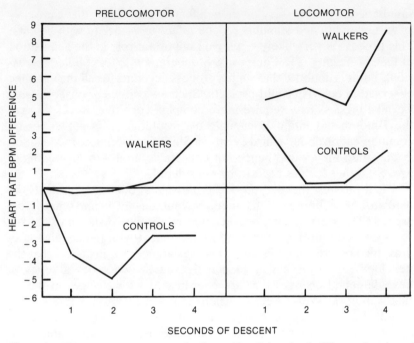

Figure 1. Heart rate responses to the deep side of the visual cliff as a function of whether the infant was locomotor or prelocomotor at time of testing, and whether the infant had had walker experience.

over, a comparison of prelocomotor walker infants with their prelocomotor controls supported the facilitating role of the walker experience because the experimental infants' cardiac responses were significantly more acceleratory than the controls' ($t = 2.04$, $p < 0.05$). Only the comparison of the two endogenously locomoting infants, the locomotor walkers and the locomotor controls, failed to reach significance, although there was a distinct trend for the heart rate reactions of the experimental babies to be more acceleratory.

The evidence seems clear and consistent: for human infants and kittens, the role of self-produced locomotion in the emergence of wariness of heights seems well established. What is unknown is the precise psychological process that is influenced by the self-produced locomotion and that mediates the aversive reactions of human and animal infants. For instance, is it the case that the onset of self-produced locomotion serves as a setting event for the infant to associate maternal emotional reactions with danger? We earlier cited the mothers' reports of a need to watch their infants carefully and to grab them quickly in order to prevent a fall. In reacting to "near falls," mothers might simultaneously utter a cry or show a fearful expression that can serve as an unconditioned stimulus for the infant to associate with heights. This process is very likely to play an important role in the acquisition of fear of heights (see Campos & Stenberg, 1981, for a fuller discussion), but it is doubtful that such a process accounts for all the variance observed in our visual cliff projects. Such a vicarious or observational learning process may require more complex cognitive processes than the 7-month old infant is capable of, insofar as it is a two-person communication about a third event—a Stage 5 sensorimotor acquisition in Piagetian theory and hence not expectable until 9 to 11 months of age. So, other factors need to be considered.

Is it possible that self-produced movement does play a role as the mediator of calibration of distance, as Kaufman (1979) and others have argued? Does the infant's appreciation of absolute distance of objects from his body undergo a marked improvement with the acquisiton of crawling and creeping? Piaget (1954) has argued, for instance, that the development of the ability to perceive depth undergoes a series of developmental changes that are coordinated with changes in the infant's motoric skills. Before vision and prehension are intercoordinated, the infant sees everything in a flat plane, much as we see the sun, and moon. After vision and prehension are intercoordinated, near space depth perception is calibrated so that infants can perceive the distance to objects with great precision, but only if the objects are within reasonable reaching distance. Finally, after vision and locomotion are intercoordinated, far space becomes calibrated, so that the infant can perceive accurately the distances to objects even when they are beyond reach.

Piaget's theoretical notions may account for the behavior we observe on the visual cliff. All the infants we have tested have well-developed skills in reaching, even if they are not locomoting on their own. Accordingly, we have observed that the infants in the cited descent paradigm studies show the placing response or extending the arms outward in preparation for direct contact with the cliff surface. The infants show this anticipatory reaction only on the shallow side, and the infants begin this placing reaction only when their hands are some 12 inches or so from the surface of the table (i.e., in near space). It may be that the onset of locomotion allows the infant to calibrate far space perception, resulting in the appreciation not only that the deep side of the cliff is beyond reach, but that it is a considerable distance away. Fear sufficient to be expressed in cardiac acceleration might then ensue.

Obtaining evidence relevant to the growth of the child's perceptual world in the third dimension is difficult. McKenzie, Tootle, and Day

(1980) recently reported, however, that 6-month-olds demonstrate substantial evidence for size constancy when the stimuli are presented at relatively near distances from the infant (0.9 meters). When the same stimuli are presented at greater distances (2 meters), however, the size constancy breaks down. Size constancy requires the perceiver to process information about the absolute distance of an object from his or her own body, or to know from prior experience the actual size of an object. The latter skill was ruled out in the McKenzie et al. study by the use of novel stimuli. Hence, it seems worth considering the possibility that 6-month-old infants possess absolute depth estimation characteristics, but only for distances relatively near the body.

Regardless of what mechanism is finally isolated as the major mediator of the effects of self-produced movement on the visual cliff behavior, there is now ample evidence that the psychological changes associated with the achievement of self-produced locomotion are not limited to the visual cliff. In a recent study, Campos, Bertenthal, and Benson (1980) investigated the relationship between locomotor ability and the ability to extract a constant form from a fluctuating display. We used a paradigm first developed by Ruff (1978). She presented 6- and 9-month old infants with a series of six familiarization trials in which infants saw two exemplars of the same configuration on each trial. Across the familiarization trials, the infants kept seeing the same configuration, but the configuration was confounded with three irrelevant dimensions—size, color, and orientation. Thus, on Trial 1, the infant might have seen two small, yellow, upright, cross-like forms. On the next trial, the forms may have been large, green, and inverted, but still cross-like. Trials 7 and 8 were test trials. The question was whether infants on test trials would look longer at a *new form* (the elements of the cross now arranged in a different configuration), or to a new instance of a familiar form (the cross). As on each familiarization trial, the infants saw both the novel and the familiarized form presented in a novel size, color, and orientation. Ruff reported that 9-month-olds consistently looked longer at the novel form in preference to the novel instance of the familiarized form, but 6-month-olds did not. From these findings, she concluded that 9-month-olds possess the capacity to extract form invariance, a skill that must be critical for both form perception and concept formation. Ruff, however, did not speculate on what might account for this startling developmental shift. We decided to test whether the onset of self-produced locomotion, which generally occurs between 6 and 9 months of age, might be playing a significant role.

We speculated that one significant consequence of moving about voluntarily in space is that the infant must notice major changes in the physical appearance of objects like tables, chairs, desks, etc. The infant can also notice, however, that the object itself does not change. We thought that self-produced movement therefore might teach the child general skills in extraction of invariances of forms from fluctuating displays. Although these skills are potentially available to the prelocomotor infant who can rotate objects in his or her hands and note the identity of the object within its variations, prelocomotor infants in point of fact do not seem to use these skills. When an object is placed in the infant's hand at 6 or 7 months, it typically is placed in the child's mouth. Although the child can also possess the capacity of noting that an object seems to change shape when the mother carries the infant about passively, it has been our impression that the infant who is passively carried is in a state of "visual idle"—staring blankly straight ahead and not focusing on single objects in the environment. We therefore thought it worth exploring the role of self-produced movement on extraction of form invariance.

We tested 30 prelocomotor and 30 locomotor infants with age held constant at 7.5 months. The locomotor infants had been moving approximately 6 weeks according to maternal reports. All infants were given as close to a replication of Ruff's (1978) procedure as possible. To maximize the likelihood of form extraction, we followed Ruff's recommendation of making the two exemplars of the form differ between themselves in the three irrelevant dimensions not only between trials, but within trials also. Thus, on Trial 1, the infant might have seen a cross-like object that was green, upright, and small together with a cross-like object that was red, inverted, and medium-sized. After six 30-second familiarization trials, there were, as in Ruff's study, two 10-second test trials. On the test trials there was a novel form paired with a novel instance of the familiarized form. Both forms were presented in a novel size, color, and orientation, which was the same for the two forms.

As predicted, the locomotor infants behaved like Ruff's 9-month-olds and the prelocomotor ones behaved like her 6-month-olds. There was much more looking ($\bar{x} = 6.3$ seconds) at the novel form than the familiar ($\bar{x} = 4.4$ seconds) one by the locomotor infants, while the prelocomotor ones looked virtually the same duration ($\bar{x} = 5.4$ seconds) at the two forms. Thus the acquisition of self-produced movement is associated with the development of form extraction abilities. Although it remains for experimental studies like the walker study to demonstrate whether self-produced locomotion determines the emergence of this skill, it seems likely that locomotor experience is playing a causal role in inducing such changes.

There are other interesting developmental shifts taking place between 6 and 9 months of age that are potentially related to the onset of crawling. Acredolo (1978; Acredolo & Evans, 1980) demonstrated that 6-month-olds do not use environmental landmarks to signify the position of an object in the environment. For instance, infants do not use a large star or blinking light display to specify where in a room a reinforcing stimulus will emerge. Rather, 6-month-olds use what Acredolo calls an "egocentric" frame of reference: Infants locate objects in relation to their own body. So, if the infant had found the reinforcer to his or her right on previous trials, he or she will look to the right even following a rotation of the body of 180° in space. Such egocentric responding occurs even though the presence of physical landmarks potentially specifies the position of the object to the child's left. By 9 months, this tendency has begun to be replaced by an "allocentric" frame of reference, in which the infant shows the ability to use landmarks to locate objects.

Bremner and Bryant (1977) reported similar findings, and speculate that the onset of self-produced locomotion may facilitate the shift from use of egocentric to allocentric frames of reference. So long as the infant is relatively stationary in space, as is the case before the onset of crawling, relating objects in the world to the body will be a reasonably accurate means of locating objects in space. Once the baby starts to move about, however, the shifting location of the body will lead to confusion over the physical location of desired objects, unless stationary environmental landmarks begin to be used by the child to "anchor" the relative positions of toys, furniture, kitchen, etc. We believe that the elegant descriptive research done so far on shifts in use of spatial codes should be extended to determine whether experimentally-induced locomotion or endogenously generated locomotion is associated with the onset of the shift in spatial coding.

The onset of crawling has effects that extend beyond the cognitive and perceptual sphere. Psychoanalysts (e.g., Fraiberg, 1969; Spitz, 1975), and ethologists (e.g., Ainsworth et al., 1978) have speculated that the onset of locomotion has major impact on the attachment relationship between infant and mother. The need to balance the child's newly developed exploratory capabilities with the need to ensure the child's safety creates new demands on the caregiver and the infant. The caregiver must become much more vigilant and more sensitive to the child, and the infant must develop means whereby he or she can explore, yet maintain proximity. We wonder whether the roots of a phenomenon which we call "social referencing" (Campos & Stenberg, 1981; Klinnert et al., 1982) are not found shortly after the onset of locomotion. Such referencing is defined as the search for emotional information from the face, voice, or gesture of the caregiver to help the child resolve uncertainties or disambiguate situations, and is clearly present by 12 months of age. Its developmental onset has not yet been traced.

SELF-PRODUCED LOCOMOTION:
IMPLICATIONS FOR THE HANDICAPPED

The important role of motor behavior as the basis for understanding, which was so strongly emphasized by Piaget (e.g., Piaget, 1960) has been challenged by some developmentalists. Kagan (1971; Kagan, Kearsley, & Zelazo, 1978), for example, has questioned whether actions on objects are always necessary for cognitive structures to develop. Moreover, gross attempts to relate variations in early motor development to later motoric proficiency as well as to subsequent cognitive levels have been largely unsuccessful (Kopp, 1979). For both theoretical and empirical reasons, then, recent psychology has discarded serious consideration of motoric development as a significant factor in psychological growth.

We have argued just the opposite, and proposed that the onset of self-produced movement is a skill with measurably important consequences for psychological development. There are at least two ways in which our position about the importance of motoric factors differs from previous ones, such as Gesell's (1929). First of all, we focus on specific motoric skills and look for consequences on rather discrete, but nevertheless important, psychological processes. We have focused on spatial perceptual and cognitive abilities as those most likely to be directly affected by the onset of self-produced locomotion. We also expect social consequences to be specific, and probably most related to the changes in caregiver-infant interaction resulting from the marked increase in vigilance and behavioral regulation that the caregiver needs to impose on the infant following the development of crawling. We are thus not surprised at the failure of the earlier attempts to link motoric activity to psychological development. Such attempts proceeded at too gross a level of analysis, and tried to draw correlations between the acquisition of motoric milestones and the development of cognitive skills with which those milestones may have nothing in common.

Furthermore, we have limited our argument to the role of self-produced locomotion for the *induction* of new psychological skills. We have not addressed other questions about developmental consequences of self-produced locomotion. For instance, is locomotion also important for *maintaining* skills that have already been achieved? Is self-produced locomotion a *facilitatory* influence, in the sense that it is sufficient but not necessary for psychological growth, or in the sense that it brings about at a slightly earlier age a process that would have developed anyway? Is self-produced locomotion *essential*, without which the infant will have permanent deficits? Are the effects of self-produced locomotion all-or-none? Or does more motoric experience lead to better information processing?

One group of children who can provide us with valuable information about the issues of induction, maintenance, and facilitation are children with temporary or permanent motoric handicaps. We would expect, from straightforward extrapolation of the studies cited in this chapter, that infants impeded from movement (e.g., because of orthopedic casting, or because of neurological problems like meningomyelocele) would show defects at least over the short term in 1) how the body is located relative to other objects in space, 2) how far an object is from his or her body, especially in far space, and 3) how the transformation of objects come about as a result of one's moving around them.

The motorically impeded child, then, can confirm whether self-produced locomotion truly *induces* these spatial cognitive skills. If the handicapped child shows the same developmental course for these skills as does a normal child, then either self-produced locomotion is not playing a role as an inducer, or the handicapped child is employing an alternative developmental pathway to achieve the same end. Moreover, if the role of self-produced movement is merely facilitatory, the motorically impeded child will show only a delay relative to the normal child. At an older age, the handicapped child would be expected to catch up to the level of spatial cognitive skills of the normal child. On the other hand, if the role of movement is necessary for the emergence of skills, then the handicapped child will show stagnant spatial development for the duration of his or her locomotor impediment.

The motorically handicapped infant can also provide us with important information regarding the precise relationship between the variables of self-produced movement and psychological processes. The studies discussed in this chapter, ranging from Held and Hein's kitten carousel work, through our visual cliff studies, to those on spatial cognition, have tested all-or-none questions by contrasting the presence and absence of self-produced locomotion. We have not determined, however, at what point further self-produced locomotor experience stops having an effect. We also do not know how variations in the timing and rate of motor development influence cognitive and social/emotional factors.[2]

Still another important issue concerns whether the efficiency of locomotion is an important variable for psychological growth. Is the experience of an infant who can move about by effortfully dragging himself or herself with elbows in "combat crawl" fashion the same as that of an infant who can use hands and knees? One way in which inefficient locomotion might inhibit development in the handicapped child is by the tremendous drain of energy and attention required for forward movement, as reflected in the child's appropriate use of exertion, space control, speed, as well as consistency of performance (Rosenbloom, 1971). The child with limited opportunities to practice locomoting may be devoting excessive energies to reach the goal, and thus may be less likely to attend to aspects of the environment that change in conjunction with movement. Rosenbloom refers to some clinical observations made by a colleague on a group of spina bifida children for whom it was noted that manipulative skills (of which they were fully capable) were depressed. These children were required to use their ostensibly normal hands for support with walking aids, or for maneuvering their wheelchairs, rather than in conventional manual exploration. The locomotor impediment thus prevented the child from devoting sufficient attention to developing manipulative skills within his or her capacities. Rosenbloom's observation leads us to wonder: does impeded locomotion similarly lead to less frequent rehearsal of perceptual and cognitive skills?

It is important to note that there are many ways in which defective motoric activity can influence psychological development besides those favored by Held and Hein, Piaget, and others. Abercrombie (1968) for instance, argued that limitations of an individual's capacity to exhibit active movement may retard perceptual development because the child may experience a conflict between attentiveness to different stimuli. For instance, a child may desire to grab an object to the left, but be unable to orient his or her eyes in the direction of what he or she wants to grasp, resulting in both motoric clumsiness and in poor perceptuo-motor feedback. Haskell, Barrett, and Taylor (1977)

---

[2] There is now evidence that locomotor experience beyond 30 days may not influence infants' visual cliff reaction either with the direct placement or the locomotor crossing paradigms (Richards & Rader, 1981a; 1981b). Taken in conjunction with our findings, this research suggests that locomotion may influence primarily the emergence of the wariness of heights. It also suggests that *when* a locomotor impediment takes place (i.e., before or after onset of self-produced locomotion) may make a great difference in the psychological makeup of the motorically handicapped child.

also suggested that cerebral palsied children may have problems with processing the abundance of perceptual information generated by inefficient movements.

If studies of handicapped infants confirm the importance of self-produced movement, then intervention strategies become readily apparent. The use of locomotor aids, rolling carts, and crawligators may enable the infant to experience an enriched environment by gaining access to objects. Although the impact of supplemental experiences might not be immediately observed, changes might become evident in a more rapid development of the infant's cognitive skills once locomotion is acquired. Note, for instance, in the walker study cited above that the effects of the walker on cardiac accelerations were clearest only in those infants who eventually acquired locomotion capacity on their own.

The social/emotional consequences of motoric impediment should not be ignored (Dècarie, 1969; Dècarie & O'Neill, 1973). Restriction of movement results in an inability of the handicapped child to profit from the exhilarating sense of exploration and self-control that characterizes the development of locomotion. In addition, an older handicapped infant can compare his or her own competence with that of normal children especially in something as visible as locomotion. The outcome of such a comparison must have depressing emotional consequences, and lead to a decrease in self-esteem. Furthermore, motoric impediment can increase dependency and decrease mastery motivation, resulting in a more passive individual and a greater difficulty in establishing the independence of the self from the caregiver (Mahler, Pine, & Bergman, 1975). Such a potential problem places important and difficult demands on the child's parents to structure the environment in such a way that the child can perform independent actions. Parents must be sensitive to those actions that are within the child's realm of possibilities and those that are not.

These brief considerations should suffice to point out the importance for both general psychology and for the clinical practitioner of engaging in studies relating motoric impediment to cognitive, perceptual, and socioemotional processes. This chapter has identified areas that are potentially fruitful for investigation with both normal and motorically handicapped children. Whether one accepts Piaget's strong theoretical position that action and not sensation is the basis of knowledge (Furth, 1968; Lamb & Campos, 1982), or whether one takes the more neutral position that action facilitates attention to environmental invariants, there is little doubt that self-produced movement is a powerful, yet neglected force in psychological growth.

REFERENCES

Abercrombie, M. Some notes on spatial disability: Movement, intelligence quotient, and attentiveness. *Developmental Medicine and Child Neurology*, 1968, *10*, 206–213.

Acredolo, L. The development of spatial orientation in infancy. *Developmental Psychology*, 1978, *14*, 224–234.

Acredolo, L., & Evans, D. Developmental changes in the effects of landmarks on infant spatial behavior. *Developmental Psychology*, 1980, *16*, 312–318.

Ainsworth, M., Blehar, M., Waters, E., & Wall, S. *Patterns of attachment*. Hillsdale, N.J.: Lawrence Erlbaum Associates, 1978.

Bowlby, J. *Attachment and loss*. (Vol. 2). *Separation*. New York: Basic Books, Inc., 1973.

Bower, T. *Development in infancy*. San Francisco: W. H. Freeman, Inc., 1974.

Bremner, J., & Bryant, P. Place versus response as the basis of spatial errors made by young infants. *Journal of Experimental Child Psychology*, 1977, *23*, 162–171.

Campos, J. Heart rate: A sensitive tool for the study of emotional development in the infant. In L. Lipsitt (Ed.), *Developmental psychobiology: The significance of infancy*. Hillsdale, N.J.: Lawrence Erlbaum Associates, 1976.

Campos, J., & Langer, A. The visual cliff: Discriminative cardiac orienting responses with retinal size held constant. *Psychophysiology*, 1971, *8*, 264–265. (Abstract)

Campos, J., & Stenberg, C. Perception, appraisal, and emotion: The onset of social referencing. In M. Lamb & L. Sherrod (Eds.), *Infant social cognition*. Hillsdale, N.J.: Lawrence Erlbaum Associates, 1981.

Campos, J., Langer, A., & Krowitz, A. Cardiac responses on the visual cliff in prelocomotor human infants. *Science*, 1970, *170*, 195–196.

Campos, J., Hiatt, S., Ramsay, D., Henderson, C., & Svejda, M. The emergence of fear on the visual cliff. In M. Lewis & L. Rosenblum (Eds.), *The development of affect*. New York: Plenum Press, 1978.

Campos, J., Emde, R., Gaensbauer, T., & Henderson, C. Cardiac and behavioral interrelationships in the reaction of infants to strangers. *Developmental Psychology*, 1975, *11*, 589–601.

Campos, J., Bertenthal, B., & Benson, N. Self-produced locomotion and the extraction of form invariance. Paper presented at the meetings of the International Conference on Infant Studies, New Haven, Conn. 1980.

Campos, J., Svejda, M., Bertenthal, B., Benson, N., & Schmid, D. Self-produced locomotion and wariness of heights: New evidence from training studies. Paper presented at the meetings of the Society for Research in Child Development, Boston, Massachusetts, 1981.

Décarie, T. A study of the mental and emotional development of the thalidomide child. In B. Foss (Ed.), *Determinants of infant behaviour*. (Vol. 4). London: Methuen & Co., Ltd., 1969.

Décarie, T., & O'Neill, M. Quelques aspects du développement cognitif d'enfants souffrant de malformations dues à la thalidomide. *Bulletin de Psychologie*, 1973/1974, *24*, 286–303.

Fraiberg, S. *The magic years*. New York: Schocken, 1966.

Furth, H. Piaget's theory of knowledge: The nature of representation and interiorization. *Psychological Review*, 1968, *75*, 143–154.

Gesell, A. *Infancy and human growth*. New York: MacMillan Publishing Company, 1929.

Gibson, J. *The ecological approach to visual perception*. Boston: Houghton Mifflin Company, 1979.

Gogel, W. The metric of visual space. In W. Epstein (Ed.), *Stability and constancy in visual perception*. New York: John Wiley & Sons, Inc., 1977.

Haskell, S., Barrett, E., & Taylor, H. *The education of motor and neurologically handicapped children*. London: Croom Helm, Co., 1977.

Hein, A. Acquiring components of visually guided behavior. In A. Pick (Ed.), *Minnesota symposia on child psychology* (Vol. 6). Minneapolis: University of Minnesota Press, 1972.

Hein, A., Held, R., & Gower, E. Development and segmentation of visually controlled movement by selective exposure during rearing. *Journal of Comparative and Physiological Psychology*, 1970, *73*, 181–187.

Hein, A., Vital-Durand, F., Salinger, W., & Diamond, R. Eye movements initiate visuo-motor development in the cat. *Science*, 1979, *204*, 1321–1322.

Held, R., & Bauer, J. Visually guided reaching in infant monkeys after restricted rearing. *Science*, 1967, *155*, 718–720.

Held, R., & Hein, A. Movement-produced stimulation in the development of visually-guided behavior. *Journal of Comparative and Physiological Psychology*, 1963, *56*, 872–876.

Kagan, J. *Change and continuity in infancy*. New York: John Wiley & Sons, Inc., 1971.

Kagan, J., Kearsley, R., & Zelazo, P. *Infancy*. Cambridge: Harvard University Press, 1978.

Kaufman, L. *Perception: The world transformed*. New York: Oxford University Press, 1979.

Kirk, R. *Experimental design: Procedures for the behavioral sciences*. Belmont, CA: Brooks/Cole Publishing Co., 1968.

Klinnert, M., Campos, J., Sorce, J., & Emde, R. Social referencing: An important appraisal process in human infancy. In R. Plutchik & H. Kellerman (Eds.), *The emotions*. New York: Academic Press, 1982.

Kopp, C. Perspectives on infant motor system development. In M. Bornstein & W. Kessen (Eds.), *Psychological development from infancy: Image to intention*. Hillsdale, N.J.: Lawrence Erlbaum Associates, 1979.

Lamb, M., & Campos, J. *Development in infancy*. New York: Random House, 1982.

Mahler, M., Pine, F., & Bergman, A. *The psychological birth of the human infant*. New York: Basic Books, 1975.

McKenzie, B., Tootle, H., & Day, R. Development of visual size constancy during the 1st year of human infancy. *Developmental Psychology*, 1980, *16*, 163–174.

Piaget, J. *The construction of reality in the child*. New York: Basic Books, 1954.

Piaget, J. *The psychology of intelligence*. Totowa, N.J.: Littlefield, Adams & Co., 1960.

Richards, J., & Rader, N. Affective, behavioral, and avoidance responses on the visual cliff: Effect of crawling, onset age, crawling experience, and testing age. Unpublished manuscript, University of California, Los Angeles, 1981 (a).

Richards, J., & Rader, N. Crawling-onset age predicts visual cliff avoidance in infants. *Journal of Experimental Psychology: Human Perception and Performance.* 1981 (b), *7*, 382–387.

Rosenbloom, L. The contribution of motor behaviour to child development. *Physiotherapy*, 1971, *57*, 159–162.

Ruff, H. Infants' recognition of the invariant forms of objects. *Child Development*, 1978, *49*, 293–306.

Scarr, S., & Salapatek, P. Patterns of fear development during infancy. *Merrill-Palmer Quarterly*, 1970, *16*, 53–90.

Schwartz, A., Campos, J., & Baisel, E. The visual cliff: Cardiac and behavioral correlates on the deep and shallow sides at five and nine months of age. *Journal of Experimental Child Psychology*, 1973, *15*, 86–99.

Spitz, R. *The first year of life.* New York: International Universities Press, 1975.

Svejda, M., & Schmid, D. The role of self-produced locomotion on the onset of fear of heights on the visual cliff. Paper presented at the meetings of the Society for Research in Child Development, San Francisco, 1979.

Walk, R. The development of depth perception in animals and human infants. *Monographs of the Society for Research in Child Development.* 1966, 31 (Whole No. 5).

Walk, R., & Gibson, E. A comparative and analytical study of visual depth perception. *Psychological Monographs*, 1961, 75 (15, Whole No. 519).

Chapter 13

SOCIAL INTERACTIONS OF HANDICAPPED INFANTS

Jeanette A. Walker

The application of developmental research to research and practice with the handicapped infant population may be approached from at least two different perspectives. First, one may define what is "normal" as a criterion against which to measure the handicapped infant, and assume that to bring the infant closer to this criterion will result in optimal progress for that infant. In this approach, theories of normal development are applied directly to practice with the handicapped. Alternatively, one may take a more indirect approach, using theory and research paradigms derived from work with normal infants for studying the development of the handicapped infant, with the goal of expanding, testing, and solidifying theory and possibly describing alternative processes of development. Such research is then used as a basis for assessment and intervention with the handicapped infant population.

The second approach may not offer the benefit of immediate direct application, yet it offers a more useful perspective for comprehensive and generalizable understanding of the development of the handicapped infant. Research derived from this more indirect approach can provide a base for early intervention that recognizes and capitalizes on the plasticity that the human infant displays across developmental systems, possibly encompassing different development patterns for handicapped infants than those which characterize the normal infant population. The purpose of this chapter is to illustrate the potential usefulness of this second and more indirect approach for describing social interactions between handicapped infants and their caregivers.

For the special education practitioner, interest in social interaction research with infants is likely to be stimulated by personal observations of social deviance or delay in populations of older handicapped children, for despite wide variations in handicapping conditions and in intellectual and motor capability, the social interactions of these toddlers often seem to the observer to have several things in common:

1. The amount of social interaction seems to be reduced, with contacts with adults being primarily of a caregiving or, if the child is in an intervention program, of a teaching nature
2. There may be little spontaneous or child-initiated social contact
3. Those interactions that do occur give the impression of being out of harmony and not truly of a socially interactive nature
4. The children may seem not to be aware of the reciprocal nature of social communication or of themselves as social partners
5. Interactions with caregivers may display unusual characteristics such as one-sided activity or extremes of activity and inactivity, accompanied by uncertainty on the part of the caregiver.

It might be expected that a handicapped child would affect the characteristics of any social interactive situation (e.g., Walker & Kershman, 1981). Certain assumptions may be made, however, that lead one to question whether poor later outcomes are inevitable, and if not, how they came about and whether they could have been prevented. For there are many handicapped toddlers whose social interactions are much healthier. What accounts for the difference?

A first assumption is that social retardation or deviance at age 2 or 3 is not a necessary correlate of being handicapped. There is a self-perpetuating aspect to delay. Handicaps tend to become cumulative, extending into areas beyond those directly affected by the handicapping condition, resulting in secondary overlays. Kearsley's (1979) notion of iatrogenic retardation may be applied to the concept of iatrogenic social retardation brought about over time through transactions between the organism and the environment. The development of social interaction patterns is affected both by the biological status of the infant and by learning and experience. The two continua of caretaking and reproductive casualty as described by Sameroff and Chandler (1975) take on a different significance with the handicapped infant because the possibility of caretaking casualty being seen both within the context of, and as contributing to the effects of, reproductive casualty. The perceptions that primary caregivers hold of the infant's capabilities, and the caregiver/infant interactions that are affected by these perceptions, may play a significant role in determining developmental outcomes across all areas.

A second assumption is that self-righting tendencies undoubtedly function in the damaged baby just as they do in other babies; there are, however, two ways to view these tendencies. First, the band of tolerance within which the handicapped infant is able to establish maximum homeostasis may be more narrow than that for the normal baby; there may be less spontaneous recovery, less incidental learning, and less self-initiated seeking of experience. In addition, however, the biological drive for homeostasis would seem to offer some promise for adaptation to differences in the social interactive system. If social communication is a basic human function, then both organisms, that is, the caregiver and the infant, might be expected to strive to overcome interactive differences through the use of alternative routes.

A final assumption is that the acquisition of developmental milestones by the infant necessarily changes the characteristics of the social interactions that are functionally appropriate for him or her at each point in time. The parent is changing, too, as are his or her expectations for the characteristics of social interaction with the infant. With the handicapped infant, passage of time is likely to mean new or recurring crises as the infant either does not change, or does not develop normal interactive patterns; the characteristics of interactions may therefore change or not change in unanticipated ways. What may be an adaptive mechanism for maximizing functional developmental progression at one period may not be adaptive for the next period.

The position adopted in this chapter assumes that although the handicapped infant presents definite impediments to the achievement of pleasurable and growth-supporting social interchanges, a great deal of variation is possible within these interchanges. There is much debate over the relationship of early experience to later development (Clarke & Clarke, 1976; Sameroff, 1979). In the case of the handicapped infant, however, early experience is of primary importance for maximizing the infant's developmental abilities. Because the primary caregiver controls the environment that is available to the handicapped infant, parent/infant social interaction as an avenue to this environment may have an impact not only on later social development but on development in other areas as well. Distinguishing the characteristics of interactions that are both functional and adaptive for the infant at each point in time, and those that are not, is therefore an investigative effort essential for providing a base for planning interventions that may attenuate the development of secondary and cumulative delay.

In addition to those more practical benefits, research into the social interactions of handicapped infants offers possibilities for addressing unique questions about the sequence and organization of development in general, and provides a challenge to theories of normal development. The presence of a handicap allows the exploration of the importance of different capabilities for social interaction and communication, and better definition of the roles of various systems, including biological, cognitive, perceptual, and social, in the development of communicative patterns. Through longitudinal description of a group known to have a greater probability of later maladaptive interaction patterns, it may be possible to determine the way in which these patterns develop.

THE NATURE OF SOCIAL INTERACTION IN INFANCY

Communication in the context of face-to-face interaction has been described by Duncan and Fiske (1977) as the establishment of a "dialogue" with certain characteristics that define it as an organized phenomenon. The dyadic interchange between two individuals offers enticing possibilities for attempting to define some of the regularities of this dialogue. Duncan and Fiske in their work with adults call these regularities the "rules" of social communication. In this sense, a communication rule is defined as any statement that describes the hypothesized relationship between two or more elements of the turn system, which reduces uncertainty as to how individual streams of behavior are combined into sequences of interrelated behaviors. Collis (1978) used similar terminology in describing regularities in parent/infant interaction.

A major goal of the social interactive exchange between parent and infant is to establish and maintain mutual involvement and to achieve affective synchrony through the regulation of content, timing, and intensity (Brazelton et al., 1975). The concept of synchrony implies that the acts of each individual are related in a nonrandom and mutually pleasurable form in both timing and content to those of the other individual, and that the cyclic phasing of attention and withdrawal is matched across the two members of the dyad. Asynchrony thus implies a mismatch in phasing, with little or no predictable relationship between the behaviors of the two individuals, or with contingent relationships that are not reinforcing across members of the dyad.

The search for patterns or rules of interaction in infancy has been based primarily on behavioral observation of naturally occurring communicative acts between parent and infant, using varying levels of observation and analysis (Parke, 1979). Characteristics of social interactions between parents and normal infants have been described in a variety of ways, two of which seem particularly useful for examining interaction between handicapped infants and their parents. These are 1) the patterns formed by the interrelationships of behaviors of the two members of the dyad, and 2) other related characteristics such as the roles played by the two individuals.

Patterns of Interaction

Reciprocity seems to be one of the major characteristics of a synchronous interaction. Gottman (1979) defined this construct in terms of each individual's actions being predictable from the actions of the other.

Each individual's behavior thus changes the probability of subsequent behaviors in the other, implying sequences of mutual attention and interactive turntaking.

During infancy, reciprocity can be usefully defined as "pseudo-reciprocity," inducing the pseudo-dialogue described by Schaffer (1977), and has been studied in terms of regularities in both timing and content across different ages in infancy. For example, Stern et al. (1975) have described the co-active vocalizing that accounts for much of the social interchange between 3–4 month old infants and their mothers, while Schaffer, Collis, and Parsons (1977) found few instances of overlaps in vocalizing between 1–2 year olds and their mothers. As verbalization assumes a more important role in information giving and receiving, overlaps would increasingly interfere, and patterns of turn-taking would change to accommodate this role, resulting in more reciprocal interactions.

Repetition is a second kind of pattern that has been described in mother/infant interactions. Stern et al. (1977) found repetition of both rhythm and content in the actions of mothers with their 13–14 week-old-infants. Thirty to forty percent of all vocal and kinesic phrases used by these mothers were repetitions of their own previous phrases. In our own research, we have observed much repetition of patterns and content, especially in social rituals such as "Oh, you're a pretty girl, you're a pretty girl." A closely related concept that has been studied is the *cyclicity* of interactions; interactions seem to occur in rhythmical repetition of *sequences* of behavior or states both within and across individuals. Synchronous interactions found between mothers and infants are characterized by the meshing of repeating *intra*-individual cycles that are not only highly predictable for each individual across the time span of the interaction but are predictable for the dyad as a unit as well. Brazelton et al. (1975) described a homeostatic curve in the cycling of attention and affect; in this curve, the typical sequence for the dyad is initiation, mutual orientation, greeting, play dialogue, and disengagement, followed again by the same sequence to form a cycle of "build-up and withdrawal." Furthermore, this cycling of intensity tends to blend together with cycles of repeating sequences of content.

Many patterns of infant/caregiver interaction seem to be highly predictable, including within-individual sequences of behavior, cross-individual contingent behaviors, and the length of chains of content and affect. It is this predictability that allows the meshing of behavioral streams into an interaction. Each member of the dyad can anticipate and match his or her own interactive behaviors not only to what has already happened but to what will happen. Predictability is also undoubtedly one of the major factors that allow the infant to learn intentional action and to gradually assume a more reciprocal role as an interactive partner.

Rather than being entirely predictable, however, interactions are characterized by predictability with *variations* in modality, speed, intensity, and length of cycles. Stern et al. (1977) described this combination of predictability and variety as "theme and variation," which allows the infant to make and test hypotheses about the environment. Als et al. (1976) interpreted this combination of predictability and variety as being ideally suited to the expansion of the infant's behavioral repertoire.

Each of these patterns of social interaction provides a useful theoretical framework for describing and understanding the social interactions in which handicapped infants are engaged. It seems clear that the attainment of a synchronous interactive relationship, insofar as it is defined by the combination of this variety of areas of research, may be extremely dependent upon the *intra*-individual capabilities and characteristics of each partner. In turn, these capabilities and characteristics may define basic assumptions made by each partner about what the other brings to the interaction. And yet a handicapped infant may violate any or even all of these predictions and may in addition make it difficult for the caregiver to fulfill the interactive roles of the adult member of the dyad, affecting the nature of the regularities that may be described for the interaction.

Social Interactions of Handicapped Infants

The differences and similarities between handicapped and nonhandicapped infants as social partners, and the accompanying differences and similarities in the patterns of dyadic interactions of these two populations are new areas of research. In order to illustrate the usefulness of this approach, some of the work that is directly related to the interactive patterns described above is reviewed. In addition to what may be drawn from the literature, data from two sources are discussed: 1) a developmental study of hydrocephalic twins (Walker, 1981), and 2) a comparative study of four deaf-blind and four normal infants (Walker & Kershman, 1981). Each of these studies is based on descriptions of dyadic interactions in play situations.

Handicapped infants may simply be less ready for engagement in social interaction, and less responsive to it in general. Even the level of affect that the infant is capable of bringing to the interaction may be disturbed, and the infant may be less readable and less fun as a social partner. Als et al. (1976) described the lack of differentiated facial signs in blind infants, and the feeling that the parent has of being incompetent in eliciting social responses from the infant. The less intense smiles of Down's syndrome babies as compared to normal babies have been described by Emde et al. (1978) as noise in early affect signals, again illustrating how handicapped babies may be more difficult to interpret.

Our own data show that inactivity accounted for almost 50% of the behavior of a group of four deaf-blind babies during a 3-minute play session with their mothers (Walker & Kershman, 1981). For a group of matched normal babies, only 11% of their behavior was coded in the inactive category. In addition, when inactivity and negative vocalization (crying) were subtracted, only 38% of the deaf-blind babies' behaviors remained available to be interpreted as communicative behaviors, and 75% of the normal babies' behaviors fit this criteria. In terms of the affective quality of the communication, the average number of consecutive interactive behaviors in which the normal infant maintained positive affect was 6.3, and for the handicapped infant it was 2.1. The deaf-blind babies were thus less affectively ready for positive interaction, and less able to maintain it once it was initiated.

The handicapped infant's ability to allow the meshing of behaviors into synchronous interactive patterns may be adversely affected by biological involvements that distort patterns of cycling, and that make him or her less predictable than the normal infant. Jones (1977) found that Down's syndrome babies make fewer initiations than nonhandicapped babies, and also engage in rapid repetition of vocalization. Our deaf-blind babies were characterized best by inactivity. Each of these characteristics interferes with the alternating reciprocal character of the interaction. In the twin study, we found a pattern in which *long* periods of silence were interspersed with extremely vigorous physical and vocal games on the part of the parent (Walker, 1981). The infants contributed little to the interaction, and consequently little reciprocal turn-taking occurred. Rather, the parent alternated activity with nonactivity; the "action" was accounted for by the parent's behavior.

Normal social interaction between infant and caregiver is characterized by repetition of both single behaviors and sequences of behaviors. Disruptions of these patterns might be expected on the basis of nonresponsiveness or unpredictable responsiveness in the handicapped infant. And, given that the caregiver may in addition not be able to enter into the already ongoing cycles of the infant's behavior, but must rather attempt to elicit responsiveness, one might expect even more parental repetition. In the twin study, we have several segments in which stereotyped repetition of kinesthetic/vocal games account for a majority of the interaction (Walker, 1981). The periods of activity that were interspersed with the long silences were characterized by repetitive games that changed little from the beginning to the end of the interaction. The play interactions in general were much more reliant on such games than seems to be true with normal infant-parent dyads. The maximum number of different games for any of our three minute observations was three, indicating little change in the types of games that were played with the handicapped infant.

In the deaf-blind study we found different parental use of repetition following different baby categories (Walker & Kershman, 1981). This was particularly true when the babies were most inactive; when the baby was doing nothing, the parent of the normal baby was more likely to change his or her approach, while the parent of the deaf-blind baby was almost equally likely to change or to repeat, indicating uncertainty about what would work, and resulting in interactive sequences that were both less cyclic and less predictable. There was ample justification for such uncertainty because the deaf-blind babies were less predictable in both the modality and the affective quality of their responses to particular mother behaviors than were the normal babies. The probability of a change in affect, given a category change from one coded behavior to the next and using the three categories of positive, negative, or neutral, was 0.90 for the deaf-blind babies, and only 0.43 for the normal babies. When the probability of a positive infant response (as opposed to no response or cry) to any given parent interactive behavior was examined, normal infants were much more predictable in terms of both the behaviors to which they would respond and the behaviors they produced. For example, for the normal infants the probabilities of positive infant responses to vocal, tactile, or kinesthetic stimulation were higher than 0.71. For the handicapped infants, the probability of response to these three modalities ranged from 0.28 to 0.46, with much higher probabilities for a no response (0.48 to 0.56). Although the probability of a positive response was thus much less certain for the handicapped infant, such responses did occur. This finding may partially explain the common observation that parents of handicapped infants seem to "try harder;" it may simply take more work to get a response. Because 50% of the behavior of the deaf-blind babies was in the inactivity category, one might say that the babies were predictable in both affect and responsiveness. As suggested, however, there may be much less predictable patterning to the cycling of the interactions, as well as less predictable responding to particular parent behaviors.

Although the patterning of interactions between normal infants and their caregivers were highly predictable across time, they were also characterized by variety in terms of the number of different types of communicative signals that were used within the rhythmic flow of the interaction. In the deaf-blind infants, one category (inactivity) accounted for about half of their interactions, and for the normal infants, one category accounted for 31%. If just one more category was added, 73% of the deaf-blind babies' behavior was accounted for, while two categories accounted for only 59% of the interactive behavior of the normal babies, suggesting more variation in the interactive categories used by the normal babies.

Variety may also be examined in terms of the different games that are engaged in and the changes that are introduced into any one repeating sequence. As already mentioned, interactions between the twins and their parents tended to be more stereotyped in terms of the number of different games that were played. When we looked within the games, however, we found variation of both content and rhythm. For example, the father of the twins repeated the same game with content variations such as "chin-nose-cheek-cheek," "chin-nose-ear-ear," and with variations in rhythm such as "chin-nose-ear-ear," "chin-nose-ear-ear-ear-ear-ear," and, "deet deet deedle, deet deet deedle, deet deet deedle deedle deedle deedle deet." Variations in emphasis were also used in some of the games. This resembles the theme and variation discussed previously, and certainly introduced elements of surprise into the interaction. Variation over developmental ages is also a critical variable for both partners; not only may the handicapped infant be much less interesting as a social partner at any given point in time, he or she may also change less over time. I have heard the mother commenting on play with one of the twins, "I wish you could learn some new tricks . . . this is so boring."

The data presented suggest that the handicapped infant may have qualities that affect his or her abilities as initiator, elicitor, responder, and maintainer of synchrony in the interactive bout. He or she may be less reinforcing, less interesting, and more difficult as a social partner. In addition, biological processes and needs may predominate over social processes, minimizing play and maximizing caregiving. As a social partner, the handicapped infant may require even greater sensitivity on the part of the caregiver than does the normal infant, plus greater willingness to adapt to what may be extreme differences, to continue the interaction despite a lack of response from the infant, and to consciously attend to the characteristics of the interaction rather than to simply engage in it. The result of these adjustments may be more positive outcomes in later social development for the handicapped infant.

More General Characteristics of Social Interactions in Infancy

The description of interactive patterns holds particular promise for understanding the social interactions of handicapped infants. Several other lines of research may also contribute substantially to this effort as each might be affected by the presence of a handicap. One of these is an examination of the roles played by each member of the dyad. In infancy, what seems to be an interactive dialogue between parent and child is undoubtedly more of a pseudo-dialogue, with the burden for maintaining the dialogic exchange resting with the caregiver. The caregiver's role seems to be that of providing repeated opportunities for interaction to take place, and initiating and maintaining the interaction by joining the infant's ongoing activity. This role has been described for a variety of types of interactions. For example, Kaye (1977) studied the alternating patterns of infant suck and parent jiggle, with the parent entering during the pauses between bursts of infant sucking. Schaffer, Collis, and Parsons (1977) found a similar pattern for vocalization, with the parent entering when the infant became silent, and becoming silent when the infant began to vocalize. Fogel (1977) described how the parent provides a "gaze frame" for infant gaze, so that when the infant looks at the parent, mutual gaze is probable. The parent's role in the interaction is one of achieving the *appearance* of a rule-governed intentional and reciprocal dialogue; the infant's role is to behave predictably enough for this to occur. As the infant achieves the ability to intentionally regulate his or her behavior in relation to that of the interactive partner, he or she is able to assume more of the burden for maintaining the dialogic quality of the interaction and to exchange roles with the parent. Individual differences between infants would be expected to have major implications for the role of the mother over time.

A second area of research with implications for the study of handicapped infants is the search for patterns or rules that seem to characterize interactions *across* different channels or modalities of interaction. Although in the adult literature this search for common patterns has most often focused on gaze and vocalization, infant researchers have begun to examine the role of other modalities, including touch and kinesics, as expressive and receptive channels of communication for both partners, and have extended the search for common communicative rules to these channels as well. Stern et al. (1977) found similar interactive patterns to be characteristic of parent behavior in both vocalization and kinesics during dyadic interactions. Fogel (1977) described an interaction in which the mother responded to a run of arm movements as if it were a run of vocalization. Brazelton et al. (1975) stated that the homeostatic curve described earlier may be essentially content-free, being characterized by changes in intensity rather than in modality. Collis (1978) also addressed this topic, and emphasized the need to study the process of communication regardless of the channel. Infant cycles may not be independent across modalities, but rather may be behavioral manifestations of underlying cycles of arousal and withdrawal (Fogel, 1977). As the infant develops, certain channels undoubtedly become differentiated as more communicative ones. In early infancy, however, it may be that the different modalities are more equivalent as expressive and/or receptive channels than is true for adults, and that the common patterns or rules identified across channels are those with which we may best describe the growth of communicative abilities. The concept of common rules across interactive channels has especially intriguing implications for the study of handicapped infants who may be delayed in one or more modalities.

Bell (1977) suggested that each participant in social interaction (or in caregiving) has upper and lower limits related to both the intensity and the appropriateness of the behavior shown by the other; in normal interactions, these limits are rarely exceeded. The width of this "band of tolerance" is, however, an open question, as are the individual characteristics to which it is related. The adaptation of interactions to match the abilities of different social partners is an area of special interest in studying the handicapped infant population. The combination of the study of content-free regularities in communication, together with the idea of duplicate systems or processes being available to meet the functions of different developmental milestones, provides particularly intriguing possibilities for the study of adaptation. Parental adaptation of interactive sequences to the present capabilities of the infant has been illustrated in a variety of ways in the study of normal infants. Snow (1972) described the variations in linguistic complexity used by mothers in interaction with their infants, while Stern et al. (1977) interpreted the repetition and exaggeration of maternal behaviors in interaction as being adaptation to the infant's level of understanding. The latter found that maternal phrases were half as long, and pauses twice as long, as those found in adult interaction. Brown and Bakeman (1977) found early differences in interactions between dyads with term infants and those with premature infants; these investigators have pointed out that different does not necessarily mean worse, and that observed differences may actually be functional adaptations to the infant. It is essential that differences found between dyads containing normal babies and those in which one member is a handicapped baby be considered with this in mind.

PROMISES FOR APPLICATION

The description of the social interactions of handicapped infants will undoubtedly contribute to the social interaction literature information that may not be available from any other population. In addition, however, the processes used to describe such interactions may offer an approach to assessment and intervention. Assessment, for example, might be based on an analysis of a visual display of the patterns of two behavior streams, one for the caregiver and one for the infant. If one were concerned with the infant's vocalization, and with determining the caregiver communicative behaviors to which such vocalizations were related, visual analysis of interactive patterns displayed across time would yield such information. In addition, levels of probability could be determined for the contingent relationship between any caregiver behavior and infant vocalization. From such probabilities, it is possible to generate hypotheses concerning appropriate intervention.

One brief example will serve to illustrate this point. We videotaped a non-interactive severely handicapped cerebral palsied 2-year-old boy in interaction with his mother. Using the process described above, we found that two mother variables, 1) moving her face close to his, and 2) imitating the baby's few vocalizations, were associated with the frequency of *his* vocalizations. An intervention that focused on these two behaviors resulted in increases in the frequency of occurrence of these parental behaviors, and in overall and contingent baby vocalization (Walker & Bushman, 1980). In addition, there were dramatic increases in the amount of everyday positive social interaction between parent and infant, indicating that as the mother learned to make use of her own behavior to increase her infant's responsiveness, he also became more fun to interact with, affecting the overall amount and quality of the interaction.

QUESTIONS, PROBLEMS, AND SOLUTIONS

The preceding sections illustrate the promise of applying theories and methods from the study of the characteristics of social interaction with a nonhandicapped population to the study of the development of social interactions between handicapped infants and their caregivers. Such description must, however, be set within the context of broader questions if it is to contribute to more general understanding of the processes of development.

First, there is a need to continue with descriptive/comparative questions related to the processes and patterns of interaction. Are differences predictable from the specific handicap or from cognitive and/or affective developmental levels? Are any patterns evident *across* handicaps? For example, do the stereotypic patterns described above differentiate handicapped from normal populations in general? Are patterns of interaction evidenced in modalities that are not the usual interactive modalities, but that may be more available to the handicapped infant? Are differences in use of modalities related to the caregiver's perception of the infant's capability?

Second, we may ask questions of a developmental nature. How do patterns of interaction change over time? Are changes (or non-changes) related to infant characteristics, to parent characteristics, or to the history of the interaction? What is the effect of crisis points in development? Are there developmental continuities that subsequently differentiate healthy and non-healthy interaction?

A third area addresses interactive differences in terms of adaptation. Are parental differences functional adaptations to differences in infant cues? Are there limits to adaptation? How does adaptation at one point in development relate to later adaptation? Does adaptation relate to differences in developmental outcomes? How can we differentiate adaptations that are functional for later development from those that are not?

Fourth, the possibilities for intervention into social interactions need to be examined. Can patterns of interaction be changed through intervention? Can caregivers learn adaptive responses to complement the infant's capabilities? Will new interactive patterns learned in one situation generalize to other situations? What are the outcomes of intervention in terms of both mutually pleasurable interactions at one point in time and effects on development across time?

Finally, there are a number of even more complex questions such as the interrelationships between behavioral systems, the minimum characteristics that are necessary for social interaction, the relationships of interactive patterns to other psychological constructs such as attachment, the role of variables that can be grouped under the term cognitive mediation, and the relative impact of previous events, social expectations for caregiving, the preceding behavior, and the context.

Although there is much to be learned from further study related to the questions above, there are also numerous practical problems facing a researcher working with handicapped infants. In general, the babies are less accessible and more heterogeneous than the normal population. In addition, because the research often involves a long-term commitment of the family to the project, those who are willing to participate may not be a representative sample. Many of the infants are in intervention programs, and have been there for different periods of time; assessing the varying amounts and types of impact that this intervention has on the research question is difficult. Sampling and control of, or even knowledge of, related variables are significant problems. The effect of these variables may vary in meaning over time for a handicapped population in ways that are different from the normal infant.

Furthermore, those measures used with the normal infant may not be equally applicable with a handicapped infant. For example, the lack of some behavior in the parent of a handicapped infant may not be interpretable in the same way if the infant is lacking a sensory modality to which the parent is adapting. Procedures too may be a problem. Families with handicapped infants are often involved with numerous support agencies, and research time may simply be seen as an overload, especially if the project is long-term or if there is no immediate benefit to the family. Even the choice of setting, for example, field or lab, may have different meanings with the handicapped infant. For example, it may be much harder for the parent of a handicapped infant to bring the infant, with accompanying therapeutic equipment, to a lab. At the same time, through multiple contacts with intervention programs, this parent may feel much more comfortable in a strange place then does the parent of the normal infant.

To overcome at least some of these problems, a review of a few of the constraints that have been traditionally imposed on research efforts is needed. It seems essential that we not only test *existing* hypotheses about normal development, but allow for the possibility of discovering new areas of study or new ways of explaining what we see. Glaser and Strauss (1967) advocated a combination of theory generation and theory testing for the field of sociology; there is much to learn from such a combination in the study of handicapped infants. The use of methods from other fields also seems essential for understanding the more elusive qualities of the interaction. Even within our own methodological orientations it seems essential to combine designs, including cross-sectional, developmental, and intervention studies. Intensive prospective case studies, replicated with different infants, may be a feasible approach to accumulating information on the development and integration of patterns of interaction across time.

Finally, a focus on particular constructs such as mutual attention would seem to be a fruitful way of approaching social interaction. By following the manifestations of such constructs over time, it may be possible to describe how functions are maintained when the usual means of accomplishing them are lacking.

SUMMARY

Despite the many complexities involved in research with handicapped infants, there are also many possible important outcomes. These outcomes may lend insight into the processes of normal development and adaptation. By studying infants with deficits in communicative abilities, we may begin to understand the role that such abilities play in human interaction. By studying a population in which disruptions in social interactions are more common than in the normal population, we may gain insights into the antecedents of deviancy. The complexities offer promise for exploring new directions in the development of social interaction and communication. Even more directly, the processes used in such research may provide a means of improving the daily social interactions between handicapped infants and their caregivers.

REFERENCES

Als, H., Tronick, E., Palmer, S., & Brazelton, T. Affective reciprocity and the development of autonomy: The study of a blind infant. Presented at American Academy of Child Psychiatry, Toronto, 1976.

Bell, R. Socialization findings reexamined. In R. Bell & L. Harper (Eds.), *Child effects on adults*. New York: John Wiley & Sons, 1977.

Brazelton, T., Tronick, E., Adamson, L., Als, H., & Wise, S. Early mother-infant reciprocity. In *Parent-infant interaction*, Ciba Foundation Symposium 33. Amsterdam: Associated Scientific Publishers, 1975.

Brown, J., & Bakeman, R. Abnormal mother-infant behavior and child abuse. Technical Report #5: Abnormal Mother-Infant Behavior and Child Abuse. Athens: Georgia State Infancy Laboratory, 1977.

Clarke, A., & Clarke, A. *Early experience: Myth and evidence*. London: Open Books, 1976.

Collis, G. Describing the structure of social interaction in infancy: In M. Bullowa (Ed.), *Before speech: The beginnings of human communication*. Cambridge: Cambridge University Press, 1978.

Duncan, S., and Fiske, D. *Face-to-face interaction: Research, methods, and theory*. Hillsdale, N.J.: Lawrence Erlbaum Associates, 1977.

Emde, R., Katz, E., & Thorpe, J. Emotional expression in infancy: II. Early deviations in Down's syndrome. In M. Lewis & L. Rosenblum (Eds.), *The development of affect*. New York: Plenum Press, 1978.

Fogel, A. Temporal organization in mother-infant face-to-face interaction. In H. Schaffer (Ed.), *Studies in mother-infant interaction*. New York: Academic Press, 1977.

Glaser, B. & Strauss, A. *The discovery of grounded theory*. Chicago: Aldine Publishing Co., 1967.

Gottman, J. *Marital interaction: Experimental investigations*. New York: Academic Press, 1979.

Jones, O. Mother-child communication with pre-linguistic Down's syndrome and normal infants. In H. Schaffer (Ed.), *Studies in mother infant interaction*. New York: Academic Press, 1977.

Kaye, K. Toward the origin of dialogue. In H. Schaffer (Ed.), *Studies in mother-infant interaction*. New York: Academic Press, 1977.

Kearsley, R. Iatrogenic retardation: A syndrome of learned incompetence. In R. Kearsley & I. Sigel (Eds.), *Infants at risk: Assessment of cognitive functioning*. Hillsdale, N.J.: Lawrence Erlbaum Associates, 1979.

Parke, R. Interactional designs. In R. B. Cairns (Ed.), *The analysis of social interactions: Methods, issues and illustrations*. Hillsdale, N.J.: Lawrence Erlbaum Associates, 1979.

Sameroff, A. Theoretical and empirical issues in the operationalization of transactional research. Paper presented at biennial meeting of Society for Research in Child Development, San Francisco, March, 1979.

Sameroff, A., & Chandler, M. Reproductive risk and the continuum of caretaking casualty. In F. Horowitz (Ed.), *Review of child development research.* Chicago: University of Chicago Press, 1975.

Schaffer, H. Early interactive development. In H. Schaffer (Ed.), *Studies in mother-infant interaction.* London: Academic Press, 1977.

Schaffer, H., Collis, G., & Parsons, G. Vocal interchange and visual regard in verbal and pre-verbal children. In H. R. Schaffer (Ed.), *Studies in mother-infant interaction.* London: Academic Press, 1977.

Snow, C. Mothers' speech to children learning language. *Child Development,* 1972, *43,* 549–65.

Stern, D., Beebe, B., Jaffe, J., & Bennett, S. The infant's stimulus world during social interaction: A study of caregiver behaviors with particular reference to repetition and timing. In H. Schaffer (Ed.), *Studies in mother-infant interaction.* London: Academic Press, 1977.

Stern, D., & Jaffe, J., Beebe, B., & Bennett, S. Vocalizing in unison and in alternation: Two modes of communication within the mother-infant dyad. *Annals of New York Academy of Sciences,* 263, 1975, 89–100.

Walker, J. Differential effects of handicapped infant twins on characteristics of parental social play. Paper presented at the Association for the Severely Handicapped, New York, October, 1981.

Walker, J., & Bushman, L. Intervention into social interaction between mother and handicapped baby. Presented at the Association for the Severely Handicapped, Los Angeles, October, 1980.

Walker, J., & Kershman, S. The deaf-blind baby in social interaction. Presented at the Biennial Meeting of the Society for Research in Child Development, Boston, April 2–5, 1981.

Chapter 14

QUESTIONS REGARDING THE EFFECTS OF NEUROMOTOR PROBLEMS ON SENSORIMOTOR DEVELOPMENT

Cordelia C. Robinson

This chapter focuses on the perspective of the clinician working with infants who have congenital or acquired problems that will have an impact on their developmental progress. At the Meyer Children's Rehabilitation Institute (MCRI), scales based on Piaget's description and theory of cognitive development during the stage he identifies as the sensorimotor period have been applied to intervention with handicapped infants and instruction of their parents. The scales that have been used primarily are those developed by Uzgiris and Hunt (1975), the Ordinal Scales of Psychological Development.

In applying information from child development literature based upon Piaget's writings regarding the sensorimotor period (Piaget, 1952, 1974), this chapter adopts what Jens and O'Donnell (this volume) described as an "as if" attitude. That is, in the absence of information that contradicts the point being addressed, it is assumed that the findings regarding nonhandicapped children are applicable to the study of handicapped children. Support for adopting the position that such findings are applicable can be found in reviews of work regarding the use of the Ordinal Scales (Uzgiris & Hunt, in press) and in other examples of applications of Piaget's theory to work with handicapped children (Dècarie, 1969; Fraiberg, 1968; Furth, 1966; Weisz & Zigler, 1979).

In the course of using the Ordinal Scales and Piaget's theory in developing interventions for young handicapped children, a number of questions have been raised about the impact that variations in a child's physical status and the environment have upon the course and rate of sensorimotor development. In this chapter some of those questions are posed, followed by a rationale as to why research designed to answer them may contribute to an understanding of the impact of handicapping conditions upon development and may offer information that can be used in the design of effective intervention for children with handicaps. Before posing these questions about sensorimotor development, a description of the context in which these questions have occurred is provided, and problems encountered in applying developmental work with nonhandicapped children to work with children with handicaps are discussed. These comments are intended as practical guidelines for clinicians (e.g., psychologists, educators, therapists) planning to pursue a course similar to that of MCRI.

CLINICAL CONTEXT

The context for the questions regarding sensorimotor development is provided by the Infant Development program at MCRI, and the Toddler Research and Intervention Program at Peabody College (Bricker & Bricker, 1971, 1972, 1973). The Peabody Program dealt with infant and toddler-age handicapped children, most of whom were retarded or had syndromes typically associated with retardation. The use of the sensorimotor scales in the Peabody Program was primarily to assess the handicapped children to determine whether Uzgiris and Hunt's findings with normal infants would replicate with this population of handicapped infants. The comparisons between the handicapped and nonhandicapped toddlers and infants indicated that many of the handicapped children followed the same ordinal hierarchy of development as nonhandicapped children (Robinson et al., 1973). Others have replicated these findings when looking at the development of object permanence skills (Kahn, 1976; Silverstein et al., 1975). The content of the ordinal scales was also used as a basis for designing activities that should be part of the day-to-day experiences of the children with whom we were working. Thus, the approach to sensorimotor intervention was analogous to the approach to intervention in the area of communication development outlined by Bricker and Bricker (1974).

Use of the Ordinal Scales in the Infant Program at MCRI differed in a number of ways from the strategies employed in the Peabody Program, largely because of the difference in populations. The population of the Infant Program at MCRI was substantially more heterogeneous than was the population at Peabody and included a high proportion of children with multiple handicaps (approximately 50 percent). Approximately one-third of this population had handicaps that were severe to profound.

The MCRI Infant Program is located in an interdisciplinary facility, and the children with multiple handicaps receive therapy from several different disciplines as well as from an Infant Program teacher. The service model is one of weekly instructional visits with parent and child rather than a daily program with groups of children. In the Infant Program the parent receives instruction focused on arrangement of the environment so as to provide appropriate experiences and instructional opportunities. Guidelines for the content of those experiences are derived from the Ordinal Scales, which include object permanence, means end relationships, operational causality, spatial relationships, verbal and gestural imitation and schemes in relation to objects. Child progress in relationship to the landmarks on the scales is monitored at regular intervals. For more details regarding the use of the Ordinal Scales in this program, the reader is referred to Robinson and Fieber (1974), Robinson and Robinson (1978), and Robinson (in press).

Questions regarding sensorimotor development have resulted primarily from observations of children with moderate to severe degrees of cerebral palsy. These children have problems in their progress through sensorimotor stages that differ from those of retarded children, blind children (Fraiberg, 1968) and children with congenital absence of limbs or parts of limbs (e.g., thalidomide children studied by Decarie, 1969). Gratch (this volume) has addressed the issue of the utility and limitations of Piagetian based scales with non-normal populations. In the case of blind children, Fraiberg, Siegal, and Gibson (1966) demonstrated a sequence of searching based upon increased competence in sound localization that parallels visual localization. Dècarie (1969) found that children with absent or truncated limbs were able to make remarkable adaptations through which they engaged in sensorimotor activities that she viewed as equivalent to nonphysically handicapped children in function if not in form.

SENSORIMOTOR DEVELOPMENT

The discussions of sensorimotor development presented here refer to Piaget's descriptions of children's cognitive development during the sensorimotor period. It is assumed that the major developments described by Piaget for that period (e.g., object permanence, means-end skills, operational causality, spatial relationships, imitation, and schemes in relation to objects) are conceptual understandings of the world, that the child must acquire before he or she can advance to further stages in cognitive development. It is not assumed that the process that Piagetian theory postulates is accurate for all children, but rather that questions regarding development of that process may facilitate understanding of developmental progress in children with handicaps.

QUESTIONS REGARDING THE
COURSE OF SENSORIMOTOR DEVELOPMENT

Is the course and sequence of sensorimotor development the same for children with specific neuromotor handicaps as it is for nonimpaired children? It is argued (Robinson & Fieber, 1974; Robinson & Robinson, 1978) that if children seem to be physically incapable of certain responses, tasks should be analyzed in an effort to determine other functionally equivalent responses. For example, we recommend accepting an "eye point" (looking at the location of the hidden object) in an object permanence eliciting situation as evidence of object permanence in children with cerebral palsy who cannot voluntarily control their limb movements for an accurate uncover, reach, and grasp response (Robinson & Robinson, 1978). The logic for such an approach comes from cognitive theory where emphasis is placed upon a given behavior as just one expression of an underlying cognitive process. This approach of modifying the physical task requirements has been used with preschool handicapped children by Haeussermann (1958).

The form of response, the relationship of that form to the underlying construct, or in Gratch's terms "the role of action" (this volume), and the need for a definition of action, has been the focus of work by Bower (1974). Bower argues for the acceptance of visual searching in response to a violation of expectancies as a reliable indicator that a child has the concept of object permanence. Fetters (1976) reported that children with cerebral palsy scored higher when the Bower's "nontraditional" criteria were used rather than more traditional indices.

With the goal in mind of generating information useful for the design of interventions for the child with cerebral palsy, three more specific questions arise. First, assuming that the alternative tasks, such as those designed by Bower, can be analyzed according to stage requirements (Fischer, 1980), does experience with a series of situations where one observes the consequences of rules or violation of rules result in learning, or an information base that is functionally equivalent to that gained by typical experience of the child acting on objects and situations and observing the consequences of those actions himself or herself? Or using another example, does experience based upon the sensorimotor actions of an intermediary (such as uncovering a hidden object or flipping a light switch on and off) result in learning that is functionally equivalent to that which comes about through direct experience? Also, does the role of direct action versus experience mediated by another person vary according to sensorimotor Stage (1–4) or conceptual area (e.g., object permanence, means-ends)? The answer to these questions is that the role of direct action/experience does seem to vary across sensorimotor stages (Robinson, in press). More specifically, once the child's behavior is mediated by language, outcomes are functionally equivalent, whether the child is personally engaging in the activity himself or herself or the child is giving some signal and another person is carrying out the activity. At sensorimotor Stages 3 and 4, clinical observation has suggested that the infant does not attend to the situation if another person serves as the mediator of the experience. This problem is consistent with Piaget's characterizations of the sensorimotor stages and perhaps can be seen most clearly in the landmarks identified for the Ordinal Scales in the areas of causality and means-end development. It is not until sensorimotor Stage 5 that Piaget attributes the ability to separate cause and effect to the child's behavior.

The issue that has not been addressed in the division of the sensorimotor period into substages is the relationship between experiences at one stage and outcomes at the next stage. Seligman (1975) argued that an individual's expectation that he or she can control events in the environment is dependent upon having experiences sometime during the course of development where he or she actually exercised control over environmental events. The experience of exercising control over environmental events and the motivational value of perceiving that control, as control, is a recurrent theme in descriptions of infant learning, whether one prefers Piaget's terminology of primary and secondary circular reactions, Uzgiris and Hunt's (1975) learning set "if I act I can make interesting things happen" or Watson's (1966) "contingency awareness." Central to each of these conceptualizations of early infant learning is the existence of a relationship between a child's action and a result. The form of the particular behavior and the form of the particular effect are generally irrelevant.

Emphasis upon the importance of experience has become the focus of clinical and experimental interventions with handicapped infants (Robinson & Robinson, 1978; Brinker, 1981) and with older handicapped individuals who are developmentally functioning at early sensorimotor stages (W. Bricker, personal communication). There seems to be considerable consensus among clinicians and developmental researchers that the experience of acting on one's environment is an important experience. Arrangement of a handicapped infant's environment so that the infant is able to experience control over visual, auditory, and tactile stimuli in the same manner as the nonhandicapped infant may be essential in the acquisition of more complex cognitive processes. There is a lack of information regarding the frequency with which the typical infant has such contingency experience before he or she develops a "generalized expectancy" (Lewis & Goldberg, 1969) that a response will produce an effect on the environment (Robinson & Robinson, 1978). Nonetheless, it seems that we may have been too restricted in our view as to what constitutes an experience that is an example of the learning set "if I act, I can make interesting things happen."

The problem does not lie with the conceptualization of the developmental stage but rather with our focus on narrow indices as evidence of the developmental stage and thereby not appreciating the variety and frequency of opportunities that the typical infant has to exercise some control over his or her environment. The following describes a specific instance that seems to be an example of a situation that should be included as an experience in this category of Stage 2 means-end/causality experience, but which in the past has not been regarded as such. Recently a colleague described holding an 8-week-old infant so the child was able to look over her shoulder. The environment was unfamiliar to the infant and one of the rooms contained a large printed fabric wall hanging with lines of high color contrast. This colleague commented that she found herself walking backwards across this room toward the wall hanging. She perceived that the infant wanted to be closer to the pictures. Once they were closer, she no longer perceived the baby as straining to get closer to the picture. The infant's "action" in this instance was fairly subtle and the outcome of the "action" mediated by another person. Characterizing this situation as belonging to the experiential set of primary circular reactions seems appropriate. Such examples suggest that the experiential base for development of a "generalized expectancy" for effectiveness or "contingency awareness" is vast, and that infants who do not have the physical ability to activate mobiles or wind chimes are also likely to have restricted experiences in an array of situations. Therefore, interventions must be much more broadly conceived.

In the MCRI program the emphasis in our instruction to parents of children in Stage 2 or 3 of the sensorimotor period has changed over the past several years. Previously the focus was on arranging the environment so that the physically handicapped child could activate visual, auditory, or tactile stimuli with a response in his or her repertoire. Such advice is still offered, but greater emphasis is given to creating an expanded range of daily activities that the infant can control, such as that described above with the 8-week-old infant. Through conversation with and observation of the infant's caregiver we try to determine how he or she interprets specific infant behavior. Documenting those behaviors and clarifying them for caregivers will enhance the infant's experiential base for developing "contingency awareness," or the generalized learning set "if I act, I can make things happen." The manner in which we enhance attention to such behaviors is illustrated in Table 1. Table 1 was prompted by conceptualizations of sensorimotor development, specifically the landmarks in the development of operational causality and means-end development (Uzgiris & Hunt, 1975), and by the work of Bates et al. (1975) and Snyder (1978) regarding functional stages in development of communication. In approaching the question regarding the functional equivalence of different forms of sensorimotor experience, a greater emphasis should be placed upon

Table 1. Procedure for analyzing communicative intent, which is based on a recording tool developed by Nancy Fieber

	Eliciting situation	Child's signal	Function	Meaning to adult
1.	Child for long period in chair	Fuss and extend	Personal-unhappy, uncomfortable	He wants out of chair
2.	Adult offers verbal cues "Want out?" Touch to child's sides	Arm movement and head movement	Instrumental responsive	He means yes, he wants out
3.	Adult guides child through pattycake. Pauses, asks "more?" Touches child's hand	Child gives eye contact, smiles moves hands to adult's hand	Instrumental responsive	He wants to play pattycake again
4.	Adult activates See "N," Say, pauses, asks, "more?"	Child hits at See "N" Say	Instrumental responsive	He wants me to activate it again
5.	Child is bounced on back on ball. Adult asks "more?" and moves ball as cue	Child kicks, kicks and smiles, kicks and smiles and vocalizes and gives eye contact	Instrumental responsive	He wants to bounce again
6.	Adult places child on tummy on ball then begins to rock child	Fuss	Personal-unhappy	He doesn't like this
7.	Mom takes child's hand forward and sings, "See Saw" as rocked on ball	Child stops fuss, smiles and lifts head slightly	Personal, OK	This way is OK. He feels safe with his mom

relating interventions to the theoretical conceptualizations of the specific sensorimotor stages (Uzgiris, 1976; Fischer, 1980) rather than specific behavioral landmarks.

A related issue concerns a practical argument between educators and physical and occupational therapists over the habilitative management of infants with cerebral palsy. In particular, the issue revolves around the use of abnormal reflex patterns. Some children are able to accomplish actions and therefore control over events in the environment through the use of abnormal motor patterns, such as the use of the asymmetric tonic neck reflex for reach and grasp. What are the tradeoffs, and consequently the implications for intervention, in allowing the child to use these atypical patterns, which permits some control over the environment, versus suppressing the use of such patterns, which may preclude most control over the environment?

In terms of this debate, several principles serve as guides for interventions with handicapped infants. These principles are based on the following assumptions: 1) that active participation in an activity by the infant is preferable to passive participation; 2) that self-selection of an activity or material by the infant is preferable to selecting activities or materials for the infant; 3) that the function that a behavior serves (e.g., locomotion) is more important to eventual development than the form of the particular behavior (e.g., crawling versus walking); and 4) that the infant should have some experience acting directly upon the environment as a foundation for use of others as intermediaries to accomplish actions on his or her environment. Based upon these assumptions the infant should be encouraged to use whatever responses are available to act on the environment. If the child is not permitted to respond, his or her motivation for environmental interaction may be significantly affected. The therapist working with a cerebral palsy child may be guided by different assumptions, one of which may be that use of abnormal reflex patterns as operant responses will reinforce them, and thus interfere with the child's developmental progress. Until empiracal work is available that verifies one or the other assumptions, the practical consequences of such a conflict between two clinicians working with the same child must be considered. The parent and child are placed in the middle of this conflict. Because the parent cannot carry out the recommendations generated from these two points of view, he or she is put in the position of selecting which alternative to follow. This is an unreasonable burden of responsibility for parents but one that they face frequently. Consequently, this issue should be a priority research area.[1]

---

[1] Another example of this issue—one that could have more devastating consequences—is the consideration of alternative modes of communication for a child who may not be an oral communicator (Chapman & Miller, 1980).

RELATIONSHIP BETWEEN
SENSORIMOTOR DEVELOPMENT AND OTHER DOMAINS

A recurrent theme in the child development literature concerns the integration and organization of development across behavioral domains (Sroufe, 1979). This theme is one that receives rhetorical attention but unfortunately tends to have less impact on clinical and research activities. Translating the findings and implications of child development research into practice requires information about the relationships among the domains of development, that is, cognitive skills, motor skills, communication skills, social skills, and daily living skills. One of the barriers to obtaining such information has been the tendency to isolate skills in the various domains from one another and in some cases to view one domain as being a more important one than others (Fischer, 1980). For example, sensorimotor skills are sometimes seen as prerequisites to development in other domains, such as development of object permanence as a prerequisite to a particular function in language development. The alternative view (looking for skills that are common across domains) is receiving an increasing amount of attention in the literature. Literature regarding development of communication in infants provides evidence of more attention being directed toward the reciprocal influences among cognitive, language, social and motor skill domains (Bates, Camaioni, & Volterra, 1975; Bruner, 1975; Newson, 1979; Stern, 1974a, 1974b).

The view that skill development in the various domains are reciprocal in their influences has practical implications for the impact of a given disability upon developmental progress. For example, a motor disability is sometimes viewed as affecting only motor development. If the disability is severe, clinicians will point out that one can expect other domains of skill development to be affected, and a secondary symptom status is then ascribed to these delays. Secondary status implies recognition that development in one domain is affected by another, but does not sufficiently emphasize the potential negative impact across domains. The study of infant development should have a positive impact in this regard. For example, the basis for development of communication is currently viewed as being influenced by the parent-infant dyad's ability to develop reciprocity in social "games" (Field, 1978; Stern, 1974a, 1974b). The infant's behavior that is interpreted as contributing to reciprocity is dependent upon increasing flexibility and control over motor responses. Thus, the child with a severe motor disability may have limited opportunities to engage in the reciprocal exchanges that seem to be a base for the development of communication and subsequent language. Interpretations of the child's responses as efforts to communicate should be made as soon as the child is identified as handicapped rather than waiting until the child is of the age where one would expect to address the issue of communicating by word, gesture, or communication board.

The issue of the integration of development raises numerous questions, one of which concerns the relationship between sensorimotor and communication skills. Specifically, does the relationship between sensorimotor development and development of specific aspects of communication pertain if a person's mode of expression is nonoral? The wording of this question assumes that a relationship between sensorimotor skills and language skills exists. Thus, an "as if" mode is adopted here. Such a mode seems appropriate given the practical problem of working on communication development with a cerebral palsied child.

Much current thinking regarding communication and development views the child as moving toward less and less idiosyncratic modes of communication. Thus, whether the form of communication is gesture or word, the movement is from less to more conventional "actions." Such development in communication is typically concurrent with increasing skill development in other domains, that is, fine motor, gross motor, and cognitive skills of representation and perspective taking. Fine motor development, for example, serves as the skill base for more refined gestures or more articulate sounds. Such refinements also allow the child to employ objects in increasingly complex ways. Using oneself or an object as a tool to obtain another object out of reach is a landmark in the means-end sequence at sensorimotor Stage 4. Using the hand reach that is frequently interpreted as "gimme" is at sensorimotor Stage 5. Thus, the skills of requesting action from another person may evolve from skills of doing something for oneself.[2]

Generally a child moves effortlessly to less idiosyncratic modes of communication. This is typically a gradual process with some spurts and sometimes lengthy plateaus. Advances in motor skills seem to form a base for greater diversity in experience and frequently wider social contacts. These social contacts are likely to be with persons less familiar with the infant's idiosyncratic communication system and less likely to "richly" interpret the infant's behavior as having communicative intent. A given dyad's idiosyncratic forms of communicating may persist beyond the point at which the child is using a less idiosyncratic mode of communicating to other persons. Such persistence can be predicted based upon the dyad's history and is not generally a cause for concern. However, problems can be encountered when attempting to change a child's mode of communication.

---

[2] The theory of cognitive development regarding the control and construction of hierarchies of skill proposed by Fischer (1980) may be a useful tool for verifying this assumption.

For example, speech therapists attempting to introduce to a 3-year-old child with severe cerebral palsy a nonvocal picture based communication system met resistance. In this case the therapists felt it was appropriate to shift this child to a communication system more symbolic than his current mode. Yet efforts to get the family and this child to consistently replace their idiosyncratic communication system with a more abstract system did not proceed well. The typical mode of therapy in cases where a new communication system is introduced is to instruct the parents in appropriate ways of responding to their child and arranging experiences for him. Such a strategy had in the past worked well with this family. The questions that were raised in this clinical context included: 1) Is it reasonable to expect parents and a child to utilize a communication system that is dependent upon carrying a device when they already have an effective, albeit idiosyncratic, mode of communication that is not dependent upon such a device? 2) Is the answer to the first question based upon skills the child has in other domains, such as sensory and motor exploration of the function of objects, or acting on situations to produce effects? 3) Is it best that such a system be introduced by persons with whom the child has had considerable experience communicating or by a less familiar person? 4) If such a child appears to be ready for a more abstract communication system, is it best to introduce it initially in circumscribed settings and with a limited number of persons, or is it best to try to introduce it pervasively throughout the child's environment? The answers to such questions have significant implications for designing habilitative programs for children who will be aided by the use of alternative communication systems.

Recommendations

One can misuse sensorimotor scales by viewing the landmarks as limited to specific behaviors, rather than as one example or index of a general competency. Thus, developmental programs, where emphasis is placed upon teaching the child to uncover a specific object as a program objective, are of concern. The emphasis should be upon identification of a general competency, for example, the recognition that the object still exists even though the child has lost sensory contact with it. The educator then tries to arrange an environment in which objects disappear and can be recovered. Instances of child behavior from which we are willing to infer that the child has object permanence are then identified.

One of the consequences of emphasizing generalized competencies is the likelihood of an accompanying emphasis upon the function of a particular behavior rather than its form. Thus, in order to accommodate children who do not have a particular mode of expression or a competency available to them, we are challenged to look for other situations that require the same underlying skill and provide them with experiences.

In taking the position that the function of a response is more important than its form, we must keep in mind that a typical child with all motor and sensory faculties available has the opportunity to interact in a wide variety of situations. These situations, in the Piagetian view, serve as the "aliments" to be assimilated into a given scheme and in the stimulus response learning perspective serve as exemplars of a class. In both views the generalization of the scheme or concept is influenced at least to some degree by the specific instances that contributed to its formation. Thus, if a child demonstrated less generalization of a concept than we might have anticipated, the question as to whether his or her experiences were limited in both quantity and quality must be considered. It may not be simply limited data that affects the handicapped child's performance. Limited opportunities to integrate information from various sources is also a likely consequence of a specific disability. We must consider that not only will the child's information base differ, his or her experiences with processing information will also differ in form from the nonhandicapped child's experience.

SUMMARY

Extensive use of scales based upon sensorimotor development in both clinical and research work with handicapped children are represented in our work and have been found to be useful tools. However, Gratch's conclusion (this volume) that the utility of sensorimotor scales is not derived from their content but rather from the tradition from which they originated is supported. Clinicians utilizing the scales should appreciate: the respect for the individual inherent in the method clinique; the emphasis upon a constructionist view of intelligence; the significance of stages; and the assumption of an underlying organization to development.

REFERENCES

Bates, E., Camaioni, L., & Volterria, V. The acquisition of performatives prior to speech. *Merrill Palmer Quarterly,* 1975, *21,* 205–226.

Bower, T. *Development in infancy.* San Francisco: W. H. Freeman, 1974.

Bricker, D., & Bricker, W. Toddler Research and Intervention Project Report, Year I. *IMRID Behavioral Science Monograph.* George Peabody College, Nashville, 1971.

Bricker, D., & Bricker, W. Toddler Research and Intervention Project Report, Year II. *IMRID Behavioral Science Monograph*. George Peabody College, Nashville, 1972.
Bricker, D., & Bricker, W. Toddler Research and Intervention Project Report, Year III. *IMRID Behavioral Science Monograph*. George Peabody College, Nashville, 1973.
Bricker, W., & Bricker, D. An early language training strategy. In R. Schiefelbusch & L. Lloyd (Eds.), *Language perspectives-acquisition retardation and intervention*. Baltimore: University Park Press, 1974.
Brinker, R. Patterns of learning of handicapped infants. Paper presented at biennial meeting, Society for Research in Child Development, Boston, April 2–5, 1981.
Bruner, J. The ontogenesis of speech acts. *Journal of Child Language*, 1975, *2*, 1–19.
Chapman, R., & Miller, J. Analyzing language and communication in the child. In R. Schiefelbusch (Ed.), *Nonspeech language and communication: Analysis and intervention*. Baltimore: University Park Press, 1980.
Decarie, T. A study of the mental and emotional development of the thalidomide child. In B. M. Foss (Ed.), *Determinants of infant behavior* (Vol. 4). London: McThuen, 1969.
Fetters, L. The development of object permanence in infants with motor handicaps. Paper presented at the Annual Conference of the American Physical Therapy Association, New Orleans, June, 1976.
Field, T. The three R's of infant-adult interactions: Rhythms, repertoires and responsivity. *Journal of Pediatric Psychology*, 1978, *3*, 131–136.
Fischer, K. A theory of cognitive development: The control and construction of hierarchies of skills. *Psychological Review*, 1980, *87*, 477–530.
Fraiberg, S. Parallel and divergent patterns in blind and sighted infants. *Psychoanalytic Study of the Child*, 1968, *23*, 264–300.
Fraiberg, S., Siegal, B., & Gibson, R. The role of sound in the search behavior of a blind infant. *Psychoanalytic Study of a Child*, 1966, *71*, 327–357.
Furth, H. *Thinking without language*, New York: Free Press. 1966.
Haeussermann, E. *Developmental potential of preschool children*. New York: Grune & Stratton, 1958.
Kahn, J. Utility of the Uzgiris and Hunt scales of sensorimotor development with severely and profoundly retarded children. *American Journal of Mental Deficiency*, 1976, *80*, 665–667.
Lewis, M., & Goldberg, S. Perceptual-cognitive development in infancy: A generalized expectancy model as a function of the mother-infant interaction. *Merrill-Palmer Quarterly of Behavior and Development*, 1969, *15*, 81–100.
Newson, J. Intentional behavior in the young infant. In D. Shaffer & J. Dunn (Eds.), *The first five years of life: Psychological and medical implications of early experience*. New York: John Wiley & Sons, 1979.
Piaget, J. *The origins of intelligence in children*. New York: International Universities Press, 1952.
Piaget, J. *The construction of reality in the child*. New York: Basic Books, 1974.
Robinson, C. A strategy for assessing motorically impaired infant. In I. Uzgiris & J. Mc V. Hunt (Eds.), *Research with scales of psychological development in infancy*. Urbana, Ill. University of Illinois Press, in press.
Robinson, C., Chatelanat, G., Spritzer, S., Robinson, M., & Bricker, W. Study of sensorimotor development in young developmental delayed and

non-delayed children. In D. Bricker & W. Bricker (Eds.), Infant, toddler and preschool research and intervention project: Report year III. *IMRID Behavioral Science Monograph, No. 23.* George Peabody College, Nashville, 1973.

Robinson, C., & Fieber, N. Development and modification of Piagetian sensorimotor assessment and curriculum in developmentally handicapped infants. Paper presented at Annual Meeting of American Academy of Cerebral Palsy, Denver, Colorado, November, 1974.

Robinson, C., & Robinson, J. Sensorimotor functions and cognitive development. In M. Snell (Ed.), *Systematic instruction of the moderately and severely handicapped.* Columbus: Charles E. Merrill, 1978.

Seligman, M. *Helplessness: On depression, death, and development.* San Francisco: W. H. Freeman, 1975.

Silverstein, A., Brownlee, L., Hubbell, M., & McTain, R. Comparison of two sets of Piagetian scales with severely and profoundly retarded children. *American Journal of Mental Deficiency,* 1975, *80,* 292–297.

Snyder, L. Communicative and cognitive abilities and disabilities in the sensorimotor period. *Merrill-Palmer Quarterly,* 1978, *24,* 161–181.

Sroufe, A. The coherence of individual development: Early care attachment, and subsequent developmental issues. *American Psychologist,* 1979, *34,* 834–841.

Stern, D. Mother and infant at play: The dyadic interaction involving facial vocal and gaze behaviors. In M. Lewis & L. Rosenblum (Eds.), *The effect of the infant on its caregiver.* New York: John Wiley & Sons, 1974a.

Stern D. The goal and structure of mother-infant play. *Journal of the American Academy of Child Psychiatry,* 1974b, *13,* 402–421.

Uzgiris, I. Organization of sensorimotor intelligence. In M. Lewis (Ed.), *Origins of intelligence: Infancy and early childhood.* New York: Plenum Press, 1976.

Uzgiris, I., & Hunt, J. McV. *Assessment in infancy: Ordinal scales of psychological development.* Urbana, Ill. University of Illinois Press, 1975.

Uzgiris, I., & Hunt, J. McV. *Research with scales of psychological development in infancy.* Urbana, Ill. University of Illinois Press, in press.

Watson, J. The development and generalization of "contingency awareness" in early infancy: Some hypothesis. *Merrill-Palmer Quarterly,* 1966, *12,* 123.

Weisz, J., & Zigler, E. Cognitive development in retarded and non-retarded persons: Piagetian tests of the similar sequence hypothesis. *Psychological Bulletin,* 1979, *86,* 831–851.

Section VI
INTERVENTION

Chapter 15

ISSUES IN DESIGNING INTERVENTION APPROACHES FROM DEVELOPMENTAL THEORY AND RESEARCH

Marci J. Hanson

Debates regarding the provision of early intervention are now a rarity. Such programs for infants are a reality of the 1980s and they run the gamut from models based solely on medical treatment to those whose major goal is to provide parent support employing systematic training with an interdisciplinary focus. Questions regarding the most effective and critical interventions, however, remain unanswered. Once children with treatment needs are identified, solutions to problems of designing appropriate educational approaches require a synthesis of basic developmental information with a perspective on the clinical needs of children and their families. The interventionist applying treatment is caught in the juggling act of seeking out and attempting to apply available data on findings from research while making clinical judgments regarding the provision of services to individual children. Thus, the process of intervention requires merging general principles derived from theories of child development with the clinical demands which necessitate individualization.

Rarely does a direct relationship exist between the findings of a given research study and its clinical application. It is more likely that advance in the one lead to shifts in the other. An examination of the development of early assessment tools provides an example of this relationship. The advent of standardized infant development assessments in the 1930s and 1940s provided the means for studying individual differences in infancy. This capability contributed to a growing research interest in describing the development of young children. Performance outcomes on these tests are acknowledged as useful indices of normative development. For this reason, these tests have made valuable contributions to the clinical field in the identification of children not performing as expected and who may be in need of services.

Now that services are available, clinical demands have evolved for more utilitarian assessments. Rather than just gross indicators of "normalcy," there are needs for more microanalytic analyses of behavior that can be used across a wide range of children including those with sensory and/or physical disabilities. Further needs exist for assessments that are predictive of later development and useful in evaluating the effects of treatment programs. As discussed in this volume (see chapters by Johnson and Sheehan) current assessments fall short on these dimensions (Lewis, 1976). Thus, research findings often form the path for delivery of services to individuals; likewise clinical needs may dictate new research directions.

This chapter reviews applications of research findings to interventions with disabled and/or at-risk infant populations and identifies issues derived from clinical practice that indicate a need for further research. This discussion is focused on issues in identification of *who* should be the target of intervention efforts, issues on *how* the intervention may be conceptualized and delivered, and issues on *what* the intervention approaches should include. Each section presents a review of research findings and applications as well as an analysis of future research needs in that specific area.

Before beginning this discussion, the rationale for early intervention is briefly considered. Few professionals today would question why treatment in the early years of life is crucial given the importance of this developmental period (Hayden & McGinness, 1977; Isaacson, 1975) and the potential far-reaching consequences of intervention on child performance outcomes and family dynamics. The case for early intervention is documented extensively in numerous books, articles, and reviews (Beller, 1979; Bronfenbrenner, 1975; Friedlander, Sterritt, & Kirk, 1975; Horowitz & Paden, 1973). Not only do these research and clinical studies establish the need for intervention, but they also converge to suggest that an early onset of treatment is most beneficial. Additionally, programs have documented the effectiveness of early intervention in a variety of settings—both home-based and clinic- or school-based. Decisions regarding the appropriateness of where the services are delivered, therefore, are probably best made taking into account the geographical and economical considerations of the target population. Research suggests that setting is not the critical variable as long as families are actively involved in treatment. Bronfenbrenner (1975) in his review of the effectiveness of early intervention emphasized this point. He concluded that those programs in which intervention was begun early in the child's life and in which the child's parents were actively involved produced the most impressive and enduring gains. Bronfenbrenner's review focused predominantly on programs with "disadvantaged" or environmentally at-risk populations. Evaluations of programs for handicapped or biologically at-risk infants produced similar conclusions concerning the importance of beginning early in the child's life and working not only with the child but with the family.

Finally, developments in special education aimed at gaining educational services and establishing rights for handicapped persons have taken place concurrently with the surge in research on early development. Parents have been a primary force behind this movement, which has led to the acknowledged importance of their involvement. This emphasis is reflected both in legislation (Turnbull & Turnbull, 1978) and in a general approach to provision of educational services (Hayden & McGinness, 1977).

WHO SHOULD BE THE FOCUS OF INTERVENTION APPROACHES?

The provision of intervention services to infants who are disabled and/or at-risk should logically begin with a definition of the target population. Influences from basic and applied research are examined as contributors to the identification of who should receive services and issues for further research in this area are listed.

Contributions from Research Findings and Practice

Infant Behavior   Research findings over the last decade and a half have formed the basis for viewing the infant as competent. These studies have indicated that infants enter the world with sensory and perceptual capabilities, equipping them to maximally benefit from environmental input and actively affect change in the world. To illustrate, in terms of visual competence, investigations have shown that the neonate can discriminate levels of brightness (Hershenson, 1964), color (Trincker & Trincker, 1967), and visually track a moving object (Dayton et al., 1964). The 3- to 4-month-old responds to facial features (Haaf & Bell, 1967) and prefers regular over distorted faces and other stimuli (McCall & Kagan, 1967). Additionally, infants seem to prefer three-dimensional over two-dimensional figures (Fantz, 1961) and with increasing age exhibit a preference for more complex stimuli (Brennan, Ames, & Moore, 1966). In the auditory domain, the neonate is equipped to interact and make complex discriminations particularly with respect to human voices (Eimas et al., 1971). More extensive reviews of infants' behavioral competencies are provided in Appleton, Clifton, and Goldberg (1975) and Kessen, Haith, and Salapatek (1970).

Caregiver Behavior   Another topic from the developmental literature of importance to this discussion is maternal stimulation to the infant. The results of several major studies reflect the general conclusions. These studies reported a positive relationship between maternal competency and infant competency in the cognitive, communication, and social behavior domains (Ainsworth & Bell, 1975; Clarke-Stewart, 1973; Yarrow et al., 1972). This literature suggests that caregiver responses to and stimulation of infant behavior are integrally linked to infant developmental outcomes.

Caregiver-Infant Interaction   Knowledge of the behavioral competence of infants has led to the recognition of the infant's contribution to human interactions, and, thus, a focus in the literature on "the effect of the infant on its caregiver" (Lewis & Rosenblum, 1974). Research on this topic has come to characterize infant behavior as an important contributor to and determinant of parental behavior.

A number of studies with "normal" infant populations have provided evidence that adults differentially respond to infants on the basis of given infant characteristics. These characteristics include: age and developmental status, sex, state, birth order, and responsiveness to stimuli.

Given the highly probable impact of these "normal" variations in infants on caregiver behavior, it is not surprising that characteristics that identify infants as at-risk or disabled may likewise exert a powerful influence on the dynamics of caregiver-infant interaction. The literature provides ample documentation that at-risk and disabled infants may differ behaviorally from "normal" babies. Studies have indicated, for example, that prenatal and perinatal complications may produce differences in infant responsivity, irritability, motor, feeding and visual responses (Beckwith & Cohen, 1978; Field, 1979; Als et al., Note 1). Additionally, in the few behavioral observations of disabled infants, marked differences have been noted. Studies have shown that the development of Down's syndrome infants, for example, is characterized by delays in affective, cognitive, and motor behavioral domains (Cicchetti & Sroufe, 1976; Hanson, 1981). Observations of blind infants similarly have documented deviations from normal development in the motor and signaling behavior of these infants (Fraiberg, 1968, 1977). As Fraiberg pointed out, these behavioral deviations may produce and/or necessitate concomitant adjustments in caregiver behavior.

Literature on caregiver-infant interaction does in fact suggest that the behavior of caregivers of atypical children may differ from that of caregivers of "normal" infants and young children. The following differences have been noted: differences in touching, talking, and gaze behavior and differences in maternal attitudes toward premature newborns (Field, 1979; Goldberg, 1978); social interaction differences in abused and failure-to-thrive populations (Klein & Stern, 1971; Shaheen et al., 1968); differences in communication and provision of stimulating activities by parents of blind infants (Fraiberg, 1977); and linguistic input and child behavior management differences in mothers of young "retarded" children (Buium, Rynders, & Turnure, 1974; Marshall, Hegrenes, & Goldstein, 1973) and physically handicapped children (Kogan & Tyler, 1973). Thus, there is support for the view that the atypical infant may be a less competent partner. This in turn may modify caregiver-infant interactional behavior.

Although not yet supported empirically, the assumption is often made that caregiver-infant interaction with a dyad that includes a disabled member is deviant or dysfunctional. This notion perhaps has evolved from the literature describing parental attitudes and reactions to the birth of a "defective" child. Regardless of origin, it seems that generalizations about caregiver-infant interaction involving atypical populations cannot be made. The majority of the interaction studies previously reviewed, suggest that parents may respond differently, report more stress, and hold more negative attitudes about their "atypical" child. A number of recent investigations, however, have reported that parents may not differ behaviorally when compared with parents of normal infants in interaction situations and/or may actually exhibit "compensatory" behavior, which serves to provide more stimulation to their youngsters (preterm babies: Field, 1979; Caesarian section delivered babies: Field & Widmayer, 1980; Vietze et al., Note 2). Furthermore, Hanson (1981) indicated that mothers of Down's syndrome infants in an early intervention program differed little in their behavior toward their infants from mothers of nondisabled infants of the same age. The birth of a child who has a disabling condition or who is at-risk for developmental problems may require caregiver adjustments. The behavior of the caregiver in interacting with the baby, however, may not differ from that of parents of "normal" children, and if differences do exist, they may be functional and positive rather than negative or deviant.

Summary   Findings from developmental research elucidate the importance of the infancy period and of the quality of caregiver-child interaction during this time. Implications from this research for the design of intervention approaches include beginning intervention early in the child's life and actively involving the caregiver. As such, the target for intervention is both the child and the caregivers.

Research Needs

Research findings have provided indices that aid in the definition of target populations for intervention. Many difficult issues remain, however. The "state of the art" on infant assessment and diagnosis indicates an inability to consistently identify those infants who are "at-risk" (determine which babies will eventually need intervention) and determine what type of intervention is most appropriate for a given child.

Extensive research efforts have been devoted to establishing an index from which to identify newborns who are at-risk for developmental delays and who may require intervention services (Parmelee & Haber, 1973; Parmelee et al., 1975). Although longitudinal and comprehensive in scope, the assessment index developed in Parmelee's research does not yet consistently discriminate or predict which newborns will be developmentally delayed. Existing standardized infant development scales and neurological examinations have been shown to be inadequate in terms of predictive validity except with severely involved children, although these assessments are useful in determining an infant's developmental status at a given point in time (Hatcher, 1976; Lewis, 1976).

Given inadequate identification and prediction tools and the tremendous needs for identifying at-risk children, clinicians have once again looked to basic research for useful strategies to assess at-risk and disabled infants. Several of these research tools, such as the habituation paradigm, may hold potential as a means of assessing "cognitive" development of children, in particular those who may be unable to participate in more conventional testing due to sensory and motor impairments. The prospective studies that are needed for prediction are not yet completed, however, and the use of such measures as clinical tools is premature (Friedman, 1975). A case in point involves the use of scales designed to measure temperament for clinical prediction or treatment (Rothbart, Note 3). These scales developed for assessing individual differences in infancy in a research paradigm are now being considered for use as "screening" tools to identify difficult babies and assist caregivers in dealing with them. Although this area is worthy of clinical and research interest, the studies needed to make such scales clinically useful have not been conducted. In addition to questions of predictive validity, serious questions arise in terms of the construct validity of such scales. Temperament is not necessarily a unified or a continuous phenomenon. What may be considered as "difficult" behavior at one point in time may not be labeled as troublesome at another time. Moreover, existing temperament scales usually require parental responses to questions regarding the infant's behavior making it impossible to determine if the measurement is tapping child behavior or parental perception of child behavior. In summary, most existing basic research tools designed for studying infant development, although clinically appealing, are not at present sufficiently analyzed to be clinically useful.

A major area for future research continues to be the development of clinical tools appropriate for prediction and identification of those children who are at-risk for future delay. Beyond that, research is needed also to match child entry characteristics with given intervention approaches so that the most efficient and beneficial treatment can be provided.

HOW SHOULD INTERVENTION BE CONCEPTUALIZED AND IMPLEMENTED?

Contributions from Research Findings and Practice

Discussion in the previous section provided the rationale for including both the child and the caregiver(s) in intervention efforts. Implicit in this rationale is the assumption of an interactive model of child development. An analysis of development from the interactive model posits that developmental outcomes are a product of the child's constitutional status and the child's experience in her or his environment (Sameroff & Chandler, 1975). Thus, contributions of both constitutional and environmental variables are considered in this model.

Using an interactional model, the interventionist may set out to intervene by altering child characteristics and environmental variables. Such a strategy might involve combining several approaches typical of many treatment programs available today for children who are at-risk and/or disabled. One approach is the traditional medical or therapy approach aimed at modifying child behavior through the provision of treatment to the child from another source (e.g., drug therapy, positioning, passive stimulation activities). Such activities center on the child but require no action on the child's part. The opposite approach focuses solely on environmental variables and involves shaping child behavior through feedback from the environment. Although both approaches have produced beneficial effects with given populations, it is likely that optimal outcomes will be achieved only when the child's active involvement with the environment is considered.

Although the interactional model takes nature and nurture variables into account, it assumes that these variables are constant over time. A more comprehensive model proposed by Sameroff and Chandler (1975) is the transactional model, which emphasizes the interdependent nature of constitutional and environmental variables. In this model, child characteristics affect the environment and the child, in turn, is influenced by the environment her or his behavior has in part produced.

Sameroff (this volume) described the transactional model more fully by indicating the influence of cultural variables on the relationship between family members and child. He suggests that a change in structure must occur to differentiate a transaction from an interaction. This transactional model provides a useful theoretical base for describing developmental outcomes with children who are at-risk or disabled. Previous discussion has highlighted the impact both infant and caregiver variables exert on interactions. At a more complex level other external variables or clusters of variables may serve also to alter developmental outcome. These "mediating" variables include medical complications (Littman & Parmelee, 1978); family stability (Drillien, 1964); and social class (Clarke-Stewart, 1973; Tulkin & Kagan, 1972). Several large scale investigations have provided evidence of the powerful effects of these variables. For instance, results from the Kauai study (Werner, Honzik, & Smith, 1968) indicated that perinatal complications alone failed to explain subsequent psychological and physical development of children tested at age 10 except when combined with other variables such as social class. Children whose development was most "retarded" were those who had undergone the most severe perinatal complications and who had experienced the least favorable environments. Similar findings were reported by Drillien (1964) who also noted a relationship between perinatal factors and social status. In that investigation, low birth-weight preterm infants from middle class homes generally fared better (had higher developmental quotients) than those reared in lower social status families. These studies provided evidence to support an interactional model of development. Further analysis of similar data may reveal a transactional effect. Drillien (1964) suggested that obstetric complications may lower the child's resistance to unfavorable environmental circumstances. If such early stress functions to affect the child's ability to process and control the environment or if it serves to influence caregiver attitudes and/or expectations regarding the child's development, effects (outcomes) may be best tested (and treatments designed) when viewed from the transactional perspective. The transactional model of development seems to provide a useful guide or structure from which to conceptualize intervention approaches.

Perhaps the major focus in intervention is on changing the child's and/or caregiver's vulnerability to environmental effects. Programmatically, what does this mean and how can this be accomplished through early intervention programs? Implications for intervention may include the following: 1) provision of treatment and direct skill training to the infant to accelerate the rate of acquisition of developmental milestones, which may result in a modification of parent expectations and thereby offer a more hopeful prognosis; 2) facilitation of the infant's active engagement with the environment, which would serve to provide the child with increased learning opportunities and the caregiver with feedback on the infant's capabilities; 3) assisting caregivers in coping and/or adjusting to the child's atypical behavior or special needs through direct training, provision of information, counseling, observation, support from other parents, and; 4) aiding parents in working with the myriad of agencies with which they must often interact in order to ensure that services be offered in a comprehensive, coordinated fashion. When viewed from this perspective intervention is seen as attenuating the vulnerability of infant and caregiver to adverse conditions and maximizing opportunities for optimal commerce with the environment.

At a molecular level, the outcomes of intervention efforts can be recorded as functional, enjoyable, reciprocal interactions between caregiver and child. At a molar level, societal values may actually be modified. Given that early intervention programs for children at biological risk for handicapping conditions have existed for 10 years throughout the country, the outcomes of such efforts are now evident. A representative case is educational intervention with Down's syndrome infants and their families. Applied investigations have documented the progress of these infants when involved in early training programs (Hanson, 1977, 1981; Hayden & Haring, 1976; Rynders & Horrobin, 1975). Further evidence has shown that the interaction patterns of caregivers and infants participating in such programs may not differ markedly from those of "normal" infants and their parents (Hanson, 1981). The impressive gains made by these children when involved in systematic training approaches seem to have created a ripple effect so that parent expectations are raised and societal roles are beginning to shift. For example, it is more likely that parents today will be counseled by social service and medical contacts to raise their child at home rather than institutionalize the child as was the common practice in the past. Reports of Down's syndrome children mastering academic skills, such as reading and being integrated into more regular school placements, have increased in the popular press and received considerable public discussion. Intervention efforts with Down's syndrome infants and their families, therefore, provides an example of the transactions that may occur—infant behavior is changed, parent attitudes and expectations are modified, and lastly, such effects ultimately may modify the view society holds of handicapped persons.

Research Needs

Intervention is conceptualized as a complex network of services to the child and family. These services emphasize an active involvement of child and family in their environment. This view raises multiple issues surrounding the evaluation of intervention approaches, namely issues regarding what and how intervention can be measured.

Evaluation efforts typically have focused on measuring child behavior change (Friedlander et al., 1975; Tjossem, 1976). When developmental outcomes are viewed from a transactional model, however, it is evident that a single measure of child behavior is insufficient to describe a comprehensive intervention effort. Rather, analysis of program effects requires the use of multiple measures. Ramey (Note 4) alluded to a similar approach in his description of the five levels of social consequences of early intervention: 1) effects on the child's behavior and attitudes; 2) effect on the child's relationships with family members (e.g., attachment); 3) effect on the family unit (e.g., work and educational patterns); 4) effect on the family's relationship with social agencies such as the Department of Social Services; and 5) effect on social and cultural institutions. He advocated various levels of data analysis to include measures of attitudes and behavior, and relevant persons and economic factors that may be affected by early intervention. Data at the levels outlined exist for the Carolina Abecedarian Project for high-risk preschoolers, described by Ramey (Note 4). To date, however, few large scale early intervention investigations have been undertaken that can provide similar data for programs involving children with established risks. Although small intervention programs are flourishing, evaluation of these efforts is difficult. Difficulties in cross program comparisons arise due to differences in target populations, approaches, and measures employed. Data pools available across programs from which to analyze results for larger groups of children are not available.

At examination of the "state of the art" of available assessments of infant and caregiver behavior reflects the critical need in this area for new instruments and approaches. Even in the area that can be best measured—infant behavior—available instruments are insufficient for evaluation purposes. Current tests such as the Bayley Scales of Infant Development (Bayley, 1969) and Griffiths' Mental Development Scale (Griffiths, 1954) provide gross behavioral indices of the child's functioning relative to normative status. Although such tests are appropriate and useful for their intended purpose of studying individual differences in infancy, they are inappropriate for use with many handicapped children (e.g., physically involved and sensory impaired) and are unlikely to reflect small changes that may result from training efforts with these children. Furthermore, as was previously discussed, these instruments fail to reflect the "total picture" as to the effects of consequences of early intervention. Other measures considered necessary to reflect the breadth of intervention services may include measures of caregiver attitudes and behavior. Although many parent attitude scales are available, few are useful with young handicapped or at-risk populations. Further work in this area, such as that by Bromwich (Bromwich, 1979, 1981) is necessary to measure caregiver behavior and interactional processes.

In summary, the model of early intervention proposed requires a complex array of services and necessitates the analysis of infant and caregiver interaction. The assessment tools and approaches for isolating the results or consequences of such intervention efforts are lacking, however, thereby underscoring a major research need.

WHAT SHOULD INTERVENTIONS INCLUDE?

Contributions from Research Findings and Practice

The literature on infant development suggests the philosophy around which an intervention curriculum should be established. Clinical practice, in turn, provides the framework within that structure for decision making and goal identification. Therefore, the discussion on content or "what should be included for intervention approaches" must focus on influences from both areas. Contributions from the developmental literature include information on the competencies and individual differences of infants, the effect of infants on caregivers, caregiver-infant interaction, and process-oriented infant learning experiences. Assumptions relevant for assisting infants to functionally interact with their environments also are examined in light of current practices in the field.

Findings from research in child development provide the underpinnings for intervention efforts with infants. First, as was previously discussed, the infant has been characterized as a competent and active learner (Stone, Smith, & Murphy, 1973) whose characteristics and behavior may exert tremendous effects on the caregivers' attitudes and behavior (Lewis & Rosenblum, 1974). Second, recent investigations on individual differences in infancy (Carey, 1973; Rothbart et al., Note 5) have contributed to a growing awareness of the importance of studying early behavior patterns. An understanding and identification of these early differences may ultimately be used to assist parents and teachers in "reading" the infant's cues and in adapting to the infant's style (Goldberg, 1977).

A focus on the reciprocal relationship between caregiver and infant represents the third, and perhaps most important, area of concern in identifying treatment strategies. The previous discussion has established the case for approaching intervention as a complex system of services for the whole family, not just the child. The research on attachment and early social learning interactions involving the parent and child reinforces this approach (Ainsworth, 1973; Schaffer & Emerson, 1964). Recent studies have postulated that even interaction within the first hours and days of life are critical for optimal infant development (Klaus et al., 1972). Many infants are deprived of this early contact and subjected to medical intrusions due to prematurity and other perinatal complications. Stimulation, typically involving increased handling and auditory and visual experiences, has produced beneficial effects on development (Powell, 1974; Scarr-Salapatek & Williams, 1973; Solkoff et al., 1969). A careful monitoring and analysis of infant response to early stimulation is necessary, however, to determine type and timing of treatment (Gorski, Note 6). The literature examining early experiences between caregivers and infants warrants attention as a focal point in the design and implementation of a treatment approach.

A final set of research findings with implications for early intervention efforts centers on the role of contingent learning in infant development (Lewis & Goldberg, 1969). In this learning paradigm the infant exercises control over her or his environment and is able to produce predictable outcomes. Thus, if the infant's behavior is responded to consistently, the infant may learn that her or his actions affect the environment. These skills are generally accepted as essential to learning, motivation, and affective and cognitive development. Studies by Watson (Watson, 1972; Watson & Ramey, 1972) on contingent learning suggest that infants receiving contingent experiences as contrasted to noncontingent controls not only learned target motor behavior, but also exhibited positive affective responses. Other investigations suggested "contingency" experiences have a generalized facilitory effect on retention and learning of other unrelated responses (Finkelstein & Ramey, 1977; Rovee & Fagan, 1976). This research suggests the potential usefulness of developing "process" oriented curricula designed to teach children to "learn to learn" (Hanson, Note 7; Lewis, Note 8).

Infant development research provides the framework for formulating general intervention goals. Contributions from applied early intervention research and clinical practice aid in the pragmatic aspects of intervention. In the haste to ensure that development occurs in target infants according to normal sequences, the functional needs of the child and family are often overlooked. The realities of daily living in our society and input from families dictate that the interventions provided establish the training of functional, adaptive skills as a principle underlying all therapeutic efforts. Infants must be able to communicate effectively, achieve mobility, and actively engage in meaningful environmental interactions. Likewise, caregivers must be able to understand and "read" their infants' cues and needs, provide stimulation and appropriate care, and engage in mutually satisfying interactions with the infants. Training efforts, therefore, should be focused on achieving functional behavior. An analysis of child behavior needed to engage in normal environmental interactions provides a means of identifying necessary skills or behavior. For instance, a survey by Vincent et al. (1980) documented the skills needed by children to survive in public preschool programs. Skills identified fell predominantly into the category of social-survival skills, which included behavior related to completing tasks without teacher direction or reinforcement. The importance of being able to work independently and in large groups was stressed. Information of this type provides valuable guidance to the intervention provider in formulating goals.

Research and Demonstration Needs

Many effective curricula are available as guides for early intervention programs designed for children who are disabled or at-risk. They include, for example, *The Portage Project* (Bluma et al., 1976), *Learning Accomplishment Profile Learning Guide* (1975), *Hawaii Early Learning Profile* (1979), *Teaching Your Down's Syndrome Infant: A Guide for Parents* (Hanson, 1977), *Teaching the Young Motor Delayed Child: A Guide for Parents* (Hanson & Campbell, in press), *Handling the Young Cerebral Palsied Child at Home* (Finnie, 1975), *Program Guide for Infants and Toddlers with Neuromotor and Other Developmental Disabilities* (Connor, Williamson, & Siepp, 1978), and the *Carolina Curriculum for Handicapped Infants* (Johnson, Jens, & Attermeier, 1979). Most infant curricula are comprised of a developmentally sequenced series of activities or tasks based on the acquisition of normal developmental milestones. Since normative information is most readily available from infant assessment tools, curriculum items and materials often closely resemble test items. By the nature of testing procedures, these assessments provide only molar indicators of normative development. Information lacking, but needed for curriculum building includes: The identification of "critical" skills or prerequisite skills for later development; an understanding of the processes of development and strategies for facilitating these processes; an analysis of component skills necessary to achieve more global milestones such as independent walking; and a description of the quality of behavior needed for more normal functioning.

In the actual training process a number of unsolved issues remain that are pertinent to intervention efforts with infants. These issues include: identification and selection of appropriate and effective reinforcers (novel vs. familiar, social vs. nonsocial); temporal parameters in the delivery of reinforcers/consequences (latency); type of reinforcement (e.g., discrete, conjugate); schedules or reinforcement; and type of exploratory experiences necessary for optimal learning (compensatory experiences if child is sensorially or motorically impaired, functional vs. nonfunctional use of objects). This list is by no means exhaustive but highlights the breadth of technical decisions that must be addressed in implementing training procedures. Empirical investigation of these issues is needed to provide guidance in intervention planning.

A final issue is the identification of viable service delivery models. These models must accommodate a variety of children ranging from at-risk infants to those with severe and multiple impairments and must include services for various "family" constellations. Above all, these models must reflect the transdisciplinary services needed for infants. Although few would argue that coordinated service efforts are needed, comprehensive and viable models for provision of these services are scarce.

SUMMARY

Educators are increasingly faced with the task of providing appropriate services for young children with special needs. The design of these early intervention services by necessity demands a synthesis of research findings on developmental processes with service delivery systems and clinical needs. The purpose of this chapter is to discuss the application of research to the identification of clinical models for early intervention. The discussion focuses first on the issue of defining *who* should be the target of intervention services. A review of pertinent literature clearly points to the importance of including both the infant and the infant's caregivers in any intervention effort. The development of clinical tools for identification and prediction with children who are at-risk for developmental delay, however, is discussed as a remaining research task.

The second set of factors considered is the issue of *how* early interventions should be conceptualized and designed. The transactional model of development is suggested as the structure through which to view and define intervention approaches. Questions surrounding the evaluation of these approaches are raised as a focus for future research. The third discussion section centers on issues of *what* should be included in intervention efforts. Curriculum design is analyzed in terms of incorporating information available on the competencies of and individual differences across infants, and on the effects of infants on their caregivers and the caregivers on infants. Additionally, issues of process vs. content curriculum and establishing goals for training functional skills are described. Finally, training issues and service delivery needs are identified.

The demand for early intervention programs is growing. Such programs will increasingly be forced to accommodate diverse groups of infants ranging from those at-risk for later delays to those with identifiable severe and multiple impairments. Given that early intervention efforts with these infants is a relatively new phenomenon having come into existence in the last 10 years, the identification and definition of intervention approaches is still an active and evolving process.

REFERENCES

Ainsworth, M. The development of infant and mother attachment. In B. Caldwell & H. Ricciuti (Eds.), *Review of child development research* (Vol. 3). Chicago: The University of Chicago Press, 1973.

Ainsworth, M., & Bell, S. Mother-infant interaction and the development of competence. In K. Connolly & J. Bruner (Eds.), *The growth of competence*. New York: Academic Press, 1975.

Appleton, A., Clifton, R., & Goldberg, S. The development of behavioral competence in infancy. In F. Horowitz (Ed.), *Review of child development research* (Vol. 4). Chicago: University of Chicago Press, 1975.

Bayley, N. *Bayley scales of infant development*. New York: The Psychological Corporation, 1969.

Beckwith, L., & Cohen, S. Preterm birth: Hazardous obstetrical and postnatal events as related to caregiver-infant behavior. *Infant Behavior and Development*, 1978, *1*, 403–411.

Beller, E. Early intervention programs. In J. Osofsky (Ed.), *Handbook of infant development*. New York: John Wiley & Sons, 1979.

Bluma, S., Shearer, M., Frohman, A., & Hilliard, J. *Portage guide to early education* (Rev. Ed.). Cooperative Educational Service Agency, #12, Portage, Wisc. 1976.

Brennan, W., Ames, E., & Moore, R. Age differences in infants' attention to patterns of different complexities. *Science*, 1966, *151*, 1354–1356.

Bromwich, R. *Manual for the parent behavior progression (PBP)*. Northridge, Cal. California State University, 1979.

Bromwich, R. *Working with parents and infants: An interactional approach*. Baltimore: University Park Press, 1981.

Bronfenbrenner, U. Is early intervention effective? In B. Friedlander, G. Sterritt, & G. Kirk (Eds.), *Exceptional infant* (Vol. 3). New York: Brunner/Mazel, 1975.

Buium, N., Rynders, J., & Turnure, J. Early maternal linguistics environment of normal and Down's syndrome language-learning children. *American Journal of Mental Deficiency*, 1974, *79*, 52–58.

Carey, W. Measurement of infant temperament in pediatric practice. In J. Westman (Ed.), *Individual differences in children*. New York: Wiley-Interscience, 1973.

Cicchetti, D., & Sroufe, L. The relationship between affective and cognitive development in Down's syndrome infants. *Child Development*, 1976, *47*, 920–929.

Clarke-Stewart, K. Interactions between mothers and their young children: Characteristics and consequences. *Monographs of the Society for Research in Child Development,* 1973, *38* (6–7, Serial No. 153), 1–109.

Connor, F., Williamson, G., & Siepp, J. (Eds.), *Program guide for infants and toddlers with neuromotor and other developmental disabilities.* New York: Teachers College Press, 1978.

Dayton, G., Jones, M., Steele, B., & Rose, M. Developmental study of conditioned eye movements in the human infant. II. An electro-oculographic study of the fixation reflex in the newborn. *Archives in Ophthalmology,* 1964, *71,* 871–875.

Drillien, C. *The growth and development of the prematurely born infant.* Baltimore: Williams and Wilkins, 1964.

Eimas, P., Siqueland, E., Juzczyk, P., & Vigorito, J. Speech perception in infants. *Science,* 1971, *171,* 303–306.

Fantz, R. A method for studying depth perception in infants under 6 months of age. *Psychological Record,* 1961, *11,* 27–32.

Field, T. (Ed.). *Infants born at-risk: Behavior and development.* New York: Medical and Scientific Books, 1979.

Field, T., & Widmayer, S. Developmental follow-up of infants delivered by caesarian section and general anesthesia. *Infant Behavior and Development,* 1980, *3,* 187–204.

Finkelstein, N., & Ramey, C. Learning to control the environment in infancy. *Child Development,* 1977, *48,* 806–819.

Finnie, N. *Handling the young cerebral palsied child at home (2nd edition).* New York: E. P. Dutton & Co., 1975.

Fraiberg, S. *Insights from the blind.* New York: Basic Books, 1977.

Fraiberg, S. Parallel and divergent patterns in blind and sighted infants. *Psychoanalytic Study of the Child,* 1968, *23,* 264–299.

Friedlander, B., Sterritt, G., & Kirk, G. (Eds.), *Exceptional infant* (Vol. 3): *Assessment and intervention.* New York: Brunner/Mazel, 1975.

Friedman, S. Infant habituation: Processes, problems and possibilities. In N. Ellis (Ed.), *Aberrant development in infancy: Human and animal studies.* Hillsdale, N.J.: Lawrence Erlbaum Associates, 1975.

Goldberg, S. Social competence in infancy: A model of parent-infant interaction. *Merrill-Palmer Quarterly,* 1977, *23,* 163–177.

Goldberg, S. Prematurity: Effects of parent-infant interaction. *Journal of Pediatric Psychology,* 1978, *3,* 137–144.

Griffiths, R. *The abilities of babies.* New York: McGraw-Hill, 1954.

Haaf, R., & Bell, R. A facial dimension in visual discrimination by human infants. *Child Development,* 1967, *38,* 895–899.

Hanson, M. *Teaching your Down's syndrome infant: A guide for parents.* Baltimore: University Park Press, 1977.

Hanson, M. Down's syndrome children: Characteristics and intervention research. In· M. Lewis & L. Rosenblum (Eds.), *Genesis of behavior: The Uncommon Child.* New York: Plenum Press, 1981.

Hanson, M., & Campbell, P. *Teaching the young motor delayed child: A guide for parents.* Baltimore: University Park Press, in press.

Hatcher, R. The predictability of infant intelligence scales: A critical review and evaluation. *Mental Retardation,* 1976, *14,* 16–20.

Hawaii Early Learning Profile (HELP). Compiled by the Enrichment Project for Handicapped Infants, S. Furuno, K. O'Reilly, C. Hosaka, T. Inatsuka, T. Allman, B. Zeisloft. Palo Alto, California: VORT Corporation, 1979.

Hayden, A., & Haring, N. Programs for Down's syndrome children at the

University of Washington. In T. Tjossem (Ed.), *Intervention strategies for high-risk infants and young children*. Baltimore: University Park Press, 1976.

Hayden, A., & McGinness, G. Bases for early intervention. In E. Sontag (Ed.), *Educational programming for the severely and profoundly handicapped*. Reston, Va: Division on Mental Retardation, The Council for Exceptional Children, 1977.

Hershenson, M. Visual discrimination in the human newborn. *Journal of Comparative Physiological Psychology*, 1964, *58*, 270–276.

Horowitz, F., & Paden, L. The effectiveness of environmental intervention programs. In B. Caldwell & H. Ricciuti (Eds.), *Review of child development research* (Vol. 3). Chicago: The University of Chicago Press, 1973.

Isaacson, R. The myth of recovery from early brain damage. In N. Ellis (Ed.), *Aberrant development in infancy: Human and animal studies*. Hillsdale, N.J.: Lawrence Erlbaum Associates, 1975.

Johnson, N., Jens, K., & Attermeier, S. *Carolina curriculum for handicapped infants (Field test edition)*. Chapel Hill, N.C.: Carolina Institute for Research on Early Education for the Handicapped, 1979.

Kessen, W., Haith, M., & Salapatek, P. Human infancy: A bibliography and guide. In P. Mussen (Ed.), *Carmichael's manual of child psychology* (Vol. 1, 3rd Ed.). New York: John Wiley & Sons, 1970.

Klaus, M., Jerauld, R., Kreger, N., McAlpine, W., Steffa, M., & Kennell, J. Maternal attachment: Importance of the first postpartum days. *New England Journal of Medicine*, 1972, *286*, 460–463.

Klein, M., & Stern, L. Low birthweight and battered child syndrome. *American Journal of Disorders in Children*, 1971, *122*, 15–18.

Kogan, K., & Tyler, N. Mother-child interaction in young physically handicapped children. *American Journal of Mental Deficiency*, 1973, *77*, 492–497.

Learning Accomplishment Profile for Infants. Compiled by Chapel Hill Training-Outreach Project, P. Griffin & A. Sanford. Winston-Salem, N.C. Kaplan Press, 1975.

Lewis, M. (Ed.). *Origins of intelligence: Infancy and early childhood*. New York: Plenum Press, 1976.

Lewis, M., & Goldberg, S. Perceptual-cognitive development in infancy: A generalized expectancy model as a function of the mother-infant interaction. *Merrill-Palmer Quarterly of Behavior and Development*, 1969, *15*, 81–100.

Lewis, M., & Rosenblum, L. (Eds.). *The effect of the infant on its caregiver*. New York: John Wiley & Sons, 1974.

Littman, B., & Parmelee, A. Medical correlates of infant development. *Pediatrics*, 1978, *61*, 470–474.

Marshall, N., Hegrenes, J., & Goldstein, S. Verbal interactions: Mothers and their retarded children vs. mothers and their nonretarded children. *American Journal of Mental Deficiency*, 1973, *77*, 415–419.

McCall, R., & Kagan, J. Attention in the infant: Effects of complexity, contour perimeter & familiarity. *Child Development*, 1967, *38*, 939–952.

Parmelee, A., & Haber, A. Who is the "risk infant"? In H. Osofsky (Ed.), *Clinical Obstetrics and Gynecology*. New York: Harper & Row, 1973.

Parmelee, A., Sigman, M., Kopp, C., & Haber, A. The concept of a cumulative risk score for infants. In N. Ellis (Ed.), *Aberrant development in infancy: Human and animal studies*. Hillsdale, N.J.: Lawrence Erlbaum Associates, 1975.

Powell, L. The effect of extra stimulation and maternal involvement on the development of low birthweight infants and on maternal behavior. *Child Development*, 1974, *45*, 106–113.

Rovee, C., & Fagan, J. Extended conditioning and 24-hour retention in infants. *Journal of Experimental Child Psychology*, 1976, *21*, 1–11.

Rynders, J., & Horrobin, J. Project EDGE: The University of Minnesota's communication stimulation program for Down's syndrome infants. In B. Friedlander, G. Sterritt & G. Kirk (Eds.), *Exceptional infant: Assessment and intervention* (Vol. 3). New York: Brunner/Mazel, 1975.

Sameroff, A., & Chandler, M. Reproductive risk and the continuum of caretaking casuality. In F. Horowitz (Ed.), *Review of child development research* (Vol. 4). Chicago: University of Chicago Press, 1975.

Scarr-Salapatek, S., & Williams, M., The effects of early stimulation on low birthweight infants. *Child Development*, 1973, *44*, 94–102.

Schaffer, H., & Emerson, P. The development of social attachments in infancy. *Monographs of the Society for Research in Child Development*, 1964, *29*.

Shaheen, E., Alexander, D., Truskowsky, M., & Barbero, G. Failure to thrive—A retrospective profile. *Clinical Pediatrics*, 1968, *7*, 255–261.

Solkoff, N., Yaffe, S., Weintraub, D., & Blase, B. Effects of handling on the subsequent development of premature infants. *Developmental Psychology*, 1969, *1*, 765–768.

Stone, J., Smith, H., & Murphy, L. (Eds.). *The competent infant*. New York: Basic Books, 1973.

Tjossem, T. (Ed.). *Intervention strategies for high risk infants and young children*. Baltimore: University Park Press, 1976.

Trincker, D., & Trincker, I. Development of brightness in infants. In Y. Brackbill & G. Thompson (Eds.), *Behavior in infancy and early childhood: A book of readings*. New York: Free Press,, 1967.

Tulkin, S., & Kagan, J. Mother-child interaction in the first year of life. *Child Development*, 1972, *43*, 31–41.

Turnbull, H., & Turnbull, A. *Free appropriate public education: Law and implementation*. Denver, Colorado: Love Publishing Company, 1978.

Vincent, L., Salisbury, C., Walter, G., Brown, P., Gruenewald, L., & Powers, M. Program evaluation and curriculum development in early childhood/special education: Criteria of the next environment. In W. Sailor, B. Wilcox, and L. Brown (Eds.), *Methods of instruction for severely handicapped students*. Baltimore: Paul H. Brookes Publishers, 1980.

Watson, J. Smiling, cooing, and "the game." *Merrill-Palmer Quarterly*, 1972, *18*, 323–339.

Watson, J., & Ramey, C. Reactions to response-contingent stimulation in early infancy. *Merrill-Palmer Quarterly*, 1972, *18*, 219–227.

Werner, E., Honzik, M., & Smith, R. Prediction of intelligence and achievement at ten years from twenty months pediatric and psychological examinations. *Child Development*, 1968, *39*, 1036–1074.

Yarrow, L., Rubenstein, J., Pedersen, F., & Jankowski, J. Dimensions of early stimulation and their different effects on infant development. *Merrill-Palmer Quarterly*, 1972, *18*, 205–218.

REFERENCE NOTES

1. Als, H., Brazelton, T., Lester, B., & Landers, C. *Caesarean section: Differential impact on newborn behavior*. Paper presented at the International Conference on Infant Studies, New Haven, Connecticut, April, 1980.

2. Vietze, P., MacTurk, R., McCarthy, M., Klein, R., & Yarrow, L. *Impact of mode of delivery on father and mother-infant interactions at six months*. Paper presented at the International Conference on Infant Studies, New Haven, Connecticut, April, 1980.
3. Rothbart, M. *Personal communication*. April, 1980.
4. Ramey, C. *The social consequences of early intervention*. Paper presented at the American Association on Mental Deficiency, New Orleans, June, 1977.
5. Rothbart, M., Furby, L., Kelly, S., & Hamilton, J. *Development of a caretaker report temperament scale for use with 3, 6, 9, and 12 month old infants*. Paper presented at the Meeting of the Society for Research in Child Development, New Orleans, March, 1977.
6. Gorski, P. *Interactive influences on development—identifying and supporting infants born at-risk*. Paper presented at Annual Meeting American Academy of Child Psychiatry, Chicago, October, 1980.
7. Hanson, M. *Curriculum development and related research with moderately and severely handicapped infants*. Paper presented at the Fifth Annual American Association for the Education of the Severely/Profoundly Handicapped Conference, Baltimore, October, 1978.
8. Lewis, M. *Institute for the study of exceptional children: Research plan*. Princeton, N.J.: Educational Testing Service, 1978–1979.

Chapter 16

PSYCHOSOCIAL RETARDATION AND THE EARLY EXPERIENCE PARADIGM

Craig T. Ramey and Lynne Baker-Ward

Scientific research is never conducted by unbiased researchers in neutral environments. In contrast to the idealized picture of the objectivity of the scientific community, empirical research normally takes place within the boundaries established by shared beliefs about nature. Thomas Kuhn (1962) introduced the term *paradigm* to define the pervasive models of reality that tell scientists about the entities that nature can and cannot contain. Typical scientific research, according to Kuhn, is addressed to the articulation of the theories and phenomena that the accepted paradigm already provides. A paradigm supplies the scientist with both a map and directions for map-making: The accepted paradigm defines the phenomena that constitute valid research problems, and directs the procedures by which these problems are addressed.

The study of human development, like other areas of scientific inquiry, has been constrained by adherence to particular paradigms throughout the history of the discipline.[1] The paradigms that form the boundaries for psychological and educational research, however, may be distinguished on the basis of their immediate application to clinical and educational practice and social policy. Hence, the pervasive model of reality that guides research in the area of psychosocial retardation also shapes practices for the identification and treatment of infants at risk for psychosocial retardation. For this reason, it is important to explore the model of reality that has determined the current understanding of psychosocial retardation.

---

[1] It should be noted, however, that there is disagreement as to whether universal paradigms as defined by Kuhn with regard to the physical sciences are extant in the behavioral and social sciences (e.g., see Buss, 1978). Although we acknowledge that paradigms in different branches of science are not isomorphic, we find the concept a useful heuristic for this discussion.

EXISTENCE OF THE EARLY EXPERIENCE PARADIGM

In the decades since World War II, a pervasive model for normal and atypical human development has been apparent. Kesson (1979) dubbed this model "the doctrine of the primacy of early experience" (p. 819). The child's experiences during the opening years of life have been widely regarded as critical determinants of later social and intellectual functioning. Yarrow (1961) observed: "The significance of early infantile experience for later development has been reiterated so frequently and so persistently that the general validity of this assertion is now almost unchallenged" (p. 459). Kagan (1979) argued that a central premise of the modern conceptualization of human development is the belief that psychological structures created by early experience are stable throughout the lifespan. Although the doctrine of the primacy of early experience has recently been challenged (Clarke & Clarke, 1976; Kagan, Kearsley, & Zelazo, 1978), large claims concerning the critical importance of the child's earliest experiences continue to be made. Klaus and Kennell (1976), for example, argued that "affectional ties can be easily disturbed and may be permanently altered during the immediate postpartum period . . . early events have long-lasting effects" (p. 52).

The conceptualization of development as critically affected by certain early experiences has inevitably influenced the way that development is studied. Hunt (1979) located 1,197 references to early experience for 1968–1977 in *Psychological Abstracts* alone; he found only 300 investigations of early experience in the literature prior to 1954. Hunt's claim that there is "exploding knowledge in this domain" is well-substantiated.

The view that early experience is a crucial determinant of behavior also has had profound ramifications for educational practices and social policy. Because experiences during the early portion of the lifespan have been assigned a causal role in the establishment of developmental outcomes, a strong environmentalism has guided practice and policy in the area of special education. Zigler and Anderson (1979) summarized the appeal of environmentalism as follows:

> Environmentalism became the Zeitgeist. . . . the public hailed the construction of a solid foundation for learning in preschool children as the solution to poverty and ignorance. (pp. 7–8)

The doctrine of the primacy of early experience has thus functioned as a paradigm in developmental psychology. It has been widely and frequently accepted without question as a tacit theoretical assumption; it has mandated the consideration of research problems germane to this model of development; it has provided the rationale for public policy. Like all paradigms, the early experience paradigm has functioned as a powerful lens through which psychologists, educators, and others have examined human development. The paradigm has focused attention on certain phenomena; magnified the significance of certain findings; and, of equal importance, has filtered out some anomalous facts and observations. The early experience paradigm has, to a great extent, affected not only what we currently think about psychosocial retardation and other aspects of normal and atypical human development; it has also been influential in defining the limits of our understanding and the gaps in our knowledge. An examination of the theoretical assumptions that underlie the treatment of children at risk for psychosocial retardation requires an exploration of the ramifications of this model of reality. This examination first requires the consideration of the scientific and extra-scientific factors that led to the establishment of the early experience paradigm.

ESTABLISHMENT OF THE EARLY EXPERIENCE PARADIGM

The idea that the individual's early experiences are of particular consequence for later development is an old one. This concept was advocated in the writings of Plato in the fourth century B.C.; reflected in the Old Testament; and acknowledged by the empiricists (see Hunt, 1979). Yet in spite of the history of the construct, the significance of early experience was advanced only intermittently in the history of Western thought. Other concepts more frequently provided the dominant models of human development. Until the eighteenth century, preformationism was the prevailing view. The process of development was seen as the growth in size of the perfectly formed homunculus thought to be present in human sperm. Predeterminism replaced preformationism in the nineteenth century, and was advanced by Galton and other proponents of the primacy of heredity in development. Predeterminism acknowledged maturational changes, but held that they were relatively encapsulated and consequently unaffected by early experiences (Gottlieb, 1971). This view induced two empirical traditions that denied the contributions of early experience to later development (see Hunt, 1979). One avenue of research followed early in the twentieth century led to the conclusion that instincts are unlearned patterns of behavior that emerge only as the result of physical maturation (e.g., Lorenz, 1937). The second denial of the significance of early experience was particularly influential in child psychology. The rate of behavioral development was seen as controlled only by maturation, which was predetermined by the child's genetic make-up (e.g., Gesell, 1946).

In contrast to predeterminism, any model stressing the importance of early experience implicitly assumes the probabilistic epigenesis of behavior. As presented by Gottlieb (1971), the probabilistic viewpoint postulates bidirectional relationships between maturation, function, and behavior. While predeterminism holds that the maturational process is relatively unaffected by experience, probabilism assumes that maturation is affected by function and behavior (sensory stimulation and motor movement). The early experience paradigm not only replaced the predetermined model of development with the probabilistic model, it also held that the presence of absence of stimulation or other experience at some critical point in development could shape the individual's ontogeny.

By the early 1960s, the doctrine of the primacy of early experience was so thoroughly entrenched in American psychology that it was accepted without challenge, as discussed above. How did this conceptualization of the critical importance of early experience come to be so influential in such a relatively short period of time? Kuhn (1962) contended that both scientific and "extra-scientific" factors are involved in the establishment of any paradigm. Such was the case with the early experience paradigm; both the scientific and the political zeitgeists contributed to the construction of this model of reality.

The Scientific Bases of the Early Experience Paradigm

Evidence from three major streams of investigations flowed together in establishing the doctrine of the primacy of early experience. Freud's theory of psychosexual development, more than any other stream of psychological thought, contributed significantly to the popular acceptance of the concept that early experience is a critical determinant of later behavior. As early as 1905, with the publication of the second of his *Three Essays on the Theory of Sexuality,* Freud implied that the early experiences of infants and young children in such commonplace situations as feeding and toilet training are associated with later personality disorders. Throughout its history, the psychoanalytic tradition has stressed the importance of the early relationships between young children and their parents, particularly the attachment between the mother and the infant (e.g., Spitz, 1945).

A second scientific tradition that contributed to the establishment of the early experience paradigm flows from ethology. The phenomena of imprinting, as presented by Lorenz (1937), were interpreted as representing a unique predisposition for learning, present for only a brief critical period. Although imprinting was observed initially and most extensively in precocial birds, it was also shown to be operational in the early attachments of mammals, such as lambs, goats, and dogs (Beach & Jaynes, 1954). The concept of imprinting was extended to humans in the work on maternal-infant attachment, a literature that merges the basic constructs of psychoanalytic theory with ethology.

The third scientific tradition contributing to the establishment of the early experience paradigm provided a neuropsychological theory for the existence of critical periods in intellectual as well as social development. Hebb (1949) emphasized the significance of early sensory experience for the formation of "cell assemblies," formulating a neurological basis for the primacy of early experiences. Subsequent investigations with animals revealed that variations in early experience affected both the organization and the biological bases of subsequent behavior (e.g., Thomson & Heron, 1954). This evidence substantiated the claim that critical periods, determined by neurological factors, exist for intellectual development.

As the early experience paradigm flowered, its roots branched from the Freudian idea that early experience is important for later social and sexual behavior to the belief that it is also critical for later intellectual and instrumental competencies. Furthermore, the conceptualization of the impact of early experience was broadened and deepened. Initially, early experience was seen to predispose an individual toward a certain personality structure and a consequent propensity to respond to certain situations in predictable ways. Later, the extension of the concept of critical periods to humans conceptualized early experience as imparting stable and irreversible neurological consequences that could set a ceiling for later problem-solving behavior. Although the empirical support for this notion was both scant and limited to investigations with laboratory animals, this interpretation of the effects of early experience formed the basis for much of the work done in the area of psychosocial retardation in the past several decades.

Extension of the Doctrine of Early Experience

Public awareness of the pervasive environmentalist viewpoint stemmed largely from the work of J. McVicker Hunt and Benjamin Bloom (Zigler & Anderson, 1979). In *Intelligence and Experience,* Hunt (1961) put to rest the idea that intelligence was genetically predetermined and fixed throughout an individual's life. As an alternative, he provided an interpretation of Piaget's work integrated with learning theory. Hunt's "concept of the match" assigned a greater role in intellectual development to the characteristics of the environment than to the hereditary make-up of the individual. Successful developmental outcomes were seen as the cumulative result of the child's successive interactions with increasingly complex stimuli. Hence, adequate intellectual development depended upon the child's receiving the appropriate stimulation at the appropriate point in development. Hunt's statement did not postulate critical periods in development, but implied that early experience was particularly important. As stated by Hunt (1979): ". . . the longer a young organism lives with experience of a given development-fostering quality, the more difficult it is to change the nature of the effect" (p. 124). Hunt's work thus gave an important impetus to the compensatory education movement by conveying two important scientific constructs to the public: 1) intelligence is developed through the child's interactions with an environment that provides stimulation appropriate to the child's current level of cognitive functioning; and 2) the provision of an appropriate environment for intellectual development early in life is particularly important.

The work of Benjamin Bloom was also important in establishing the primacy of early experience as a pervasive model of reality. In *Stability and Change in Human Characteristics,* Bloom (1964) made two major points that provided the impetus for preschool intervention. First, he posited that intellectual growth occurred most rapidly in the first four to five years of life, and tapered off by the time the child had entered grade school. Second, Bloom argued that the first 5 years of life were a critical period for intellectual development. Intellectual development was characterized by plasticity only during the early years of life. Consequently, the first few years provided the only opportunity for facilitating intellectual development by enriching the child's environment.

Extra-scientific Bases of the Early Experience Paradigm

The political zeitgeist was also an important determinant of the early experience paradigm. Public attention was directed in the early 1960s to widespread poverty in the United States (see Zigler & Anderson, 1979). Nine million Americans were reported to have an annual income below $3,000 in 1963; 40% of the young men called for military service were found to be unfit for duty because of deficiencies in their educational backgrounds or health. Explanations and solutions that would not disturb middle-class consciences and pocketbooks were sought by politicians. Consequently, the government embarked upon a strategy for eradicating poverty that would later be called "blaming the victim" (Ryan, 1971). Economic deprivation was construed as cultural deprivation; it was argued that early education could compensate for this cultural deprivation. Although policy makers had not been provided with formal sufficient investigation of compensatory education[2], the social and political appeal of the early experience paradigm compen-

---

[2] See the following discussion of the work of Kirk (1958). Although, in effect, a pilot study for Head Start existed, it was virtually ignored prior to the implementation of the project (Clarke & Clarke, 1976). The selective inattention given to this study by both social scientists and policy analysts evidences the existence of the early experience paradigm.

sated for its lack of empirical verification. The environmentalist view-point and the emphasis on intellectual attainment in the compensatory education movement harmonized well with the American ethos (Keesen, 1979).

A more pragmatic political concern contributed further to the immediate implementation of Project Head Start, the center of the compensatory education movement and the educational embodiment of the early experience paradigm. The War on Poverty was threatened by the opposition of local governments to Community Action Programs (CAP), which were designed to place both program funding and administration directly in the hands of the poor. Consequently, the administrators of the War on Poverty sought a community action program that would benefit the poor without misaligning local governments (Zigler & Anderson, 1979). It was determined that programs for the 12 million children whose families were below the poverty line would meet the mandate to attack the roots of poverty. As a service for the children of poverty, program administration by the poor was less threatening to local governments. Furthermore, the program's common sense appeal was an asset to its acceptance. At the same time, the Head Start program diverted attention from more controversial CAP programs.

Hence, several factors were instrumental in the establishment of the early experience paradigm in psychology and education: Extension of scientific traditions examining the psychosocial and physiological effects of early experience; the compatibility of the resulting environmentalism with American values and traditions; and the extant political climate. A strong emphasis on the importance of early experience in determining intellectual development involves the corollary that positive changes in the child's environment could result in increases in measured intelligence. This corollary formed the rationale for the compensatory education movement. The early experience paradigm purported to identify the causes of psychosocial retardation, and to specify the means by which it could be eradicated. According to the early experience paradigm, intellectual deficiencies arose from the inadequacy of the poor child's environment. These deficiencies and the resulting cycle of poverty could be shortcircuited by providing the poor child with compensatory education during the preschool years, the putative critical period for intellectual development.

IMPLICATIONS OF THE EARLY EXPERIENCE PARADIGM

Scientific Implications

Kuhn (1962) suggested that science normally proceeds by documenting shared beliefs and by substantiating existing theories. Normal scientific enterprise consists of further articulating the existing paradigm. Research and its application in psychosocial retardation have been defined by the early experience paradigm in just this way. The early experience paradigm has mandated selective attention to certain existing empirical studies, and a selective inattention to other data that argue against the paradigm. This paradigm has determined the phenomena that are researched, and directed the manner in which they are examined. Furthermore, it has diverted scientific resources from the investigation of problems inconsistent with the early experience paradigm.

The selectivity that characterizes research and practice is apparent in the early experience paradigm when the empirical basis for early intervention is examined. The work of Skeels and his colleagues (Skeels & Dye, 1939; Skeels, 1966) was often cited in the 1960s as demonstrating the effectiveness of early intervention. Zigler and Anderson (1979) argue that the original Skeels and Dye study provided the empirical basis for the creation of Head Start and other compensatory education programs. It should be noted, however, that the study was met with skepticism when it first appeared, and has been repeatedly criticized on methodological grounds (Clarke & Clarke, 1976). Nonetheless, Skeels and Dye's results were seen as a dramatic demonstration of the potential impact of environmental stimulation on intellectual development.

Skeels and Dye formed one experimental group and a contrast group from an orphanage population of 25 children. While the contrast group received routine care in the orphanage, the children in the experimental group were reared in an institution for the mentally retarded where they were "adopted" by older retarded girls. Consequently, the experimental group received much more social stimulation than did the contrast group. After 2 years, the children in the experimental group had gained 28.5 IQ points on the average; those in the contrast group had lost a mean of 26.2 IQ points during this period. Twenty-one years later, Skeels (1966) conducted an extensive follow-up to this original study. He found that the initial IQ difference between the groups was reflected in the quality of life (i.e., occupation, marital status, and income) evidenced by the members of the experimental group.

Given the existing zeitgeist, Skeels' work was widely interpreted as evidence for the life-long effects of early experience. A fresh examination of these studies presents diametrically opposed but equally viable alternative interpretations (Clarke & Clarke, 1976). In spite of early trauma, including institutional care during Bowlby's (1958) alleged critical period for the formation of the mother-infant bond and relatively late adoption, the children in the experimental group grew up to be rather average citizens. Furthermore, an examination of the developmental outcomes achieved by the members of both the experimental and the contrast group reveals that adult status was markedly related to continuing, life long environmental changes rather than to early experience alone.

Educational Implications

In contrast to the widely cited work of Skeels and his colleagues, a study with equally important implications for the understanding of the effects of early experience was virtually ignored during this period: Kirk's (1958) investigation of the effects of early preschool education. Kirk examined 81 preschool children with initial IQs between 45 and 80. The experimental children attended either a community preschool or an institutional preschool; two contrast groups receiving no preschool intervention were formed, one in the community and one in an institution for the mentally retarded. Each child in the two experimental groups participated in the preschool program for between 1 and 3 years. After completion of the first year of public elementary school, each child in the experimental and contrast groups was re-evaluated. Kirk's results revealed that preschool intervention was effective in facilitating intellectual development. From the beginning until the completion of preschool attendance, children in the Community Experimental Group showed an average increase of less than one point in the Binet IQ over the same period. During the same time span, children in the Institutional Experimental Group showed an average gain of 12 IQ points, while those in the Institutional Contrast Group, on the average, lost more than 7 IQ points. The support that the compensatory education movement could have received from these findings, however, was limited by the follow-up conducted after the children's first year of primary school. The children in the Community Contrast Group gained, on the average, 7.5 IQ points, while the scores of the Community Experimental Group children were virtually unchanged. Furthermore, no group differences in reading achievement scores were found. Hence, the results of a lengthy preschool experience were reduced, due to either the accelerating development of the contrast group, or the decreasing rate of development of the experimental group children.

Kirk's study, reported 6 years before Head Start was planned, in effect constituted a valuable pilot study for preschool intervention programs. The reader who comes to Kirk's work with knowledge of the results of the evaluations of Head Start is filled with an amazing sense of *deja vu*; Kirk's results neatly anticipated the outcomes of later compensatory education programs. Yet, Head Start planners virtually ignored the study, and publicly bemoaned the fact that time pressures precluded the possibility of accumulating any pilot data (Clarke & Clarke, 1976). Why was Kirk's extensive and well-controlled investigation given such little attention? The results of this study were published and distributed in 1958 by a prominent university press; consequently, a lack of accessibility to Kirk's findings is not a viable explanation. A second possibility concerns the validity of Kirk's findings. Was the work methodologically flawed, so that its applicability was questioned? Kirk's study utilized a quasi-experimental rather than an experimental design. Subjects were not randomly assigned to the experimental conditions in the community groups; the institutional experimental and contrast groups were intact in separate facilities. Careful assessments of the initial status of the children in each group was conducted, however, and the data suggest that the groups were initially comparable. Detailed case studies as well as statistical analyses of group differences seem to substantiate Kirk's claim that "the aim . . . was to set up an ideal experimental design and approximate it as closely as possible" (p. 10). Furthermore, questions about the methodological procedures used in the Skeels study did not limit its application to policy. A further question about the direct applicability of Kirk's work to Head Start concerns the characteristics of the children suspected of mental retardation because of cultural deprivation; Kirk's study included children with mental retardation of both organic and social etiologies. Kirk, however, defines as one of the primary aims of his study the delineation of the differential effects that training might have on organic and environmental retardation. Hence, the study would be particularly germane to the design and implementation of Head Start.

The possibility that the study was virtually ignored because its conclusions were inconsistent with the prevailing early experimental paradigm seems to be the most tenable explanation. Kirk (1958) concluded that the child's cultural milieu, including schooling, could influence intellectual development only within genetically determined limits. In this way, Kirk's results and their interpretation argued eloquently against the prevailing radical environmentalists.

The early experience paradigm functioned as a lens that magnified the importance of Skeels' positive assessment of an environmental intervention. It also filtered out the contradictory evidence presented by Kirk's extensive and controlled examination of a formal preschool intervention program. The early experience paradigm has also focused the attention of social scientists on research problems defined by the paradigm, to the extent that potentially significant observations have been ignored.

The early experience paradigm provides the following syllogism with regard to psychosocial retardation:[3]

1) The social and intellectual experience provided by the poor child's early environment is inadequate
2) The experience provided by the early environment is the major determinant of the child's intellectual growth
3) Therefore, as a result of the early environment and its power to determine intellectual development, the poor child develops deficient intellectual processes.

Operating within the early experience paradigm, social and behavioral scientists set out to substantiate the assumptions derived from the paradigm. A copious literature was assembled, delineating the differences in the environment of the deprived child and the more advantaged middle-class child. Bernstein's work (1961, 1964) clearly implicated the mothers of poor children as contributors to environmental disadvantage. Bernstein argued that a variety of child-rearing practices common among mothers of lower social and economic status retarded the child's intellectual development. Hess and Shipman (e.g., 1967) and others, operating within the theoretical framework erected by Bernstein, explored differences in the behavior of mothers from different social classes toward their children. In general, lower-income mothers were found to be less involved with their children's activities, less positively reinforcing than middle-class mothers, and seen as more commanding and more directly controlling of their children (for a review of this literature, see Ramey et al., 1978).

In the push to delineate the differences believed to exist in the environments of disadvantaged and advantaged children, several critical oversights occurred. First, as Ginsburg (1972) points out, the differences in the behavior of lower SES and middle SES mothers were statistically significant, but not massive. In many regards, the behavior of the two groups of mothers was characterized by more similarities than differences. The desired maternal teaching behaviors were not absent from the task performance of the lower SES mothers; they were

---

[3] These assumptions are similar to those described by Ginsburg (1972) as constituting the "myth" of the deprived child in the educational system. Ginsberg argued as follows:

a) The poor child's environment is inadequate
b) Environment is the major determinant of the child's intellectual growth
c) As a result of the environment and its power to shape human behavior, the child develops deficient intellectual processes
d) Schooling should be designed to remove and correct intellectual deficits (pp. 190–192)

simply observed less often. Nonetheless, drastically different child outcomes were traced to discrepant maternal teaching styles. Second, a causal linkage between maternal behavior and child intelligence was such an accepted construct that the concurrent relationship between the mother's teaching behavior and the child's task performance was not a central focus of empirical investigations. That results obtained in the widely-used teaching tasks revealed trivial or insignificant correlations between maternal behavior and the child's task performance was not a central concern of empirical investigations. Nonetheless, the cognitive socialization imparted to the child by the lower SES mother was assumed to be an important causal factor in the etiology of psychosocial retardation. In addition to the inattention given the concurrent relationship between maternal behavior and child performance, the predictive validity of the observed differences in parental behaviors was not assessed.

More empirical attention has recently been given to the predictive validity of differences in the home environments of advantaged and disadvantaged children. For example, Bradley and Caldwell (1976) examined the relationship between the quality of stimulation available in infants' homes and subsequent mental development through 54 months of age; Elardo, Bradley, and Caldwell (1977) investigated the effects of aspects of infants' home environments on language development at age 3; and Ramey, Farran, and Campbell (1979) explored the utility of predicting the child's IQ at age 36 months from mother-infant interaction patterns. These investigations relied on process-oriented research strategies and longitudinal data. In examining the relationship between aspects of early experiences and later development, such work may help remediate a critical deficiency in the literature. Pointing to this long-standing empirical deficiency is not to argue that differences in the early environments of children are unimportant. The studies cited above help to demonstrate the importance of certain aspects of early experience for subsequent intellectual development. Rather, we submit that educational psychology was so thoroughly entrenched in the early experience paradigm that critical assumptions were accepted without sufficient empirical research. It was assumed that the poor child's environment provided inadequate social and intellectual stimulation. Until recently, research efforts were directed toward providing empirical evidence to substantiate this assumption, rather than toward answering questions that were clearly germane to meeting the needs of disadvantaged children through educational intervention.

The early experience paradigm posits that the experience provided by the early environment is the major determinant of the child's intellectual development. The less than critical acceptance of this central tenet of the early experience paradigm led to a further critical oversight: Variability within the disadvantaged population was either ignored or dismissed as error variance. Begab (Note 1) has estimated that approximately 10% of the poor in the United States are likely to be mentally retarded. The vast majority of the children who grow up with the psychosocial disadvantage do not develop psychosocial mental retardation; rather, they become self-sufficient, productive members of society. The failure to examine the differences between the early environments of disadvantaged children who vary in intellectual accomplishments has been an obstacle to the understanding of the causes of psychosocial mental retardation and, consequently, to its prevention and amelioration. A focus on the differences between the home environments of disadvantaged children who develop intellectual competence and those who demonstrate impaired intellectual performance could significantly advance insight into the specific family variables associated with intellectual development. This avenue of inquiry has been neglected because of the early experience paradigm. The ingrained belief that early psychosocial disadvantage results in impaired intellectual development diverted attention from the vast majority of poor children, those who become adequate students and productive citizens.

The conclusion that poor children develop deficient intellectual processes generated data documenting the impaired cognitive development of disadvantaged children. As a consequence of the effort to identify the differences in the cognitive performance of lower-income and middle-income children, important similarities in their abilities were given little attention. Ginsburg (1972), argues that "poor children do not suffer from massive deficiencies of mind" (p. 139). As reviewed by Ginsburg, research has often revealed no differences in the performances of relatively advantaged and disadvantaged children on Piagetian tasks; studies reporting significant results have shown few differences in the task performance of the two groups.

The belief that early deprivation caused a permanent intellectual impairment probably facilitated the ubiquitous use of IQ scores in psychological research and educational practice concerning psychosocial retardation. In all probability, many factors were involved in the almost universal insistence on the inclusion of IQ scores in research and evaluation of compensatory education. Surely among these factors were the demonstrated psychometric properties of standardized IQ tests. The belief, however, that a central, stable characteristic of the child is affected by early experience figured in the establishment of IQ as the criterion variable for assessments of the efficacy of educational intervention. Furthermore, this belief made it easier to disregard concerns about the ecological validity of laboratory assessments of children from widely divergent backgrounds.

In summary, the early experience paradigm was a central determinant of the importance assigned to empirical findings and the research problems selected for investigation. Of equal importance, the paradigm was a critical factor in the designation of certain findings and issues as inconsequential or uninteresting. Normal scientific enterprise substantiates the assumptions derived from the prevalent paradigm. In this way, the early experience paradigm, like all scientific paradigms, was self-perpetuating.

CRISIS IN THE EARLY EXPERIENCE PARADIGM

Operating within the early experience paradigm, a body of literature documenting widely-held beliefs and substantiating generally accepted theories was compiled throughout the 1960s. The science of human development progressed as science, according to Kuhn (1962), normally does. Yet, in spite of the selective attention and self-perpetuation characteristic of a scientific paradigm, an anomaly appeared and persisted: compensatory education did not keep its promises. The alleged failure of compensatory education forced the scrutiny of the basic assumptions of the early experience paradigm.

A nationwide evaluation of Project Head Start, the best known and most extensive of the educational intervention programs, concluded that no long-lasting intellectual benefits from the program could be found. The positive effects of Head Start attendance, moreover, were small in magnitude as well as short-lived (Circirelli, 1969). This pattern of results was also obtained in evaluations of other intervention programs. In an address to the American Psychological Association reporting on his review of early intervention projects for the National Academy of Sciences, Bronfenbrenner (1974, Note 2) concluded: The effects were at best short lived and small in magnitude, with substantial overlap in the distributions for experimental and control groups (p. 2).

The attack on compensatory education inevitably became a battle against the early experience paradigm. In 1969, Jensen argued that compensatory education had been tried but had failed, and attributed psychosocial retardation to genetic limitations rather than to environmental deprivation. Along with the controversy aroused by the Jensen article, the traditional nature-nurture dichotomy was resurrected. If the early environment could no longer be considered the prime determinant of intellectual development, then it was assumed that the genetic make-up of an individual must be the critical factor.

Arguing *against* the early experience paradigm, however, is still arguing *within* the paradigm. More data can be collected to argue that early experience is effective; more evidence can be amassed to suggest that it is not. This approach, however, entails the risks that thought will continue to be restricted by a particular view of psychosocial retardation—a view that may not convey a complete picture of human development.

BEYOND THE EARLY EXPERIENCE PARADIGM

Seen outside of a zeitgeist conducing and even coercing environmentalist interpretations, the research evidence suggests no simple model for the specifications of the role of early experience in human development. Although some animal studies have documented direct and permanent effects of early experience on adult behavior, a more complex relationship between early stimulation and subsequent development characterizes ontogeny in higher mammals. Hunt (1979) observed that the slower rate of neurological maturation apparent with movement up the evolutionary scale has two consequences for consideration of the effects of early experience. First, early experience can be hypothesized as having significance for longer periods of time with movement up the phylogenetic ladder. Second, the effects of early experience are increasingly reversible as behavior becomes more complexly organized and affected by multiple determinants. For these reasons, postulating direct causal linkages between early experience and subsequent human development has been questioned. Clarke and Clarke (1976) reviewed the evidence on the effects of early experience, and found that the hypotheses derived from the general notion that the first years of life are critical for later development have not been supported. These hypotheses include widely-held ideas about the adverse effects of early mother-child separations; the existence of critical periods for intellectual and social development; and the inefficacy of late adoption in reversing the effects of early adversity.

Changing opinion about the primacy of early experience does not mean, however, that early experience is considered unimportant. Development has been characterized as a continuous process, a cumulative series of transactions between individuals and their environments (Sameroff & Chandler, 1975). This cumulative nature of development, rather than the existence of a critical period for the effects of early experience, renders the early years of human life still highly significant for later development (Ramey & Baker-Ward, 1983). The level of skills and competencies that individuals attain early in their lives affects their abilities to respond to later situations requiring adaptation and complex behavioral organization. In addition, potential plasticity in development may be lessened by the tendency of a society to associate particular experiences such as schooling with limited age spans. In spite of the special importance of the early years in the continuous epigenetic process of human development, later experiences can also have significant effects. If the quality of the fostering environment improves during the lifespan, the debilitating effects of early adversity can be mitigated. Similarly, if the environment becomes less supportive, early developmental gains can be lost. In contrast to the view prevalent in the 1960s, then, every phase of human development is increasingly acknowledged as a "critical period" (Ramey & Baker-Ward, 1983).

The early experience paradigm need no longer constitute the pervasive model of human development to justify early education. Following the crisis presented by the alleged failure of compensatory education, psychologists and educators have begun to re-evaluate their basic assumptions regarding child development. At the present time, no one theory is established well enough to achieve paradigmatic status. Clarke and Clarke (1976) argued that empirical research is currently insufficient to build a clearly formulated model of development. It is apparent, however, that a fully articulated model must meet certain specifications.

An adequate model must acknowledge the total fusion between the classic determinants of developmental outcomes: heredity and environment. Factors endogenous as well as factors exogeneous to the organism must be incorporated into the model. The continuous interplay between these factors in development must be the focus of research attention.

Developmental psychology, like philosophy before it, has traditionally focused on a nature-nuture dichotomy. Psychologists have increasingly come to recognize the fallacy of this dichotomy, but have been unable to go beyond models stressing either genetic influences or environmental factors. The absurdity of an extremist position on the nature-nurture question has long been acknowledged. Obviously, any genotype develops in some environment; any environment acts upon some genetic material. In an influential article published in 1958, Anastasi eloquently argued for an interactionist model of development. She called for investigation into ways in which both heredity and environment operate to produce a given phenotype, such as an individual's measured intelligence. According to Anastasi, the important question is not "how much" heredity or environment contributes to the expression of a given trait, but rather "how" they interact in development. Anastasi's advice was acknowledged, but not followed. Two schools of thought purported to present interactional models of development (Ramey & Finkelstein, 1981). The models share fundamental concepts, but place different emphasis on the contributions of genetic and environmental factors. The genetic-social model, represented by Jensen (1969), acknowledges the contributions of environmental factors but holds that the greater amount of variance in intellectual traits is contributed by genetic factors. The alternative model, the social-genetic model, acknowledges that genes play a role in the expression of intelligence, but posits that environmental factors more parsimoniously account for the differences between individuals. Both of these models are generally tested by deriving estimates of heritability for traits, especially intelligence.

The social-genetic model, of course, was an integral part of the early experience paradigm. Unfortunately, the accumulation of evidence against his model did not lead to a restructuring of thought regarding the process of development. If environmental factors did not solely determine intelligence, it was concluded that genetic factors must. This is a position reversal instead of the needed reconceptualization. The heredity-environment debate has been the bad penny of developmental psychology: it keeps turning up, and we simply keep flipping it over.

In contrast to the counter-productive nature-nurture dichotomy, a useful model of development must acknowledge the constant interchange between the organism and the environment. The potential productivity of this approach is illustrated by a study conducted by Zeskind and Ramey (1978). They examined full term infants who were fetally malnourished, as defined by low ponderal indices, who had been randomly assigned to either a supportive day care environment or to a presumably nonsupportive environment characterized by the presence of high risk factors for mental retardation. By 2 years of age, the infants in the supportive environment had significantly higher IQs, as measured by Bayley and Stanford-Binet scores. Furthermore, the infants who were reared in the supportive environment interacted more positively with their primary caregivers. A potentially dysfunctional condition hence had differential consequences in different social environments.

The fusion between the child's biology and environment is a critical construct for understanding psychosocial mental retardation (Ramey & Finkelstein, 1981). Psychosocial disadvantage has a significant impact on the organism even before birth. Poor mothers are less likely than more advantaged mothers to receive adequate prenatal care. The biological consequences of the social conditions include factors that predispose the child toward mental subnormality. Furthermore, the quality of the environment interacts with biological factors through time; consequently, developmental outcomes are not predictable from either factor alone. As Sameroff (1975) has demonstrated, the impact of early biological difficulties is dependent upon the quality of the caregiving environment.

The early experience paradigm posits a simple, mechanistic model of development. The effects of early experience are seen as universally consistent among individuals of different biological make-ups, and stable throughout time. In contrast, development might be better conceptualized as continuous transactions between a child and various environments. Because development is continuous, later experience as well as early experience is important. Because biological and social factors are coalesced at every point in development, even before conception, the effects of experience can never be consistent across individuals of differing biological integrity.

Another important characteristic of any viable model of human development must be an emphasis on the bidirectionality of effects. This is an integral component of any transactional model. Psychologists have come to recognize the importance of the child's impact on other people. The early experience paradigm presents the child as the passive recipient of stimulation. In contrast, even young infants are now presented as eliciting and selecting unique experiences from relatively constant environments (Bell & Harper, 1977).

A reformulated model of development must also acknowledge the interrelated contexts of childrearing. Bronfenbrenner (1979) argued that mainstream developmental psychology has emphasized the primacy of interpersonal processes on the evolution of behavior. As a consequence, a great deal is known about the power of such mechanisms as modeling, identification, reinforcement, and social learning. Unfortunately, little has been established about the distribution of these processes across different contexts of child rearing; about the ecological conditions that facilitate or debilitate the operation of such mechanisms; and about the potency of these processes in interchanges involving more than two people. The early experience paradigm has perpetuated these inadequacies by focusing attention almost exclusively on early mother-child interactions. But psychosocial retardation is a construct defined by differences between the prevalent societal standard and the individual's circumstances. The critical questions concerning the interactions of the context of development—family, neighborhood, school, and society—have yet to be answered.

SUMMARY

Science inevitably operates within paradigms. The early experience paradigm will, in all likelihood, ultimately be replaced by an alternative model of reality that will just as effectively focus our attention and magnify our biases. Even science can yield no objective, inevitable truths. A transactional model, or any other model, is a human construction. It is worthwhile only to the extent that it advances knowledge and understanding. The early experience paradigm has left two important legacies for understanding how science must look at human development. First, the shortcomings of the model of development it presented, made apparent in the revolution against the paradigm, have suggested an alternative route to follow in understanding development. As discussed above, this route must include the coalescence of biological and social factors; the bidirectionality of effects; and the relationships between the contexts of child rearing.

Second, the era described by Scarr and Weinberg (1977) as "environmentalism run amok" bequeaths a warning to those involved in meeting the needs of the disadvantaged. In the wild zeal for the early experience paradigm, the need for accountability among the scientific community was given short attention. As the work of Lazar and his colleagues has begun to reveal (Lazar et al., 1977), compensatory education failed only when measured against the goals set for it by its proponents. Because its promises were not kept, the opportunity to establish a revolutionary system of early education with far-reaching benefits for society was lost and cannot easily be regained. By its very nature, a scientific paradigm renders it difficult to make explicit the assumptions it embodies and the rationale for practice it provides. Only through deliberate restraint, multi-disciplinary collaboration, and constant scrutiny can we avoid being controlled by the paradigms we may create. Santayana's warning to attend to the mistakes of the past is particularly appropriate in the economy of the 1980s. Although the problems presented society by psychosocial disadvantage must be addressed, we cannot afford to repeat the excesses of the 1960s.

REFERENCE NOTES

1. Begab, M. *Issues in the prevention of psychosocial retardation.* Paper presented at a colloqium at the University of North Carolina Mental Retardation Center on Issues in the Prevention of Psychosocial Retardation, Chapel Hill, N.C., December, 1978.
2. Bronfenbrenner, U. *Experimental human ecology: A reorientation to theory and research on socialization.* Paper presented as the presidential address to the Division of Personality and Social Psychology at the meeting of the American Psychological Association, New Orleans, 1974.

REFERENCES

Anastasi, A. Heredity, environment, and the question "How?" *Psychological Review,* 1958, *65,* 197–208.
Beach, F., & Jaynes, J. Effects of early experience upon the behavior of animals. *Psychological Bulletin,* 1954, *51,* 239–263.

288   Ramey and Baker-Ward

Bell, R., & Harper, L. *The effect of children on parents.* Hillsdale, N. J.: Lawrence Erlbaum Associates, 1977.

Bernstein, B. Elaborated and restricted codes: Their social origins and some consequences. *American Anthropologist,* 1964, *66,* 55–69.

Bernstein, B. Social class and linguistic development: A theory of social learning. In A. Halsey, J. Floud, & C. Anderson (Eds.), *Education, economy, and society.* New York: Free Press, 1961.

Bloom, B. *Stability and change in human characteristics.* New York: John Wiley & Sons, 1964.

Bowlby, J. The nature of the child's tie to his mother. *International Journal of Psychoanalysis,* 1958, *39,* 350–373.

Bradley, R., & Caldwell, B. The relation of infants' home environments to mental test performance at fifty-four months: A follow-up study. *Child Development,* 1976, *47,* 1173–1174.

Bronfenbrenner, U. Contexts of child-rearing: Problems and prospects. *American Psychologist,* 1979, *34,* 844–850.

Buss, A. The structure of psychological revolutions. *Journal of the History of the Behavioral Sciences,* 1978, *14,* 57–64.

Cicirelli, V. *The impact of Head Start: An evaluation of the effects of Head Start on children's cognitive and affective development.* Athens, Ohio: Westinghouse Learning Corporation, 1969.

Clarke, A. M., & Clarke, A. D. B. *Early experience: Myth and evidence.* New York: Free Press, 1976.

Elardo, R., Bradley, R., & Caldwell, B. A longitudinal study of the relation of infants; home environments to language development at age three. *Child Development,* 1977, *48,* 595–603.

Freud, S. *Drei Abhandlungen zur Sexualtheorie.* Vienna: Deuticke, 1905. (Translated as *Three essays on the theory of sexuality,* 1962.)

Gesell, A. The ontogenesis of infant behavior. In L. Carmichael (Ed.), *Manual of child psychology.* New York: John Wiley & Sons, 1946.

Ginsburg, H. *The myth of the deprived child.* Englewood Cliffs, N.J.: Prentice Hall, 1972.

Gottlieb, G. *Development of species identification in birds.* Chicago: University of Chicago Press, 1971.

Hebb, D. The organization of behavior. New York: John Wiley & Sons, 1949.

Hess, R., & Shipman, V. Cognitive elements in maternal behavior. In J. Hill (Ed.), *Minnesota Symposium on Child Psychology* (Vol. 1). Minneapolis: University of Minnesota Press, 1967, 57–81.

Hunt, J. McV. Psychological development: Early experience. *Annual Review of Psychology,* 1979, *30,* 103–143.

Hunt, J. McV. *Intelligence and experience.* New York: Ronald Press, 1961.

Jensen, A. How much can we boost IQ and scholastic achievement? *Harvard Education Review,* 1969, *39,* 1–123.

Kagan, J. Family experience and the child's development. *American Psychologist,* 1979, *34,* 886–891.

Kagan, J., Kearsley, R., & Zelazo, P. *Infancy: Its place in human development.* Cambridge: Harvard University Press, 1978.

Kessen, W. The American child and other cultural inventions. *American Psychologist,* 1979, *34,* 815–320.

Kirk, S. *Early education of the mentally retarded: An experimental study.* Urbana, Ill.: University of Illinois Press, 1958.

Klaus, M., & Kennell, J. *Maternal-infant bonding.* Saint Louis: C. V. Mosby Company, 1976.

Kuhn, T. *The structure of scientific revolutions.* Chicago: University of Chicago Press, 1962.

Lazar, I., Hubbell, V., Murray, H., Rosche, M., & Royce, J. *Summary: The persistance of preschool effects: A long-term follow-up of 14 infant and preschool experiments.* Ithaca, N.Y.: College of Human Ecology, Community Services Laboratory, Cornell University, 1977.

Lorenz, K. The companion in the bird's world. *Auk,* 1937, *54,* 245–273.

Ramey, C., & Baker-Ward, L. Early stimulation and mental retardation. In B. Wolman (Ed.), *International encyclopedia of neurology, psychiatry, psychoanalysis, and psychology.* New York: Van Nostrand Reinhold, 1983.

Ramey, C., Farran, D., & Campbell, F. Predicting IQ from mother-infant interactions. *Child Development,* 1979, *50,* 804–814.

Ramey, C., Farran, D., Campbell, F., & Finkelstein, N. Observations of mother-infant interactions: Implications for development. In F. Minifie & L. Lloyd (Eds.), *Communicative and cognitive abilities: Early behavioral assessments.* Baltimore: University Park Press, 1978.

Ramey, C., & Finkelstein, N. Psychosocial retardation: A biological and social coalescence. In M. Begab, H. Garber, & H. Haywood (Eds.), *Causes and prevention of retarded development in psychosocially disadvantaged children.* Baltimore: University Park Press, 1981.

Ryan, W. *Blaming the victim.* New York: Pantheon Books, 1971.

Sameroff, A. Early influences on development: Fact or fancy? *Merrill-Palmer Quarterly,* 1975, *21,* 267–294.

Sameroff, A., & Chandler, M. Reproductive risk and the continuum of caretaking casualty. In F. Horowitz (Ed.), *Review of child development research* (Vol. 4), Chicago: University of Chicago Press, 1975.

Scarr, S., & Weinberg, R. Rediscovering old truths or a word by the wise is sometimes lost. *American Psychologist,* 1977, *32,* 681–682.

Skeels, H. Adult status of children with contrasting early life experiences. *Monographs of the Society for Research in Child Development,* 1966, 105.

Skeels, H., & Dye, H. A study of the effects of differential stimulation on mentally retarded children. *Proceedings and addresses of the American Association on Mental Deficiency,* 1939, *44,* 114–136.

Spitz, R. Hospitalism: An inquiry into the genesis of psychiatric conditions in early childhood. *Psychoanalytic Study of the Child,* 1945, *1,* 53–74.

Thompson, W., & Heron, W. The effects of early restriction in activity in dogs. *Journal of Comparative and Physiological Psychology,* 1954, *47,* 77–82.

Yarrow, L. Maternal deprivation: Toward an empirical and conceptual reevaluation. *Psychological Bulletin,* 1961, *58,* 459–490.

Zeskind, P., & Ramey, C. Fetal malnutrition: An experimental study of its consequence on infant development in two caregiving environments. *Child Development,* 1978, *49,* 1155–1162.

Zigler, E., & Anderson, K. An idea whose time had come: The intellectual and political climate for Head Start. In E. Zigler & J. Valentine (Eds.), *Project HEAD Start: A legacy of the war on poverty.* New York: Free Press, 1979.

Chapter 17

DYADIC AND CONTINGENT ASPECTS OF EARLY COMMUNICATIVE INTERVENTION

Laurel Carlson and Diane D. Bricker

INTRODUCTION

Over the last decade, knowledge of the infant's perceptual, social, and learning capacities has steadily increased. As early as the first few months of life, the infant differentiates between the animate and inanimate social environment (Richards, 1974), differentially responds to familiar social stimuli (Sherrod et al., 1978), and habituates to redundant stimuli (Kagan, Kearsley, & Zelazo, 1978). In learning about the world the infant is an active participant using sensory, social, and cognitive skills to process and organize diverse types of information from the environment. Despite the growth of a substantive body of data reflecting the competency of the infant, knowledge about the evolution of language from earlier skills or capacities remains limited (Nelson, 1979; Bricker & Carlson, 1981). In particular, knowledge of the specific relationships between environmental arrangements and consequences and the infant's biological proclivities impedes progress toward the formulation of intervention strategies for infants experiencing problems in acquiring effective communication and language skills. Unfortunately, the field cannot await a "perfect" theory before cautiously applying newly acquired information or perspectives to the intervention process. Therefore, the purpose of this chapter is to provide an experimental framework for the interventionist concerned with enhancing the acquisition of effective language behavior in the at-risk or handicapped infant. In particular, the focus is on understanding communication as a dyadic and contingent process as the basis for formulating an approach to early language intervention.

Preparation of this chapter has been supported in part by Grant No. G007901289 to the Center on Human Development, University of Oregon from the Office of Special Education, USOE.

291

In tracing early language learning, the assumption of developmental continuity is implicit although controversial (Self & Horowitz, 1979). Developmental continuity assumes that the acquisition of formal language processes is tied either directly or indirectly to earlier forms of social-affective, communicative, and cognitive behavior (Bates, 1979; Nelson, 1979). Such a position concerning the origins of language does not attempt to imply that early social-communicative and cognitive skills determine the acquisition of language or that prelinguistic behaviors are directly continuous with semantic or grammatical structures. Rather, early social-communicative and cognitive experiences are viewed as providing a basis for the acquisition of more formal language structures. A key to describing the antecedents of formal language in the preverbal period lies in the identification of complex sets of generative communicative, conceptual, and social skills that become coordinated and integrated over time (Bricker & Carlson, 1981; Bruner, 1977). The evolution of these skills is evidenced through the infant's interactions and manipulations of the social and physical environment. In addition, the baby becomes increasingly competent in expressing specific communicative functions preverbally and in referring to and classifying objects, actions, and events. The development of such generative skills is subject to experiential substitutability (Uzgiris, 1981). That is, experiences of differing quality and intensity in a variety of social and physical contexts seem sufficient to permit their construction. The notion of substitutability will be emphasized repeatedly throughout this chapter.

Consideration of the nature of developmental processes is useful in examining the preverbal strategies and skills that may be important for the acquisition of language. Current models of development deemphasize the undirectional perspective. The infant is viewed as a dynamic organism that both affects and is affected by the environment. The social environment and the infant exhibit a plasticity as both actively participate in verbal and nonverbal exchanges. During the early developmental period the primary caregiver constitutes a major environmental influence on the quality and direction of the infant's growth. The intertwining of the caregiver's behaviors with those of the infant seems to significantly affect the infant's acquisition of the skills necessary to attend, organize, and act upon the environment. The caregiver's behavior is also subject to modification through the interactive process (Thoman, 1979; Lewis & Rosenblum, 1974). Careful scrutiny of the content, sequence, and timing of social contextual events is therefore necessary in the study of early processes that may serve as precursors to language acquisition. The nature of these processes makes it imperative that they be studied in the communicative context of the wide variety of interactive sequences during which the infant learns the dual roles of speaker and listener.

The Nature of the Dyadic Process

Infants develop an effective communication system with their primary caregiver long before they develop language. Increasing documentation of the sophistication of the infant as an active participant in early transactions with the caregiver has become available since the mid-70s. Unfortunately, many interventionists working with at-risk and handicapped infants have failed to acknowledge these findings.

The interactional process between the infant and caregiver may be conceptualized as a jointly or mutually regulated system in which each member of the dyad modifies and adapts his or her behavior to dovetail with that of the other. From the first few weeks of life the infant and caregiver assume the roles of initiator and responder, each influencing the other's behavior in a reciprocal manner.[1] The balance of reciprocity changes over time, with the normal infant's participation increasing with age. The caregiver seems to reduce his or her dominance in the interaction as the baby becomes capable of initiating and directing activities. As the infant approaches the end of the first year, a more balanced reciprocity is attained in normal caregiver-infant dyads (Vietze et al., 1978). The handicapped or at-risk infant may either introduce unexpected variability or fail to initiate interactions. Either of these patterns inhibits the establishment of a mutually rewarding reciprocal relationship without compensatory adjustments by the caregiver.

From the first few weeks of life, most infants and caregivers display organized interactions, which appear as structured cycles of affective and attentional responses (Brazelton, Koslowski, & Main, 1974). These cycles reflect periods of caregiver-infant activity and engagement as well as inactivity and disengagement. In striking a balance between the mode and intensity of the behavior of both partners, these cycles typically consist of the following sequence of responses:

Initiation—Infant vocalizes while looking at caregiver to attract attention

Mutual Orientation—Infant vocalizes and caregiver focuses on his or her face

Recognition—Infant smiles when seeing caregiver thereby establishing a joint reference

---

[1] The application of a systems model to the caregiver-infant relationship appropriately stresses the total interaction relationship (Thoman, 1979). The interpretation of caregiver-infant interactional data in terms of the effects of isolated behaviors may be an oversimplification of a complex phenomenon.

Reciprocal Play-Dialogue—Caregiver vocalizes and infant gurgles
Disengagement—Caregiver vocalizes and infant looks away

The disengagement or looking away phase probably reflects the baby's need to control the amount of stimulation he or she can process during a period of intense social interaction (Field, 1980; Osofsky & Connor, 1979).

These cycles or response sequences cannot be characterized as having either a fixed pattern or behavioral content but rather exhibit substitutability (Uzgiris, 1981). That is, infants and caregivers can enter the cycle at any point with widely varying behavioral content.

To successfully engage in a synchronous interaction, certain prerequisites are required of the dyad's participants. Caregivers must contribute their unique sensitivities and environmental experiences to the interaction when reading and responding to the infant's signals. Equally important, the infant must clearly and predictably signal his or her state and needs as well as remain receptive and responsive to the caregiver's ministrations (Thoman et al., 1978). Without the establishment of a match between initiator and respondent, the dyadic relationship may not evolve into a healthy context for the infant's social-communicative development.

The biologically intact infant seems predisposed to initiating social interaction with the social environment (Maccoby, 1980; Goldberg, 1977). This predisposition is so compelling that when it is absent the infant's caregivers may fail to facilitate social interactions. Some physically handicapped and developmentally delayed infants either cannot or do not elicit or maintain the social dialogue necessary to ensure their own exposure to the experiential information essential for the successive restructuring and organization of behavior into increasingly complex patterns in development (Jones, 1980; Gaussen, 1979).

Within the social medium of the caregiver-infant relationship, the infant acquires a series of key generative skills that may be fundamental to the development of communicative competence and language. Participation in the engagement and disengagement cycles in relation to social stimuli, successfully eliciting the caregiver's attention, learning to establish and sustain joint action routines, and maintaining social relationships may be functionally necessary to the acquisition of the pragmatics of later-developing language. Experiences provided by the caregiver for role-taking in dialogue-like exchanges and intentional expression through vocal-gestural routines also seem to provide a basis for later communicative ability (Trevarthen, 1977; Sugarman, 1981). In addition, the rudiments of reference may be cultivated early in dyadic exchanges as objects are presented and named by the caregiver during play episodes (Nelson, 1979).

A key element in the infant's acquisition of communicative and conceptual skills important for language thus seems to reside in the relationship the infant forms with the primary caregivers. In the social context of the dyad, the caregiver plays an influential role as he or she serves as the baby's primary communicative and social partner as well as the infant's liaison with the world of objects (Yarrow et al., 1975). In arranging the physical environment, the caregiver provides the context for the infant's acquisition of social-communicative skills. An implicit pedagogy may be observed on the part of the caregiver as he or she solicits information from the infant, interprets early intentions, references objects and events, and establishes joint communicative exchanges in which the regulatory rules of conversation are followed.

The Nature of Contingency Experiences

Within the context of caregiver-infant interactions, the infant explores the salient social and physical features of the environment. Through these encounters a repertoire of communicative, conceptual, and problem-solving skills and strategies is constructed. An important foundation for the acquisition of these competencies is the establishment of contingency experiences. A contingency experience is defined as the recognition that one's behavior is related to a predictable outcome (Lewis & Goldberg, 1969). Watson (1967) has suggested that newborn infants are preadapted to seek out social contingency experiences. That is, babies seem to have a natural proclivity for smiling and cooing to social stimuli which, in turn, tends to elicit a social response. For most infants, the primary caregivers are the major source of opportunities for learning social contingencies.

Contingency experiences are provided by the object world as well. Physical stimuli can provide consistent information as an outcome. For example, a baby quickly learns that batting a ring attached to his or her crib reliably results in an interesting consequence. However responsive the physical world is for the infant, it seems that the social world is most salient in the early months as it provides more opportunities for the development of contingency relations (Lewis & Brooks-Gunn, 1980).

Both members of the infant-caregiver dyad provide mutual contingency experiences. From the earliest stages, certain salient behaviors of the infant effectively evoke social responses. For example, the infant's cry is capable of eliciting adult proximity and intervention, while the cessation of the sucking response during feeding seems to trigger a jiggling-stimulation response from the caregiver (Kaye, 1977). From the perspective of the caregiver, a similar pattern of events may be traced. Through interactions with the infant, the caregiver learns that his or her actions and certain outcomes are related; for example, holding the infant close to the body soothes the baby and eliminates crying. The successful elicitation of contingent feedback from each member of the dyad may be instrumental in generating feelings of effectiveness (Lewis & Goldberg, 1969). Without the establishment of contingent feedback by either or both of the partners, disruption of the dyadic interaction may occur (Vietze et al., 1978; Thoman et al., 1978).

The lack of social responsiveness of blind infants in the early months can affect the caregiver-infant interactions as the work of Fraiberg (1977) suggests. The absence of expected social signals such as eye contact and smiling by the infant tends to deprive the caregiver of the contingent feedback necessary to maintain an effective communicative interaction. In lieu of the conventional visual signal systems used by sighted babies, the mothers of blind infants must learn to compensate by providing tactile and kinesthetic simulation. In addition, the caregiver must learn to attend to alternative signals and cues such as the infant's hands rather than his or her face for feedback. Such modifications must be integrated into the caregiver's repertoire if mutually satisfying contingent interaction is to develop.

Certain environmental settings reduce opportunities for the establishment of contingency relations between the infant and caregiver. For example, institutional environments that have fixed care-giving schedules fail to provide the infant with experiences in which his or her actions produce a specific outcome, which is apparently essential to establishing contingency relations (Moss, 1967). In relation to communicative competence, Sugarman (1981) hypothesized that institutional settings provide fewer opportunities for the child to evolve an elaborate signal system to enlist the participation of the environment. When removed from such noncontingent, unsupportive environments, failure-to-thrive infants often seem to "recover" miraculously. In addition to changes of a basic nature such as proper nutrition, one could speculate that the increased vigor and activity seen in these infants is, in part, produced by an increased responsiveness of the environment to the infant's behavior.

Thus, within the social-communicative exchanges of the infant and primary caregiver an important repertoire of cognitive and communicative skills is acquired. As Bruner (1977) suggested, these capabilities provide an important foundation for the conceptual and pragmatic structures of later language development. A fundamental mediating influence in the infant's acquisition of these competencies consists of the interactions with the primary caregiver. As a facilitator, the caregiver serves as the baby's primary communicative partner eliciting social stimulus as well as the main liaison with the object world (Yarrow et al., 1975).

The remainder of this chapter concentrates on describing potentially useful intervention strategies designed to eliminate or attenuate problems in caregiver-infant dyadic relationships that result from disruptions of the interactional processes we have just considered.

A Model for Communicative Interaction

Although our concern is with the dyadic relationship of the caregiver and infant, the focus of the intervention effort necessarily must be on the caregiver. The caregiver's behavior is certainly more amenable to verbal modification than is the infant's. In addition, the caregiver has considerably more latitude in arranging the environment and overtly shifting consequences. The role of the interventionist is to assist the caregiver in becoming a more sensitive observer of the infant's behavior, and a more effective provider of contingent experiences that will engage the baby in actively acquiring early social-communicative competence.

The intervention model we are proposing can be conveniently divided into three sections: 1) a content for communicative intervention; 2) key processes for communicative intervention; and 3) a strategy for facilitating infant-caregiver communication.

Content for Communicative Intervention

The literature on early communicative development is sufficient to extract a tentative sequence of behaviors exhibited by infants. In a small sample of infants, Sugarman (1978) has traced the development of early sensorimotor (object) behaviors and social behaviors from simple schemes to the coordination of those schemes into prelinguistic communicative functions called protoimperatives and protodeclaratives. The onset of these coordinated behaviors has been reported to co-occur with the onset of other prelinguistic functions (e.g., refusals, asking, and greetings) and initial lexical forms (Halliday, 1975). Our research with a group of Down's syndrome infants suggests that they closely parallel the developmental sequence of the Sugarman infants, although coordinated behaviors were acquired later by the delayed group (Bricker & Carlson, 1980b). Initial observations began when both samples of infants were less than 7 months of age and revealed that the proportion of simple action schemes (e.g., banging objects, smiling at mother) greatly exceeded the proportion of complex (e.g., chains of simple responses such as banging, mouthing and then throwing a toy) and coordinated (e.g., using objects to attract the caregiver's attention and using the caregiver to obtain desired objects out of the infant's reach) action schemes. In fact, during these early months no infant engaged in coordinated responses. As expected, monthly observations revealed a gradual increase in the proportion of complex action schemes produced by both delayed and nondelayed infants. This increase in complex schemes was associated with a decrease in simple action schemes. At approximately 11 months, the nondelayed infants produced a small proportion of coordinated schemes (approximately 10%), whereas coordinated behaviors began to appear in the delayed infant's repertoire at approximately 17 months (Bricker & Carlson, 1980).

Figure 1 contains a schematic of the developmental sequence outlined above beginning with simple preverbal social and object action schemes and moving to the production of lexical items. In considering such a speculative sequence, it is important to keep in mind the notion of substitutability. Within a particular generic sequence (e.g., simple social schemes), a wide variety of appropriate contents can be expressed within each individual dyad.

Figure 1 is intended to outline a sequence of early social-communicative and sensorimotor behaviors that may provide the foundation for the acquisition of language. From the perspective that communicative development is an important precondition for language acquisition, the gradual growth in complexity and coordination of object and social schemes seems to represent the evolution of the infant's increasing clarity in expressing a communicative purpose or function. By the middle of the second year of life, the infant can successfully express a variety of social-communicative functions through clusters of coordinated social and object transactions (e.g., vocalizing, looking at mother, and then pointing to an out-of-reach object) without relying on lexical forms. The object and social world provide the settings and props for these transactions.

Overlaying the gradual increase in the infant's proficiency at expressing communicative purposes is a second set of communicative skills that are being acquired within the framework of caregiver-infant social exchanges. Functionally related to the pragmatics of language, these skills may be classified as the constituents of dialogic exchange. Certainly this proposed separation of object schemes and dialogic responses is artificial, but we believe it to be a useful heuristic as an invervention perspective. The separation emphasizes for the interventionist the need to attend to the content and to the interactional nature of the infant-caregiver system in the acquisition of early communicative behavior.

Key Processes for Communicative Intervention

The dialogue sequence proposed in Figure 1 is derived from current research (viz. Bruner, 1975; Trevarthen, 1977; Snow, 1977). Prior to the acquisition of formal linguistic skills, the infant seems to acquire a number of precursor responses. As noted in Figure 1, the infant first

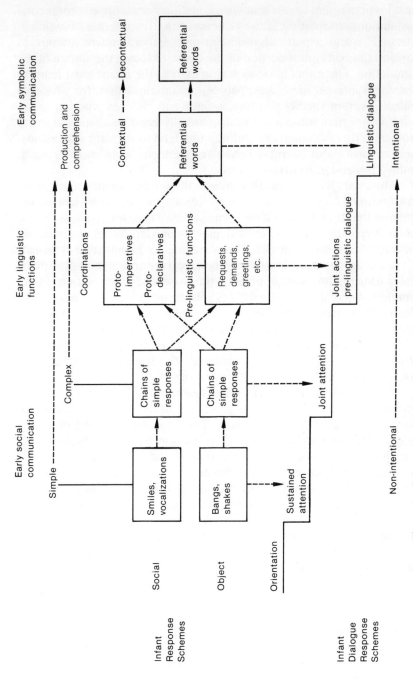

Figure 1.   Schematic of the developmental sequence for early communication.

must learn to orient to relevant visual, auditory or tactile environmental stimulation. Orientation is the selection from the infant's "blooming, buzzing" world a particular content and the subsequent attempt to position the body, or a portion of the body, to locate the source of the stimulation. Once this basic skill is acquired, the infant must learn to sustain an interest in objects, people, or situations that, for whatever reason, warrant further scrutiny. Infants and children who fail to acquire appropriate attentional skills generally have significant learning problems. By teaching these children to attend to relevant dimensions, their acquisition of adaptive behaviors seems to be enhanced considerably (Beveridge & Brinker, 1980).

Most caregivers seem sensitive to the infant's ability to maintain an attentional focus early on as they often select specific environmental features that they believe have some saliency or attractiveness for the infant. Typically, a variety of strategies are used to attract and maintain the infant's attention, including the "making" or highlighting of aspects of the environment. In most cases the caregiver accompanies the physical marking of an event or object with associated conversation. In our monthly observations of Down's syndrome infants we generally found that mothers talk to their infants about the focus of their mutual attention. If mothers do not spontaneously offer comments, the infant may seek to elicit them with a communicative signal. Establishing joint attention seems, logically, essential to learning the rules of communication.

Caregivers of intact infants are reported to engage in a "natural" pedagogy in which the infant is gently led to focus on the topic of the mother's communicative behavior. This repeated focusing of the infant's attention on the topic of conversation builds, we believe, into a prelinguistic dialogue between caregiver and infant.

Joint attention can be established by the infant as well as the caregiver. Most caregivers seem to be sensitive to the infant's line of gaze or general focus of attention and will, during these episodes, provide a verbal commentary on the infant's focus of attention. In addition to learning to establish joint attention, the infant must learn the rules for becoming a speaker and a listener. Potential precursors of the speaker-listener roles have been reported to appear early in the infant's repertoire (Stern et al., 1977). That is, within the first year the infant begins to acquire the communicative cycle of vocalization-pause-vocalization-pause. Interestingly, normal infants and mothers are reported to overlap vocalizations relatively infrequently (Stern et al., 1977), while the overlap between mothers and handicapped infants is reported to be more frequent (Jones, 1980). The normally developing infant seems to effortlessly acquire the duality of the speaker-listener roles and subsequently moves to substituting words for the previously used prelinguistic communicative signals.

As the infant and caregiver reciprocally interact with each other in the natural environment, their social-communicative interactive exchanges are connected and are mutually contingent on one another (Gottman, 1979). By 3 months, contingency games in which the behavior of the partners is mutually rewarding are played with increasing frequency. Social stimulation successfully elicits social-communicative feedback from the infant just as the infant's expanding communicative repertoire effectively elicits adult attention and communicative responses.

The contingent feedback provided by the caregiver to the infant's signals thus seems to be instrumental in fostering the development of communication just as it increases the baby's ability to control the environment. In normally developing mother-infant relationships, the caregiver naturally provides opportunities for the infant to achieve control of his or her surroundings. Unfortunately, such efficacy is more difficult to establish in some handicapped and developmentally delayed infants. Studies comparing the interactive patterns of mothers and their delayed and at-risk infants have identified differences between groups in the quantity and latency of feedback provided by the partners (Gaussean, 1979; Emde, 1979; Jones, 1977). In an observational investigation of mother-infant vocal contingencies, with a group of developmentally delayed children and normally developing infants, Vietze et al. (1978) showed that the contingency relationships between infants' vocalizations and parent vocal onset and parents' vocalizations and infant vocal onset were not well established in the dyads with a severely delayed child.

A Strategy for Communicative Intervention

Within the early social-communicative exchanges between infants and caregivers, a basic repertoire of sensorimotor and social-communicative skills is acquired. As we and others have argued (Bricker & Carlson, 1981; Bruner, 1977), these skills may provide a foundation of essential behavioral precursors for the child's acquisition of later developing linguistic and cognitive systems. Although our interest is in language, the assumption of continuity has shifted our focus to include the preverbal period of infancy and to expand our intervention efforts to include the stage prior to formal language acquisition. Due to space limitations as well as the magnitude and complexity of early prelinguistic development, this chapter offers only a proposal for prelinguistic intervention involving selected aspects of the caregiver-infant dyadic interaction. In limiting the scope, a number of problems are created. First, as Thoman (1979) has indicated, the interactional system between the infant and caregiver is a multidimensional intertwining of responses of considerable complexity. Such a reality forces those designing interventions to oversimplify as intervention areas are selected. Second, in making an effort to specify an intervention, a dilemma is created by response variability or the notion of substitutability (Uzgiris, 1981). That is, no set patterns of interactions seem to be necessarily appropriate for particular caregiver-infant dyads; and consequently, specificity of the response mode or content is highly questionable. As Bromwich (1981) pointed out, satisfactory caregiver-infant interactions must be idiosyncratically determined by both participants and the relevant environmental constraints. This reality leads to the formulation of an intervention approach focused on general process strategies rather than precise specification of stimulus-response procedures.

The information and perspectives discussed in the introductory section of this chapter can be synthesized into an intervention approach that has the potential of significantly enhancing educational or habilitative efforts with at-risk and/or handicapped infants during the preverbal period of development. The intervention strategy is focused on the preverbal period with particular emphasis on selected aspects of the caregiver-infant interactive process and content.

Taking into account the nature of the dyadic process and its content, a proposed strategy for communicative intervention has been formulated consisting of three phases: 1) observing and monitoring of the infant's responses; 2) organizing and structuring of the environment, and 3) arranging contingencies to teach the essential communicative roles to the infant.

Observing and Monitoring the Infant

The initial phase of intervention focuses on assisting the caregiver in becoming a sensitive observer of his or her infant's behavior. If the caregiver-infant interaction is not satisfactory or if the infant is not progressing toward the acquisition of essential communicative responses, a variety of problems may result. Careful observation of the infant's behavior by the caregiver and interventionist may yield valuable clues. Such observations may reveal that the caregiver is not responsive to the infant's signals or the infant may emit such subtle or infrequent cues that the caregiver is unable to detect changes in the baby. Furthermore, the infant and caregiver may have not learned to synchronize their behavior—when the infant is tired, the mother may choose this time for stimulation and be disappointed when the infant cries irritably.

The caregiver and interventionist should attempt to determine the infant's daily cycles of alertness and other factors that may impinge on the success of the interaction. Our observations of a small sample of mothers of Down's syndrome infants suggest that these mothers tend to respond too often and too quickly for their handicapped babies to be able to provide suitable reciprocal responses. The baby may still be processing previous information while the mother is introducing new and different stimulation.

Organizing and Structuring the Environment

Carefully conducted observations of the infant-caregiver dyad should produce information that can be used in subsequent organization and structuring of the intervention. There seem to be at least two dimensions that need attention: matching or timing of the interactive behavior and the attention-response cycle.

Matching, timing, or synchrony of caregiver to infant covers at least three areas: content, emotionality, and form or mode. If the dyad is not synchronous or the caregiver cannot adequately read the cues of the infant's emotional state, problems may arise. When the infant is distressed and needs assurance, the caregiver should be able to provide the necessary feedback and support. If the caregiver is upset because, for example, he or she has not adjusted to the seriously handicapped infant, he or she may be unable to respond with appropriate emotional feedback for the infant and thereby will not provide adequate positive affective behavior.

A primary problem for the handicapped infant seems to be the caregiver who tries to compensate for the infant's deficiencies. As mentioned, the caregiver may provide an excess of stimulation, not leaving adequate time for the infant to process incoming information and not allowing the infant sufficient time to produce an overt response. There may be a second problem associated with the match or synchrony between the infant and caregiver's response. That is, input cannot be too discrepant or an infant cannot assimilate and accommodate to the input. On the other hand, in the absence of disequilibrium no change in the infant's behavior is likely to occur (Hunt, 1961). Although there is considerable controversy over the source of motivation for such change (Nelson, 1979), the reality for the interventionist is that the environment should be arranged to elicit or support change and modification in the infant. For the nonhandicapped infant, the "naturally" occurring responses of the caregiver may be sufficient to stimulate repertoire change; however, for the at-risk or handicapped infant, infrequent or poorly timed feedback may not be adequate to compensate for the infant's particular problem or disability. A more carefully organized approach is necessary.

According to Brazelton, Koslowski, and Main (1974) among others, infants often engage in a general behavioral response pattern that includes orientation, recognition, expressive response, and a feedback or latency period. It seems likely that the point at which the caregiver/teacher intervenes in the orientation-recognition-response-feedback sequence may facilitate or hamper the subsequent acquisition of new responses by the infant. For example, if the caregiver response does not allow ample time for the orientation and recognition phase, the infant may lose the opportunity to fully attend to the stimulus array before a new set of antecedent conditions occur. One is tempted to predict that too many missed opportunities in which insufficient time is available for the infant to "get set" might result in the development of non-attentional or apathetic behavior—a state often apparent in handicapped infants. It is possible that such apathy or nonresponsiveness may be developed as a protective mechanism for dealing with a world that passes by too quickly, or said another way, the infant has not been allowed the chance to develop contingency awareness (Watson, 1979). The notion of learned helplessness or lack of learned contingent responses could well account for such behavior in infants (Lewis, 1978; Seligman, 1975). Interestingly, both of these theories rest on the notion that the infant has not had the opportunity to develop an appropriate response system.

We believe the orientation, recognition, response, and latency cycle can be observed when the infant is engaged with the social and non-social environment. Our research with Down's syndrome infants reveals similar chains or patterns that seem to reflect this sequence. For example, an infant will look toward a toy the mother is shaking, smile in apparent recognition or pleasure at seeing the toy, reach out to be given the toy, shake or throw the toy, and then pause before initiating further activity.

In the establishment of early communicative behaviors with delayed infants the caregiver may be making three errors: 1) responding at the wrong time in the infant's behavior cycle; 2) responding too rapidly; or 3) providing stimulation that clearly is a developmental mismatch for the child. To offset these problems we are proposing a simple intervention procedure. The strategy we suggest employs an imitation paradigm; however, rather than the caregiver or the interventionist providing the model, the infant provides the model.

The Imitation Approach

When the infant responds, and the form or modality is not of great importance, the caregiver should wait briefly and then imitate the infant's behavior. Upon completion of the imitative response, the caregiver should emit a positive social response and then wait for the infant to respond again. When the next response occurs, the caregiver should again imitate the response accompanied by some positive affective behavior. Such a paradigm will be effective for a number of reasons: first, imitation of the infant forces the caregiver to attend closely to the infant's behavior in order to imitate the infant's previous response. Second, the infant's behavior precedes the caregiver's and forces the caregiver to follow the infant's lead. Third, since it can be presumed that the infant is engaging in self-reinforcing behavior, the motivational factor for the infant is accounted for. Fourth, the infant will begin to get a sense of contingency control. That is, the infant is discovering that his or her behavior elicits some systematic, predictable effect from the environment. Fifth, the infant can control the timing of the cyclical interactions with the caregiver, thus adjusting the speed of responding to his or her comfort zone. Finally, this procedure is so simple and straightforward that implementation should require minimal training.

One cannot expect an adult to engage only in imitative behavior for extended periods without becoming dissatisfied; however, the responsiveness of the infant should increase and this should, in turn, be reinforcing to the caregiver. Each partner is participating in the development of a contingent system. The caregiver can be helped to slowly introduce changes into the infant's repertoire. For example, once the baby and mother have initiated and maintained a vocal imitation pattern, the caregiver may introduce a minor variation in his or her imitated response, from for example ba-ba to be-be, and watch to see if the infant responds differently. When retrieving objects that are being dropped, the mother might introduce slightly different ways of returning the desired object so the baby will have to accommodate the reach and grasp a little each time. Other simple extensions of the imitation method are easily developed.

Once the caregiver has learned to match the infant's content, timing and affectivity, gradual rearrangement of contingencies to assist the infant in acquiring the rules of communicative dialogue can be undertaken. Thus, the goal of providing a prelinguistic interactional foundation for linguistic interchange will be served.

SUMMARY

A goal of this volume is to develop a more functional liaison between research and practice. This chapter focuses on providing a brief synthesis of current findings generated by investigators who are studying early social-communicative behavior. We have used this synthesis to argue for the importance of early dyadic exchanges and contingency awareness as a foundation for the development of language. In particular, we outline the possible effects that handicapping conditions may have: hampering the infant's exploration and control of the environment and disrupting the acquisition of early precursors to adaptive communicative exchanges. Finally, we propose a strategy for intervention that could potentially enhance the at-risk or delayed infant's contingent relationships with the social environment which should, in turn, enhance the dyadic exchanges believed to be so fundamental to language.

ACKNOWLEDGMENTS

The authors would like to thank David Littman and Susan Edginton for their helpful editing of this chapter.

REFERENCES

Bates, E. *Emergence of symbols: Cognition and communication in infancy.* New York: Academic Press, 1979.
Beveridge, M., & Brinker, R. An ecological-developmental approach to communication in retarded children. In M. Jones (Ed.), *Language disorders in children*. Lancaster: MIT Press, 1980.
Brazelton, B., Koslowski, B., & Main, M. The origins of reciprocity: The early mother-infant interaction. In M. Lewis & L. Rosenblum (Eds.), *The effect of the infant on its caregiver*. New York: John Wiley & Sons, 1974.
Bricker, D., & Carlson, L. The relationship of object and prelinguistic social-communicative schemes to the acquisition of early linguistic skills in developmentally delayed infants. Paper presented at the Conference on Handicapped and At-Risk Infants: Research and Application, held at Asilomar, Monterey, California, April, 1980b.
Bricker, D., & Carlson, L. Issues in early language intervention. In R. Schiefelbusch & D. Bricker (Eds.), *Early language: Acquistion and intervention*. Baltimore: University Park Press, 1981.
Bromwich, R. *Working with parents and infants*. Baltimore: University Park Press, 1981.
Bruner, J. From communication to language—A psychological perspective. *Cognition,* 1975, *3,* 255–287.
Bruner, J. Early social interaction and language acquisition. In H. Schaffer (Ed.), *Studies in mother-infant interaction*. London: Academic Press, 1977.
Emde, R. *Levels of meaning for infant emotions: A biosocial view*. Unpublished manuscript. Denver, Col. University of Colorado Medical Center, 1979.
Field, T. Interactions of preterm and term infants with their lower- and middle-class teenage and adult mothers. In T. Field (Ed.), *High-risk infants and children*. New York: Academic Press, 1980.
Fraiberg, S. *Insights from the blind*. New York: Basic Books, Inc., Publishers, 1977.
Gaussen, T. Analysing parent-child interactions in clinical practice: The development of a procedure and method of reporting. *Child: Care, Health and Development,* 1979, *5,* 111–134.

Goldberg, S. Social competence in infancy: A model of parent-infant inter-action. *Merrill-Palmer Quarterly,* 1977, *23,* 163–177.

Gottman, J. *Marital interaction.* New York: John Wiley & Sons, 1979.

Halliday, M. *Learning how to mean.* New York: Elsevier North Holland Publishing Co., 1975.

Hunt, J. *Intelligence and experience.* New York: Ronald Press, 1961.

Jones, O. Mother-child communication with pre-linguistic Down's syndrome and normal infants. In H. Schaffer (Ed.), *Studies in mother-infant interaction.* New York: Academic Press, 1977.

Jones, O. Prelinguistic communication skills in Down's syndrome and normal infants. In T. Field (Ed.), *High-risk infants and children.* New York: Academic Press, 1980.

Kagan, J., Kearsley, R., & Zelazo, P. *Infancy: Its place in human development.* Cambridge, Mass.: Harvard University Press, 1978.

Kaye, K. Toward the origin of dialogue. In H. Schaffer (Ed.), *Studies in mother-infant interaction.* London: Academic Press, 1977.

Lewis, M. The infant and its caregiver: The role of contingency. *Allied Health and Behavioral Sciences,* 1978, *1* (4), 469–492.

Lewis, M., & Brooks-Gunn, J. Social cognition and the acquisition of self. New York: Plenum Publishing Corp., 1980.

Lewis, M., & Goldberg, S. Perceptual-cognitive development in infancy: A generalized expectancy model as a function of the mother-child interaction. *Merrill-Palmer Quarterly,* 1969, *15* (1), 81–100.

Lewis, M., & Rosenblum, L. *The effect of the infant on its caregiver.* New York: John Wiley & Sons, 1974.

Maccoby, E. *Social development.* New York: Harcourt Brace Jovanovich, 1980.

Moss, H. Sex, age, and state as determinants of mother-infant interaction. *Merrill-Palmer Quarterly,* 1967, *13,* 19–36.

Nelson, K. The role of language in infant development. In M. Bornstein & W. Kessen (Eds.), *Psychological development from infancy: Image to intention.* Hillsdale, N.J.: Lawrence Erlbaum Associates, 1979.

Osofsky, J., & Connors, K. Mother-infant interaction: An integrative view of a complex system. In J. Osofsky (Ed.), *Handbook of infant development.* New York: John Wiley & Sons, 1979.

Richards, M. *The integration of a child into a social world.* London: Cambridge University Press, 1974.

Seligman, M. *Helplessness: On development, depression, and death.* San Francisco: W. H. Freeman, 1975.

Self, P., & Horowitz, F. The behavioral assessment of the neonate: An overview. In J. Osofsky (Ed.), *Handbook of infant development.* New York: John Wiley & Sons, 1979.

Sherrod, K., Crawley, S., Petersen, G., & Bennett, P. Maternal language to prelinguistic infants: Semantic aspects. *Infant Behavior and Development,* 1978, *1,* 335–345.

Snow, C. Mothers' speech research: From input to interaction. In C. Snow & C. Ferguson (Eds.), *Talking to children.* Cambridge: Cambridge University Press, 1977.

Stern, D., Beebe, B., Jaffe, J., & Bennett, S. The infant's stimulus world during social interaction: A study of caregiver behaviours with particular reference to repetition and timing. In H. Schaffer (Ed.), *Studies in mother-infant interaction.* London: Academic Press, 1977.

Sugarman, S. Some organizational aspects of pre-verbal communication. In
I. Markova (Ed.), *Social context of language*. New York: John Wiley &
Sons, 1978.

Sugarman, S. The development of preverbal communication: Its contribution
and limits in promoting the development of language. In R. Schiefelbusch
& J. Pickar (Eds.), *Communicative competence*. Baltimore: University Park
Press, 1981.

Thoman, E., Becker, P., & Freese, M. Individual patterns of mother-infant
interaction. In G. Sackett (Ed.), *Observing behavior (Volume I)*. Baltimore,
Md.: University Park Press, 1978.

Thoman, E. *Origins of the infant's social responsiveness*. Hillsdale, N.J.:
Lawrence Erlbaum Associates, 1979.

Trevarthen, C. Descriptive analyses of infant communicative behaviour. In
H. Schaffer (Ed.), *Studies in mother-infant interaction*. London: Academic
Press, 1977.

Uzgiris, I. Experience in the social context: Imitation and play. In R. Schiefelbusch & D. Bricker (Eds.), *Early language: Acquisition and intervention*.
Baltimore: University Park Press, 1981.

Vietze, P., Abernathy, S., Ashe, M., & Faulstich, G. Contingency interaction
between mothers and their developmentally delayed infants. In G. Sackett
(Ed.), *Observing behavior*, Vol. I. Baltimore: University Park Press, 1978.

Watson, J. Memory and "contingency analysis" in infant learning. *Merrill-
Palmer Quarterly*, 1967, *13*, 55–76.

Watson, J. Perception of contingency as a determinant of social responsiveness. In E. Thoman (Ed.), *Origins of the infant's social responsiveness*.
Hillsdale, N.J.: Lawrence Erlbaum Associates, 1979

Yarrow, L., Rubenstein, J., & Pedersen, F. *Infant and environment: Early
cognitive and motivational development*. Washington, D.C.: John Wiley
& Sons, 1975.

INDEX